EARLY SETTLERS AND INDIAN FIGHTERS

OF

SOUTHWEST TEXAS

BY
A. J. SOWELL
AUTHOR OF "TEXAS RANGERS" "BIG-FOOT WALLACE," ETC.

*FACTS GATHERED FROM SURVIVORS OF
FRONTIER DAYS*

Southern Historical Press, Inc.
Greenville, South Carolina

This volume was reproduced
from a personal copy located in
the Publishers private library

All rights reserved. No part of this publication may be reproduced,
stored in a retrieval system, transmitted in any form, posted
on the web in any form or by any means without the
prior written permission of the publisher.

Please direct all correspondence and book orders to:
SOUTHERN HISTORICAL PRESS, Inc.
1071 Park West Blvd.
Greenville, SC 29611

Published 1900 by:
 ISBN #978-1-63914-631-4
Printed in the United States of America

PREFACE.

In the following pages the author has attempted to recite what is yet the unwritten history of life on the border, especially in Southwest Texas. Many brave and heroic men have lived and died, and did their country glorious service upon the frontier of Texas, whose names as yet have found no place in history. They were the men who cut the brush and blazed the way for immigration, and drove the wild beast and wilder men from the path of civilization. They bore the heat and burden of the day, and their deeds should live like monuments in the hearts of their countrymen. Where commerce now holds its busy and prosperous marts was then the camping ground and rendezvous of these rangers and pioneers. The incidents of history herein contained have been gathered from sources most reliable, and he who peruses this volume may feel assured that he is not reading fiction, but facts which form a part of the frontier history of Texas. If this work serves one of the purposes for which it was written, i. e., that the names of these good and brave men and women be not forgotten and the writer occupy one fresh, green spot in the folds of their memory, he will not think his labor has been in vain. And now, to the pioneers of Texas and to their descendants is this work dedicated by

THE AUTHOR.

CONTENTS.

Atascosa County, Early Settlers of	249
Adams, James M.	582
Boales, J. A.	295
Berry, Mrs. Hannah	46
Burrell, Joseph	141
Brucks, Judge Bernhard	159
Binnion, Mrs. M. A.	337
Briggs, Rev. E. A.	343
Bowles, Doke	383
Brucks, Henry	368
Bramlett, W. M.	397
Battles With Indians	399
Bowie's Old Fort	405
Buckalew, Frank, Captured by Indians	587
Buckalew, Berry C.	591
Battle Between Rangers and Indians	642
Beardy Hall Killed by Indians	736
Burney, R. H.	841
Castro, Henry	105
Conrads, Joseph	114
Castro's Diary, Part I	119
Castro's Diary, Part II	126
Castro's Diary, Part III	131
Carr, James C. (Buckskin)	165
Castroville Founded	137
Charobiny, Rudolph	347
Cañon de Uvalde	401
Click, M. C.	508
Clark, Amasa	519
Calahan's Expedition	530
Cox Family as Indian Fighters	602
Captured an Indian	692
Carr, Col. J. C.	761

CONTENTS.

Colonel Carr's Courtship in Arkansaw 765
Camp Verde 710
Colwell, Capt. Neal 720
Davenport, A. J. 106
Dove Creek Fight 265
Davenport, Aunt Mary 291
Davenport, L. C. 472
Desperate Run for Life 607
Disastrous Battle With Indians in Kerr County 645
Death of Capt. Phillip Dimmitt 677
Early History of Guadalupe County 409
English, Ed. 567
Etter Family 782
Frontier Tragedy 268
Fight Between Rangers and Indians 271
Fiftieth Anniversary of the D'Hanis Settlement 280
First Settlement of D'Hanis 443
Forty Immigrants from Darmstadt 663
Fenley, J. D. 672
Four of the Dowdy Family Killed 740
Fight Between Settlers and Indians 742
Frontier Incidents 735
Family History 789
Haby, Nichalus 97
Huffman, Jack 828
Highsmith, Ben F. 1
Haller, Louis 155
Hays, Capt. Jack 331
Huehner, Herrman 375
Haby, Jacob 480
Hicks, F. L. 527
Hunter, Judge James M. 561
Hartman, Henry 575
Incidents of Frontier Life 275
Incident of Ranger Life 148
Indian Fight in Sabinal Canyon 381
Incident of Victoria's Raid 731
Jones, Mrs. Mahala 468
Joe Wilton Killed by Indians 539

Jarvis, Charles G.	620
Jack, Hardy, Captured by Indians	704
James, Rev. A. L.	713
Kinchaloe, Mrs. Sarah J.	90
Kennedy, Mrs. R. D.	257
Kelly, Mrs. Nancy	460
Killed an Indian	525
Kennedy, Ross	651
Lawhon, Jesse, Killed by Indians	246
Last Indian Raid in Frio Canyon	513
Lowe, Judge M. F.	634
Leakey, John	612
Miller, Jack	229
Mann, John L.	170
Massacre of Peddlers and Battle of El Blanco	434
Moore, Lon	595
Maney, Judge Henry	683
Metzgar, Capt. Fred	776
Nowlin, Dr. James C.	696
Old Settlers	453
Old Settlers of D'Hanis	441
Outlaw, Y. P.	458
Patterson, John W.	188
Putnam Children Captured by Indians	339
Peters, Charles	745
Rothe, August	233
Reinhart, John	195
Richarz, Capt. H. J.	202
Rees, Capt. Alonzo	638
Rogers, Capt. John H.	624
Saatoff, M.	811
Shane, Henry	483
Smith, Seco	477
Siege and Fall of the Alamo (Poetry)	772
Sevier, Col. T. F.	774
Scull, Mrs. Amanda	835
Tinsley, F. G.	303
Thompson, Gideon	206
Tom, Capt. John	32

BENJ. F. HIGHSMITH.

TEXAS INDIAN FIGHTERS.

BENJAMIN F. HIGHSMITH.

Came to Texas in 1823.

"Uncle Ben" Highsmith, as he is familiarly called by all who know him, is one of the most interesting characters at this time (1899) in Southwest Texas. He lives in Bandera County, on Blanket Creek, between Sabinal and Frio Canyons. In 1897, when the writer went to interview the old veteran for the purpose of getting a sketch of his life for publication in the Galveston News, he found him sitting in front of his door, with his hat pulled down, shading his eyes, for he is nearly blind, and he has to almost feel his way when stirring about. His general health, however, is good, and he has one of the most remarkable memories of incidents, names, and dates. To my greeting, he called out, "How are you, Jack? I know your voice, but I can not see you. Get down."

Uncle Ben was born in Lincoln County, Mississippi, on the 11th day of September, 1817. His father, A. M. Highsmith, was in the British war of 1812, and served as scout and ranger. Mr. Highsmith came to Texas with his father in 1823, and crossed the Sabine River on a raft the day before Christmas of the above date. There were four other families along, thirty-three persons in all, and all relatives except one.

The Highsmiths moved on up the country after landing on Texas soil, and first settled on the Colorado River two miles above the present town of La Grange, on the west side of the river. This place was afterwards called Manton's Big Spring. At that time it was called Castleman's Spring. It was named for John Castleman.

The Indians soon gave trouble, and these outside pioneers had to come back to the settlement below, where lived the families of Zaddock Woods and Stephen Cottle. This settlement was finally abandoned on account of Indians, and all went to Rabb's Mill. The settlement here and those who came for mutual protection now numbered six families. Bread was a very scarce article, as farming at this time was on a very small scale.

The Comanche Indians, who had up to this time been on friendly terms with the whites, now informed them that they must leave or they would come next moon and kill all of them. The settlers were not strong enough to disregard such a warning as this, and consequently broke up and scattered. Most of them went down to Old Caney and Columbus. The Cottles stopped at Jesse Burnham's and the Highsmiths at Elliot C. Buckner's. This was in 1829.

Mr. Highsmith first visited San Antonio in 1830. On this occasion he went on a trading trip in company with James Bowie, W. B. Travis, Ben McCulloch, Winslow Turner, Sam Highsmith, and George Kimble. They arrived there on the first day of April. It was far out on the frontier, and consisted of scattered grass-covered houses, mostly.

After returning from this trip, Mr. Highsmith moved with the other members of the family to Cedar Lake and stopped on the Harrison place, and was the only family there at that time.

In 1832 a disturbance commenced with the Mexicans, which culminated in the

BATTLE OF VELASCO.

The causes which brought about the collision were these: In 1831 Bustamante had overthrown Zacatecas, who was President of Mexico, and who had formulated the famous Constitution of 1824, which guaranteed to Americans the right to govern themselves. Bustamante told his followers that it gave the Americans the right to govern Mexico also, and at once sent troops to garrison San Antonio, La Bahia, Velasco, Anahuac, and Nacogdoches. General Cos was sent to San Antonio, Filisola to La Bahia (Goliad), Ugartechea to Velasco, and Bradburn to Anahuac. Santa Anna now arose against Bustamante and the Americans espoused his cause, thinking he was their friend and would uphold the Constitution of 1824.

To show their fidelity to the cause of Santa Anna, the American settlers began to raise men to attack the garrisons which had been placed in the Texas towns by Bustamante. Capt. Elliot C. Buckner raised one of the companies and proceeded with other captains against Velasco. Uncle Ben joined this company, having to run away from home to do so on account of his youth, being then only 15 years of age. The following are the names of those whom Mr. Highsmith can still remember who belonged to this company: Peter Powell, Joe and Horace Yeamans, Billy Kingston, Moses Morrison, Isaac Van Dorn, Hamilton Cook, Caleb R. Bostick, Tom Tone, Dan Ralls, Andrew Castleman, Leander Woods, and a Mexican named Hosea, who lived with Captain Buckner.

When the Americans under Buckner, about 100 in number, arrived at Velasco they went into the town at a full charge, and being supported by other troops the battle commenced with great fury. The Mexicans numbered about 500, and met the Americans with a heavy fire of musketry and artillery. In less than an hour the battle of Velasco was over and the Mexicans defeated. While many Mexicans were killed, the Americans did not come unscathed out of the fight. Out of Buckner's company, he himself was killed, the Mexican, Hosea, Leander Woods, and Andrew Castleman. One man of this company ran when the firing commenced, but soon checked up and seemed about to come back, but about this time the Mexican artillery fire commenced, and away he went again and returned not. When the boys joked him about it afterwards he said: "Boys, I will tell you the truth. I have got as brave a heart in me as any man that lives, but the most cowardly pair of legs that was ever fastened on to a man. Now, while my legs were carrying me off I was protesting and trying to persuade them to bring me back into the fight, and did actually get them to stop and turn me around, but at that critical moment the cannon fired, and away they went again, and I failed to get them to hold up any more within range of the battle."

About the middle of November, 1833, Ben Highsmith and his father were camped at Croft's prairie, eight miles below Bastrop, cutting logs to build a house, when the "stars fell," as that extraordinary meteoric display which occurred at that time was called.

BATTLE OF GONZALES.

In 1835 Santa Anna, who had overthrown Bustamante, was now President of Mexico, and wanted to govern Texas also. He went about to bring this to pass by ordering General Cos, his brother-in-law, who was still in command at San Antonio, to send a company of soldiers to Gonzales and bring off a little cannon which the Americans had in their possession, and which had been furnished them by the Mexican government for defense against the Indians. The settlers at Gonzales refused to give up the cannon, and the soldiers went back to San Antonio and reported the same to their commander. Another company was sent with an order from Santa Anna to take it by force. In the meantime a runner had been sent from Gonzales to the settlements on the Colorado, informing them of the action of the Mexican government, and calling on the settlers for assistance to repel with force this plain violation of the Constitution of 1824. The fact of the business was that Santa Anna had become alarmed at the number of Americans that were settling in Texas and wished to disarm and drive them out, although this immigration had been invited and extra inducements offered to get it, and these settlers were actual citizens of Mexico.

The appeal from Gonzales was responded to with alacrity by the Colorado men, and companies were formed and moved with great dispatch. Mr. Highsmith left his home on the Colorado, and on arriving at Gonzales joined the company of Capt. John Alley, the whole being under the command of Col. John H. Moore. The cannon in question was a small affair, had never been used by the settlers against an enemy, and they had no balls to fit it, and did not know how it would shoot if occasion offered. However, they concluded to try it before the Mexicans came. John Sowell, a gunsmith of Gonzales, hammered out a ball on his anvil to fit the cannon, and it was loaded at his shop. Col. James Neill, an experienced artillerist, was present, and he aimed the gun at a small sycamore tree which grew on the bank of the Guadalupe River, about 300 yards distant from the shop. The tree was hit and considerably splintered, and part of the top fell off. When the Mexicans came they crossed the river above town and the settlers went up there before day to fight them, carrying the cannon with them, which had been loaded with slugs at Sowells' shop. It was not yet daylight when they arrived in the vicinity of the Mexicans, and very foggy,—the strangest fog, Mr. Highsmith says, he ever saw. It was clear of the ground a short distance of half a foot or more, and by lying down one could see the legs of the Mexicans, who were on the ground, and also that of the horses of those who were mounted, 150 yards away. Mr. Highsmith found this out by dropping something and stooping down to pick it up. He called the attention of Colonel Neill to this fact, and the colonel said that it beat anything in the fog line that he had ever witnessed. Colonel Neill had charge of the cannon, and was about to direct its fire on the Mexicans, when the battle very unexpectedly and accidentally commenced. This was brought about by two scouts, one from each of the opposing forces, coming in contact and firing at each other at close range in the fog. The fight was of short duration. The cannon was fired five times, mixed with rifle shots, and the Mexicans retreated across the river. The fog lifted, and shots were exchanged after they crossed. Dr. John T. Tinsley got a fair bead on one who had stopped to take a look back, and, from the way he cursed in choice Spanish as he continued his retreat, must have hit him. The gunsmith John Sowell brought his shop apron full of slugs to the battleground to load the cannon with. The Mexicans continued their retreat to San Antonio, and most of the Colorado men went back home.

BATTLE OF MISSION CONCEPCION.

Captain Alley's company and a good many of the Gonzales men after the fight at Gonzales joined Gen. Stephen F. Austin, who, seeing war was inevitable now with Mexico, was raising a force to capture San Antonio. Mr. Highsmith remained with his company, and says one night the command camped on the Cibolo Creek while en route to assault the city, and that two of the men ate so many green pecans that it killed them. This was in the fall of 1835.

General Austin went into camp on the San Antonio River below the city, and then sent Colonels Fannin and Bowie up to near the old Mission Concepcion with ninety-two men, as an advance guard. They went into camp in a pecan grove in a bend of the river and put out guards. Next morning, about the break of day, as some of the men had arisen and were kindling fires, 400 Mexican morales troops attacked them. It was foggy, and the Mexicans had advanced a nine-pound cannon and placed it in close range of the position of the Texans and commenced firing before the guards discovered them. At the first fire of the gun, one of the Texans sang out, "That cannon is ours!" Fannin and Bowie were cool, brave men, and soon had their small force well in hand and to some extent protected by the bank of the river, where they were told to form and shoot when they liked, and not to wait for orders. The cannon shots had no effect, as the Texans were sheltered also by pecan and hackberry trees. The rifles soon cleared the gunners from the piece, and as the fog lifted they could see the Mexican infantry coming with trailed arms to protect it. This line was soon checked by a deadly rifle fire, and then a portion of the Texans made a charge from their position and captured the cannon. The Mexican infantry fired and then retreated, but formed again and still continued to fire at longer range. The cannon was only fired three times before it was captured and brought into the Texan camp.

When the firing commenced Dave Kent, Jesse Robinson, and John Henry Brown had just arrived at the Mission San Jose with some beef cattle, and at once hurried to the battle.

There has been some controversy as to who was in command of the Texans in this fight, Bowie or Fannin. Mr. Highsmith says that on the morning of the fight Bowie gave the order to "Get your guns, boys; here they come," when the Mexicans first fired on them. Only one man on the side of the Americans was killed. His name was Richard Andrews. He and Ben Highsmith stood beside the same hackberry tree during the hottest of the fire, and Andrews exposed himself in getting a shot. His companion said, "Look out, Dick; they will hit you." He fired, however, and stepped back to reload, and then leaned from the tree again to look and to shoot. Highsmith said again, "Look out; you will get shot." About this time a ball struck the side of the tree, and, glancing, went through Andrews, going in at the right and coming out at the left side, lacerating the bowels in its progress. The wounded man lived until night and died in great agony. So great was his pain that he would place a finger in each bullet hole and try to tear them larger in the vain effort to get relief. He was buried on the battleground, under a large pecan tree. During the battle the Mexican cavalry was stationed back east in the prairie on the La Bahia road, about half a mile from the battleground, with their ropes ready to lasso the Texans when they were driven out of the timber across the open flats. The Mexicans had not learned yet what it was to round up a bunch of Texans. In the end the infantry and cavalry retreated back to San Antonio, with the loss of one cannon and about sixty men.

THE GRASS FIGHT.

After the Concepcion fight General Austin came up with the main body of his troops and all moved to the head of the San Antonio River above the city and began to invest the place. General Burleson had arrived with the Colorado men, and Ben Milam was also there. The Mexicans were in a precarious situation. They could not leave the city, and no supplies could reach them. Their cavalry horses were nearly starving. One night a party was sent out west of town to cut grass and bring it in for the horses. They succeeded in loading about fifty burros with the prairie grass, but daylight came upon them before they could get back to town, and they were discovered by Colonel Bowie, who with part of his men were on the lookout for a reinforcement which was expected from Mexico to relieve the beleaguered city. Bowie at once attacked them, although a large force of soldiers was with the grass cutters. The Mexicans commenced a rapid retreat to town, followed by the yelling Texans, and a lively fight and chase took place. The grass-laden jacks kept the road, braying at every jump, and the Mexicans fired back as they ran. One Texan was hit a glancing shot in the forehead and he fell from his horse. When the suburbs of the town was reached the Texans turned back, as the firing was attracting a reinforcement with artillery. The fight commenced on the Alazan Creek, and the road to Castroville now crosses the battleground. A party came back to see about the man that fell from his horse, and he was found sitting on the bank of a small ravine and holding his forehead with both hands. One of the party, John McGuffin, said, "Hello, here; what are you doing? Catching your brains in your hands?" The wounded man was tenderly cared for and recovered. Uncle Ben was in the fight, but does not remember the man's name. In writing this sketch I only give accounts of battles that Mr. Highsmith participated in, and only allude to others in a general way.

General Somerville was present during the siege, and one day a sentinel named Winslow Turner made him mark time for trying to pass him without the countersign. It is more than likely the officer was trying the soldier to see what kind of a guard he was.

STORMING OF SAN ANTONIO.

On the 5th day of December, 1835, while the siege was dragging slow and the men impatient and inactive, Col. Ben Milam called for volunteers to storm San Antonio. General Austin, who was not a military man, but a statesman, and who was at the head of the great immigration scheme of bringing colonists from the States to Texas, had quit the service, and Gen. Edward Burleson was in command of the Texans now before San Antonio. When Milam made the call for men to enter the city, 300 responded and were led in by Milam and Col. Frank W. Johnson. General Burleson held the reserves up at the old mill. Bowie also, with part of his men, was there ready to give assistance at a moment's notice. Mr. Highsmith went in with Milam, but was not by him when he was killed, being on the west side of Soledad Street, and the gallant old colonel was killed on the east side at the Veramendi House. After Milam was killed Colonel Johnson took command and continued the assault to a successful finish. Col. J. C. Neill made a demonstration against the Alamo with artillery to draw the attention of the Mexicans to the east side of the river, while Milam and his men were entering on the other.

Mr. Highsmith noticed two men get peculiar shots near him while a storming party were making their way toward the plaza. Sam Evitts was shot in the mouth and the ball came out under his right ear, and James Belden had his right eye shot out. Both men recovered. John Harvey was killed, and Captain Ware and "Deaf" Smith were wounded at the Veramendi House when Milam was killed.

General Cos surrendered his men, and they were all paroled and sent back to Mexico.

FRONT OF THE VERAMENDI HOUSE ON SOLEDAD STREET, SAN ANTONIO, TEXAS, WHERE COL. BEN MILAM WAS KILLED.
The marks of bullets are seen on the doors, which are of cedar, heavy and thick, and have swung there since 1720.

THE GRAVE OF BEN MILAM, SAN ANTONIO, TEXAS.

After the surrender many of the Texans went back home, thinking the war was over. Colonel Fannin had been sent to La Bahia, or Goliad, before the taking of San Antonio, and was in command there. Col. James Neill was placed in command of the Alamo until relieved by Col. William B. Travis. Mr. Highsmith stayed in the Alamo with Colonel Travis until the approach of Santa Anna from Mexico with a large army, and he was then sent by his commander with a dispatch to Colonel Fannin ordering that officer to blow up the fort at Goliad and come to him with his men. Mr. Highsmith was gone five days, and on his return Santa Anna's advance of 600 cavalry was on the east side of the river, riding around the Alamo and on the lookout for messengers whom they knew the Texan commander was sending from the doomed fort.

Mr. Highsmith sat on his horse on Powderhouse Hill and took in the situation. The Mexican flag was waving from the Church of Bexar across the river, and the flag of Travis from the Alamo. The country was open and nearly all prairie in the valley around San Antonio, and objects could be seen some distance from the elevated points. There was a great stir and perceptible activity in the town, and the forms of some of the doomed men at the Alamo could be plainly seen as from the walls of the fort they watched the Mexican cavalry.

The daring messenger saw there was no chance for him to communicate with his gallant commander, and slowly rode north towards the San Antonio and Gonzales road. The Mexican cavalrymen saw him, and a dense body of them rode parallel with and closely watched him. Finally they spurred their horses into a gallop and came rapidly towards him. Highsmith took one last look towards the Alamo and the trapped heroes within, and then, turning his horse east, dashed off towards Gonzales. He is the last man alive to-day who talked with Bowie and Travis at the Alamo. The Mexicans pursued Uncle Ben six miles—two miles beyond the Salado Creek—and then gave up the chase. He went on to the Cibolo Creek, eighteen miles from San Antonio, and then halted on a ridge to rest his horse. While here his quick ear caught the sound of cannon as the dull boom was wafted across the prairie. The siege and bombardment of the Alamo had commenced. Mr. Highsmith thinks that David Crockett went into the Alamo with George Kimble, A. J. Kent, Abe Darst,

Tom Jackson, Tom Mitchell, Wash Cottle, and two 16-year-old boys named Albert Fuqua and John Gaston. Crockett had a few men who came with him to Texas, and some think he did not come by Gonzales, but straight across from Bastrop to San Antonio. The men mentioned above all came from Gonzales and were led by Captain Kimble. The names are not all given here. There were thirty two of them in all. They came down the river in the night and fought their way into the Alamo by a sudden dash.

When Mr. Highsmith arrived at Gonzales he found Gen. Sam Houston there with about 300 men on his way to succor Travis, and Highsmith's report was the last reliable news before the fall. Scouts were sent back to within a few miles of San Antonio to listen for the signal gun which Travis said he would fire at sunup each morning as long as held the fort. On Monday morning, March 7, 1836, the scouts listened in vain for the welcome signal. The sun arose and began to mount into the heavens, and still no token came; all was silent in the west. The scouts mounted their horses and set off again for Gonzales to inform General Houston that the Alamo had fired her last gun. On the 6th the Alamo had been stormed and all the defenders perished.

When Mr. Highsmith reported to General Houston the situation at the Alamo, he sent Uncle Ben and a boy named David B. Kent again to Colonel Fannin, ordering him to demolish the fort of Goliad and retire to the east bank of the Guadalupe River and form a junction with him. When they arrived at Goliad and handed the message to Fannin he read it, but said nothing. When asked what reply they must carry back he said, "Tell him that I will not desert the fort." Colonel Fannin had made an attempt to join Travis at the Alamo, but his frail transportation carts had broken down and he had to return to Goliad, having no means to convey his supplies or artillery. The readers of Texas history are familiar with the terrible scenes that were enacted around the fort of Goliad after the departure of these last messengers to Fannin. A large Mexican army came and the commands of Ward, King, and others were massacred. Fannin attempted also to leave, but was cut off and surrounded in the Coleta prairie, and after a hard battle against largely superior numbers, surrendered the remnant of his command, who were then massacred, only a few escaping the general slaughter.

The young lad Kent, who was sent with Highsmith to Fannin,

THE OLD CHURCH OF BEXAR.
From which waved the blood-red flag of Santa Anna during the siege and storming of the Alamo.

was the son of David Kent, who was killed in the Alamo. The writer has seen this messenger Kent, and had many talks with him. He died a few years ago in Frio Canyon, Uvalde County.

Highsmith and Kent returned to Gonzales and found General Houston and his men still there, and made their report. Houston was greatly distressed. There was great commotion in town. Mrs. Dickinson had arrived and confirmed the report that the Alamo had fallen and its defenders been all slain. There was wailing and weeping among wives and mothers. The Gonzales men and boys to the number of thirty-two had perished with Travis. Mrs. Dickinson was the wife of Lieut. Almon Dickinson, who was killed in the Alamo. She had been spared and had made her way to Gonzales.

BATTLE OF SAN JACINTO.

The Mexican army divided at San Antonio after the Alamo was taken, Santa Anna coming to Gonzales, Cos by Bastrop, and Urrea to Goliad. It was the latter that fought Fannin. Mr. Highsmith went on with the army from Gonzales, and blames General Houston for several things. In the first place, he said they should have fought the Mexicans at the Colorado, as more men were together there than at any subsequent time, and that the burning of Gonzales, Columbus, San Felipe, Harrisburg, and New Washington by order of Houston was useless, as the Mexicans could have done no more. He said if the battle could have been fought at Columbus it would have saved much property. Be this as it may, however, all is well that ends well. The Texans under Houston, few as they were, gained a great and glorious victory when they did fight on the historic plain of San Jacinto.

Uncle Ben went into the battle in the company of Capt. William Ware. He says the dead Mexicans lay thickest around the breastwork and were considerably scattered on the prairie. The breastwork, he said, was composed of brush, dirt, packs, etc. A great many prisoners were taken, and he says they held them in camp that night by stretching ropes around the trees, building large fires so as to keep a good light, and by keeping guards posted on the outside circle of ropes. During the night the grass caught fire and burned among some boxes of captured paper cartridges, and many of them exploded. When the cartridges commenced to go off the Mexican prisoners, 700 in number, became greatly alarmed, not knowing the cause of the fusilade, and thinking the Texans had commenced to shoot the prisoners.

After the battle and pursuit was over the wounded Mexicans who were able to travel were marched to the camp of the Texans, some having to travel two miles. They never groaned or complained, and a casual observer would not have known they were wounded except by their bloody clothes. There were about 300 of them in all, and thirty of them died in the Texan camp that night.

Mr. Highsmith says, from the amount of guns picked up on the field, there could not have been less than 2200 Mexicans in line of battle. Their line was twice the length of that of the Texans and more densely packed.

There was a man named Bob Love in the battle, and during the first charge the men were ordered to fall forward at the flash of the cannon to avoid the shots; but Love had not heard this order, and when the men went down at the flash he turned back and ran to camp and told the guard detail there that all of Houston's men had been killed at the first fire except himself. He then went on towards the Sabine and told all the people that he saw the same tale. The date of the battle was April 21, 1836.

FIGHT BETWEEN INDIANS AND SURVEYORS.

In 1838 Mr. Highsmith went out with a surveying party under the leadership of Captain Lynch. Their course was westward, and they finally established their camp between Salt and Cherokee creeks, where the land lay which they wanted to run off. This place is now covered by Lampasas County. There were twenty-five white men in the party, including the hunters. Work progressed all right. Game was plentiful and no signs of Indians. Nothing occurred worthy of note until the morning, when preparations were being made to break up camp and return to the settlements, the work having been completed. At this time the men were surprised and thrown into momentary confusion by the furious onslaught of about forty Indians who had approached their camp through some thickets. The most of the white men were frontiersmen and good Indian fighters, and order was soon restored and the Indians driven back to cover by a well-directed rifle fire. The men had time to reload before another charge came, and the Indians were again driven off after circling around the position of the whites, yelling and discharging a good many arrows, but without much effect. This kind of fighting was kept up for nearly an hour, when the Comanches, seeing it was going to cost them too much to continue it longer, drew off. There was but one white man killed, and that was the brave Captain Lynch. He was shot through the body with a bullet, and died instantly, without speaking. His body was buried on the battleground by his comrades, and they then returned to the settlement without further incident.

FEDERATION WAR.

This is the name Mr. Highsmith gives to the disturbances which occurred along the Rio Grande in 1839. He says the Mexicans were raiding on the Americans who had commenced to settle on the lower Nueces between that stream and the Rio Grande. These Mexicans were in some force, and were led by one of their countrymen named Parbon. John N. Seguin, a Mexican of Spanish descent, but loyal to Texas at that time, raised a company of ninety-five men to go and fight Parbon and his party. Sixty of this company were Americans and the balance Mexicans. Mr. Highsmith, ever ready to go on an expedition, joined the force under Seguin. The latter had a fine ranch below San Antonio on the river of the same name. On a creek called Santiago, between San Patricio and Laredo, they met Parbon and his men, and a fight occurred in the brush and prickly pears. A parley was finally agreed on, and while this was in progress one of Parbon's men told Juan Cantu, who belonged to Seguin's company, that the latter intended to sell his company out. When the men heard this they broke up and came back to San Antonio. Captain Seguin had some trouble with the Americans near his ranch, and thinking he had been wronged by them, turned traitor to Texas, removed to Mexico, and returned with the invading armies of Vasquez and Wall in 1842.

When Vasquez made his raid Mr. Highsmith joined the company of Capt. H. M. Childress. The Mexicans held San Antonio a few days and then went back to Mexico without a fight, not waiting until the Texans could assemble. The latter kept their forces in the city a while before disbanding. While here, Highsmith learned through Juan Cantu, who was loyal to the Texans, that Seguin was at the Calaveras ranch, thirty miles down the river, and applied to Captain Childress for twenty-five men to go and capture him. This was granted, and Captain Highsmith set out for the Calaveras ranch, guided by Juan Cantu.

The party arrived at the ranch in the night and surrounded it. The owner, Calaveras, was called out and asked if Seguin was there. He said "No." "You lie," said Cantu, and proposed then and there to hang him. A rope was produced, put around his neck, and he was drawn up, but was told he would be let down when he told where Seguin was. Calaveras, however, persisted in his first statement that Seguin was not there, and that he did not know where he was. He was drawn up three times, but finally released and left nearly dead. No doubt Seguin had been there, but was gone. Highsmith and his men went back to San Antonio and disbanded.

It is a pity that Captain Seguin should have had any trouble with the Texans. He commanded a small company of Mexicans at San Jacinto, fighting against Santa Anna, and it was he and his men who collected the bones of the men who were killed and partly burned at the Alamo. They buried these remains about seventy-five yards from the northeast corner of the Alamo.

CHEROKEE WAR.

In 1839 an attempt to remove the Cherokee Indians from East Texas to the Indian Territory, which had been set aside as the home of the Indian tribes, caused a short conflict, in which the Indians were defeated and the intentions of the government carried out. Two chiefs, Bowles and Big Mush, commanded the Indians, and the whites were led by Gen. Thomas J. Rusk. The battle was fought near Nacogdoches in a thick woods of pine, white oak, gum, etc. Both Indian chiefs were killed, and among the whites killed was Capt. John C. Crane, one of the captains under Milam at the storming of San Antonio in 1835, and who was well known to Mr. Highsmith, who was near him when he fell and helped to bury him. Uncle Ben in this fight belonged to Capt. Ed. Burleson's company.

THE FIGHT AT MILL CREEK.

In 1839 Gen. Vincent Cordova, a disaffected Mexican living at Nacogdoches, raised a motley crowd of Mexicans, Indians, and negroes and started to Mexico. Gen. Ed. Burleson got wind of him on the Colorado, and went with a company of rangers to intercept him. Ben Highsmith and Winslow Turner were members of the company. The trail of Cordova was struck between Webber's Prairie and Austin, and the band overtaken on Mill Creek, in Guadalupe County, about five miles east of the little village of Seguin, then just starting. It was a running fight and did not last long, as it was nearly sundown when it commenced. It could not be ascertained how many of the enemy were killed, as they fell as they ran and were badly scattered. The father of the writer lived at Seguin at the time, and was on the battleground next morning. He said there were two negroes, one Mexican, and one Indian dead on the ground where the fight first commenced. Cordova intended to capture and pillage Seguin. The dead Indian had his head cut off. Mr. Highsmith says that Dr. Venters, who was with the rangers, had a personal combat with an Indian and killed him. I have heard my father say that a doctor who was in this fight cut off the head of a dead Indian and carried it away with him for medical examination. Likely this was the one.

INDIAN FIGHT ON BRUSHY CREEK.

In 1839 the Comanche Indians in large force made a raid on the settlement below Austin, and after killing some of the Coleman family and robbing the house of Dr. Robinson in his absence, traveled a northerly course towards Brushy Creek, carrying one of the doctor's negroes with them. Mr. Highsmith was at Bastrop, and when he heard the news of the raid set out for Austin in company with his old comrade of many battles, Winslow Turner. When they arrived at Austin Capt. James Rogers was raising men to pursue the Indians, and the two Bastrop men joined him. Gen. Ed. Burleson, the Indian fighter and leader on the Colorado, was away at the time. Captain Rogers with thirty men left Austin in pursuit and came up with the Indians twenty miles northeast from Austin, on Brushy Creek, not far from the present town of Taylor. The Indians saw the white men coming across the prairie and made ready to fight them. The Indians charged when Rogers and his men came near, and after firing the captain saw that his force was not sufficient to cope with them, especially in open ground, and ordered a retreat to a mott of timber on a hill. Here his intention was to dismount his men and make a fight. As soon as the men started the Indians followed with fearful yells, and by the time the timber was reached considerable confusion prevailed among the white men. Only three men dismounted in obedience to orders, and the balance passed on. Captain Rogers, seeing he could not carry out his plans, also passed on. The three men who had dismounted at the trees were Ben Highsmith, Winslow Turner, and Jacob Burleson. The Indians were crowding the settlers closely and firing at them, and the dismounted men, seeing the stand was not going to be made, hastily remounted and followed. Their order as they left the trees was Turner in front, Burleson next, and Highsmith last. About this time the Indians, who were close upon them, fired a volley with rifles. Highsmith felt the wind of a ball close to his ear, and at the same time saw the dust rise from the crown of Burleson's hat, who was directly in front of him. The next instant the gallant young man reeled and fell from his saddle, shot in the back of the head. The men were not to blame for making this retreat, as they were greatly outnumbered, and many more would have been slain had they stayed. Some were young men who had never seen Indians before.

The Indians did not pursue far, and the men all got together and went back towards Austin. Captain Rogers was greatly dejected. Before getting back, however, they met Gen. Ed. Burleson coming rapidly with twenty men. He was informed of the disastrous fight, and that his brother Jacob was killed. General Burleson now took command of all the men and went back to give the Indians another fight. He, like Jack Hays, had never been defeated by Indians. They first went to the spot where Jake Burleson fell, and there found his body, stripped and badly mutilated. He was shot through the head, as Highsmith had told them, and his right hand and right foot cut off, scalped, and his heart cut out. The Indians went back to Brushy Creek and there strongly posted themselves. The creek here made an acute bend, and the Indians were in the lower part of it and concealed from view except when some of them showed themselves in order to watch the movements of the white men.

General Burleson moved his men around the position of the Comanches and occupied the upper bend of the creek, and the fight soon commenced across the space between them, which was in short rifle range. The battle lasted a long time and was hotly contested—rifle against rifle. The Indians seemed to be nearly all armed with guns and were good shots, and still outnumbered the white men. The latter, some of whom were old Indian fighters, were cautious, exposing themselves as little as possible. The Indians did the same. They evidently recognized Burleson as their old enemy, and they dared not leave cover and charge his position. One Indian crawled out of the bed of the creek unperceived and took a position behind a large bunch of prickly pears, where he lay flat on the ground and watched his opportunity to shoot as some settler would expose some part of his body. He did execution, and it was some time before he was located, but the smoke of his gun finally betrayed him. Winslow Turner saw where the smoke came from, and quickly ascending a small tree at great risk of his life, got sight of the Indian, fired quickly, and came down again. The Comanche jumped at the crack of the gun and tumbled over the creek bank. This Indian had on Dr. Robinson's coat and vest, as was noticed when he jumped away from his position. The coat and vest were found when the fight was over, covered with blood and a bullet hole in them. The Indians, after losing many of their warriors, gave up the fight and retreated down the creek and then into the hills. They carried off their dead, but the bloody ground they occupied told the tale of their loss.

After the battle was over the loss of Burleson in killed was Jack Walters, Ed. Blakey, and James Gilleland. The latter was a Methodist preacher. Of the four men killed three were shot in the head. Gilleland was shot between the point of the shoulder and neck, the ball ranging down and going through the lungs. Mr. Highsmith helped to carry Blakey to the house of Noah Smithwick, at Webber's Prairie, twenty miles distant from the battleground. Smithwick was brother-in-law of the wounded man. They carried the dying youth on a blanket stretched between two poles, between a pair of horses. He was shot late in the evening, and died at sundown on the next evening. The other dead were carried off to their respective homes by friends. Heartrending scenes were enacted when the bloody remains were slowly brought to their homes by sorrowing comrades. Walters was a young man and his mother was a widow.

BATTLE OF PLUM CREEK.

In 1840 a large body of Comanche Indians, about 500 in number, made a most daring raid through Texas and burned and sacked the town of Linnville on the coast. When the news of this raid was generally circulated men began to gather from all points where there was a settlement to intercept and fight them on their way back to the mountains from whence they came. Mr. Highsmith heard the news at his home in Bastrop, and at once saddled his horse, got his gun, and started. Among the leaders who were gathering men to fight the Indians were Felix Huston, Ed. Burleson, Jack Hays, Matthew Caldwell ("Old Paint"), and the McCullochs, Henry and Ben.

Mr. Highsmith joined the company of General Burleson. The Indians came up Peach Creek and then across Tinny's Prairie towards Plum Creek. Scouts kept Burleson informed as to the route of the Indians, and he cut across with his men to intercept and fight them at Plum Creek, but when he arrived there the Comanches had crossed the creek and were out in the prairie. They had many pack animals, besides squaws and warriors, and presented an imposing spectacle as they moved along singing and exploiting on their horses, and altogether covering a mile in extent. Burleson moved out towards them and charged, commencing the fight with eighty-two men. The warriors divided and moved towards Burleson, firing and yelling, which was spiritedly replied to by the men from the Colorado. About this time a reinforcement arrived of 125 men under Gen. Felix Huston, who were following on the trail from below. The fight now became general and quite extended, as the Indians began to quail before the fire and to move off, following in the wake of the squaws and pack animals. Other reinforcements in small squads continued to arrive, attracted by the firing to the course the battle was following. The pursuit lasted many miles, and wound up where the present town of Kyle is situated, between San Marcos and

Austin. It commenced three miles east of the present town of Lockhart, in Caldwell County.

Many personal encounters took place during the long-extended and scattered battle. One Indian in the chase has his horse killed, and after leaving him and running a short distance on foot, returned to the dead horse to secure his bridle, but was killed and fell across the horse's neck with the bridle in his hand. Another Indian presented a very humorous and grotesque appearance. When the stores at Linnville were looted this fellow proceeded to rig himself from head to foot in regular full dress fashion, except the pants, having on a beegum hat, fine calf boots on over his naked legs, and a broadcloth long forked-tail coat, which was resplendent with a double row of brass buttons in front. This dusky dude, however, had no valet de chambre to put on his coat for him, and consequently got it on wrong, having the front behind and closely buttoned up to the back of his neck. He also had an umbrella hoisted, and was riding with head erect and a little thrown back, singing loudly, when the battle commenced. The sight of him and the humorous figure he cut caused loud laughter among the Texans who were near him. He lost his hat and umbrella during the fight, but himself escaped, although fired at repeatedly. He was a dexterous rider and dodger. Mr. Highsmith saw a white woman lying under a tree with an arrow in her breast. Some men had dismounted beside her, and a doctor from Gonzales was extracting the arrow. One of the men was well known to Mr. Highsmith. He was Z. N. Morrell, the noted pioneer Baptist preacher. The wounded woman was a captive, and the Indians shot her when they commenced to run from the whites.

The horse which was killed when the Indian also lost his life trying to save his bridle belonged to Colonel Bell, who was killed off of him at Kitchen's ranch as the Indians were coming back from Linnville. Several men shot at this Indian when he was killed, among whom were Mr. Highsmith and Andrew Sowell. The latter's ball hit the shield.

During the charge across the hogwallow prairie many horses fell and threw their riders. Bones of Indians were found years after along the route of pursuit.

BATTLE OF BANDERA PASS.

Soon after the Plum Creek battle President Houston commissioned the famous Jack Hays to raise a company of Texas rangers for the protection of the frontier against Indians and lawless characters. The latter were thick around San Antonio, and did pretty much as they pleased. Jack Hays at the time was a young surveyor, and not much known. He distinguished himself at the battle of Plum Creek. General Houston, who had been elected President of the young Republic of Texas, recognized his ability, and seeing the necessity of having such a man with a company of like spirits around him, at once put him in the field, and well did he sustain the trust and confidence which the hero of San Jacinto placed in him. Under Hays the Texas rangers gained a name and reputation which was world-wide.

Mr. Highsmith joined the company of Hays, and they were stationed at San Antonio. They soon established law and order in the Alamo City, and the name of Hays and his rangers soon become a terror to evildoers. The red man of the plains felt the weight of his mailed hand and learned to dread an encounter with him. In four pitched battles they were utterly routed, namely, Nueces Canyon, Pinta Trail Crossing, Enchanted Rock, and Bandera Pass. No account of these battles will be given in this sketch except those Mr. Highsmith was engaged in. The main scouting ground of the rangers was in the mountains west and northwest of San Antonio, up the Guadalupe, Medina, Sabinal, Frio, and Nueces rivers.

In the spring of 1841 Captain Hays started on a scout with forty men. His camp at this time was seven miles west of San Antonio, on Leon Creek. They went a northwest direction up Medina River and camped for the night at a point about where the center of Bandera town now is. Guards were well posted, and the night passed without any disturbance. Some people would be surprised to know that the Texas rangers under Hays were many of them men of education and refinement. Around the campfire at night it was not uncommon to hear men quoting from the most popular poets and authors, and talking learnedly on ancient and modern history. It is true they looked rough in the garb they wore. The wide hat was to protect them from the sun in long scouts across the prairies. The leggings of buckskin or cowskin protected the legs from the thorny brush and cactus. The large clinking spurs put new life into a tardy pony if occasion demanded. The intention of Hays was to turn north from this place and go out through the famous Bandera Pass and into the Guadalupe valley, and then scout up the river to the divide. The pass was about ten miles from the night camp of the rangers.

After the rangers left camp and were riding over the open country towards the pass, which could be seen plainly, quite a different looking crowd were assembling there. A large band of Comanche Indians were also on the warpath, and had started across the country by way of the pass to the Medina valley. They arrived there first, and, seeing the rangers coming, laid in ambush and awaited there to fight them.

The pass was named for General Bandera of the Spanish army, who was stationed at San Antonio when the missions were first built there. All of this country and Mexico then belonged to Spain. The pass was the home of the Apache Indians, and they raided upon San Antonio. General Bandera was ordered to follow them to their stronghold and chastise them. He found them at home in the pass and strongly fortified among the rocks. A long and desperate battle took place and many were killed on both sides, but at last the Spanish arms prevailed and the Indians gave way and retreated through the hills further towards the west. They never came back, but settled in New Mexico. Now, after the lapse of a century or more, another bloody battle was about to be fought here.

Hays and his men arrived at the pass about 11 o'clock in the morning and began to ride through it, as yet having seen no sign of Indians. The pass was 500 yards in length by 125 in width, and from 50 to 75 feet high on both sides, very steep, and covered with rocks and bushes. The Indian chief dismounted his men and placed them among the rocks and bushes on both sides of the pass, leaving their horses in the rear, and also concealed in a deep gulch which cut into the pass from the west and well up towards the north end.

The first intimation the rangers had of the presence of Indians was being fired on by bullets and arrows on all sides, and the terrible warwhoop of the Comanche resounded through the gorge. For a few moments there was some confusion among the rangers on account of the plunging of frightened and wounded horses, who would turn and try to run back through the pass in spite almost of all their riders could do. This was a trying and most critical time and the Indians knew it. They charged down into the pass and almost mixed up with the rangers and plunging horses. The white men could not well use their guns and hold their horses, too. To add to the disadvantage and confusion, some of the rangers were killed and wounded and were falling from their horses. As soon as a horse would find himself free of his rider he would gallop madly back through the pass.

All this took place in less time than it takes to write, and it was the first time Jack Hays was ever caught in a trap; but he was equal to the occasion. His clear voice now rang out sharp and quick, "Steady there, boys; dismount and tie those horses; we can whip them; no doubt about that." Order was soon restored, and in a moment the rangers were on the ground, and the Indians were falling and giving back before a deadly rifle and pistol fire. They came again, however, and several hand to hand conflicts took place. Mr. Highsmith, who was in the fight, dismounted near a ranger named Sam Luckey, who was soon shot through by a bullet. It entered under the left shoulder blade and came out below the right nipple. Highsmith caught him when he commenced falling and let him down to the ground easy. At this time the rangers had fastened their horses near the south entrance of the pass and were fighting in front of them. The wounded Luckey called for water, and Highsmith gave him some out of a canteen. At this time the fight was raging and the pass was full of Indians, rangers, and horses. The Comanche chief during this close fight attacked Sergt. Kit Ackland and wounded him. Ackland also shot the chief with a pistol, and then they clinched and both went down. Both were large, powerful men, and the combat was terrific. Both had out their long knives and rolled over and over on the ground, each trying to avoid the thrust of the other and himself give the deadly wound. The ranger was finally the victor. He got up covered with blood and dirt, with the bloody knife in hand. The chief lay dead, literally cut to pieces.

Mr. Highsmith loaded and fired his rifle many times, and was finally wounded in the leg with an arrow. The wound did not disable him, but after getting the arrow out he continued to load and fire until the fight was over, which lasted an hour. The Indians finally gave way, retreated to the upper end of the pass, and left the rangers masters of the situation. It was a dear bought victory. Five rangers lay dead and as many more wounded. Many horses were also wounded and killed. Of the wounded were Highsmith, Ackland, Tom Galbreath, James Dunn ("Red"), Sam Luckey, and one other whose name is not now remembered. While the fight was going on some of the Indians were carrying their dead back to where their horses were, at the north end of the pass. Hays carried his dead and wounded men back to the south entrance of the pass, where there was a large water hole, and there spent the night burying the dead rangers and taking care of the wounded. The writer was not able to get the names of those killed except one, whose name was Jackson. It has been fifty-six years since the battle was fought, and Mr. Highsmith can not now remember the others. At the time of the fight he had not been in the company long, and the names of those killed were not as familiar to him as the survivors became in after years.

From the pass Hays carried his wounded men to San Antonio, where they could get good medical attention.

Jack Hays never had a better crowd of fighting men than was with him in the Bandera Pass fight. Some of them are as follows: Sam Walker, Ad. Gillispie, P. H. Bell, Ben McCulloch, Kit Ackland, Sam Luckey, James Dunn, Tom Galbreath, George Neill, Mike Chevallier. Some of these became noted men in after years, but were then all young Texas rangers. Sam Walker was a lieutenant-colonel in the Mexican war of 1846, and was killed at the battle of Humantla. Gillispie commanded a company also, and was killed at the storming of Monterey. Ben McCulloch commanded a company, and was also a Confederate general in the civil war, and was killed at the battle of Elkhorn. George Neill was the son of Col. James Neill, who commanded the artillery at the storming of San Antonio. Chevalier was a captain in the Mexican war, as was also Ackland. Sam Luckey was a famous humorist, singer, and story-teller around the campfires. P. H. Bell was afterwards Governor of Texas. Ben Highsmith participated in eighteen battles, and was the last man to carry a dispatch from Travis at the Alamo. All of them made records as good fighters.

The Comanches buried their chief at the upper end of the pass, and the spot can still be pointed out by some rocks that are over the grave.

BATTLE OF SALADO.

In 1842 Mr. Highsmith was still a member of Jack Hays' ranging company, and stationed at San Antonio. In September of the above year Gen. Adrian Wall came from Mexico with about 1200 men and captured San Antonio. The rangers were out on a scout at the time, and failed to discover the approach of the Mexicans. Some of them came in, not being aware of the changed conditions, put up their horses, and were captured after some slight resistance. The balance of the rangers had gone down the Medina River with Captain Hays, and when they came back discovered there were Mexican soldiers in town, and made their escape, although hotly pursued by a large body of cavalry. Mr. Highsmith was with this party with Hays. The rangers went into camp on the Salado, and Captain Hays sent runners to Seguin and Gonzales and other points informing the people of the situation and calling for help. Lieut. H. E. McCulloch was very active in spreading the news and raising men. Spies from the ranger camp kept watch on the Mexicans around San Antonio. The people east, as was their wont in time of danger, responded with alacrity, and soon Gen. Matthew Caldwell took the field with a force and established his camp on the Salado, seven miles northeast from San Antonio. Captain Hays was then sent with part of his rangers to draw the Mexicans out to Caldwell's position. They advanced to within half a mile of the Alamo, and cut up many antics on their horses in a bantering way to get the Mexican cavalry to pursue them. In this they succeeded, for soon 400 cavalry came out and charged them. A lively chase now commenced back to the position of Caldwell. Mr. Highsmith was not in this chase, but remembers the following names of those who were: H. E. McCulloch, Kit Ackland, Stuart Foley, Creed Taylor, Andrew Sowell, Big Foot Wallace, Ad Gillispie, Sam Walker, Sam Luckey, and a man named Jett, who was killed in the battle which followed on the creek. The Mexican army soon came out and a severe battle was fought, in which Wall was defeated. Caldwell's force has been variously estimated. The writer once heard Gen. Henry McCulloch say that there were 201.

Before the fight commenced, and while the Mexicans were preparing to charge, the Baptist preacher, Z. N. Morrell, asked permission of Caldwell to make the men a short talk. The request was granted, and the general added, "I wish you would; it will do the boys good."

The preacher was listened to with profound respect, and he wound up the address with these words: "And now, boys, my impression before God is that we will win the fight." The men cheered their appreciation. The Mexicans made some desperate charges, but shot wild. Sometimes they would come within fifteen yards of the Texans, yelling like Indians. General Cordova, who had the fight with Burleson's rangers on Mill Creek in 1839, was killed in this fight by Wilson Randle of Seguin. John N. Seguin was also here in command of a company fighting the Texans. Capt. Nicholas Dawson, from Fayette County, tried to get to Caldwell's position with fifty-two men, but was cut to pieces and himself and thirty-two of his men were killed and the balance captured, except two—Gon. Woods and Aulcy Miller. Woods fought his way through the Mexicans and got to Caldwell; Miller went the other way to Seguin. Wall, being defeated by Caldwell, went back to San Antonio, but did not tarry there long, and set out for Mexico. He was followed by the Texans and overtaken, and a skirmish took place called

THE FIGHT ON THE HONDO.

The Mexican army in their retreat from San Antonio traveled towards the foot of the mountains and crossed the Medina River two miles above the present town of Castroville, and then traveled up between two ravines to a high ridge near the Hondo River. The advance of the Texans was led by Jack Hays and his rangers, who crowded close on the rear of the retreating Mexicans. The Texans were badly scattered, coming on in companies under their respective leaders. This want of order and a thorough understanding in regard to commanders and plan of battle caused the pursuit to be a failure. Captain Hays and his men came upon the Mexicans at the ridge where they had halted to give battle, and he halted his men to await the arrival of the remainder of the American forces, but they came in disordered squads, and the Mexican commander, seeing that he was not going to be immediately attacked, moved on across the Hondo and made another stand there. One battery was placed in position on the east side of the creek with twenty men with it, supported by infantry, and the main army formed in the flats on the west side with a cannon in position to bear upon any approach to the one on the east.

Captain Hays had sent a runner back to inform General Caldwell of the fact when the Mexicans made the first halt on the ridge. When the general came up he told Hays to follow on with his men, and when he came upon them again to charge and bring on the battle, and he would support him with the rest of the men. In the meantime Hays had sent Ben Highsmith, Sam Luckey, Tom Galbreath, and some others to follow close after Wall's army so that he could get accurate information as to the disposition of their forces in case a stand was made to fight. When the scouts arrived at a point a short distance above where the little village of New Fountain is now, in Medina County, they halted, for they were close upon the rear of the Mexicans. There was a great commotion among the latter, and they made a great deal of noise,—a perfect babel of voices, carts rattling across the rocky bed of the Hondo, officers giving commands, teamsters and artillerymen shouting and cursing, mules braying, and the occasional yelling of a lot of Cherokee Indians who were with the Mexicans. While the rangers were sitting here on their horses listening to all this they were startled by a rifle shot, and Sam Luckey reeled in his saddle and would have fallen to the ground had not Ben Highsmith caught him. The shot came from a dry branch of the Verde Creek, and the spot was located by the smoke of the rifle of the hidden marksman. Some of the rangers charged in that direction, but only the glimpse of a fleeing Cherokee Indian who did the work could be seen. These Indians were good shots and armed with rifles. They did more damage to the Texans at Salado and at Dawson's massacre than the Mexicans.

Luckey was hit under the right shoulder blade, and the ball came out just below the left nipple, barely missing the heart. This shot was just the reverse to the one he received the year before at the Bandera Pass, and by a strange coincidence Ben

Highsmith was near him on both occasions and caught him before falling, laid him down, and each time gave him water. Captain Hays and quite a lot of his men now came up, and he told the men that he was going to attack the rear guard of the enemy, and that the troops in the rear would support them. One man was left with the wounded Luckey, and the balance advanced to the attack. Hays soon found out the position of the enemy and told his men to charge and capture the battery on the east side of the creek, and then turn it upon the Mexicans beyond.

Quite a large force of Texans were now close by, and Hays though it was all right to make the charge. The men, about fifty in number, who now collected around their gallant captain to make this desperate charge were men who had been beside him in many bloody conflicts, and he knew they could be depended upon. One inducement that nerved the men to make this daring attack was the fact that in the Mexican lines on the other side of the creek, held as prisoners, were twelve of Dawson's men who had been captured at the massacre, many of the citizens of San Antonio, including members of the district court which was in session when the town was taken, and a few of Hays' rangers—their own comrades. When all was ready Hays led the way and the charge commenced. The rangers fired as they went and were soon among the cannons, which raked them with grape shot as they came up. The work was short and quick at the guns. The men who worked them either ran or were killed. Some sought refuge under the pieces to avoid the fearful rush of the mounted rangers, and Mr. Highsmith says he saw Kit Ackland lean from his saddle with pistol in hand and shoot some of them between the spokes of the cannon wheels. Although the rangers had driven in this force and captured the guns, they could not hold them. They were exposed to a severe fire of musketry and also a cannon from the other side of the creek. In vain the rangers looked for help from the rear and listened for the answering shout to their wild yells as they were spurring their horses among the cannon and artillerymen. This help did not come, and after holding their position a short time they were forced to retreat. Mr. Highsmith rode his horse under a mesquite tree and stopped after the Mexicans had been killed and driven from the cannon. While here a solid shot from the cannon beyond the Hondo struck the top of the tree and cut it off. The fragments fell upon him and his horse, which badly frightened the latter, and he wheeled and ran off with the limbs hanging all over him.

The rangers wounded in the charge were Arch. Gibson, "Dutch" Perry, John Castleman, Anderson Herrell, and William G. Cook. Herrell's horse was badly wounded, and Nick Wren's horse was killed under him in forty yards of the cannon. A grape shot hit him in the breast and went lengthwise through him. Captain Hays' horse was also wounded. Big Foot Wallace was in the charge on a mule.

While all this was going on there were more than 200 men a few hundred yards in the rear, idle spectators. It seems at the very last moment there was a misunderstanding as to who would lead the charge as commander of the whole force. The Baptist preacher, Z. N. Morrell, had a son who was a prisoner, having been captured with Dawson's men. He learned also in San Antonio that he was wounded. This man of God was in the desperate charge, hoping to rescue his son, and when the rangers returned to the main body bitterly reproached the latter for not coming to their assistance. What was the feelings of the Texas prisoners when they saw the assault fail? No doubt some of the captured rangers recognized their comrades and captain when the cannon was taken by such a bold dash, and felt sure of their liberation.

No further attempt was made on the Mexican position, and some time during the night the Mexican commander continued his retreat. A council of the Texan officers was held and the pursuit abandoned. The volunteer companies scattered back to their various homes, and the rangers went back to their quarters at San Antonio. The failure to defeat General Wall on the Hondo caused the prisoners in his hands to spend three years in the dungeons of Mexico before they were released.

Mr. Highsmith was in the Somervell expedition in 1843, but came back with Captain Hays when the expedition was abandoned, and missed the chance of drawing a bean for his life, as others did who selected commanders and went on to the invasion of Mexico after the expedition was declared off. A full account of this expedition will be given in the sketch of Big Foot Wallace, who was with it.

BATTLE OF PALO ALTO.

When the war broke out between Mexico and the United States, in 1846, Jack Hays raised a regiment of Texas rangers and joined General Taylor's army. Some of the old rangers who had been with Hays so long on the frontier raised companies for his regiment and many others went as privates. Among those who raised companies were Ad Gillispie, Kit Ackland, Ben McCulloch, Mike Chevalier, and some others. Sam Walker was lieutenant-colonel. Mr. Highsmith joined the company of Gillispie.

The cause of this war was the boundary line of Texas. When Texas applied for admission into the Union of States she claimed the Rio Grande River as her boundary line in the southwest. Mexico asserted that the Nueces River was the line, and would fight for that boundary. War was declared, and both countries began to raise armies and to march towards the disputed territory. The consequence was that the two armies came into collision on May 8th at a place called Palo Alto, on the east side of the Rio Grande. While the battle was not of long duration, there were so many cannons fired, coupled with that of the small arms, that a great deal of smoke was produced, and Mr. Highsmith says that in some charges that were made the Mexicans and Americans became badly mixed and separated from their commands. There was no breeze stirring, and the smoke lay close to the ground like a fog.

The Mexicans retreated from Palo Alto towards the Rio Grande, but halted next day at Resaca de la Palma and again gave General Taylor battle. During this battle Mr. Highsmith was helping to support a battery led by Captain May, and his horse was killed. In order to keep from being run over by the dragoon he stepped aside into a chaparal thicket. A Mexican officer saw him go in there and came to get him. The latter, however did not know what it was to go into a thicket after an old Texas ranger. Highsmith killed him and got his horse, and rode the captured steed back into the battle. He kept this horse all during the war and rode him back to Texas.

The Mexican army being defeated here, retreated into Mexico and the Americans followed. Matamoros was taken without much fighting, and the next battle Mr. Highsmith was in was

AT MONTEREY.

This was a hard-fought battle, and many American soldiers were killed. Here Mr. Highsmith lost his captain, the brave and gallant Gillespie. He did not see him killed.

During the battle Capt. Ben McCulloch got into a very close place and was about to be cut off by some Mexican lancers. A ranger named Boseman Kent went to his assistance, but with an empty gun. The lancer who was crowding McCulloch the closest turned and ran when Kent aimed his gun at him, and then the ranger pursued him. All at once horse and Mexican went out of sight and Kent saw a deep gulley in front of him, but could not check up in time to avoid it. He pulled on his horse, gave him the spur, and leaped it. As he went over he saw the gay lancer and his horse at the bottom.

The next and last battle Uncle Ben participated in was

BUENA VISTA.

This battle was fought the 23d of February, 1847. General Taylor had 5000 men, opposed by Santa Anna with 20,000. The battle commenced early in the morning and lasted all day. The rangers and many other volunteers from the States made some most desperate charges. In one of these, about the middle of the forenoon, Uncle Ben was hit by a large musket ball in the leg. He had a large silk handkerchief around his neck, and with this he bound up his leg and went on after the command. It soon became so painful, however, he was obliged to stop. When the doctor dressed the wound he pulled the handkerchief through it four times in order to cleanse it of clotted blood. When the war was over Uncle Ben came back to Texas and joined a company of rangers commanded by Capt. J. S. Sutton. They scouted out towards the Rio Grande, but had no fights.

He made Bastrop his home from 1833 to 1882, when he came west and settled in Sabinal Canyon, near the place where he once killed a buffalo while on a scout with Jack Hays in 1842. He draws a pension as a Mexican war veteran and for two wounds. He has many relatives about Bastrop who are prominent men in legal and official circles. Uncle Ben has a whetrock in his possession which he has owned ever since 1830, and carried it in his shot pouch in all the battles he was engaged in. It was given to him by Jacob C. Trask, at Matagorda. It is about three inches in length by one and a half in width, and is much smaller than when he first came in possession of it. On one side is a deep groove, made there by sharpening his awl in the days when he made moccasins and buckskin clothes. The following old-timers have sharpened their knives on it around the campfires and elsewhere: Sam Houston, James Bowie, Thos. J. Rusk, W. B. Travis, Ben Milam, Jack Hays, Ben McCulloch, P. H. Bell, Stephen F. Austin, James W. Fannin, Deaf Smith, M. B. Lamar, Ed. Burleson, and Asa, John, and Andrew Sowell, three of McCulloch and Hays rangers.

Uncle Ben saw the first paper published in Texas, the Telegraph, issued at Columbia by Gail and Thomas Borden.

CAPTAIN JOHN TOM.

Came to Texas in 1835.

The writer, while on a trip in Frio Canyon in 1898, had the pleasure of spending a few hours with the old veteran Capt. John F. Tom, one of the few survivors of the famous battle of San Jacinto. Captain Tom has a beautiful home in the Frio valley a few miles above the town of Leakey, where he is spending the evening of life in quiet and peace, surrounded by a pleasant family and genial neighbors. He was born in Maury County, Middle Tennessee, in 1818. His father, William Tom, was a soldier under Gen. Andrew Jackson in the war with the Indians, and was present at the famous battle of Horseshoe Bend. His uncle John Files on his mother's side was a soldier under Jackson in the British war of 1812, and was killed at the battle of New Orleans on the 8th of January, 1815. His great-grandfather was killed by the tories in South Carolina during the revolutionary war of 1776.

Captain Tom came to Texas with his father in 1835, landing at the mouth of the Brazos in February. Quite a lot of people came to Texas in those days who were refugees from justice and bore bad characters generally. Mr. William Tom brought with him the following recommendations of good character and citizenship, which were shown the writer and allowed to be copied:

"State of Tennessee, Maury County, November 15, 1834.—Whereas William Tom, a citizen of the State of Tennessee and county of Maury, is about to remove from here to the province of Texas with his family, consisting of the following members: His wife Kissiah, his oldest son John, second Charles, third Alfred, fourth James, fifth a daughter named Sarah, these being children of his first wife, Mary Files; Hughes, Caroline, and William, children of his second and present wife, Kissiah.

"And whereas, we whose names are assigned below, being citizens of the State and county aforementioned, and being neighbors and acquaintances of said William Tom, and some of us knowing him as a citizen of said State and county for the most part of twenty years, do hereby certify said William Tom is an orderly citizen of honest character and industrious habits, and that the above respecting his family and all herein mentioned is correct.

"Samuel Whiteside,   B. Erwin,
"Eli Asken,   John Kingston,
"James Lusk,   James Lessoms,
"James Cathey,   Henry Higgins,
"John Prewitt,   Archibald Brown,
"Thomas Kindrick,   William Brown,
"W. J. Young,   William Gounett,
"Samuel Lusk,   Gideon Strickland,
"James Lusk,   Wm. C. Malone,
"Samuel Johnes,   Jonathan Talle,
"S. C. Aydetalatt,   S. Whiteside,
"Robert L. Brown,   Isaac O. Whiteside,
"Dudley A. Lobeston, Milton Whiteside,
"Pen Gill,   John Eddring,
"Robertson Whitehead, George W. Sessums,
"Michael Higgin,   Jourdan Thompson,
"Joseph Tom,   John Neilser,
"Francis Bell,   Daniel Neilser."

Following this is a certificate of County Clerk Thomas J. Porter and Justice of the Peace Alexander Cathey, of good character, etc. Also the following from the Governor of the State, showing that these certificates were by proper authority:

"State of Tennessee, Executive Department.—I, William Carroll, Governor in and over the said State, do hereby certify that Thomas J. Porter, whose signature is annexed to the foregoing certificate, is now and was on the day of the date thereof the clerk of the court of pleas and quarter sessions for the county of Maury, in the said State, and that his official acts as such are entitled to full faith and credit, and that said certificate is in due form of law. In testimony whereof, I have hereunto set my hand and caused the great seal of the State to be affixed, at Nashville, the 22d day of December, 1834. By the Governor,
                                          "WILLIAM CARROLL.
"SAMUEL G. SMITH, Secretary."

This is rather a unique document, and I do not suppose there is another of the same character in the State of Texas. It is carefully preserved and highly prized by the Tom family, as it should be.

In the summer of 1835 the Tom family were living in Washington County, where they settled after leaving the mouth of the Brazos. In the fall of the same year the Mexicans came to Gonzales, on the Guadalupe River, which place had been settled by Green DeWitt's colony, and demanded a small cannon which had been furnished to the settlers by the Mexican government for their defense against Indian attacks. The Texans refused to give up the cannon, and a fight ensued in which the Mexicans were defeated, and they went back to San Antonio, from which place they came, without accomplishing their mission.

Gen. Stephen F. Austin, who was called the "Father of Texas," then raised a small army and proceeded to San Antonio, where General Cos was in command of the Mexican forces. William Tom and his son John, the subject of this sketch, joined Austin's command and went out to San Antonio to fight Cos and his army. They participated in the battles of Mission Concepcion and the "Grass fight," and then father and son joined the artillery under Colonel Neill, who was an old comrade of the elder Tom in the Creek war under General Jackson.

Some ditching was done and cannon planted within 600 yards of the Alamo and fire opened upon it, but the pieces were too light and no impression was made upon it. When the Mexicans opened fire on their position the Texans lay low and avoided their shots, and when night came they retired to the old mill at the head of the river. This demonstration against the fort of the Alamo was to draw the attention of the Mexicans from Col. Ben Milam, who was entering the city with about 300 men west of the river. After some terrible fighting the city was taken and Cos and his men surrendered. Before this was accomplished, however, the brave Milam lost his life, with many others who followed him.

After the capture of the city William Tom and his son went back home, and in March, 1836, John joined the army of Gen. Sam Houston on the Colorado.

On the release of General Cos and his men they went back to Mexico, and President Santa Anna, who was a brother-in-law to Cos, at once invaded Texas with a large army and recaptured San Antonio and stormed the Alamo, which was garrisoned by

CAMP GROUND OF THE TEXANS THE NIGHT BEFORE THE BATTLE OF SAN JACINTO. From a Photo.

less than 200 men under Col. William B. Travis, all of whom perished, fighting to the last.

Colonel Fannin met a like fate at Goliad, and none now were left of the defenders of Texas except the small army that had assembled under General Houston.

Young Tom joined the company commanded by Capt. W. W. Hill. However, when the battle of San Jacinto came off, the captain was sick, and the men were led into the fight by Bob Stephenson.

When the final day for battle came the Texans were impatient. They had retreated constantly before the dictator of Mexico, and had now made a stand between Buffalo Bayou and the San Jacinto River. John Tom at this time was only 17 years of age, boyish in appearance, and wore a pair of girl's stockings and buckskin moccasins.

Santa Anna crossed the bayou and encamped with the men under his immediate command, about 1500, and that night was joined by the treacherous Cos with 500 more. He had violated the parole granted him after the surrender at San Antonio, and returned with the invading army under the Mexican president. To oppose this force Houston had 732 men.

The Texan commander seemed to be in no hurry to bring on the battle, although both armies were in close proximity. He sat quietly and calmly in his tent until 4 o'clock in the evening of the 21st of April. In the meantime, however, he had sent Deaf Smith, his trusty scout, with one companion to cut down the bridge across Vince's Bayou, which was the only outlet of escape for a defeated army. When the general thought ample time had elapsed for this to be accomplished, he ordered the twenty-two captains who commanded the companies present to come before him. There was a great stir now in the patriot camp when the men saw their captains assemble and the horse of their general saddled in front of his tent. He came out with his sword buckled around him, and in a few words told the captains to parade their men in line. When the order was communicated to the respective companies the men obeyed with alacrity, and soon formed in one rank and quite extended out into the prairie. General Houston rode down the line and gave his orders, telling the men that he was going to attack the enemy, and for them to move slowly and orderly at first, and not to crowd or pass the two small cannons which were in the center, and which were to be loaded and fired as they advanced when they came within range of the enemy. One of these guns was commanded by Ben McCulloch, afterwards Confederate general in the civil war, and who was killed at the battle of Elkhorn. As the men stood in line grasping their guns, with eager, expectant faces, listening to their commander, they presented a strange and motley group in individual contrast. Beside the gray-haired veteran of other wars stood the beardless youth, with wide open eyes, throbbing heart, and quick, short breath, anticipating his first battle. Shoulder to shoulder with the better dressed men from the towns in the east stood the buckskin-clad hunter from the west; the merchant had left his counter and stood by the farmer in line with gun in hand; the doctor had left his office and drugs behind, and was handling a long rifle instead of his pill boxes, with shotpouch and powderhorn over his shoulder; the lawyer had quit his briefs and clients, and was parading in line gun in hand and pistol in belt, with his patent leather boots touching the moccasined foot of the plainsman. All were there with but one object in view—love of liberty. The cowards, tories, and scallawags had long since deserted Houston's ranks, and the men who now stood in line with their faces to the foe were the true patriots and heroes. When the advance was ordered the men started with a firm step in good order. When they came in view of the Mexicans they noticed them in great confusion, and their cannon soon began to play on the advancing line of Texans. The "Twin Sisters" replied, and soon things began to get lively. The men commenced to double-quick and yell, and soon passed the cannons. They were left behind on the prairie, one of them loaded. The Mexicans sent a plunging fire of musketry at the yelling Texans as they came sweeping towards them, and men began to get hit and fall out of line. General Houston shouted his orders for no man to stop to assist a fallen friend or comrade, but to press on straight ahead and not to fire until they could see the Mexicans' eyes, and to penetrate the Mexican line and engage them hand to hand. The men went at a full running charge, with trailed arms and yelling loudly. Their comrades dropped out here and there stricken by the musket balls that were dropping among them like hail. John F. Tom, the boy with the moccasins, was in all this wild charge, but was finally hit and knocked out of line. The men were true to the orders they had received and pressed on. Some of his neighbors only gave him a quick glance as he went down with his left leg badly shattered by a musket ball. The hand-to-hand fight, pursuit, and great slaughter of the Mexicans has already been written many times and needs no repetition here. Mr. Tom lay on the field until the battle was over, but two of his friends—Milt Swisher and Louis Clemens—remembered where he fell, and coming back to the spot bore him away to the camp. The young soldier suffered great pain for many days and was carried home as soon as possible, where kind and affectionate hands dressed his wound and nursed him until the limb was cured. Mr. Tom still limps from that shot.

In 1846 Captain Tom moved to Guadalupe County, before it was organized, and in 1856 was elected sheriff of the county, which office he held four years, that being the limit in that day and time. In 1862 he moved to Atascosa County, which was then just being settled and which was on the frontier. The Indians were very hostile and made many raids through this county, and in 1863 Mr. Tom received a commission to raise a company of rangers for frontier protection. While acting in this capacity the Indians made a raid and killed some people, besides carrying off a lot of stock. Captain Tom pursued them with his rangers and came upon the hostiles at the head of San Miguel Creek, and a fight ensued. Both parties attempted to get to a pile of rocks for their protection during the battle, and the Indians beat the rangers to the coveted spot. In the fight that followed the Comanches were defeated with loss. Of the men in the fight the old captain could only remember Calvin S. Turner, Lot Miller, and a boy named McCombs. After the fight the rangers followed the Indians to the Frio waterhole on the divide, but could not again bring them to battle, and the pursuit was abandoned.

In 1873 Captain Tom was sent to the Legislature from Atascosa County and made a true and faithful representative for his people. He moved to Frio Canyon several years ago, and in 1893 had the misfortune to get a leg broken in attempting to dismount from his horse. This, coupled with the old Mexican wound, compels him to use crutches. Captain Tom was made a Mason in 1867, Pleasanton lodge No. 383.

CAPTAIN JAMES W. WINTERS.

SAN JACINTO VETERAN.

Came to Texas in 1834.

Once in a great while and badly scattered, the writer, while in pursuit of Texas history, comes upon a San Jacinto veteran. One of these, Capt. James W. Winters, lives near the Big Foot postoffice, in Frio County.

Mr. Winters was born in Giles County, Tennessee, on the 21st of January, 1817, near the town of Pelasca. His father, James Winters, was born in North Carolina, and came to Tennessee at an early day. He was married to Miss Rhoda Beal, daughter of Benjamin Beal, during the war with the Creek Indians. The marriage took place in a fort while the people were gathered there to make a defense against the Indians.

Before the war was over he joined General Jackson's army and took part in the battle of Talladega. While with the army Mr. Winters made the acquaintance of Sam Houston, and afterwards met him in Texas, and they recognized each other.

During the revolutionary war the house of the Winters family was robbed by the tories in North Carolina. The grandmother of the subject of this sketch had a sugar bowl full of silver money, and when she saw the tories coming carried the bowl to a trunk, but instead of putting it inside slipped it underneath. The trunk was one of the old colonial kind, heavy and on rollers, and standing several inches from the floor on short legs. When the tories came into the house they took everything out of the trunk and carried it away, but failed to find the money. They took the feather beds into the yard, and, emptying the feathers, carried away the cloth, like our western Indians here in Texas. The elder Winters moved from Giles County, Tennessee, and settled on the Forked Deer River, and then from there to Shelby County, near Memphis. From this place the family came to Texas in 1834. A family named Bankhead came with them. James W. Winters had six brothers,—William C., Orin L., John F. W., Benjamin Franklin, Elisha Willis, and

Billington Taylor. James W. was the fourth son, coming between John and Benjamin. All of these came to Texas at the same time except Orin, who was engaged to be married when the family left the old States, and did not arrive in Texas until 1840.

The Winters family first settled in Texas at a place called Big Thicket, twelve miles below where Huntsville now stands. At that time all was a wilderness. When counties were first organized the place where they settled came within the limits of Montgomery County, and they lived on a little creek now called Winters Bayou. When James W. was about grown he left home and worked at the blacksmith trade at the new town of Montgomery, which was about twenty miles from home. He set in to learn the trade with Thomas Adams, but the latter on one occasion went off to buy tools and failed to return. Trouble with the Mexicans commenced in 1835, and young Winters left Montgomery and set out for San Antonio in company with his father and brother John to join the army of Gen. Stephen F. Austin, who was investing the place with a small and hastily gathered army. On arriving at San Felipe they learned that the Mexicans had surrendered. Here also they met Gen. Sam Houston, and he and the elder Winters recognized each other, and they talked about the battle of Talladega. The general also told him at parting to go back home and raise all the corn he could, for "next spring," said he, "we are going to have it out with the Mexicans, sure." James W. went back to Montgomery and stayed there until the spring of 1836, but when the news came of the fall of the Alamo he again started to meet the Mexican invaders. On again arriving at San Felipe and learning the particulars of the fierce fight at the Alamo as given by Mrs. Dickinson, who was present during the assault, and that Santa Anna was overrunning the country, a small company was at once formed on the Bernard and Capt. William Ware was elected to command. The elder Winters stayed at home during this time, but two more sons, William C. and John F. W., were present. The first lieutenant of the company was Job Collard, George Lamb second, with Albert Gallatin first sergeant and William C. Winters second. The company went on to the Colorado and there waited a few days, and by this time 200 men had collected there. General Houston was coming on from the west with the main army, and struck the river at Mercer's farm below Columbus, which then consisted of but a few houses. Ware's company with the others were at Dewees' ford, above Columbus, and remained there to prevent the Mexicans from crossing if they came that way. They did come to the opposite side of the river and shots were exchanged with them. Not being able to hold the ford, the Texans retreated and went on to the Brazos and stayed there several days in a bottom at a place called "Groce's Retreat."

Here they formed a junction with the main army under General Houston when he arrived. While here news came that the Mexicans were on the river below San Felipe, but Houston waited several days for some cannon to arrive which he expected. They finally came—two brass six-pounders ("Twin Sisters")—and the army moved on to Dunman's, where Hempstead is now. Only one night was spent here. Next morning they went to the head of a prairie which runs down to Houston; stayed one night in the prairie, and the next, on the 18th, opposite Harrisburg, which had been burned.

Deaf Smith the day before while out on a scout had captured a Mexican mail rider, and General Houston found out where Santa Anna was. On the 19th he went down Buffalo Bayou three miles and crossed, and then went down to Lynch's ferry at the mouth of the bayou where it empties into the San Jacinto River. Vince's bridge was crossed on the way down. It spanned a small bayou on the west side of Buffalo. The Mexicans went from Harrisburg to New Washington, on the bay, and then came up into the prairie and went into camp on the San Jacinto. Houston's men were now ahead of the Mexicans, having moved back up the bayou to a skirt of timber and there went into camp. Scouts came in and reported the Mexicans in camp three-quarters of a mile away, south. On the 20th the Mexicans made an attack on the camp of the Texans at long range from a mott of timber bordering a marsh 200 yards away. The Texans replied, but little damage was done. Two or three Texans were wounded, one of whom was Col. J. C. Neill, severely.

Another portion of the Mexican army was in a low depression of the prairie where cannon were planted and breastworks made. General Houston went to all the messes of his men, encouraging them and telling them that if they gained this battle all of them would be captains. After the battle, and while Santa Anna was a prisoner in the camp he expressed his surprise at the quick annihilation of his army by an inferior force. "Nothing curious about that," said the Texan general, "my whole command were captains."

Next day, the 21st, General Houston late in the evening moved his men out and made an attack on the Mexican camp. The Winters brothers were in the second regiment, commanded by Colonel Sherman, and on the extreme left of the formation in the charge, and which brought them in contact with the Mexican right, which was posted in the timber and high grass. Colonel Sherman bore to the left to rout these. They were lying down and commenced firing on the Texans in that position as they came towards them at a double-quick charge. Mr. Winters says he heard the order to fire three times before he saw anything to shoot at, and all the men ran up close to the enemy before firing. They could see the smoke from the Mexican guns coming out of the grass near the ground in the edge of the timber, but none of them moved until they arose to run.

In the meantime, however, the bullets from the Mexicans were striking among the Texans and several had already gone down, among whom was Lieutenant Lamb and Sergeant Winters. James W. did not see his brother William fall, and kept on in the charge. When the Texans came within fifty or sixty yards of the Mexicans they sprang up quickly and ran away, and seemed to be very numerous. The Texans now opened up a rapid fire with terrible effect. The ground was almost covered with dead and disabled Mexicans. Those not hit went in rapid flight through the timber towards the breastworks, followed by the Texans, who by this time were yelling loudly. The fight was hard at the cannon, and the bullets flew among and over the Texans as thick as hail. Mr. Winters had a long flintlock rifle, and stopped beside a Spanish oak tree to ram a tight ball, and while so doing a large ball struck the side of the tree and threw so much bark in his face and with such force that for a few moments he thought he was wounded from the pain it created. At this time the right wing of the Texans had reached the works and a terrible hand-to-hand fight was taking place with clubbed rifles, bayonets, and sabers. Mexicans and Texans were one writhing, surging mass. This, however, did not last long, as the Mexicans soon ran, some in one direction and some in another.

Part of them went to Vince's bridge, hoping to escape across that; but "Deaf" Smith had destroyed it that morning, and they huddled there like a bunch of cattle, and many were killed. Some of them tried to keep in the timber along the marsh and escape towards the bay shore. Nearly all of them, however, were overtaken and killed or captured. Many ran into the marsh to escape the Texans, and forty of them were taken out of there the next day. Mr. Winters loaded and fired his rifle eight times during the battle and pursuit. He was with those who cut off the Mexicans towards the bay shore, and it was nearly night when he returned to the main battleground. He became separated from his brothers during the fight, but saw John just as the pursuit ended, and asked him if he knew anything of William. He said no he had not seen him since the fight commenced. The two brothers now hastily went to camp, but hearing no tidings there, hurriedly returned to the bloody field and began a diligent search there until darkness put an end to all further work in that place. Once more they returned to camp, greatly distressed. They knew William too well to entertain the thought for an instant that he had shirked the battle, and grave fears were now entertained that he had been slain in some out-of-the-way place during the pursuit, fallen perhaps in high, marshy grass, and his body would never be recovered. On arriving at camp this time, however, they found the missing brother, who had just been brought into camp badly wounded. He was hit in the charge before reaching the timber and fell out of line without being seen by either of the other brothers. When the ball struck him he had his foot clear of the ground and leg bent, charging, and the missile, which was a large musket ball, struck just above the knee and ranged back, coming out at the large part of the thigh on the under side. In its course the ball grazed the thigh bone and so paralyzed the limb that Sergeant Winters was unable to arise from the ground after he fell, and had to lie there until dark before being carried away.

Captain Ware's company was small—only eighteen—but they were under a close fire and suffered more than some of the larger companies. The casualties were as follows: Second Lieut. George A. Lamb, killed; Sergt. William Winters, severely wounded; Sergt. Albert Gallatin, slightly wounded; Private E. G. Rector, slightly wounded; Private G. W. Robinson, severely

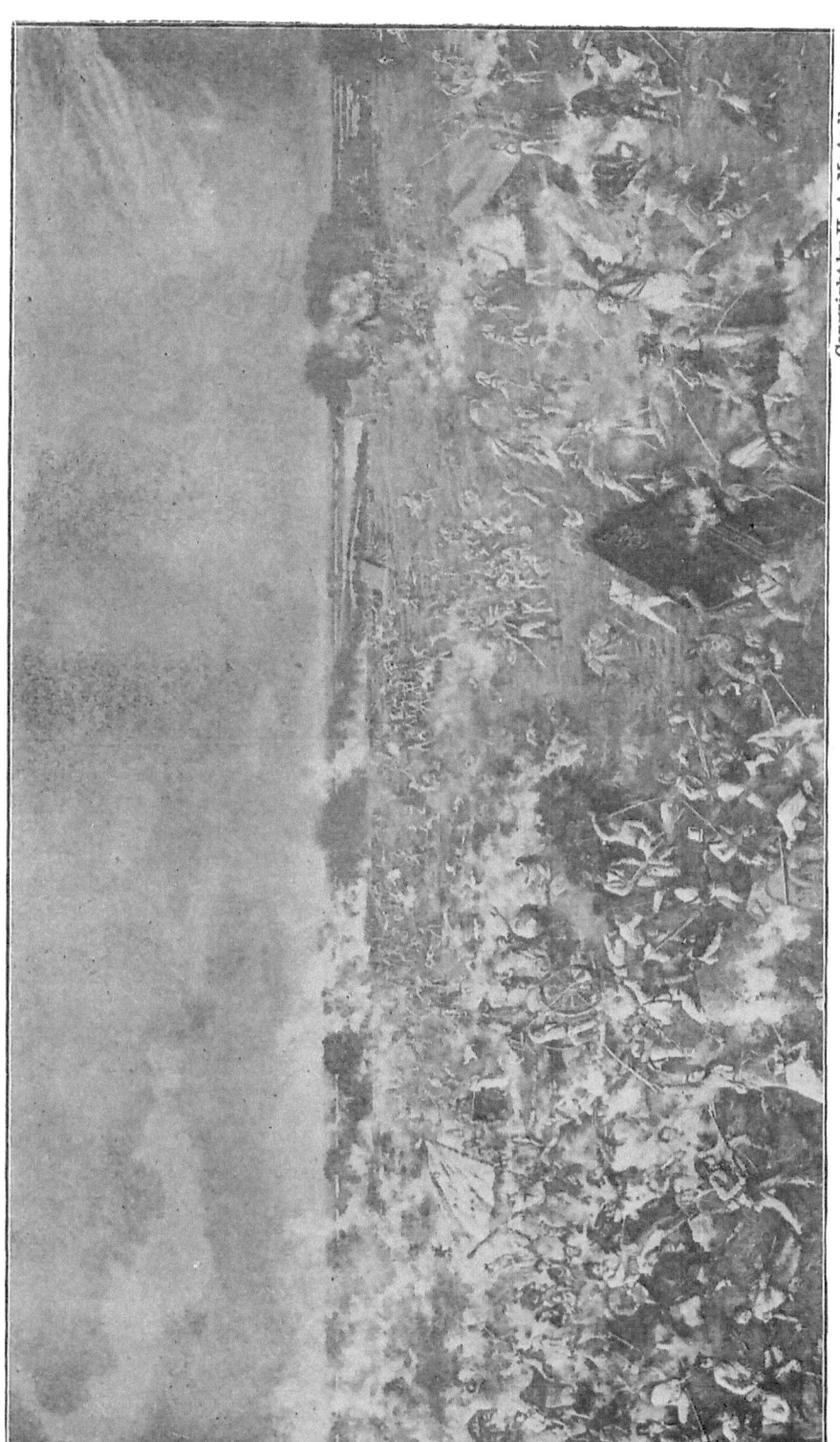

THE BATTLE OF SAN JACINTO.
From a painting.

wounded. The ball which hit Albert Gallatin first struck his powderhorn, cut through the shotpouch, and entered the side, carrying the strap of the shotpouch into the wound.

Mr. Winters says that Captain Ware was like a wild mustang, and when the charge was ordered leaped to his place in front and shouted, "Come on, boys!" Mr. Winters remained seven days on the battleground attending to his wounded brother, and at times going over the battleground. He said the Mexicans had made their breastworks out of brush and packs of camp equipage. The Mexicans lay thick in many places, and none of them were buried. The Texans had to move their camp on account of the stench emanating from the dead bodies which lay thickly south of of them. In a few days the Mexicans presented a fearful sight, swelling to enormous sizes. No buzzard or wolf came about them. From the battlefield the army went up to Harrisburg, and here Mr. Winters left them and went home. The wounded brother was carried home by John from the battleground. The elder Winters died in the Big Thicket on the first place settled by him in Texas. He had a good farm there.

In 1837 the Indians made a raid in that country and killed a Mrs. Taylor, whose husband also had been killed by Indians a month before that time. Mrs. Taylor, at the time she met her death, was at the house of a neighbor named Hadley. The attack was made in the night, and Mrs. Taylor tried to leave the house with her children, three in number—two boys and a girl. The Indians found them out in their flight, and killed the mother and little girl and shot one of the boys in the hand with an arrow. This occurred near where the town of Anderson now is. Mrs. Taylor was delivered of another child in her dying struggle after being shot. A man named Kindred went to Montgomery to give the alarm and made a most remarkable ride. It was thirty-five miles to the town, and he started from Hadley's after daylight, rode there, raised twenty-five men, and was back at Hadley's on the following night. Mr. Winters was one of the twenty-five men who went from Montgomery. After an organization took place Jerry Washam was chosen captain, and the pursuit of the Indians commenced. They had taken a westerly course out of the country. The command crossed the Navasota River and went up between that stream and the Brazos, passing within three miles of Fort Parker. Twenty-five miles beyond the fort, at a horseshoe-shaped prairie belted by timber, the Indians scattered and the trail was hard to keep. Finally buzzards were seen in a point of timber where the prairie circled around it, and the men cautiously went in. The Indians had seen the white men and hastily left, leaving bows, shields, arrows, etc. While making a close examination of the camp Mrs. Taylor's scalp was found. There was also a large amount of cooked meat in camp. The Indians were all on foot and not more than ten in number. They were trailed across the prairie on the other side of the timber, and here they again scattered and it was impossible to follow them, so the pursuers commenced their return. There was one timid man along, named Hardwick. One night he and Winters were on guard at the same time but in different places. Hardwick fired at something (or nothing) and raised an alarm. Winters saw the fire from Hardwick's gun, but not knowing what the matter was, remained at his post and awaited developments. Hardwick when he fired ran into camp with all the balance of the guards, ten in number, except Winters. The roll of the guards was called and all answered except Winters. A man by the name of Tullis said he would bet that Hardwick had killed Winters. The frightened guard had said that he did not know what he shot at. He was then asked what the thing was doing when he fired—walking upright or crawling. "Both," he says; "kinder pokin." At this they all laughed, and some of them went to hunt for Winters, whom they soon found all right.

Not long after this Indian chase Mr. Winters married Miss Pearcy Tullis, near Montgomery. Her father and brother were both in the Indian pursuit above mentioned.

In 1842, when General Wall captured San Antonio, Mr. Winters with others went to aid in defeating him. When they arrived at San Antonio their force amounted to 200 men, but the battle had been fought and the Mexicans gone back to Mexico. Mr. Winters, however, stayed out and went on with the Somervell expedition. His captain was Albert Gallatin, who was wounded at San Jacinto. Winters came back when the command had the split on the Rio Grande, and missed drawing a bean for his life,—a chance which befell those who went over into Mexico.

In 1850 he came out further west and settled on the San Marcos River, three miles above Prairie Lea, and helped his brother

William to build a mill. He stayed here two years, when he went into the mercantile business and got broke up. He moved further west then, and went into the stock business on shares with Berry Crane and others, and settled on the Nueces, near Oakville, in Liveoak County. Here he had to contend with Indians, Mexicans, and white cow-thieves. One party of six Indians made a raid and, getting into a fight with cowmen, were all killed.

When the civil war broke out Mr. Winters raised a company of ninety men and offered them to the Confederacy. They were accepted, but Mr. Winters did not go with it as captain, but was kept back as an enrolling officer, and was also commissioned as provost marshal. Guards were kept between the Nueces and Rio Grande as mounted rangers. Mr. Winters went with them part of the time. He remained on the border during the war with the rank of captain. On one occasion horse-thieves made a raid and were followed by Captain Winters with two men. They rode sixty miles in one day and caught the thieves, who were Mexicans, at sundown, charged them, killed one, and rescued eight head of horses and brought them back.

After the war he went to Tuxpan, Mexico, and lived there eight years, farming, etc. He came back to Bee County, Texas, stayed there two years, and then came to Frio County, where he still resides, eight miles southeast from Devine.

Mr. Winters had three sons in the Confederate army,—James, Josephus, and Francis Marion. James, the eldest, was captured at Arkansas Post, and was in Bragg's army after the exchange. Marion died in San Antonio before leaving Texas. Josephus was in the Fort Donelson fight, and also helped to capture the Harriet Lane at Galveston.

The old veteran, now in his eighty-second year, lives with his son William on an adjoining farm to his own. His first wife died in Mexico, and the second died in 1895.

MRS. HANNAH BERRY.

Came to Texas in 1828.

One of the most interesting characters now in Texas is Mrs. Hannah Berry, who lives in the Upper Sabinal country, in Bandera County. Mrs. Berry was born in Catahoula Parish, Louisiana, on the 2d day of November, 1812, and is the daughter of Jesse Devoe. Her father and a company of men were in hearing of the battle of New Orleans, and made all haste to get there to take part in the engagement, but were too late. They were greatly stimulated in their exertions to reach the battleground by the constant roar of cannon, which was heard for many miles.

Mrs. Berry moved to Mississippi when quite a small child, and started to Texas from "Jackson's new purchase," 150 miles above Vicksburg, in 1826. The family made several stops on the route, and arrived in Texas and settled in Liberty County in 1828. In 1831 she married John Berry, of Kentucky, who came to Texas in 1826. Mr. Berry was a gunsmith by trade, and his services in the new country were almost indispensable. He received a league of land from the Mexican government as one of Robinson's colonists.

In 1834 the family moved to Bastrop, and Mr. Berry made knives, guns, and pistols, and mended all the broken ones in the country. In 1836, when Col. David Crockett of Tennessee came to Bastrop on his way to join Col. William B. Travis at the Alamo, in San Antonio, he had with him a very fine gun, but it had been broken off at the breech, and he was very anxious to have it mended before reaching San Antonio. Some one said to Colonel Crockett when the broken gun was mentioned, "Take it to John Berry; he can fix it for you." Crockett came to Berry's shop in company with John McGee and brought the gun with him. Mr. Berry examined it, and saying he could fix it all right, at once set about the work. A large silver band was placed around the broken place, and so securely fastened that it was as strong as ever and very ornamental when polished and flowered off. Colonel Crockett was well pleased, and said it was now better than it was at first. The gun was lost in the Alamo when

Crockett was killed in the famous battle. Mention has been made several times of Crockett's beautiful silver mounted rifle which was taken by the Mexican army to Mexico when the war was over. The silver part of it was the band over the broken place put there by John Berry. Mrs. Berry says she would know the gun now if she could see it by the silver band she watched her husband put there. She remembers well how Colonel Crockett looked, and says he did not wear a cap while at Bastrop.

Mrs. Berry heard many an Indian yell during the "bloody days of Bastrop," and once saw 500 Comanche Indians at one sight. She saw Wilbarger after he was scalped by the Indians, and says he lived ten years after. When the Alamo was taken a messenger came and told the people to retreat back out of danger until the settlers who were rallying under Gen. Sam Houston could meet the victorious Mexicans in battle. The people of Bastrop left the town and traveled by various methods and to different places. Mr. Berry's family and a few others went to Fort Parker. Gen. Edward Burleson was in the Texan army, and his stepmother and her five children and one of the Burleson children went in Mr. Berry's wagon. Also of the party were the Harris and McKinney families. Dr. McKinney it was said was the cause of the Indians being so hostile in those days and killing so many Bastrop settlers. In some transaction with the Indians he made a present to them of a keg of sugar which he had poisoned, and which caused the death of a great many of them. The Indians in revenge for this killed Dr. McKinney and some companions at a place afterwards called Bone Hollow. The bones of the men had been found and buried there, hence the name. Mrs. Berry says she saw the rail pen which had been placed around them. During the stay of the fugitive families at Fort Parker Col. Benjamin Parker, who was in command of the fort and who was also a Baptist preacher, held services regularly and preached to the people. These were long, anxious days to those in the fort, especially to those who had sons and husbands in Houston's army. Mr. Berry did not go to the army, as he was getting old; but three of his sons by his first wife had gone to strike a blow for liberty.

The families stayed three weeks at the fort. Mrs. Berry knew the famous Cynthia Ann Parker well, who was then a very small girl. Mrs. Plummer was also there, who suffered so much as a captive among the Comanche Indians afterwards. There was also a strange boy at this fort named Robert Foster, whom the people who lived there called "the prophet." It was said that he told many things which had come to pass. Every morning while awaiting news from the seat of war some one would ask this boy what news he could tell them, but for a long time he would say that he had nothing to tell. One morning, however, he arose early and told the people that they could go home if they wished, as the men of General Houston had killed nearly all of the Mexican army, and that a beardless boy had captured Santa Anna. The same evening two men came in sight running their horses and firing pistols. Mr. Berry answered with several shots from the fort, and in a few minutes the men came up. They were messengers from San Jacinto, bringing news of the victory. There was great rejoicing, and those who did not live at the fort soon made preparations to go home. When the Berrys arrived at Bastrop they found their house burned and all of their stock driven off by the Mexicans. Three of the Berry boys were in the army, to wit, John Bates, Andrew Jackson, and Joseph. The two first took part in the battle, but Joseph arrived too late. Cornelius Devoe, brother of Mrs. Berry, was also in the battle. He was from Liberty County, and had not seen the Berry boys for a long time. They recognized each other during the heat of the combat, but having no time to talk or shake hands, shouted their greetings amid booming cannons and rattling musketry.

The boy Foster at Fort Parker, three days before the fearful massacre at that place, arose early one morning and told all the people to leave the fort if they did not want to get killed, as the Indians were coming and would take the place. They did not do so, and Mrs. Berry says she supposes the boy was killed with the balance, as she never heard of him afterwards.

In 1840, when the Comanches made the famous raid through Texas and burned the town of Linnville on the coast, the Berrys were living in Burleson County. When they heard the news, John Bates Berry and his brother Andrew Jackson mounted their horses and took a prominent part in the battle of Plum Creek, where the Indians were badly defeated. This battle was fought about three miles east of the present town of Lockhart, in Caldwell County.

In 1842 Bates and Joe Berry joined the Somervell expedition

and were with the party who crossed over into Mexico and fought the battle of Mier. Just before the battle Joe had the misfortune of falling into a ditch and breaking his leg while acting as a scout to ascertain something of the enemy. His brother Bates and some others carried him into an old outhouse in the town, and while there the battle commenced. The Mexicans were trying to storm Cameron's position where he had barricaded the streets and houses, and were in rifle shot of the old house in which Joe and his three companions were. It was agreed that they would not let themselves be known until the battle was over, as they would be at the mercy of the Mexicans. One of the men, however, in the excitement during a charge on the position of the Texans, aimed his rifle through an opening and fired. Joe now told them to all run and save themselves if they could and leave him alone to his fate, as the house would now be attacked and all killed. The men acted on this advice of the brave, unselfish boy, and, opening the door, made a desperate run for Cameron's position. They were met by a volley from the Mexicans, who were advancing with a small force under the command of a lieutenant to assault the house. One of the men fell dead in his tracks, but John Berry and the other man fought their way through the Mexicans and gained the position of the Texans.

In making the run and fight through the Mexicans, John Berry recognized the lieutenant in command as a man whom he knew in San Antonio. The fate of poor Joe was sealed. The Mexican officer went into the room where he lay helpless and killed him with his sword. He then came out flourishing the bloody weapon and bragging about the deed. He was afterwards killed in Texas by the Berry boys. John Berry was captured with the balance of the Texans when the surrender took place, and was in the desperate chance of drawing a bean for his life at Salado. He drew a white one, but one of his neighbors named Porter drew a black one, and bewailed his fate in such a forcible way that Berry, rendered almost desperate by the death of his brother and the terrible scenes through which he had passed, thought of swapping beans with him and being shot in his place. After the fight he had passed many long, weary hours in prison. Then came the fight at Salado, where, unarmed, they rushed upon the guards, wrenched the weapons from their hands, and fought their way to liberty. Then came days of famine and thirst, lost in the mountains, trying to make their way to Texas. The recapture, brutal treatment, and being marched from town to town, exhibited like so many wild beasts, and at last to stand up and draw beans for the little miserable life that was left in them. No wonder he thought of taking his comrade's black bean and ending it all. The thought of home, however, and the old mother watching and waiting for her boys, one of whom was already gone, decided him, and he stood by and saw his neighbor shot. After twenty-two months of hard labor on the streets of the towns in Mexico, he was released and made his way back home. A man named Whitfield Clark made his escape and informed the Berry family of Joe's death before John got back.

Mrs. Berry's husband drew a pension for services in the war of 1812, and when he died it was transferred to her, which she still receives—one of the very few left who draws a pension of that character. Mr. Berry served also against the Indians under General Harrison, and fought at the battles of Tippecanoe and the Thames. He volunteered from Kentucky and served in the company commanded by Capt. William Smithers, Hopkins' regiment. Mrs. Berry was the mother of twelve children, as follows: Mary, the eldest, married John Compton; Emanuel, married Delilah Cox; John, married Hixa Jane Donnell; Jane, married Lieut. James Ramsey, now of Corn Hill, in Williamson County; Julia and Catherine, twins; the first named married Robins; the second Jackson. Joseph, a Confederate soldier, who died at the age of 18 years at Bayou Boeuff, La.; Silas, married Sarah Hutchinson; Clarissa, married Henson Mitchell; Patrick Henry and Virginia, twins; the former died young, and Virginia married George Murphy; the last George Washington, making the twelve. The Joseph mentioned above was her own son, and the one killed at Mier in Mexico was her stepson, and on account of their great love and attachment for him this one was named Joseph also. Two of her sons, Emanuel and John, went through the civil war and helped to capture the Harriet Lane at Galveston. Emanuel limps now from injuries received in crossing the long bridge going from the mainland to the city. He is a Missionary Baptist preacher and has been for more than twenty-five years. During the battle of Galveston he saw a woman going through the street with two children, one of whom was killed by a piece of bombshell. Mrs. Berry also had two nephews in the battle, Cornelius Hampshire and Barney Hampshire. Old man John Hampshire lived on elevated ground at Bolivar Point, and two shells from the Harriet Lane fell in his yard but did not explode. While Mrs. Berry was on a visit to the Hampshires some years later, these shells were shown her. Young Joseph Berry, who died in the Confederate service, belonged to Captain Hally's company, of Belton. Lieutenant Emory of the same company was also from Belton. Colonel Mullins, who commanded the regiment, was from Florence, Williamson County. Grandma Berry has belonged to the Baptist Church ever since 1841. The first Missionary Baptist Church in Williamson County was organized in her house by Revs. Garrett and Talafero. The latter preached there fourteen months. Mrs. Berry knew the old pioneer Baptist preacher, Z. N. Morrell, well.

One of the daughters-in-law of Mrs. Berry, who was a Donnell, had a brother killed during the war at Yellow Bayou. In the old family Bible the writer found the following entry:

"Wiley H. Donnell was wounded in the fight on Yellow Bayou on the 18th of May, 1864, and died of his wound on the same night at 9 o'clock, aged 24 years, 2 months and 11 days. Had been in the Confederate service two years and nine months."

Donnell was killed by a wounded Federal soldier while lying on the ground and not able to get up.

Grandma Berry has seventy-four grandchildren that she knows of, and one hundred and twenty-four great-grandchildren, and two great-great-grandchildren. Her oldest daughter is 64 years old. Emanuel, her oldest son, is 64. Her next, John, is 60, and her youngest is 40 years old. Very few people live to see their children become old and gray around them, or such a numerous offspring of grandchildren. She is a small woman, with hair white as snow and a healthy-looking round face without many wrinkles, considering her age.

"BIG FOOT" WALLACE.

"BIG FOOT" WALLACE.

Came to Texas in 1837.

William Alexander Anderson Wallace, better known as "Big Foot," was born in Lexington, Rockbridge County, Virginia, on the 3d day of April, 1817. His ancestors came from the highlands of Scotland at an early day, and took part in the war for American independence on the side of the colonists. He had two uncles killed at the battle of Guilford Courthouse. The Wallaces were all powerful men physically. The subject of this sketch when in his prime was 6 feet 2 inches in his moccasins, and weighed 240 pounds. He had one uncle who was nearly 7 feet, and one brother who was 6 feet 5 inches. "Big Foot" had long arms and large hands, and his hair was black, thick, and inclined to curl.

Nothing of interest occurred in the life of Wallace until he was about 20 years of age. At that time war had commenced in Texas between the American colonists and the Mexicans. Many brave young men went from the States to assist the Texans against the dictator, Santa Anna, and among these was Samuel Wallace, brother of Big Foot, or William, as he was then only known. Samuel was killed in the massacre of Fannin's men at Goliad, as were three other relatives. When the news reached Lexington, Va., great was the grief in the Wallace family, and William took an oath that he was going to Texas and spend his life killing Mexicans. One reason of this bitter hatred was the fact that his brother and all the others were killed after they had surrendered and been disarmed.

As soon as he could get ready William set out for New Orleans, and from there took shipping for Galveston. A terrible storm occurred on the way and many vessels were wrecked. The one Wallace was on, the Diadem, rode out the gale well and arrived safe and sound at her destined port. Galveston, however, had nearly been destroyed, and ships were high and dry in the town. The Diadem came to anchor in Galveston Bay on the 5th day of October, 1837, and Wallace for the first time set foot on Texas soil.

The war was over in Texas. Santa Anna had been defeated and captured the year before at the famous battle of San Jacinto, and Texas was now an independent republic. Wallace drifted up to Bastrop, on the Colorado, and only found a few families there. Among them were Egglestone, Manlove, and Mays. After a short stay here he went on up to where a settlement was starting at La Grange. Col. John H. Moore owned the land where the town was afterwards built, but was the only resident there when Wallace arrived.

Shortly after coming here Big Foot had his first experience with Indians. They made a raid among the scattered settlers in the vicinity of La Grange or the Moore settlement, and were pursued by five men, among whom were Gorman Woods, William Wallace, and a man named Black. The Indians were overtaken and a running fight of several miles across a prairie took place, in which two of the Indians were killed and one wounded. Wallace killed one of them.

Wallace was fond of the woods, and hunted almost continually while at La Grange. On one occasion, while out on Buckner's Creek alone, he was suddenly surrounded by a large party of Lipan Indians and captured. They carried him to their camp and kept him for a week or more, but at the end of that time he eluded them and got back to the settlement.

In 1838 Wallace made his first trip to San Antonio, arriving there on the 14th day of April. Shortly after arriving he went and took a look at the Alamo. Signs of the fierce battle were on every side. An outer wall inclosed the fort in front and reached out into the plaza, where was an entrance through two large gates. The walls had been partly demolished by cannon shots, and the gates had been torn and twisted around and piles of rock had been thrown up here and there. The ashes were still to be seen where the slain Texans were burned, with small pieces of charred bones among them. Wallace stayed in San Antonio some time and killed many deer in the prairie around. When Austin was selected for the capital in 1839, Wallace went there and found a town of small cabins and tents. As many new buildings were going up, Wallace obtained a job to hew logs at a salary of $200 per month and board. He worked at this two months, and then went into a partnership with a man named William Leggett to raft cedar down the Colorado from high up in the mountains. Austin was on the extreme frontier, and nothing but one vast wilderness beyond, in which Wallace delighted. It best suited his roving disposition and hermit-like nature. He loved the wild woods and gloried in all the primeval scenes of nature,—her lofty rock and cedar-capped mountains, deep canyons, dark brakes and forest, clear springs and swift-rushing river. The deer, turkey, buffalo, wild horses, and the painted savage all had charms for him. He would take extensive rambles up the Colorado and then make wide circles back to the settlements, shooting game by the way, and eating and sleeping when and where he felt disposed to do so.

In Austin at this time was a good natured, jolly Irishman, named William Fox, who went into partnership with Wallace, and, renting a small cabin in town, kept "bach" there together. They took contracts for work, and one of these was to haul rock from the mountains to build houses, and they made a great deal of money. Also in this country at that time was a noted Indian called Big Foot, who gave the settlers much trouble. He was a Waco, and had a band of eight with him. He would come into the town at night, kill who he could, and carry off horses and other property. He was a wily rascal, and the settlers tried in vain to kill him. His tracks measured fourteen inches with his moccasins on; hence his name. He was also powerful physically, being 6 feet 7 inches in height, muscular, and weighing about 300 pounds. Wallace was anxious to kill him, and many miles he trailed him. He saw him three times, but never was close enough at those times to shoot. A man named Thomas Green shot him once and wounded him in the knee. This man Green was afterwards Gen. Tom Green, and was killed at the battle of Blair's Landing during the civil war. Some think that Wallace received the name of Big Foot from killing this Indian, but when the writer interviewed the old captain a few years ago and asked the question, he said: "No; Ed Westfall killed him on the Llano. I trailed him many times and saw him three times at a distance, but never shot at him."

"Then," said I, "there is another account in circulation that the Mexicans gave you that name while a prisoner in their hands in Mexico after the battle of Mier, because they could not find a pair of shoes large enough for you in the City of Mexico."

"No," said he, "that is not so. There were men in the command who had larger feet than I. The Mexicans all have small feet, and they could not find shoes to fit any of us. My feet are not large in proportion to my body. See? (and he held them out for my inspection, and it was even so—No. 9½). But 10's," he said, "fit easy. But," the old man continued, "I did get my name from the Big Foot Indian, but not because I killed him."

The story is this: One night in 1839 the Big Foot Indian came into the town of Austin, and in prowling about committed some theft on the premises of a man named Gravis, and then went to the cabin occupied by Fox and Wallace. Next morning Gravis trailed the Indian to the doorstep of Wallace, and without trying to trace it any further roused Wallace and accused him as the depredator. Wallace also wore moccasins and made a large track, but he was so incensed at Gravis that he was about to whip him on the spot, and made a grab at him. Gravis got out of the way and told Wallace to prove himself clear and he would apologize, and there would be no fight. Wallace said he could do that, and at once went to the Indian's track and placed his foot in it with the moccasin on, and made Gravis come up close enough to look at it, and showed him how much longer the Indian's track was than his. This was convincing, so Gravis begged pardon and walked off. During this episode Fox came to the door and took notice of the whole transaction, and while Wallace was standing in the Indian's track, laughed and said, "Now, Wallace, when the Big Foot Indian is not around we will call you Big Foot." Others took up the name, and so it came about that when some one would make a remark about Big Foot another would ask, "Which do you mean, the Indian or Big Foot Wallace?" So the name stuck to him and has been famous along the border for more than half a century.

It is a strange coincidence that the man who gave Wallace the name of Big Foot was finally killed by the Big Foot Indian. Fox was one day hoeing a small patch of corn surrounded by a brush fence in the suburbs of the town, when Big Foot shot him from the fence. Wallace wanted now more than ever to kill the Indian, and after burying his partner took the trail, but was unsuccessful. He killed one of the band, however, at Mount Bonnell on the Colorado, above Austin. We will have to skip over many interesting incidents in the life of Wallace, and only mention the most important of battles, etc.

In 1840 William Wallace, now known as Big Foot, once more visited the historic city of San Antonio. His restless spirit, however, could not be confined to the streets of a city. He soon went further southwest and camped and hunted along the Medina River. Finally he built a cabin on the west bank of the stream, ten miles below the present town of Castroville, in Medina County.

We now come to that period in the life of Big Foot Wallace when he began to serve the young republic in the capacity of a Texas ranger under the famous Jack Hays, who stands pre-eminently at the head of that long list of ranger captains. In 1840 the situation around San Antonio, which was then on the extreme frontier, was anything but encouraging to those who wished to settle in the country and lead quiet lives and make good citizens. Besides the numerous raids of hostile bands of Indians who roamed at will from the line of New Mexico to the coast region of Texas, horsethieves, desperadoes, gamblers, and fugitives from justice who had fled from other States, swarmed around all the border towns, and more especially San Antonio. No one was safe who was in opposition to this element. It was almost impossible to keep horses. They would dig through adobe houses to get them. A strong hand was needed here to awe this class and hold them in check. There was one man in western Texas at the time who was equal to the emergency. His name was John Coffee Hays, better known to history as Jack Hays, the famous Texas ranger. He was a surveyor by profession, brave and energetic. He had already made himself known and felt at the famous batle of Plum Creek. General Houston recognized the ability of the young surveyor, and seeing the necessity of an armed active force at San Antonio to hold both Indians and lawless characters in check, commissioned Jack Hays to raise a company, to be stationed at San Antonio as headquarters, and to follow horsethieves or Indians anywhere he wished, and to shoot horsethieves on the spot if necessary.

Big Foot Wallace heard of the organization, and at once applied for admission and was enrolled as one of the company. Captain Hays was very particular as to the kind of men he enlisted, and that is one reason why he had the best set of Indian fighters, taken as a whole, that Texas ever produced. A man had to have courage, good character, be a good rider, good shot, and have a horse worth $100. In this first company the writer has learned the names of Wallace, Woolfork, Joe Tivey, Mark Rapier, Kit Ackland, Jim Galbreth, Tom Buchanan, Coho Jones, Peter Poe, Mike Chevalier, and Ad Gillespie. Among those who came later and followed the fortunes of Hays, and helped to fight his battles and gain a reputation for him as an Indian fighter which is almost world-wide, were Sam Walker, Sam Lucky, George Neill (or Nail as he was called), James Dunn, Ben McCulloch, Henry McCulloch, Ben Highsmith, Tom Galbreth, Andrew Sowell, John Sowell, P. H. Bell, Creed Taylor, Sam Cherry, Noah Cherry, John Carlin, Rufus Perry, Joe Davis, Pipkin Taylor, Josiah Taylor, Rufus Taylor, James Nichols, Calvin Turner. Milford Day, Lee Jackson, and many other gallant men whose names can not now be obtained.

During the years 1840-41 Hays and his men captured many horsethieves in and around San Antonio and shot several of them. On one occasion they captured a notorious Mexican freebooter named Antonio Corao, and such was the nature of his crimes that it was decided to put an end to his existence. Four men were detailed to shoot him, namely, Big Foot Wallace, Chapman Woolfork, Sam Walker, and William Powell. The execution took place at the head of the San Antonio River.

During the stay of the rangers in San Antonio they did a great deal of scouting and fought several battles with the Indians. Things went on in this way until the fall of 1842, when the Mexicans under Gen. Adrian Wall made a sudden descent from Mexico and captured San Antonio. Prior to this event, however, there was a suspicion that something was wrong, from the fact that all at once no ammunition could be bought in San Antonio by the Americans. It had all been secured by Mexicans at various times. Wallace also told Captain Hays that there were at least a dozen strange Mexicans in town who did not live there. Hays now sent Wallace and another ranger named Nathan Mallon to Austin to get a supply of powder and lead. Captain Wallace told the writer that Mallon was afterwards sheriff of Bexar County. While in Austin the Indians made a raid and killed Capt. William Pyron and a man named Donovan, north of Austin about two miles. Wallace and Mallon went out and helped to bring the bodies in and bury them. They then obtained their ammunition and started back to San Antonio. Wallace had a full keg of powder rolled up in a blanket and tied to the pommel of his saddle. Mallon had a supply of caps and lead. As there were no settlements between Austin and San Antonio, they providentially went back by way of Seguin to get corn for their horses. San Antonio had been captured during their absence, and if they had gone directly back, they and their ammunition would have fallen into the hands of the Mexicans. At Seguin they found Captain Hays and his lieutenant, Henry E. McCulloch. The town (San Antonio) was suddenly captured, and part of the ranger force fell into the hands of the Mexicans. Hays and some of his men escaped. The whole country east was now rallying under Gen. Matthew Caldwell to advance upon San Antonio and give battle to this large band of 1500 freebooters and robbers. The Texans, 200 in number, advanced to the Salado Creek, seven miles northeast of the city, and Captain Hays with what rangers he had under his command was sent to draw the Mexicans out. What few rangers there were in town when the Mexicans entered made a short fight, in which the bandmaster was killed, and also the horse of General Wall.

Hays and his men went so near town and gave the Mexicans such a dare that the whole force of cavalry and infantry came out. An exciting chase now commenced across the prairie back to the position of the Texans. Four hundred cavalry chasing and firing at the small squad under the gallant Hays. When the infantry arrived with cannon the main battle came off, and the Mexicans were badly defeated.

When the Mexicans captured the quarters of the rangers in San Antonio they obtained among other things a pair of pantaloons belonging to Big Foot Wallace. During the battle now he was on the lookout to kill a big Mexican and get another pair to replace them and get even. During a close charge by the Mexicans one daring fellow charged Wallace, and presenting his carbine at him, cried out, "Take that, you d—d cowthief," and fired in his face. The large ounce ball from the escopet grazed the nose of Wallace and almost blinded him with smoke. Big Foot fired, but missed. Henry Whaling, standing near, said, "D—n such shooting as that," and aiming his rifle, quickly sent a ball through the Mexican's body, who fell against a mesquite tree and soon died.

During the next charge, one of the rangers said to Wallace:

"Big Foot, yonder is a Mexican who has on a pair of pants large enough to fit you." The Mexican in question was at this time assisting some of the wounded back to the rear. Wallace was a conspicuous figure during the fight. His dress, massive frame, and actions, while talking about the big Mexican, attracted the attention of General Caldwell, who rode up to him and said, "What command do you hold, sir?" "None," says Wallace. "I am one of Jack Hays' rangers, and want that fellow's breeches over yonder," at the same time pointing out his intended victim. Before the battle was over he killed him and secured the coveted prize, which was made of splendid material, and Wallace wore them the following year while a prisoner in Mexico after the unfortunate battle of Mier.

The saddest finale to the battle of Salado was the massacre of Dawson's men, who were cut off and nearly all killed or captured while trying to make their way to Caldwell.

The Mexicans soon left for Mexico, and were followed as far as the Hondo River, and the rear guard attacked by the rangers under Hays and some cannon captured, but failing to be supported by the main body had to retreat back. Wallace was in this fight, and the mule he rode was slightly wounded.

In 1843, in retaliation for the invasion of Texas under Wall, an expedition started to Mexico under General Somervell. Captain Hays and his rangers were along, but the expedition went to pieces on the Rio Grande and most of the men came back. Among these were Captain Hays and most of his men. Five captains, however, determined to go on in the invasion of Mexico if they could get men enough. Three hundred men came over to them. Among these were Big Foot Wallace, Sam Walker, and others of the rangers. The captains were William S. Fisher, Ewing Cameron, Eastland, Reese, and Pierson. After the separation they went down the river four miles and went into camp. Next day they elected Captain Fisher to the command and continued their march down the river. On the 21st of December, 1842, they encamped opposite the town of *Mier*. Ominous name! How the hearts of the readers of Texas history now thrill at the mention of it. Then it had no significance.

The town of Mier was six miles from the camp of the Texans. On the following morning they crossed the Rio Grande, marched to the town, and made a requisition on the alcalde for provisions and clothing. He promised that the articles should be delivered the next day at the river, but below the camp of the Texans. The Texans, however, when they went back to their camp brought the alcalde along with them as surety for the delivery of the goods. On the 23d the Texans moved their camp opposite the place where the goods were to be delivered, but the day passed off, and the next, and still the goods did not come. The Texas spies who had been kept on the west side of the river on the morning of the 24th captured a Mexican, who reported that General Ampudia had arrived in Mier with troops and prevented the fulfillment of the alcalde's promise. The Texans then determined to again cross the river and give them battle. By 4 o'clock in the evening they had all crossed and were on their march to the town. Captain Baker had command of the spies, and first met the Mexicans who sallied out from Mier. Ampudia retreated before the Texans, and at dark again entered the town.

The Texans advanced to the Alcantra Creek, east of the town, and halted for some time. This little stream ran very rapidly and it was difficult to find a crossing in the night. They finally succeeded, however, in getting over. By this time a lively fight had commenced between Baker's spies and the Mexican cavalry. Five of the Texans were cut off and captured. Among these were Dr. Sinnickson, Sam Walker, Beasley, and "Legs" Lewis. Others made narrow escapes. It was a hand to hand fight, and the Texans who were cut off were compelled to abandon their horses and take themselves across fences and ditches. Sam Walker was caught by a powerful Mexican and held down, while others tied him. One man named McMullins was caught by the legs while getting over a fence, but his boots pulled off and he made his escape. They had all emptied their guns and pistols in the fight and had no time to reload. Wallace had advanced to the edge of town, but saw the Mexican cavalry coming and went back. He passed "Legs" Lewis and said to him, "You had better run; the Mexicans will get you, sure."

After the main body of the Texans had passed the creek they advanced to the town and Wallace came in with them. They passed down a street leading to the public square, where the Mexicans had planted cannon. While doing so they were fired on and a man named Jones was killed. He was the next man in the rear of Wallace as they came in single file, and Big Foot felt the wind of the bullet that killed him. He was a well dressed man, and the Mexicans attempted to strip his body. The Texans halted and turned back, and a sharp fight ensued in which twenty Mexicans were killed. When the Texans arrived at a point near the cannon they received a discharge of grape shot which swept the street and caused them to seek shelter behind the buildings. It was now dark, Christmas evening, 1842. The only chance for the Texans to advance was by opening passage ways through the buildings and advance in this way towards the cannons. All night they worked, and when daylight came they were in fifty yards of the cannon. Their horses had been left in camp under a guard. While engaged in this work Wallace found a Mexican baby that had been abandoned during the hasty exit of the occupants of the house on the approach of the Texans. It set up a terrible squall when the white men got into the room where it was, and Big Foot took it up, and advancing to a wall inclosing a yard, climbed up and dropped it over, at the same time shouting out in Spanish for some one to come and get the muchacho. He soon heard a woman's voice on the outside and supposed it was taken care of.

At daylight portholes were opened in the various rooms the men had gotten into, and soon the deadly crack of the rifles were heard as they commenced firing on the artillerymen. The cannons were soon silenced, for it was death for a Mexican to go near them. During the day three desperate attempts were made by the enemy to storm and carry the position of the Texans, but each failed with fearful loss. Wallace said the Mexicans came so thick it was impossible to miss them, and the bravest of them were the presidio ales (town guards) who wore black hats with white bands around them. They were nearly all killed. In one of the rooms occupied by the Texans, and where Wallace was, a strong Mexican drink "aguadente" was found. The men at once commenced drinking it to excess, and even one of their officers drank so much he fell on the floor and was wounded by a bullet while in that condition. The men were so worn with the night's work that when they found this liquor they drank it out of tin cups like water. Wallace, seeing it would render them unfit for service, although he loved it as well as any of them, turned the balance of the firewater out on the floor.

Before the fight commenced, Captain Wallace says one of their scouts, Joe Berry, fell down a bluff and broke his leg. His brother Bates Berry and some others who were with him carried Joe to a vacant house in the outskirts of town. During the battle they were discovered and attacked by Mexicans. A rush was made by the Texans to reach the position of their comrades, but were all killed except Bates. He only left his wounded or crippled brother when he saw there was no chance to save him, and at the earnest solicitation of the latter, who no doubt thought the Mexicans would spare him. One of the men killed in the sally was a bugler named Austin. A Mexican lieutenant named Algerette, who was in command of the party who assaulted the position where the unfortunate Joe Berry lay, went in and killed him with his sword as he lay helpless, and then bragged about it after the surrender and exhibited the blood-stained sword. During the night battle, bugles were constantly sounding, and it was reported that the Mexicans were being largely reinforced. The Texans, however, were undismayed, and continued to load and fire their rifles with such deadly effect that great confusion prevailed among the Mexicans, who continually uttered cries of rage and pain amidst a constant blast of bugles. After it was no longer possible for the Mexicans to go near the cannons, and their charges had been repulsed, they occupied the house tops and other places convenient to shoot from, and kept their bodies hid as much as possible. Many of those killed were shot in the head. Wallace said he loaded and fired his rifle fifteen times, always waited for a good chance, and had a bead on a Mexican every time he touched the trigger. The Mexicans tried to recover their cannon by throwing ropes around them from the corners of buildings, and succeeded in getting some of them away.

During the fight after daylight on the 26th the small guard which had been left on the east side of the Alcantra Creek attacked about sixty of the Mexican cavalry and routed them, but seeing a large reinforcement coming, made a desperate attempt to join their comrades in the town. Out of the nine men who made this attempt two succeeded, four were killed, and three were captured.

During one close charge many were killed and wounded on both sides. Colonel Fisher himself was severely wounded. Captain Cameron had fortified himself and men in the rear of the building occupied by Fisher and his men, and had also been exposed to a fearful fire, during which he had three men killed and seven wounded. The bugles of the Mexicans began sounding a charge from different parts of the town, and Cameron hastily entered the room occupied by Fisher and asked for reinforcements to help defend his position. About that time a white flag was brought out by Dr. Sinnickson, one of the Texans who had been captured as before stated. He was ordered to do so by General Ampudia, and to tell the Texans he had 1700 troops in the city and 300 more on the road from Monterey, and that it would be useless for them to continue to resist, and that if they would surrender they would be treated as prisoners of war; if not, no quarter would be given. The prospect was gloomy for the Texans, and although they had fought as men worthy the name of Texan, and had caused the streets of Mier to almost run with Mexican blood, they still saw no chance to win. They were on foreign soil, hemmed in on all sides by their enemies, their number reduced, and the survivors almost worn out. Some, however, were not in favor of a surrender, and thought they could make a sally from their barricaded positions, and by keeping together fight their way out of town and back across the Rio Grande. This would have been child's play compared with what they did attempt later on. Many among Fisher's men were in favor of a surrender, and Cameron hurried back to his own and exhorted them to continue the fight. Others under the different captains favored a surrender, and commenced leaving their positions and giving up their guns in the streets. When Fisher's men commenced going out to surrender, Wallace, who had been with them most of the time, left and ran to the position of Cameron. Others now left their commands and came to Cameron, until forty or fifty stood around him and asked him to take command and continue the battle or make a rush and fight their way out. At this time great confusion prevailed; some were surrendering and others firing. Every few minutes barricades would be torn away and men would march out four or five at a time and surrender. Cameron held his position until all the balance had surrendered, and seeing that all hope was gone, said to his men, who with stern but anxious faces stood around him: "Boys, it is no use for us to continue the fight any longer; they are all gone but us." The men stood for a few minutes and looked at the hordes of Mexicans, who were now making a grand display, the cavalry charging up and down the streets, and others carrying away the guns of the Texans, who were now prisoners and herded together on the plaza. The Mexican soldiers and the citizens of the town were making a great outcry and cheering for victory. A gallant officer named Thomas J. Green, who was with Cameron, broke his sword before he would give it up. Wallace was opposed to the surrender. He remembered the fate of his brother and other relatives after the surrender at Goliad, and expected nothing else for himself and those with him on this occasion, and told them so. The gallant Cameron, however, wishing to save the lives of his men, took the lead and they followed. They were met by a strong detachment of Mexicans as they emerged from their position into the street, and the painful work commenced of handing over their guns, pistols, and knives. Wallace stayed back until the last, closely watching every incident of the surrender, thinking it might be necessary to kill another Mexican if the slaughter which he expected should commence too soon. Finally, however, he handed up his arms and was the last man to do so at Mier. Big Foot said as they were marched to the plaza his shoes became red with blood where the Mexicans bled who were killed or wounded in those desperate charges. He also saw blood in the gutters and on the house tops. He says a Mexican whom General Somervell raised and educated was killed in the fight on the Mexican side, and had the general's rifle with him.

The Mexican loss in the battle, considering the numbers engaged, was fearful. Their own report was 500 killed out of a force of 2000. The Texans had 260 men in the town, sixteen of whom were killed and thirty wounded. The Mexicans had forty artillerymen killed.

Captain Wallace told the writer he thought 800 Mexicans were killed, and while the results were not so great, it was a harder fought battle than San Jacinto. The Texans were carried up to the square from where the surrender took place, and Wallace says he saw four rows of dead Mexicans reaching across the plaza, and the priests were among them saying mass.

While this was being done the bodies of the slain Texans, stripped of their clothing, were being dragged through the streets by the cavalry, followed by crowds of yelling Mexicans of all sizes and ages.

During the last days of December General Ampudia set out with his prisoners for the City of Mexico, leaving the wounded at Mier in charge of Dr. Sinnickson. On January 9, 1843, the captive Texans arrived at Matamoros, and on the 14th set out from that place for Monterey, guarded by a troop of cavalry. On the march it was one grand jubilee with the Mexicans. They starved the prisoners and made them travel on foot all the distance until their shoes were worn out, and they were thin and haggard. The Mexicans made grand demonstrations in passing through the towns, their approach being heralded with bugles and prancing, charging cavalry. The Texans were marched through the principal streets, followed by yelling mobs of men and boys. The women with but few exceptions pitied the half-starved, healf-dead Americans, some of whom were beardless boys, and when they arrived at Monterey the women came with provisions and fed them. They stayed here from the 18th to the 20th, and were then started to Saltillo. At this place they found six of the Texans who were captured at San Antonio in September of the year before, when Wall captured that place. Big Foot was at this time still wearing the pants of the Mexican whom he killed at the battle of Salado.

At Saltillo Colonel Barragan took charge of the prisoners and proceeded with them to the Hacienda Salado, 100 miles further on, where they arrived on the 10th of February, and were there placed in prison. For some time the Texans had contemplated making an attempt to escape and had formulated a plan at Monterey, but one of their own officers disclosed the plot to the Mexicans and the attempt was not made. Now it was set on foot again without detection, and carried out. There had been an addition to the number of Texas prisoners by a portion of the Santa Fe prisoners who had gone on the ill-starred expedition to New Mexico and had all been captured and sent over into Old Mexico and confined with the Mier prisoners. A few survivors of the Dawson massacre had also been placed with them. Among the Santa Fe prisoners were Drs. Brennan and Lyons, who were anxious to make the attempt to escape. When all was ready, Captain Cameron gave the signal by throwing up his hat, and Lyons and Brennan led the charge on the guards. Cameron and Samuel H. Walker, who was captured before the battle of Mier,

THE MIER PRISONERS CHARGE ON THE GUARD, AND VICTORY AT SALADO.

each charged a guard and succeeded in disarming him. This was at sunrise on the 11th day of February, 1843.

As soon as the first charge was made and the guards were disarmed at the door of the prison, the Texans rushed into the outer court of the building, where 150 infantry were guarding the arms and cartridge boxes. There were about 200 Texans and without hesitating an instant they rushed upon the Mexican soldiers with their naked hands, and a most desperate struggle commenced for the possession of the guns and cartridges. Where in all the world's history will we find deeds recorded of any braver men than these who, on that February morning in the prison yard of Salado, rushed empty-handed on regular soldiers, faced the leveled muskets with unflinching eye, received their fire, and then closed in on them? The Mexicans inside the prison court surrendered or fled after the first fire, but still the Texans were not masters of the situation. Another company of infantry was stationed at the gate, and a force of cavalry outside. Without hesitating, the desperate men rushed on these and a terrible fight ensued. Most of the prisoners had secured guns when this second hand to hand fight took place. Big Foot Wallace had as yet secured no gun; but he rushed upon a Mexican who had fired his gun and tried to disarm him. The fellow had a bayonet on his musket, however, and made a vicious thrust at the big Texan, who seized the bayonet, and a hard struggle commenced for the mastery. The bayonet came off in the hands of Wallace, and another unarmed prisoner came up behind and seized the gun by the breech and obtained possession of it. The Mexican then fell to his knees, held up his hands, and in Spanish called for mercy, which was granted him.

The fight at this time was fiercely raging, and Wallace went into the thick of it, brandishing his bayonet, which he used until the fight was over. In vain the Mexicans tried to keep the Texans from going through the gate which would give them their liberty. The contest was short but bloody, and the noise and confusion was awful. The Mexicans uttered screams and yells of terror and surprise as the Texans rushed among them with clubbed guns after the first discharge, and delivered blows right and left. The cavalry became terror-stricken and fled, and the infantry at the gate began to throw down their arms and try to surrender, but for a time no stop could be put to the carnage.

At length the voice of Cameron was heard calling on his men to desist as he went among them and begged for the disarmed guards. This put a stop to it. They all loved the brave, unselfish Cameron, whose ancestors came from the highlands of Scotland. Many Mexicans lay dead on every side, while others were moaning with broken heads and gunshot wounds. Lieutenant Barragan, son of the commander of the Mexican force, displayed great bravery during the fight, and refused to surrender except to an officer. Six Texans who had secured guns with bayonets on them confronted him and demanded his surrender. Backing against a wall, he brandished his sword and refused to do so except to an officer. Six bayonets were now thrust at him, but he so successfully parried all of them that not one point touched him. His saber made such rapid movements that it was hardly visible. About this time Big Foot Wallace came up, and some one told him to get a loaded gun and shoot the fellow. Wallace said no; that a brave man like him should be spared. The brave young Mexican now called for Captain Cameron. He came at once, and the sword was then turned over to him. With a proud look the Mexican stepped back and folded his arms. His father, Colonel Barragan, had quit the field in cowardly flight some time before. Other Mexicans who had surrendered and were looking on during this episode said the lieutenant did not derive his courage from his father, but from his mother, and that he looked like her. The Texans did not come unscathed out of the fight; five lay still and motionless among their dead foes, and many more were wounded. Among the dead were the brave and fearless Brennan and Lyons, who led the charge at the prison door. The Texans now being masters of the situation, dictated terms to the Mexicans, one of which was that their wounded should be taken care of. Those who were able to travel prepared for instant flight. This was their only chance for safety, as they knew a large force would soon be on their trail.

Some of the Mexican cavalrymen who had tied their horses and were not by them when the onset was made ran away without mounting, and other horses were found in the town, so that all the men were mounted by 10 o'clock a. m., and set out towards the Rio Grande. Now, kind reader, if you have tears to shed, "prepare to shed them now." We will see these gallant men back again ere long in chains, all walking skeletons, drawing beans for their lives.

Big Foot Wallace secured a fine dun pacing mule which belonged to Captain Arroyo, who had run away on foot and left him. By midnight the Texans were fifty miles from the scene of their battle, and a short halt was made and the horses fed. Twelve miles more were traveled and another halt was made, and the men slept two hours. Early the next morning they left the main road so as to go around the city of Saltillo. On the 13th they struck the road leading from Saltillo to Monclova, but on the next night abandoned it and took to the mountains on the left. This was a fatal mistake, as events which followed will show.

The troubles and hardships of these brave men now commenced in earnest. When too late they saw the mistake which they had made. The country was a barren waste of mountains, without water or anything in the shape of food. Six days were spent in trying to get through. The men were perishing with thirst and starvation. Horses were killed and eaten and their blood drank by the desperate Texans. Wallace killed the mule of Captain Arroyo, and he and others devoured quantities of it with a most ravenous appetite and quaffed cupfuls of the red blood with a gusto and apparent relish, as if they were drinking to one another's health in the saloons of San Antonio.

Sitting around our firesides at home, surrounded by our families and home comforts, we can hardly realize the gravity or horribleness of the situation, and turn from it with loathing. The dry, lonely canyon where the horses were killed to sustain human life; the bloody feast, akin to savage orgies, can only be understood rightly by those who participated in it and knew what hunger and thirst means after days of abstinence, coupled with anxious, toilsome flight. They could not long remain here; swarms of cavalry with pack mules carrying provisions and water were on their trail. Leaving the remains of the slaughtered horses for the coyotes and buzzards to finish, the Texans once more plunged into the dark mountains in a vain endeavor to reach the Rio Grande, many of them now on foot, and soon all of them, for the poor horses also failed and died of thirst. They were hopelessly lost, and once more thirst began to torment them. They could no longer keep together as a body.

All were now on foot, the horses which had not died being abandoned. Many became delirious, wandered away, and died in lonely, dry ravines, or on top of lofty mountains amid huge rocks. Most of the guns were cast away, and the men toiled on. Some would sink down with their heads dropped on their breasts and their feet pointing in the direction they wished to go. Big Foot Wallace had partly dried some of his mule meat in the sun and was carrying it in a haversack, and would from time to time partake of it until thirst became so intense he could no longer do so. His tongue was dry and swollen. Five more days he spent without water, but during that time his legs never failed him. The men were now badly scattered. Wallace and three companions stayed together and toiled on with their faces in the direction, as they thought, of the Rio Grande. His comrades were Captain Cameron, Tom Davis, and James Ogden.

The Mexican cavalry who were on the trail of the Texans finally began to come upon those who were behind and to capture them. The main body, which had remained together and still had some guns with them, refused to surrender when overtaken unless they could do so as prisoners of war. It was a strange sight, this small force of half-dead men, with hollow eyes and sunken cheeks, boldly facing their robust, well-fed foes, and demanding of them an honorable capitulation, saying they would fight if it was not granted. The Mexicans promised them all these things, and the surrender was made. Wallace and his three companions were headed off and captured within 150 yards of a pool of water. They surmised from the looks of the country that water was near, and were using their last remaining strength to get to it. The Mexicans doled out the water sparingly to the Texans, fearing they would kill themselves if allowed to drink all they wanted at once. While they were dispensing a small cupful to each man, Wallace noticed a cavalryman near him who had the water gourd which had been taken from him at Mier, and thinking they would all be shot anyway, sprang at him and said in Spanish, "That is my gourd; give it up." The Mexican soldier at once complied, saying, "Pobrecito" (poor fellow). Wallace turned up the gourd, and said that first swallow of water was the best he ever tasted. He continued to gurgle it down, and Tom Davis ran up to him and said, "Give me some, Big Foot." Wallace said he could not turn it loose, and Davis was unable to pull it away from him. A Mexican officer now took notice of what was going on in regard to the gourd episode, and said in Spanish, "Hell, take the water away from that fellow; he will kill himself." Three or four soldiers then tried to take the gourd away from the big Texan, but were unable to do so until he had emptied it. He was so much taller than the Mexicans he could hold it almost out of their reach and drink, and kept whirling around while doing so, and stretched his neck and held his head as high as he could. It was a gallon gourd, and was nearly full when Wallace commenced on it. After the water was drank Wallace dropped down on his knapsack and said he never felt as good in his life. In a few moments he was asleep. He had not slept any for five nights, except in short, troubled naps, with visions of running water constantly before him. When he fell down the officer said, "See, now, he is dead."

It seems that the officers in command of this squad were humane men and treated these four prisoners well, even Captain Cameron. They camped here for the night, so that the worn and weary men could rest. Through the night a little more water was given occasionally to all except Wallace. He slept all night without once rousing up, and the soldiers said he would never wake, but die that way. When morning came, however, Big Foot waked up refreshed and hungry, and opening his knapsack began to make a hearty meal of his remaining mule meat. One of the Mexicans said: "Look at that man; he is not dead; watch him eat." Another one came to him and asked what he was eating. "Mule meat," said Wallace, as he looked the Mexican in the face. "Whose mule was it?" was the next question. "My mule," says Wallace. "It was not," said the Mexican. "He belonged to Captain Arroyo." "Why did he not stay with him, then?" said Big Foot, as he continued to eat, and then resumed: "The coward ran off and left him, and I got him. So then he belonged to me, and when I got hungry I killed him and ate him. Mule meat is good—better than horse meat."

The Mexicans made diligent search and brought in all they could find, but of the 193 who made their escape, five died of thirst and starvation, four got through to Texas, and three were never found or heard of.

The party who had Wallace and his companions next day after their capture went back to the main body, who by this time were taken. A few were taken and brought in every day for several days, and then the march commenced for Saltillo. The Texans, 160 in number, were tied together with ropes and marched in strings. On the 27th they were brought into the city, and an order was there to the commanding officer from Santa Anna to have the Texans shot. The officer refused to comply, and said he would resign his commission before he would do so. The British consul also interfered and had it stopped. One of the prisoners, James C. Wilson, was a British subject, and the consul proposed to set him at liberty, but he refused to accept it, saying he was a Texan and would die with his comrades if necessary. He lived to get back to Texas, and was honored by all who knew him. He died in Gonzales County. Wilson County was named for him. His son, Judge James C. Wilson, lives in Karnes County, and is judge of the district in which he lives.

The prisoners were now all ironed and marched back to Salado, the scene of the fight. It was now the 24th day of March. What a sad return,—haggard, poor, half dead, and in irons! Here another order was received from Santa Anna. This was to shoot every tenth man. The irons were kept on them and the guards doubled. When the prisoners arrived at the scene of their recent break for liberty, Wallace and Henry Whaling were near each other, and noticed some Mexicans digging a ditch. Whaling remarked, "That ditch is for us." The words were prophetic, as far as he was concerned. He drew a black bean, was shot, and buried in the ditch with his companions who met the same fate.

In decimating the prisoners, it was decided among the Mexican officers to let them draw lots, so that each man would have a chance for his life. The lots were to be determined by drawing black and white beans,—the white life, the black death. A pitcher (or jar, Big Foot Wallace called it, and says it was shaped like a ninepin) was procured and ten white beans to one black one was placed in it, corresponding to the number of men.

When all was ready the Texans were marched out a short distance and formed in line. An officer now approached bearing the fatal jar, in which were 159 white beans and 17 black ones. Few men even in regular war times pass through such a fearful ordeal as did the men who drew beans for their lives at Salado.

For a few moments the men stood in silence, and then the drawing commenced. No severer test could have been made of men's nerve than on this occasion. Soldiers will rush to almost certain death in the excitement of battle, but to stand and decide their fate in a second by the drawing of a bean was worse than charging to the muzzle of a blazing cannon. The Mexican officers were very anxious to kill Captain Cameron, and were in hopes that he would draw a black bean. To make this almost certain the black beans were placed on top and he was made to draw first, but the balance came in alphabetical order. As he reached for the pitcher, which was held high so that no one could see into it, one of the captives (William F. Wilson) said, "Dip deep, captain." He was a close observer, and no doubt had an idea of the job that was put up. Cameron acted on the suggestion, ran his fingers to the bottom, and pulled out a white bean. A look of satisfaction passed over the faces of the Texans, for they all loved the brave and unselfish Cameron. The Mexicans scowled. The drawing now went on rapidly. All "dipped deep," and it was some time before a black bean was drawn.

Although the men knew that some would be compelled to draw the black beans, they could not help showing their satisfaction as friend after friend brought forth the bean which gave them life. What keen pangs, however, wrenched their hearts when a fatal black bean was brought to light, held by a dear comrade who had stood by them in the midst of battle or in the desolate mountain wilds, now compelled to die—shot like a dog, far from home and the loved ones there. Most of the men showed the utmost coolness, scarcely a tremor passing over their faces as the drawing went on. One noted gambler from Austin, when his time came to draw, stepped up with a smile and said, "Boys, this is the largest stake I ever played for." When he drew forth his hand a black bean was between his thumb and forefinger. Without changing the smile on his face, he took his place in the death line and remarked, "Just my luck." The prisoners were chained together in couples, and as fast as the black beans were drawn the unfortunate holder was placed in the death line. If two chained together both drew black beans they were not separated, but moved together to the fatal line. "When one was taken and the other left" the chains were taken off and the condemned fastened to one of his companions in distress.

Young Robert Beard was sick and not able to stand in line to draw his bean, and the pitcher had to be carried to where he lay on a blanket guarded by a Mexican soldier. Before his time came to draw he told his brother, who was present, that if he himself drew a white bean and his brother a black one, he wanted to exchange and be shot instead of his brother. The brother refused, but both drew white beans and lived to return home.

It is generally believed and told that Big Foot Wallace drew two beans at Salado; that one of his comrades, a young man, expressed such great fear that he would draw a black bean, that Wallace gave him his white one and said he would take another chance. When the writer asked the old captain about this matter, he said: "No, I never drew but one, and had no idea of giving it away;" and continuing said: "I could not have done so if I wished, for I heard a Mexican officer say that there would be no swapping of beans when the Beard brothers were talking about doing so, and I suppose it was from this incident that the story started in regard to me."

One young fellow, almost a boy, drew a black bean, and giving one appealing look to his comrades, asked them to avenge his death.

"Talking" Bill Moore, when it came to his turn to draw, said, "Boys, I had rather draw for a Spanish horse and lose him." He was a lively fellow, and helped to keep up the spirits of the balance. Good fortune favored him, and he drew a white bean. While the drawing was in progress some of the petty Mexican officers did all in their power to annoy the prisoners. When one drew a black bean they expressed great sorrow, hypocritically of course, and then said, "Cheer up; better luck next time," when they knew this was the last chance the poor fellow would ever have.

Wallace was chained to a man named Sesinbaugh, and said if there ever was a Christian it was him. His time came first to draw, and as he put his hand forward to get his bean he prayed for himself and Big Foot Wallace. He drew a white bean. Wallace said that afterwards, in the dark dungeon of Perote, chained to the floor, at the midnight hour he sang and prayed and thanked God that it was as well with him as it was.

As the drawing went on the chances for Wallace grew less, his letter (W) coming at the bottom of the list. The boys had "dipped deep" until nearly all the white beans had been dipped out. When he drew there was as many black beans in the jar as white ones. When his time came his hand was so large he had difficulty in squeezing it down to the beans, and they were so scarce he scooped two up against the side of the vessel and got them between his fingers and carefully felt of them. He was under the impression that the black beans were a little larger than the white ones. The Mexicans were watching him closely, and one of them told him to hurry up, and that if he pulled out two beans and one was a black one he would have to take it. Big Foot paid no attention to this. Life was at stake now. After feeling the beans a few seconds one seemed to be a little larger than the other, and he let it go. The one he pulled out was white, but he was satisfied the other was black. When Wallace drew his hand out of the jar a Mexican officer took hold of it to examine it, and called up several others to look how large it was. The next two men to draw after Wallace both drew black beans. They were Henry Whaling and W. C. Wing.

The black beans were now all out, and the last three men on the list did not draw. An officer turned up the jar and three white beans fell to the ground.

W. C. Wing, the last man to draw a black bean, was visibly affected. He was young, and when at home was very religious, but had left the beaten track of christianity and had gone sadly astray, which fact seemed to trouble him very much. He referred to it repeatedly during the short time before his execution.

When the drawing was over and the condemned men stood in the death rank, chained two and two together, their roll stood as follows: L. L. Cash, J. D. Cocke, Robert Durham, William N. Eastland, Edward Este, Robert Harris, S. L. Jones, Patrick Mahan, James Ogden, Charles Roberts, William Rowan, J. L. Shepard (cousin of the writer), J. M. N. Thompson, James N. Torrey, James Turnbull, Henry Whaling, and W. C. Wing.

Henry Whaling asked for something to eat, saying, "I do not wish to starve and be shot, too." Strange to say, the Mexicans complied with his request and two soldiers' rations was issued to him. He ate it with relish, and then said he was ready to die. During a few minutes before the execution, while preliminaries were being arranged, the decimated men stood in silence, intently watching their captors. Not a movement escaped their notice. When the firing squad was detailed and counted off, some little sign of emotion was seen on the countenances of a few. There was a nervous twitching about the mouth. Their bosoms heaved and their breath came short and quick. Others stood as calmly as if on parade.

The irons were now taken off and they were led away to execution, bidding their more fortunate comrades farewell as they marched off. Many tears were seen running down the cheeks of the emaciated and sun-burned faces of the fortunate ones as they responded to this last good-bye.

When they arrived at the place of execution, which was just outside of the village, the Texans asked permission to be shot in front, but this was refused. Henry Whaling asked to not be blindfolded, saying he wished to look the man in the face that shot him, and show them how a Texan could die. This was also refused. The Mexicans stood close to their backs when they fired, and all fell to the ground. The bodies were then stripped and piled up like a cord of wood. The firing party then went back to the town. The Texans were all dead except J. L. Shepard. His wound was in the shoulder, although the muzzle of the Mexican's gun was in a few feet of him when discharged. He feigned death so well that he was stripped and stacked up with the balance and escaped detection of having life. When the Mexicans left he went away into the mountains, but in ten days was retaken and shot. The Mexicans discovered one was gone when they came to remove the bodies to the ditch which had been prepared for them, and scouts were sent out in all directions to hunt for him.

After the execution of the Texans, the survivors, heavily ironed, were started on foot for the City of Mexico. It is impossible to describe their sufferings. They were carried through the principal cities and towns on the route, driven like so many cattle, and half starved. They were derided, hooted at, and maltreated all the way by the populace. The shackles on Big Foot Wallace were too small, and cut deep into the flesh. His arms swelled and turned black, and when they arrived at San Luis Potosi the Governor's wife came to look at the prisoners and noticed the condition of Wallace. Her woman's sympathies were at once aroused, and she ordered the chains taken off. The officer in command refused to do so, saying only the Governor had authority to give such an order. The woman replied that she was the Governor's wife, and ordered him again to take them off.

This time he complied, and sent for a blacksmith, who removed them. The good woman then, with her own hands, bathed the swollen arms of Wallace with brandy. Seeing signs of suffering among other prisoners who had gathered around, she had the chains taken off of all of them. Before she did this, however, she asked the officer if he was afraid of his prisoners without chains on, to which he replied that he was not. Big Foot Wallace told her that she ought to be President of Mexico.

On the march to the capital, after the chains were taken off, Wallace made good use of his long arms. The writer will say here that Captain Wallace had the longest arms of any man he ever saw outside of a show. He would reach and get cakes and tamales from stands as they passed them. The owners would make a great outcry, but the soldiers would laugh. Sometimes they would meet one carrying a tray or board of good things on his head. Wallace was so much taller than the Mexican that he could get a handful of things and the owner would be none the wiser. Big Foot, with his powerful frame and long arms, was a great curiosity to them. He could pass a cake stand and then reach back and get the articles off it.

When they arrived at a little Indian village eighteen miles from the City of Mexico an order came from Santa Anna to shoot Capt. Ewing Cameron. This order was kept a secret from the balance of the prisoners for fear they would make a demonstration. That night they put Cameron in a room alone under a separate guard. The balance of the prisoners were crowded together in a small room, and they almost suffocated. They were suspicious, however, from the transaction in regard to Cameron that foul play was intended, and when they were all marched out on the following morning to a tank for the purpose of washing each Texan filled his bosom full of rocks, determined to fight for their captain and die with him if an attempt was made on his life. The guards asked them why they were getting the rocks, and were told that it was for ballast, so that they could walk better. They made no attempt to take them away—in fact they were afraid to, as they saw the Texans looked desperate. The march was again commenced early in the morning. The prisoners asked about Cameron, and wanted to know if he was going to be shot. The Mexicans said no, and for them to go on and he would soon follow. When the prisoners got one mile from this place, on rising ground, they heard a platoon of guns fire back at the village, and knew that the gallant Cameron had met his fate. It was a refinement of cruelty on the part of Santa Anna to have Cameron executed after he had drawn a white bean. He met his fate unflinchingly, and died as none but the brave can die.

Before arriving at the capital the captives were again put in irons and convict garbs placed upon them. In this condition, and with grand display, they were marched into the historic city of the Montezumas.

Before leaving San Antonio Wallace had some long shirts made which almost came down to his knees, and when his pantaloons wore out until there was but little left except the waistband, and before the convict garb was put upon him, some of the Mexicans along the route thought he was a priest, and called him "padre," and some would give him bread.

While being conveyed up the streets of the capital the populace were unusually noisy—hooting, yelling, and offering many insults. One old woman ("squaw," Wallace called her) singled him out for her especial taunts and jeers. She was very ugly, bare headed, and had a long, grizzled neck. Her hair was loose, parted on the back of her neck, and hung down in front. She would come in front of him, walk backwards, grin, and make all kinds of wry faces at him. The shackled Texan was desperate and smarting with his chain, and would have struck her if he could, but his hands were chained together behind him. Watching his chance, however, when her back was turned, he sprang forward and caught the back of her neck with his teeth, thinking to bite a piece out, but the old woman squalled like a panther and jerked loose from him. Wallace says that was the toughest meat he ever tried to bite. He could make no impression on it, and his teeth slipped off and popped like a horse pulling his foot out of a bog. The soldiers laughed very heartily at this, ridiculed the old woman, and bravoed the tall "gringo." (name for Americans).

The British consul had a good deal to say about the killing of Cameron, and had a personal interview with Santa Anna in regard to it, condemning his action.

It will be remembered by our readers that Texas was not one of the United States at this time, but was an independent Republic. The United States had nothing to do with protecting citizens of Texas, and the young Republic was not able to invade Mexico with an army and release her citizens. The Texas prisoners arrived at the City of Mexico on the 1st day of May and remained there until the following October. During this time they were confined and closely guarded at night, and worked the streets in chains during the day. Part of their work was to carry sand in sacks to make a fine road up a hill to the bishop's palace, where President Santa Anna lived. The work was slow and tedious, walking the lock-step with chains around their ankles. Even at this, however, the Texans played off a good deal by punching holes in their sacks and letting the sand run out as they went along. Part of the time they worked at Molino del Rey, one and a half miles from the city, and here four prisoners made their escape by scaling a wall. They were Samuel H. Walker, James C. Wilson, and one Thompson and Gatis. It was late in the evening, just before sundown, and all the prisoners had been brought in for the night and placed in different rooms, but all surrounded by a wall. Before the regular guard was put on for the night, which was always doubled, the four men above mentioned scaled the wall while the sentinel's back was turned.

The man Thompson had played off on the march and while at work by wrapping bloody rags, which he managed to secure in some way, around his feet and legs, and limping terribly and making many wry faces. The Mexicans let him ride all the way coming to the city. He would grimace and fall as soon as they put him on his feet. The men all knew there was nothing the matter with him, and thought it strange the Mexicans did not investigate his lameness. Wallace said that he would rather walk or work than to make the faces and contortions of body that Thompson went through. When the sentinel went into the room where he had left the prisoners a few seconds before and found it empty the truth flashed across his mind at once, and bringing the butt of his gun down on the floor with considerable force exclaimed, "Caraja!" (Mexican oath). He, however, did not report the loss, through fear, and it was not found out until the following morning; then no one knew how it occurred. What most surprised the Mexicans was that the crippled man had got away —scaled a wall. The four Texans all made their way safely back to Texas. In October the prisoners were all sent to Perote, distant about 300 miles from the capital. Here they were confined in a damp, loathsome dungeon. They had walked all the way there, but without chains on. The air was so foul in the dungeon that forty of them died. Wallace, with ten others, went wild and had to be tied down. All died but Wallace, and he was tied down fourteen days. The Mexican doctors who were in attendance had their assistants to rub Big Foot to keep up circulation. In doing so one of them rubbed a plaster off of his sore back, and he knocked the one who did it clear across the room. This was after reason had returned again. The sore was made on his back in his struggles when tied down on the stone floor of the dungeon. The writer has seen these scars, and also on his arms and ankles where the chains cut into the flesh.

Seeing they would all die if too closely confined, they were carried out through the day to work.

Many Mexicans came in to look at Wallace while he was crazy, to watch his actions, and hear him yell. One day after he had about recovered two young Mexican women of the upper or wealthy class desired to visit the prison and see the wild Texan. They made this known to the padre of the city, and he came with them to the prison. When they arrived at the entrance and the guards threw back the prison door, the dusky damsels drew back alarmed when they heard the clanking chains of the prisoners. The good father assured them, however, that there was no danger; that trusty guards were at hand, and the "mucho grande loco Americano" was unusually docile. In the meantime some of the Texans who had seen the party enter, divining the import of the visit, informed Wallace of the fact. He was lying on a cot, but at once raised up to a sitting position with his feet on the floor and enveloped himself completely in a sheet except the eyes, and looked as much like a ghost as possible. When the party came in front of Wallace and the shy maidens were tremblingly viewing "el loco hombre" (the mad man), Wallace threw off his sheet, and uttering a yell that would have made a Comanche Indian turn pale, sprang at them. With one long, wailing scream of terror the two Mexican girls sank to the floor, and Wallace caught one of them by the foot. Great excitement now prevailed. The guards rushed in and seized Wallace and tried to loosen his grip on the girl, but not being able to do so, dragged them both about over the cell in a vain endeavor to pull him loose. The girl still screamed, and Big Foot yelled and roared by turns. The

THE SURRENDER OF SANTA ANNA.

Mexican soldiers cursed, and drawing their sabers said they would cut him loose. To add to the excitement, the prisoners were rattling their chains and with upraised manacled hands were threatening to dash out the brains of the guards if they used their sabers on Wallace. The unfettered girl regained her feet, and went flying almost out of the prison. The priest stood his ground, but called on all the saints he could think of to save them. Seeing the guards dare not use their sabers, he in sheer desperation threw himself upon Wallace himself, and then told the soldiers to pull. The strain was too great now when they did so, and he relaxed his grip. The girl sprang to her feet like a frightened deer, and with flying hair made a hasty exit, followed by the padre.

As soon as Wallace was able he was put out to work with the balance. Sometimes they were hitched twenty-five to a cart and made to haul rock from the mountains down to town. During this time the Texans let three carts get away from them on the side of the mountain (accidentally, of course), and they were smashed to pieces by running off a bluff. On one occasion they hitched Wallace to a cart alone to haul sand in town. A spirit of devilment came over him, and pretending to get scared at something, he gave a loud snort and ran away. He ran against things and tore the cart all to pieces before he could be stopped. It was a funny sight to the Mexicans to see a man run away with a cart and could not be stopped or headed off until it was demolished, and they gave way to loud peals of laughter.

During this long confinement a man named Joe Davis, one of the old rangers of Jack Hays, conceived the idea of digging under the dungeon wall. It was five feet in thickness, and twenty-two feet to get under the foundation. There were twenty-seven confined in this apartment, and all agreed to the plan and went to work. They dug at night and hid the dirt as best they could. Some of the dirt was carried out in their clothing as they went to work on the streets in the daytime, and scattered gradually so as to escape detection. In this way they succeeded in digging under and out. This made a hole of forty-four feet. Twenty-four of the number succeeded in getting out, but the plot was discovered before the others could go. Only one man could travel at a time in the excavation. Wallace heard that all the prisoners were escaping in that room and hurried in there, but found it full of Mexican officers and soldiers, so hurried back to his own again. Four of those who got out were recaptured and brought back and chains put upon all of them again, which for a time had been taken off. They were compelled to work harder, and nearly starved. Many weary nights now passed away, and clanking chains could be heard at all hours of the night. Many rats invaded their prison den, and so near starved were the Texans that they were caught and eaten. The rats would come up the wall to a little cross-barred window where the sentinel stood, and going through would drop into the dungeon. When the sound of the rodent was heard hitting the floor chains would rattle all over the prison, as each man was on the alert to catch him.

The captain in command here was a wooden-legged fellow with a long Spanish name which the Texans could not remember, and the more irreverant of them called him "Limpin' Jesus." He would come limping in with a great splutter of official dignity to inspect the prison, and one of the men drew a picture of him on the wall. This made him very angry, and he had it defaced.

If all the minute particulars were written of the interesting incidents through which the captive Texans passed it would make a good-sized book. The main points have been given, and enough of minor details to give the reader a clear conception of the situation.

During all these tedious months of captivity friends in the United States were using their best endeavors to have the prisoners liberated. Texas alone was not able to send an invading army into Mexico and strike the chains from her citizens, but did all she could in conjunction with others to have it done by the Mexican authorities. The wife of Santa Anna, who was an invalid and a good woman, pleaded with the stern dictator for their release. He was greatly attached to her, and would grant almost anything she asked.

Not long after this four of the prisoners were released through the intervention of influential friends in the United States. These four were Big Foot Wallace, Thomas Tatum, James Armstrong, and William F. Wilson.

Thomas Tatum, who was a native of Tennessee, gained his liberty through the influence of Gen. Andrew Jackson.

William F. Wilson, a native of Virginia, was released through the influence of Governor McDowell.

The chains dropped from the manacled wrists of James Armstrong through the good offices of Thomas Benton, of Missouri.

Big Foot Wallace was liberated through his father and Governor McDowell of Virginia. Their plantations joined, and they were friends of long standing.

On the 5th day of August, 1844, the four men in question walked out from the dark dungeon of Perote free men, after a confinement of twenty-two months, and on the same day the wife of Santa Anna died, loved and regretted by every Texan who wore the chains in Mexico.

Soon after the death of the President's wife an order came for all the balance of the Texas prisoners to be released. Santa Anna had promised his wife on her deathbed that he would release them, and let it be said to his credit that once in life he kept his word.

When Big Foot and his three companions once more breathed free air they set out on foot for Vera Cruz, having one dollar each, which was given them for expenses out of the country. From Vera Cruz they took shipping for New Orleans.

Wallace at last found his way back to his old cabin on the Medina River. He soon found out that he had neighbors. The Germans were settling Castroville, ten miles above, having recently been brought there in a colony from Europe by Henry Castro.

The balance of the life of Wallace can not be given in a sketch like this for the want of space, and can only be noticed briefly. Some of his Indian battles will be given more in detail in the sketch of Ed. Westfall, who was with him on several expeditions.

After getting back to the Medina, Wallace spent his time in hunting and following Indians until the breaking out of the Mexican war of 1846. Part of this time he also served as a ranger again under Jack Hays. When the war broke out between the United States and Mexico on account of the boundary line of Texas, which had now become one of the Union of States, Jack Hays raised a regiment of rangers. Many of his old rangers were captains in this organization, among whom was Ad. Gillespie, Kit Ackland, Mike Chevalier, and Ben McCulloch. Samuel H. Walker, who figured in the Mier expedition, was lieutenant-colonel. Wallace joined the company of Gillespie and went out as second lieutenant.

This regiment of Texas troops did good service in Mexico.

Many of them had old scores to settle with the Mexicans. Only three years before some of them had drawn beans for their lives and worked on the streets in chains. Wallace recognized several places during the campaign where he had toiled along the dusty road in chains and nearly starved. He was in all of the fighting around Monterey, and in the desperate assault on the bishop's palace, where his captain was killed.

At the winding up of the battle, and while the bugles were sounding a parley and the Mexicans were surrendering, Wallace was seen to aim his gun at a Mexican who had a flag. Officers interfered and one of them said, "Lieutenant, don't you know a parley when you hear it sounded?" Wallace said, "No; not when I am in front of that man." The Mexican in question was the one who held the fatal bean-pot when the Texans were drawing for their lives at Salado, and called up others to look at the big hand of Wallace, and in many ways tantalized the wretched man. Wallace now accosted him angrily, and asked him if he had any bean lottery here. "Look at that hand. Do you know it? Ever see it before?" The Mexican said "No." "You have," said Wallace, "and called up others to look at it." The Mexican hung his head and Wallace cursed him for all the low-down Mexican cowards in the calendar, and then let him go.

During the storming of Monterey the Texas troops forced the upper part of the city and fought their way to the Hidalgo Hotel, and there made a halt. The Mexicans had all left except the cooks, and they were badly frightened when the Texans took possession and swarmed through the apartments looking for something to eat. The men, however, told them they had nothing to fear, but they must cook them something to eat. This seemed to be out of the question, as all the provisions had been carried away. Some of the men now went in search of something, and soon came back with thirteen sheep which they had found in a pen and killed. The cooks now went to work and soon had them well cooked, but there was no bread to eat with them.

A dried-up little Mexican, who did not seem to think anyone would want to hurt him, was hanging around, and said that for a dollar he would bring them a blanketful of bread. Wallace handed over the dollar and told him to skin out and get it. The Mexican soon returned with as much light bread as he could walk under, tied up in a blanket. One of the Texans said he was afraid to eat the bread, as it might be poisoned. Wallace said he would soon see whether it was or not, and calling up the Mexican picked up a loaf that had some cracks in it and told the fellow to sit down there and eat it. He refused to do so at first, but Wallace cocked his revolver on him and he took the dry loaf and went to work. It was hard work, but he finally got it all down. Wallace then selected another loaf and told him to try that one. The Mexican rolled his eyes and made signs that he was choking to death. A quart of water was handed him to wash it down with, and the bread placed in his hand. He took it and went quickly to work on it, but soon choked, and Wallace handed him more water. The Mexican again hesitated after swallowing the water, but Big Foot encouraged him to proceed by pointing the pistol at his right eye. This loaf was finished, and the Mexican looked glad and even smiled at the pleasant little joke of Big Foot. His countenance changed, however, when Wallace handed him another loaf and motioned for him to proceed. Before taking this loaf the Mexican made the cross and called on the saints. When he choked, Wallace would give him more water, and the Mexican would look in despair towards the pistol. When the third loaf was eaten, he was told to sit still awhile and see if it would kill him. As he did not show any signs of toppling over in two minutes, and the well cooked mutton was steaming hot before them, the hungry Texans pitched in.

While this dinner was being eaten, which was not on the bill of fare of the Hidalgo Hotel that day, the cannons were booming and soldiers cheering in the lower part of town, where General Taylor was slowly carrying one street after another towards the center. The little Mexican sat and rubbed his stomach while the Texans were eating, and once exclaimed, "Yo sentir, yo comer, no mas por semano" (I could eat no more in a week). When told he could go he went quickly.

After General Taylor's battles were over in Northern Mexico part of the rangers were sent back to Texas to protect the frontier. Among these was Wallace, and when his term of enlistment was out he returned to his old cabin on the Medina. The Indians made a raid in the Medina valley in 1848 and carried off a great many horses. Wallace went after Westfall, who lived on the Leona, west of Wallace, and they raised about thirty men and followed the Indians. Their camp was found at the "Frio waterhole," on the divide, and a battle ensued in which ten Indians were killed and some of the stock retaken.

Wallace had four dogs which he prized very highly. Their names were Rock, Ring, Speck, and Blas. Rock was his Indian dog. Wallace could always tell by his actions when Indians were around, and if it was night would take his blanket and gun and the dogs and stay in a thicket near by until morning. The dogs would lie down by him without making any noise. On one occasion Rock gave the sign of Indians just before daylight, and Wallace took his gun and watched until dawn. He then hissed the dogs out to see if they could find the trail, and soon heard them baying loudly. Coming to the spot, he saw an Indian down in a gulley, and the dogs around him. He was keeping the dogs from taking hold of him by throwing his blanket over their heads. Wallace raised his gun to shoot, but seeing the Indian was not armed, desisted, and calling the dogs off, made signs for the Indian to come out. A search revealed no weapon but a small knife, and it was broken. The Indian now told Wallace in Spanish that he had been a captive among other Indians, and had made his escape. Having no arms to kill game, he was nearly starved. He had broken his knife trying to open a terrapin. Wallace took him to his cabin, gave him all he could eat, and then, leaving his dogs to watch him, went and got his horse and carried the Indian to Castroville. This place by this time, about 1849, was building up fast and had county officers. Wallace carried his Indian around over town for people to look at, and would occasionally take a drink of whisky, until he got pretty full. A county officer now came and said he would take charge of the Indian. "No you won't," said Wallace. "This is my Indian; I caught him. If you want an Indian, go catch you an Indian." A large crowd had gathered around Big Foot and the Indian, and all laughed at the idea of the officer out trying to catch him an Indian. One of the party present that day and who heard Wallace say that is Mr. Chris Batot, of D'Hanis. Soon after this episode Wallace carried his Indian to San Antonio and turned him over to Major Neighbors, who was at that time Indian agent. About this time Wallace received a commission from Gov. P. H. Bell to raise a company of rangers. Ed. Westfall was his lieutenant.

The hardest fight they had with the Indians during this term

THE SPANISH DAGGER WHERE WALLACE'S STAGE GUARD WAS KILLED.
FROM PHOTO. BY MISS EDITH DILLARD.

of service was at the Black Hills, near the present town of Cotulla, in La Salle County. Wallace had nineteen men and defeated them, killing twenty-two of their number of eighty or more. Wallace had several men badly wounded.

After his time was out in this service he obtained a contract to drive the stage from San Antonio to El Paso. The distance was about 600 miles, and frontier all the way. He and his six guards had many encounters with Indians. Once on Devil's River five Indians were killed and two guards wounded. On another occasion the Indians attacked the stage at night, but were beaten off. In 1861, with forty settlers, he defeated a large party of Indians at the head of the Seco.

The writer had the pleasure of spending several weeks with the old captain at the house of Mr. Doc Cochran, near Devine. I never tired of listening to him talk. He was an intelligent and educated man, and had read many books, but he loved the woods best of all. He never married. He said he was engaged once while living at Austin, in 1839, but had a severe spell of sickness and his hair all come out. He left town as soon as he was able, and went into a cave in the mountains and lived there until his hair grew out, but in the meantime his girl married another man. Her name was Mary Jackson.

In October, 1898, the writer received a communication from Captain Wallace, that if I would come down and go with him and take care of him he would go to the Dallas fair and reunion of the old rangers. Accordingly I did so, and we had a fine time. Big Foot Wallace was as great a show as anything else on the grounds. All had heard of him, and wanted to talk to him and take him by the hand.

We got back about the 20th of October, and I bade him farewell at the home of Mr. Cochran and family, with whom he lived. That was the last time I ever saw him. Shortly after Christmas he took something like pneumonia, and on the 7th day of January he died, in his eighty-third year. He never wore spectacles, and could read any kind of print up to almost the day of his death. He never lost a tooth, but wore them off smooth to his gums. His remains were buried in the Devine graveyard, in Medina County, but did not rest there long. During a session of the Legislature shortly after a bill was introduced by Capt. E. R. Tarver, of Laredo, to have his remains taken up and deposited in the State cemetery at Austin. In the city he helped to build, and in which he dug the first well and ran the last herd of buffalo through town that ever made a track there, he lies, the last of the great ranger captains.

"BIG FOOT" WALLACE, AT 60 YEARS OF AGE.

MRS. SARAH J. KINCHALOE.

Born in Texas in 1838.

The lady whose name appears at the heading of this article is one of the true heroines of the west. She was born in Montgomery County, Texas, April 6, 1838, and was the daughter of Capt. William Ware, who commanded a company at the battle of San Jacinto. From Montgomery County she moved with her parents and family to Kaufman County, Texas, and from there to the Cibolo Creek, near the line of Bexar County. The next move from this place was the Sabinal Canyon, in 1852. Captain Ware was the first settler in the canyon, but he came at first without his family to look out a location in the west, and remained some time before returning for them. In the meantime Gideon Thompson came with his family, and his wife and children were the first white family to enter the lovely valley. Shortly after the arrival of the Ware family there came a young man named Robert Kinchaloe, whom Sarah J. Ware afterwards married.

Mr. Kinchaloe was a hardy frontiersman and Indian fighter, serving for a time as a ranger under Capt. H. E. McCulloch. They were stationed at the forks of the North and South Llano, where Junction City now is.

Mrs. Kinchaloe has passed through all of the horrors of a frontier life, and bears the scars of eleven wounds on her body inflicted by the hands of hostile Indians. She saw the bloody body of John Davenport after he was killed by Indians and then carried by friends to his home on Rancheros Creek. Mr. Davenport was killed on the spot where Sabinal station now is, and his ranch was a few miles east. She remembers how frightful his head looked where the scalp was taken off. The same Indians killed John Bowles on the Sabinal River, below where the station now is. Mr. Bowles had prior to that time killed three Indians one night near his ranch.

In 1866 Mr. Kinchaloe was living on Little Creek, three miles northeast from the present village of Utopia. His family at that time consisted of his wife and four children. The oldest was 8 years old and the youngest 8 months. Up to this time the Indians had killed but two people in the canyon, but others had been killed in the near vicinity. There was also at this time a man named Bowlin living near Mr. Kinchaloe. On the morning of the fearful frontier episode now to be narrated Mr. Kinchaloe, in company with Mr. Bowlin, went up the canyon about twelve miles to gather some corn which they had bought from a man who had moved away. During the absence of the two men Mrs. Bowlin and her family came to spend the night at the Kinchaloe ranch, as the husbands were not expected back until next day. That night the wily Indians were prowling about the premises and the dogs barked at them all night, and just before day some one entered the house. Mrs. Kinchaloe thought it was a Mexican herder whom Mr. Kinchaloe had in his employ, and who lived in his camp not far away. Getting up, she secured a gun, and told him if he did not leave she would kill him. The person then ran out, and was pursued by the dogs so closely that he took refuge from them on top of the smokehouse. Mrs. Bowlin was very much frightened, said she knew the Indians would kill her, and said her mother told Mr. Bowlin when they were preparing to move out west on the frontier that he was bringing her daughter out here to be killed by Indians. The next morning, Sunday, October 11, 1866, Mrs. Bowlin went back to her house to see about things, and on her return told Mrs. Kinchaloe that the Mexican herder was there and was tearing up the place, and that she believed he was a white man, as he was changed. Mrs. Kinchaloe, who was a fearless woman, at once returned with Mrs. Bowlin to see about the herder, and sure enough, when they arrived he was seen to be as white as any man. He was surly, and would neither speak to nor look at them. He was afraid of Mrs. Kinchaloe when she had a gun. The two women now returned to the Kinchaloe place, and soon after arriving there saw two Kickapoo Indians running after one of Mr. Kinchaloe's horses, which they finally roped. They now came galloping towards the house. Johnnie Kinchaloe, 6 years old, who was standing watching them as they came towards the house, said to his mother, "They are not white men; see how they throw their legs about." When the Indians got to the house they opened the gate and rode into the yard as unconcerned as if they were at home. The cowardly scoundrels knew none but women and children were there. The woman now closed the door, and Mrs. Kinchaloe got the gun and presented it as if about to fire, when the Indians ran around the house, pursued by the dogs. Johnnie now wanted to take the gun, but his mother would not let him have it. Poor Mrs. Bowlin was so badly scared she could hardly move, but her two daughters, Ella and Anna, dressed themselves in men's clothing and cursed the Indians, thinking they could frighten them away. Mrs. Kinchaloe told them to hush, as she could not stand that. The heroic woman, with the fighting blood of the Wares now up, put on a bold front and aimed the gun again at the Indians, who had returned to the front of the house. Her attempt to fire failed, for the gun snapped. At this the savages cried out, "No buena" (not good), and dismounting from their horses again went to the rear of the house. This frontier dwelling, where no lumber could be had, was a long picket house, and the space between the upright pickets was open. There were two doors, but one of them had no shutter and was partly nailed up, leaving a large opening. One of the Indians now shot Mrs. Kinchaloe with an arrow through this half-closed door, and the other one lanced her through a crack between the pickets. The brave woman, however, continued at her post and vainly endeavored to fire the gun. The weapon in question was a Spencer carbine, with a magazine in the breech containing the cartridges, which were thrown into the barrel with a lever. This Mrs. Kinchaloe did not know how to work, as it was a gun she was not familiar with, and therefore was unable to discharge it. She attempted to fire it as she would a common rifle, by pulling the hammer back and pressing the trigger. If an old-time shotgun or rifle had been in her hands she would have won the battle, but, still unable to shoot and covered with wounds and blood, she stood between the savages and her children, receiving the lance thrusts from the cowardly Kickapoos with a fortitude and heroism that would have done honor to a veteran soldier of an hundred battlefields.

While this terrible scene was being enacted the children all went under the bed except the baby. At last, covered with wounds and almost exhausted from loss of blood, Mrs. Kinchaloe handed the gun to Mrs. Bowlin, and told her to keep the Indians back if she could and not let them carry off the children. As for herself, she said she would not live five minutes longer, and sank down upon the floor. When the Indians saw this fearless pioneer woman fall they came into the house, one at each door, and stood near the fireplace, facing the helpless woman who now had the gun and was standing motionless in the center of the room gazing upon their hideous faces without making any effort at resistance. In this position they raised their bows and shot Mrs. Bowlin through the heart with two arrows. While she was falling to the floor one of the Indians took the gun from her hand and placed it in the quiver at his back. When Mrs. Bowlin sank down to the floor her two small children ran to her and commenced crying. She told them their mother was gone, and immediately expired. Mrs. Kinchaloe now exclaimed, "O, my God, the time has come now for me to die." She was lying in pools of blood upon the floor, well nigh exhausted. The Indians did not tarry long. They had consumed so much time in the fight with Mrs. Kinchaloe that they feared some settler might ride up. They made no further attempt to kill anyone, but hastily secured such things as they fancied, mounted their horses, and rode away, taking the one they had roped with them. They also took the trunks out into the yard, broke them open, pillaged the contents, tied up the articles in sheets, and carried them away.

Little Johnnie Kinchaloe now came to where his mother lay beside the dead body of Mrs. Bowlin, and said he must go and tell some one to come or she would bleed to death. She told him no, that the Indians might get him; but to pull the arrows out of her, especially the one in the shoulder, which was very painful. This the gallant little fellow did, and then brought camphor for his mother to drink, which revived her some. He then, in company with Anna Bowlin, left the house to give the alarm. Two more of the Kinchaloe children, Betty and Charley, now came out from under the bed crying, and asked their mother if she would live. She told the weeping children that she did not know, but there was little hope. Betty, 4 years old, said, "Mamma, will you go to the good man if you die?" "I hope so," was the reply. Betty then turned to Mollie Bowlin, who was sitting by the dead body of her mother, and said, "I know my mamma will go to the good man if she dies."

The nearest neighbor except the Bowlin place was Mr. Snow, two and a half miles distant, over on the Sabinal River, and thither the two children wended their way, the tall grass coming up almost to the top of little Johnnie Kinchaloe's head. The family were eating dinner in company with several neighbors when the two young messengers bearing the sad news of savage barbarity arrived and told it. The neighbors present at Mr. Snow's house were Messrs. Wish, Alexander, James O'Bryant, and Jack Dillion. One of them remarked as they arose from the table, "Now our troubles have commenced." The two last named men at once mounted their horses and rode to the scene of the tragedy. The little children were greatly rejoiced to see them. When they came into the house Jack Dillion said, "Here is Mrs. Bowlin, dead; let's take her up and take care of her." O'Bryant said, "No; here lies Mrs. Kinchaloe nearly dead. Let's take care of the living first, and then the dead." Mrs. Kinchaloe had become very cold, and they wrapped her up in a blanket and laid her on the bed. The news was soon carried to other settlers, and great excitement prevailed in the canyon.

On that day the Rev. John L. Harper was preaching at the house of John C. Ware, brother of Mrs. Kinchaloe. The news was rapidly carried to this place by Mr. Wilson O'Bryant, who had arrived upon the scene. It was on the river about three miles distant, and the old homestead of Capt. Wm. Ware, who died soon after settling there. This was a short distance below the present Utopia, and was known as Waresville. When the messenger arrived the men present at the service ran for their horses and guns. John Ware was the first one on his horse, and calling out, "Gentlemen, I am ready," galloped off, followed by the men as fast as they could mount. Among those who went to the scene of the killing were Rev. Harper, Mr. Simpson, B. F. Biggs, and Judge James McCormick. Mr. Ware came to the bedside as he thought of his dying sister, and weeping bitterly asked about her wounds. "I am shot all to pieces," she said. "My God!" said the brother. "O, that I could have been here to have saved you." The wounded woman told her brother not to weep; that she now believed she would get well. The country was thinly settled, and most of the people soon got there. Jake O'Bryant went after Mrs. Binion, the only doctor in the country, and made a most remarkably quick trip. The good woman doctor said she could revive and restore Mrs. Kinchaloe. Gideon Thompson and James Snow went after Mr. Kinchaloe and Mr. Bowlin, who at once mounted their horses and set out. The latter seemed dazed and almost paralyzed by the news. He knew that his wife was dead and that he could not succor her. With Mr. Kinchaloe it was different; his wife still lived. He rode furiously, urging his horse to his utmost speed, leaving his companion in distress far behind. Mrs. Thompson said when he passed their house he looked like a dead man, and on arriving home fell fainting at the door. After being revived he looked at his blood-covered wife and fainted again. He soon rallied again, however, and composing himself went to the bedside and promised her that as soon as she got well he would leave the frontier. The plucky woman told him no; she did not want to leave. On raising Mrs. Kinchaloe to dress the wounds where she had been deeply lanced in the body her sister, Mrs. Fenley, said, "She is bound to die." Some one said, "No she won't; she is a Ware, and you can not kill a Ware."

Who can describe the feelings of Mr. Bowlin when he arrived and stood by with his motherless children clinging around him? The body of his wife was buried near Waresville. Mrs. Kinchaloe was carried to the house of her brother, and after many days of suffering she recovered, with the scars of a dozen or more arrow and lance wounds on her body, one of which was a dangerous one in the neck. Although diligent search was made for the Indians they could not be found, and the sheep herder had also disappeared. No doubt he was in with the Indians and wanted to get a sum of money which Mr. Kinchaloe was supposed to have in the house from the sale of his wool. But he did not get it, the money being in San Antonio.

Mrs. Kinchaloe still survives at this writing, midnight, January 1, 1899, for the writer hears the bell at the church ringing in the new year. Part of this article was written in 1898 and the balance in the new year of 1899. The remark that Mrs. Kinchaloe would not die,—that you could not kill a Ware,—reminds the writer of some desperate wounds that others of this connection recovered from. William Ware, Jr., her nephew, on one occasion dropped a pistol from his hip pocket at the home of his father, John C. Ware, and it fell with the muzzle up, the hammer striking the floor with such force that it fired, the ball striking Ware in the lower part of the body and ranging up, going clear through and coming out in the right breast, penetrating the lung in its passage, and from this wound he recovered and still lives in the canyon. Last fall Mrs. Kinchaloe's son

Richard, while running a cow, was thrown from his horse and sustained such injuries about the head that he lay unconscious thirty days, without speaking, food being given him in a liquid state mostly by injection. Drs. Meer and Bowman were his physicians during the time, and kept sacks full of ice around him constantly. Twice he was pronounced dead, and one time the account of his death was written for the Galveston News by the writer of this, who was four miles away on his farm when the news of Richard's death was brought to him. The account was then written, and sent to the postoffice by Trueman Hill, who lost in on the way and it failed to be sent. Finally the doctors decided to take out part of the skull and relieve the brain on one side and see what effect it would have. The consequence was that he was soon able to be about. The portion of the skull cut out was placed carefully and scientifically back, and soon adhered and healed up.

Mrs. Kinchaloe now keeps the Utopia Hotel.

NICHALUS HABY.

Came to Texas in 1843.

Mr. Nichalus Haby, one of the pioneers of Castro's colony, was born in Alsace, Germany, in 1821, and started to Texas in company with his brother Joe and many other colonists in September, 1843. The ship in which they came was very old and came slowly, consuming 121 days in the passage from Europe to Galveston, Texas. The weather was good, and no accident happened on the trip. From Galveston they came to Port Lavaca, and there disembarked and made preparations for the long trip by land to San Antonio. Port Lavaca at that time consisted only of a few small houses. All of the colonists who came on the ship at that time with Mr. Haby are dead except his brother Joe and Mrs. Steinly, who now (1898) lives in Castroville.

Six wagon loads of the colonists came on to San Antonio and stayed about four months there, while Mr. Castro was getting ready to move his people to his grant of land west of the Medina River. When everything was ready the start was made, Castro himself taking the lead with his family in a buggy. Of this party also was Charles De Montel. The people enjoyed the beautiful scenery and herds of deer they saw while en route. The country was open then, and many miles of prairie could be seen covered with grass, and dotted about over this, some far and some near, were the herds of deer and wild horses, the latter called mustangs. Along the timbered streams were droves of wild turkeys. After the people became somewhat settled Mr. Haby became quite a hunter, and in one year killed more than 200 deer, ten bears, and some panthers. Mr. Castro, having his family with him and keeping house, paid Mr. Haby many dollars for venison and other wild meats, as he did not hunt any himself. Deer skins were very cheap, worth only 12½ cents apiece. Mr. Montel killed a great many deer. He had a fine rifle and was a good shot. At this time the famous pioneer Big Foot Wallace lived alone on the Medina River, ten miles below the Castro colony, and often came up to Castroville to spend a few days or hours, as the case might be, with his new neighbors. Mr. Haby says he saw him many times, and that he was as fine a marksman with a rifle as he ever saw. One day when Mr. Haby was out hunting he saw Capt. Jack Hays and twelve of his men out scouting for hostile Indians, who had began to prey upon the stock of the newly-arrived German settlers. Some of the Indians at this time were friendly, and often came into Castroville to sell turkeys and deer hams. They would also run horse races and show the whites how well they could ride, performing some brilliant but daring and dangerous feats of horsemanship. These were mostly Lipans, but sometimes the Comanches and Kickapoos would come in, especially when a new treaty was to be made with them. Mr. Haby says one reason the Indians became hostile was that they did not want to work, but loved to steal horses and kill white people when they got a good chance, and the settlers wanted them to leave the country.

Early in 1846 Mr. Haby went back to Germany after his father and brothers and sisters. His mother had died in 1843. His brothers were George, Jacob, Ambrose, and Andrew. There were two sisters, Mary and Margarette. On the way back to Europe the ship in which Mr. Haby sailed encountered a terrible storm which she could make no headway against, and was driven backward twenty-five miles. The only accident was to the kitchen, which was completely demolished. The weather was good coming back, and they again landed at Galveston and then came on to San Antonio, and from there to Castroville.

When the Indians became hostile Capt. John Conner raised a company of rangers and was stationed at Castroville for the protection of the people. The Habys were good frontiersmen and were not afraid of Indians. They were called by some the "fighting Habys."

In the winter of 1846, after the Comanches had again raised the tomahawk and unsheathed the scalping-knife, M. F. H. Golled, Joe Jonnes, Vincent Jonnes, and a boy 12 years old named Joe Bassiel, went up the Medina above Castroville to open up a farm. The first night in camp they were attacked by Indians and all killed. They went to sleep by their fire, leaving their guns stacked against a tree several yards away. The bodies lay where they were killed four days, and were then discovered by Mr. Nichalus Haby, who was out hunting. He first saw the guns of the murdered men standing against a tree, and thinking likely it was a camp of Indians, crept upon them very cautiously until he learned the situation. The mutilated remains of the three unfortunate men and the boy were covered with snow and ice. It was in December, and near Christmas. Mr. Haby only saw three of the bodies at this time—the boy and the two Jonnes brothers. Next day, when a party returned to the spot led by Mr. Haby, the body of Mr. Golled was found about 150 yards from the others. Mr. Golled, it seemed, had waked up when the onslaught was made and ran and fought them, breaking two lances in the fearful struggle. He was wounded in the back, and also in the hands, where he had grasped the lance points. Joe Jonnes, 17 years of age, had a lance wound in the neck which went downward and came out through the thigh. Vincent had several lance wounds through the body. Evidently he had turned quickly when the first lance thrust was made and broke the weapon, as part of it was still in the body. The boy, it seems, was held down, his breast cut open, and his heart pulled out and left hanging by his side. These three were killed on their pallets near the fire. Two of the bodies were placed in the same coffin and carried to Castroville, but were then placed in separate graves. When the coffins were made only three of the bodies had been found.

During the progress of the Mexican war of 1846 Mr. Haby enlisted in company D, Texas mounted volunteers, commanded by Captain Veach, and at once went to Mexico and did service until the war was over. After his return from Mexico the Habys settled on the Medina River, several miles above Castroville, and commenced farming, stock raising, and fighting Indians. Mr. Nic. Haby settled on the west bank of the river on a high bluff overlooking the surrounding country. Here he had many adventures with the Indians, but held his ground, still lives there, and gave the writer a cordial welcome when calling upon him for an interview. It was at this place that Mr. Haby killed one Indian that he caught stealing. It was in 1870, when the hostile Indians made their last raid on the Haby settlement. They made their first appearance below Mr. Nic. Haby's place and stole horses from his brothers Joe, Ambrose, and Andrew, and also from another settler named Monier. They then went to Mr. Wilmer's, who was a freighter, and stole his mules. Andrew Haby came up to his brother Nic's about midnight and told him of the horses being stolen, and for him to look out for his, and then returned home to protect and guard his family. Nic Haby had two horses loose in a small pasture of about eight acres on the north side of the house, and had trained them to come to him when he whistled. So after the departure of his brother he went out and gave the peculiar call and they at once came, and were tied up to a little log house in the yard. Mr. Haby then got his shotgun, which was well charged with buckshot, and went to a large liveoak tree standing near the pasture fence on the north side of the house, and distant fifty yards from where the horses were tied. The moon was shining brightly, and Mr. Haby sat down in the shadow of the tree with his back against it, facing west. The pasture fence ran north and south, and thirteen paces in front of Mr. Haby was the west line, which ran close to the house and only a few yards from where the horses were tied. With his shotgun across his lap and finger on the trigger the old pioneer watched and waited, knowing that the Indians would have to pass near him to get his horses. The fence was made of rails, and was what is called a straight fence. Two pickets were placed in the ground close together and opposite each other, at regular distances apart, and then a short piece of plank or board was nailed to each at the top to hold them from spreading when the rails were filled in. When the panels were filled in to the proper height a rail was then elevated on top of the cross board, leaving a space of a foot or more between this rider and the next rail in the panel.

After several hours of patient waiting the horses began to snort and move about uneasily and look north up the pasture fence. Mr. Haby knew the Indians were near, and cocked his gun. The horses commenced to rear and to make frantic efforts to break loose and get away. Mr. Haby at the same time saw the Indians in the bright moonlight coming in a trot, stooped over, and close to the fence on the outside, and making direct for the terrified horses. Before reaching the horses they would have to pass Mr. Haby. By the time he got his gun in position to shoot the foremost Indian was opposite him, but suddenly stopped and looked over the fence towards where Mr. Haby was bringing his gun into position to shoot. The Indian was looking between the top rail and the rider, which was about his height. At this time, and taking place quicker than it can be told, the shotgun was fired and the Indian fell. Mr. Haby turned his gun quickly to fire at the other two, but they were gone,—vanished like a vision of the night. Mr. Haby remained for a short time in his position, listening and waiting, and watching the spot where he saw the Indian fall, but no sign or move came from there, so he ventured to the spot or fence and looked over, keeping his gun in position, ready to shoot at a moment's warning. The Indian was lying prone and motionless. Being satisfied he had killed him, Haby went to the house, got a pair of blankets, returned and spread them on the ground opposite the Indian, only the fence intervening between them. Then he lay down there and spent the balance of the night watching, thinking the other Indians would come back to see about their companion and he would get another one of them. They did not come, however, and when daylight came Mr. Haby crossed the fence and examined the dead hostile. Eight buckshot had struck him in the face and forehead, and two had struck him in the mouth, knocking out nearly all of his teeth. The Indian had fallen on his gun, a long flintlock rifle, and it was at full cock. It is evident that the Indian had discovered Mr. Haby and cocked his gun, but was uncertain what it was he saw, and before he could determine, the buckshot came and he was ushered quickly into the happy hunting grounds. He had on a shotpouch and a fancy powderhorn. He also had a bow and quiver of arrows at his back. A knife, rope, and blanket was around his waist. He was about 6 feet in height, strong, well made, and seemed to be about 25 years of age. His hair came nearly to the waist, thick and black. The news of the dead Indian at Nic. Haby's soon spread through the settlement, and many came to look at him.

There was an old gentleman stopping with Mr. Haby who had at one time lived in this settlement and had a horse stolen by the Indians, and in the pursuit which followed the horse was found dead on the trail and his entrails cut out. The old man was very mad, and said if he ever saw a dead Indian he was going to cut his entrails out; and as he was standing by the body on the morning after the killing he suddenly jerked out his knife and ripped it open. There was another man present who said he would like to have the hair of the Indian, but did not like to take it off. There was a boy also in the crowd named Frank

Haby, who had a sharp knife, and he proposed to cut it off for the man. This he did very neatly, close to the skull, but without cutting the skin, and presented the fine long hair to the man who wanted it. The distance from the oak tree to where the Indian lay was thirteen steps, and the writer sat at the root of the tree and took the notes from which this sketch was written. Mr. Haby also showed the writer the powderhorn, which was beautifully carved and finished. He does not know what became of the gun; he kept it and used it many years, and finally some one carried it away. The body of the Indian was dragged about 200 yards from the house and left for the hogs to eat. Mrs. Haby would eat no hog meat for several years after. In about eight days the Indians came back to see what became of their companion, but were afraid to come close to the house. Their tracks were seen in the field and the dogs barked all night. It is likely that they found fragments of the body and were satisfied as to his fate. Mr. Haby says the Indian was a Kickapoo. The boy Frank Haby, who cut off the Indian's hair, is now a well-to-do stockman, and one of Bandera County's most reliable citizens. He lives on Seco Creek, near the Bandera road, about twelve miles from Utopia.

Mr. Nichalus Haby draws a pension for services in the Mexican war, and exhibited to the writer a medal of which he is justly proud. The medal is bronze, heart-shaped, two and one-half inches in length by two inches in diameter. Between the medal and pin at the top is a thick piece of red, white, and blue cloth, which connects the medal and pin. The latter is for the purpose of fastening it on the front of the coat or vest in a parade or reunion of veterans. On the front side of the medal at the top is the cut of a ship, in the left hand corner on the right is a cannon unlimbered, as if ready for action. Between these are two guns crossed near the muzzles, one with and one without a bayonet. A sword then crosses both, and a large pistol is between the butts of the guns at the bottom. Below the guns is the name Mexico, and then comes a prickly pear and maguay plant. Below this is an old fort, and under it the date 1846. This is encircled by a wreath, with the name of Scott at the bottom. To the left and right of this name is that of Perry and Taylor, the whole then surrounded by stars. On the margin around the medal in raised letters are following names of battles: Tobasco,

Vera Cruz, Palo Alto, Buena Vista, Cerro Gordo, Cherubusco, Chapultepec. On the pin at the top is the following: "Patented March 7th, 1876." Below this is "National Association of Veterans." On the under side of the medal is the following: "Nichlas Haby, Ninth Texas Cavalry."

HENRY CASTRO.

HENRY CASTRO.

Came to Texas in 1843.

Henry Castro was born in France in July, 1786, of rich parents, and descended from one of the oldest Portuguese families, one of his ancestors, Zoas of Castro, having been the fourth viceroy of the Indies for the king of Portugal. In 1805, at the age of 19, he was selected by the prefect of his department (Landes) to welcome the Emperor Napoleon on the occasion of his visit to that department. In 1806 he was one of the guard of honor that accompanied Napoleon to Spain. In 1814, being an officer in the first legion of the National Guards of Paris, he fought with Marshal Moncey at the gate of Clichy. Having immigrated to the United States after the fall of Napoleon, in May, 1827, he was consul at the port of Providence for the king of Naples, having become an American citizen by choice the same year. He returned to France in 1838, was the partner of Mr. Lafitte, the banker, and took an active part in trying to negotiate a loan for the Republic of Texas at Paris. Having received large grants of land under certain conditions of colonization, he immediately proceeded to comply with his contract, and after great expense and labor succeeded in bringing to this State 485 families and 457 single men, in twenty-seven ships, from the year 1843 to 1847. He died at Monterey, Mexico, while on his way to visit the graves of his relatives in France.—[Thrall's History of Texas.

A. J. DAVENPORT.

Came to Texas in 1843.

One among the old-timers and Indian fighters of the West is A. J. Davenport, familiarly called Jack by his many friends. He has a fine farm and ranch near Sabinal Station, and a stock ranch in Little Blanco Canyon. It was at the latter place the writer found him busy salting cattle. Some of these old settlers are very modest and loath to tell their experience, saying they had done nothing worth recording. Their main business in the early days was to raise cattle and trail and fight Indians, and one was almost as commonplace as the other, and hence their view of the insignificance of Indian raids, etc. People, however, who have had no experience in such things take a different view altogether, and look upon one of these old pioneers as being above the ordinary. The time has passed now for men to gain any notoriety as Indian fighters, and when we look upon one of these men who has trailed and faced and fought the wild, painted Comanche, looked into his fierce, gleaming eyes, and heard his loud war-whoop; seen his matchless riding and lightning-like dexterity with the bow as he sent his barbed and feathered arrows cutting and hissing through the air, at the same time swinging from side to side of his horse to avoid also the white man's rapid shots from a revolver;—we stand before him and look at his gray locks and sun-tanned face with great respect, akin to awe.

Mr. Davenport was born in Johnson County, Missouri, in 1843, and came to Texas the same year with his father, John Davenport, and settled in Kaufman County. John Davenport was a soldier under General Jackson in the wars with the Creek Indians and the British war of 1812.

The subject of this sketch came to the Sabinal Canyon in 1853. The following named men had already arrived and settled: William Ware, Gideon Thompson, Aaron Anglin, John and James Davenport, and Henry Robinson. His brother John was killed by the Indians near where Sabinal station is now, not long after Jack came to the canyon. His brother John, who at that time lived below the mountains, had gone early on the

SCENE OF WOLFE AND HUFFMAN'S INDIAN BATTLE.

morning he was killed to Blanco Creek after a yoke of oxen, and was returning with them when attacked. Some Mexicans witnessed the fight, but were afraid to go to his assistance. They said that he shot two of the Indians with a sixshooter. When the Indians left the Mexicans went to Davenport, and he tried to talk to them but was not able to do so. He was badly shot and scalped, and soon died. When the news of his death reached the settlement his relatives came and carried the body to his home on Rancheros Creek and buried it. His young brother Jack said that if ever he had the opportunity he would take an Indian scalp and get even on that line for that of his brother John. This retaliation was accomplished in later years while a Texas ranger under Captain Montel.

The Indians who killed John Davenport were pursued by the settlers and a desperate battle fought with them. One of the Indians killed in the fight had been badly wounded by Davenport in their fight with him. His sixshooter was also recovered.

These same Indians also killed John Bowles lower down the country.

In 1860 Judge Davenport sent word from his ranch for all the men who lived on Rancheros Creek that could, to meet him at the Kinchaloe prairie, near D'Hanis, in Medina County. The Indians, he said, were on a raid in large force, and were now going out towards the mountains with a large drove of horses. The men who responded to this call were Jack Davenport, Ross Kennedy, John Kennedy, and Frank Hilburn, the latter a noted Indian fighter, who had already killed two Indians single-handed. When they arrived at the place designated they were joined by the Hondo settlers under the leadership of Big Foot Wallace. The trail of the Indians was soon taken up and went by the way of the Comanche waterhole, now a noted place for deer hunters to camp. From this place the trail went straight to the foot of the mountains and led up Big Seco Canyon. The Indians were overtaken at the head of the creek. The fight which followed has already been described, but each witness brings out new facts that were forgotten by others. Mr. Davenport says that their party stopped and ate their dinner in plain view of the Indians, who lay in ambush and had tied a horse on the side of the mountain in view as a decoy to bring the white men up that way. Several impetuous young men went ahead to be first to get hold of the horse, and received the first fire of the Indians, which wounded Bill Davenport, son of Judge Davenport, and drove the balance back to the main force of thirty or more men. In front, when the advance up the hill was made, were Jack Davenport, Lewis McCombs, and Jasper Kinchaloe. The Indians made their first fire with shotguns which they had taken from settlers killed in this raid. Firing down hill, they overshot the men in front and struck among those lower down. The attack from the Indians, however, was so fierce that all retreated back to the foot of the mountain, where they tied their horses and acted on the defensive. During the fight an Indian sat on a black mule a long distance off, on top of a mountain, intently watching the combat. Ross Kennedy, who had an Enfield rifle, said he could move him, and raising the sight of his gun took aim and fired. The Indian sat a few moments after the gun fired, then all of a sudden the mule jumped nearly from under him, and soon got out of sight in the rocks and bushes. Evidently the mule was hit. After the fight six shotguns were found on the mountain where the Indians left them, also the pistol of Murray, the assessor, who had been killed by them. The men went that night to Sabinal Canyon and next day followed the Indians again. There came up a terrible sleet, and the men spent the night about where Henry Taylor now lives. As before stated, they ambushed the Indians at Ranger Springs, and the whole plan was frustrated by Hilburn firing too soon. Jack Davenport says that Captain Wallace planned this ambush splendidly, and if order could have been kept, would have almost annihilated this band of red marauders.

In this same year Huffman and Wolfe, two young stockmen who lived on Seco, came out west of the Sabinal River, below the mountains, to hunt stock. When they arrived at a point on the prairie about where the hay farm of Mr. Ed Kelley now is, they came upon a band of mounted Indians. It was a mile or more east to the river, where there was some protection along the banks and in the rocks and scrubby brush and scattered timber. To this point the two men turned their cow ponies and made a desperate run for life. The Indians came on in swift pursuit, yelling loudly. At this time, just across a swell in the prairie at a place called the "rock pile," William Davenport was on his way to Uvalde with a two-horse wagon, and saw the dust rising and heard Indians yelling ahead of him. The road he was traveling ran southwest, and the Indians were running the cowmen in a northeast or east direction, and hid from view as before stated by rising ground. Mr. Davenport knew well what all this meant, and turning his horses around whipped them into a gallop and made his way back home at the Blue waterhole on the Sabinal river, at the mouth of the canyon. The distance was about three miles. Had the cowboys known that Davenport was over there and gone to him, the three might have stood off the Indians with the wagon for shelter. Not knowing this, however, they kept straight for the river, firing at the Indians as they ran. The Comanches finally ran around and in the midst of the boys, and they dismounted at a liveoak tree, turned their horses loose, and fought desperately for their lives. The tree was stuck full of arrows. The boys finally made another run on foot towards the Sabinal, but likely both were wounded by this time, as the Indians had circled the tree on their horses and shot arrows from all sides, as those sticking in the tree indicated. In this run they were soon surrounded and went down under numerous arrow wounds, firing their last shots at close quarters on the open prairie. This spot is now just across the river from the home of Mrs. Nancy Kelley and her son Robert. This same band of Indians had the evening before killed the Mexican herder of Mr. Ross Kennedy, first stripping and then torturing and scalping him. Among the settlers who got together to pursue the Indians were Jack Davenport, William Knox, Ross Kennedy, John Kennedy, Dock Lee, Ambrose Crane, and Albin Rankin. Knox was chosen captain. They soon found the trail of the Indians and commenced the pursuit. When they arrived in the prairie where the old Uvalde road runs through the Kelley pasture the trail of the Indians abruptly turned east towards the river, and they knew from the signs of the torn-up earth that some one had been pursued by them, but who they could not tell. It was here the run was made on Huffman and Wolfe. Various articles were picked up such as cowmen carry to their saddles—cups, coffee-pots, wallets, etc. Out some distance from the river stood a live-oak tree in which the trailers noticed a large black object while yet some distance away. They rode straight for that now, and on coming to the spot discovered that the object in the tree was a dead Indian. He was closely wrapped in a blanket, his eyes were closed tightly with red paint, and his bow was hanging on a limb by his head. His body was astride a limb and lashed to another with a rope to keep it in an upright position. He had a bullet hole in his neck, in what is usually called the sticking place. The settlers had deviated from the trail by seeing the Indian in the tree, and did not at this time discover the bodies of the slain cowmen, which were lying in the grass about 150 yards away. The trail of the Indians from the tree led northwest across the prairie towards the mouth of Big Blanco Canyon, several miles distant. As yet the trailers had no idea who had fought the Indians or how they came out in the struggle. The trail was followed rapidly and the Indians overtaken before night in the canyon, at a place called the "sinks of the water." Here the Blanco River sinks and leaves the channel dry. The Indians had dismounted and evidently intended camping there. They were surprised by the sudden appearance and charge of the whites and ran into the cedar brakes, leaving their horses, which were all captured. Several shots were fired at the fleeing Indians, but none were killed on the ground that could be found. It was nearly night, and there was not much time to look around after the skirmish was over. Among the horses were found Huffman's mule, saddled and bridled, and his pistol hanging to the pommel of the saddle in the scabbard. One Indian tried to mount the mule, but he was fired at and ran off on foot. Jack Davenport knew the mule as one owned by Huffman, and told the men he was satisfied it was him that had been chased by the Indians and had killed one, and was evidently slain himself. The horses of the Indians were gathered, and the men returned that night to the settlement on Rancheros Creek. The place where they encountered the Indians, called "the sinks," is just below where the ranch of Mr. Charles Peters now is.

Next morning the men all started out again to search for the body of Huffman, not knowing as yet that Wolfe was with him and had also been killed. When they arrived at the scene of the fight they soon discovered the tree sticking full of arrows where they first dismounted to fight. A short search around soon discovered the bodies, mutilated and full of arrows. How many Indians they hit or killed besides the one found they could not tell. Huffman's pistol was empty, and the Indians had put it back in the scabbard, which was fastened to the horn of the saddle. Wolfe's pistol was not found. The bodies of the unfortunate young men were buried near where found, but were afterwards taken up and reinterred at D'Hanis. The Catholics took charge of the body of Huffman, as he had no relatives in this country.

In 1861 Jack Davenport joined a company of rangers commanded by Capt. Charles de Montel. They were stationed at Ranger Springs, on the Seco. While they were here the Indians made a raid below the mountains and were followed by settlers from below to the head of the salt marsh in Sabinal Canyon, about five miles west from the present village of Utopia. In the meantime a runner had been sent to the ranger camp, and a scout was sent out to intercept them. The rangers and settlers got together at the head of the salt marsh and continued the pursuit. Among the rangers were Lieut. Ben Patton, commanding; Jack Davenport, Ed Taylor, Cud Adams, Demp Forrest, Dan Malone, Charley Cole, Jasper Kinchaloe, Lon Moore, and John

Cook. The trail led in a northeast direction over a rough, mountainous country, towards the head of the Frio River. At length, arriving on a high mountain about three miles west of the present ranch of Mr. Sam Harper, in Sabinal Canyon, Lieutenant Patton discovered the Indians. They had camped in a valley, but on elevated ground, between two deep gullies, with a cedar brake in their rear. They were engaged in cooking horse meat, mending moccasins, etc. Without being seen by the Indians, Patton dismounted his men, left their horses, went down the mountain, and struck the creek about half a mile below the Indian camp, and came up keeping well concealed, until they approached the high banks of the gullies in less than fifty yards of the unsuspecting hostiles. Jack Davenport, having it on his mind to avenge his brother, kept his gun well in hand, and when the charge was ordered kept by the side of Lieutenant Patton, who led. The men went up the banks in various places and with great rapidity, and were almost among the Indians and firing upon them before they were aware of the presence of an enemy. The onset was so fierce and the firing so fast and fatal that the Indians made a poor fight, and soon sought safety in the cedar brake near by. Davenport and Patton both fired their first shot at the same Indian, who fell near the fire. Another one fell fifty yards from the fire, and the third ran about 200 yards and fell. Many of the Indians were wounded but made their escape, leaving trails of blood behind them. One wounded Indian was found under the roots of a large cedar tree which had been blown down, and was pulled out and scalped alive by one of the white men. The Indian made a very wry face during the process of scalping, as if in much pain, and pointed towards the sky, as if threatening the man with the vengeance of God. In this fight John Cook shot twelve times at one Indian running, emptying two revolvers without bringing him down. Sometimes an Indian can carry off almost as much lead as a California grizzly bear. When the fight was over Jack Davenport went to the Indian whom he knew he had shot, and scalped him, saying as he did so that he was now even with them for his brother John. Be it said to his credit, however, his Indian was dead when he scalped him.

During the civil war Mr. Davenport belonged to Colonel Duff's regiment, Thirty-third Texas, company F, commanded by Captain Davis, from San Marcos, Hays County. He was in the fight at Powderhorn, where they fought the Union troops under General Ross. Was on picket duty, and saw the Union army land at Point Isabel. At the close of the war his command was in Arkansas, and was there disbanded.

Mr. Davenport is a successful stock raiser, and one of the solid citizens of Uvalde County, honored and respected by all who know him.

JOSEPH CONRADS.

Came to Texas in 1843.

Mr. Joseph Conrads, who lives in Castroville, is one of the original pioneers of Medina County, and has many interesting things to tell of the long ago, when times were not what they are now.

Mr. Conrads was born in Prussia, near Saar River, in 1832. His father, Nicholas Conrads, with his family set sail for America from Havre de Grace, France, in 1843. They came in the ship Obre as part of the colony of Henry Castro. They had a long, tedious trip of seventy-five days in crossing the ocean, and some of the passengers died at sea. The immigrants were all French except two families—Conrads and Wilkes. Many of them were really German, but all spoke French, being Alsatians. On New Year's day of 1843 the good ship landed at Galveston, and the tired and almost worn out colonists gladly set foot on Texas soil, although it was a strange and foreign country to them, thousands of miles from the place of their nativity. The elder Conrads started from Galveston with his family to Houston, but turned back at San Felipe and stopped on Buffalo Bayou and died there. Peter, the eldest brother of Joseph, went back to Galveston and the family became scattered. However, finding that a good living could be made in Galveston, he came back and got the family together and returned there with them.

In 1846 the family of Castro landed in Galveston direct from Europe, and the Conrads family came on out with them to Castroville, the future home of the colonists, part of whom had already arrived under the leadership of Castro and commenced erecting rude shelters. The Indians at that time were friendly to the newcomers and furnished them all the wild game they wanted, very cheap. The Indians were the Lipan tribe. The colonists were not possessed of suitable firearms to kill game with, and greatly appreciated the bountiful supply of fat turkey and venison. The writer will say here that the Lipans were a branch of the Comanche tribe. Some time previous to the advent of the American pioneers into Texas there were two powerful rival chiefs among the Comanches, one of whom was named Lipan. This chief finally quit the tribe and wandered far away from them, but was followed by a band of his friends and admirers, and in time a new tribe was formed which took the name of their chief and waged a constant and bitter war against the old tribe, and many desperate and cruel battles were fought with alternate success for both parties. Two of the colonists, Young and Kingle, hunted with the Indians and helped to keep their friends in town from starving. Hostilities commenced with the Indians by the latter having some trouble with Americans who were moving to the west. The Indians stole their horses, and they killed some of the Indians. Some ex-Texas rangers also had trouble with the Lipans, in which one of the latter was killed.

On one occasion Messrs. Conrads, Gerhardt, and Ihnukers went out on a horse hunt and also to see if there were Indians about. They camped for noon at the Mustang waterhole on the Francisco, and while there saw a band of Indians coming towards them. They at once ran away, leaving all of their things in camp. The chief of the party ran after them, and holding up a sack in which he had provisions told them to stop, "Indian no hurt." Seeing they could not easily get away, the three colonists stopped, and after some talk the Indians went on and the white men quickly returned home. These same Indians went on to the Quihi settlement and captured a woman and carried her way. (This was likely Mrs. Charobiny, who escaped from them on the same day she was captured.)

Some of the people in those days made a living making boards and shingles out of the cypress which grew along the Medina River. They found a market for such things in San Antonio. This was the only chance for people living there to get anything except grass with which to cover their houses. The people in and around Castroville lived on deer meat and corn meal. There were no cattle in the country at that time except as men would work in San Antonio, buy a cow with the money, and then bring her on out to the colony. In 1846-47 Mr. Conrads and his brother ran Mr. Castro's wagon to bring in colonists from Port Lavaca. The nearest place to get cornmeal was the Guadalupe River. One night when the Indians were hostile a Frenchman tied his horse to the bedpost to make sure of him until morning, but during the heavy hours of the night, while the Frenchman slumbered, a wily and very wideawake savage slipped up, cut the rope, and carried the horse away.

In 1848 Mr. Conrads moved to San Antonio, which by this time was improving very fast. In 1849, however, he moved back to Castroville. People were coming in all the time, and that place was improving fast. Mr. Conrads says people enjoyed themselves then better than they do now. They did not have much, but appreciated all they could get and make. There were but few wagons among the settlers in those days. Some of the people carried corn on their backs to the mill after one was built nine miles below San Antonio, a distance of thirty-five miles from the colony. The people dressed in a different way compared to this time. Their everyday clothes were their Sunday clothes, too, and some people would be ashamed to wear such now. Mr. Conrads knew Capt. Jack Hays and Big Foot Wallace well, and says both were good Indian fighters and were a great help to the people.

In 1852 Mr. Conrads and a party went out on a hunting expedition, and ate their dinner one day near where Mr. H. Rothe now lives. During the time a severe sleet began to fall, and they came upon a trail of Indians, which they followed, and came upon them near night while they were eating supper near a cedar brake. The white men dismounted, crawled near them, and fired upon them. The Indians scattered into the brush and the whites took possession of their camp, and while picking up such things as they wanted they heard groans in the brake not far away. On investigating they found a wounded Indian, who had his leg broken, besides a wound in the shoulder. He had tried to kill himself by sticking an arrow in his heart. He soon died and was scalped, and a strap taken from his back. Afterwards other Indians were found dead in the brake. This was between the Verde Creek and the Hondo, not far from the Peach Tree waterhole. The men who composed this party, besides Mr. Conrads, were Bob Harper, Tom Malone, William White, William Adams, Henry Adams, and the two Boones. There were some others, but their names are not remembered.

In 1857, Peter, brother of Joseph Conrads, went out to hunt a cow, and on ascending a liveoak hill saw something run into the brush. Not thinking it was an Indian, he went in there and soon came upon a dead mare belonging to his brother. Going back and giving the alarm, five or six men went back, among whom was Joseph Conrads. They soon met another mare of Joseph's running with a buffalo lariat on. The Indians were near by, and hearing the whites talking ran away about 300 yards. The chief was soon discovered, and was seen to fire a pistol in the air. Some Mexicans were out hunting oxen, and part of this band of Indians were running them, and the chief fired the pistol to recall them to help fight the white men, whom he had now discovered. The Indians had some horses, and instead of stopping to fight they ran away and carried the horses with them. The white men ran the Indians to the Mustang prairie, firing at them all the way, which was returned by the Indians. Here Mr. Joseph Conrads dismounted to load his gun, and his horse, being frightened, got loose from him and ran away. The balance of the men soon stopped the horse, and Peter Conrads ran between the horse and the Indians and tried to cut off the balance of the horses which the Indians had in their possession. His firearms consisted only of a pistol. The Indians were now very near the settlers, and Joseph Conrads, as soon as he got his gun loaded, shot one Indian, who dismounted from his horse and sat down by a tree. The white men now retreated and the Indians followed them. One man who had a loaded gun tried to shoot, but at the same time his horse fell with him and his gun went off in the air. Joseph Conrads, having again reloaded his gun, stooped down so as to get a good shot at another Indian, but the fellow at whom he was about to fire, seeing his actions, got behind a mesquite tree. He had a squaw with him who was armed with a bow, and she shot several arrows at Conrads. The latter now determined to shoot her, as she was in plain view, but when he made the attempt he could not pull the hammer of his rifle down. The Indians soon after gave up the fight and went off. When Conrads made an examination of his gun to ascertain the cause of its failure to shoot, he discovered that he had not pulled the hammer far enough back, and only had it on the half-cock.

These same Indians killed two men at Black Hill, not far from where Benton City now is, and on their return to the mountains killed Wolfe and Huffman on the Sabinal. The Indians were followed by another party farther west and a scalp taken from them, which they supposed to be a woman's, but which proved to be that of Bilhartz, one of the men who was killed at Black Hill. He had long curly hair. The other man killed with him was named Jungman.

On one occasion when Mr. Conrads went out to hunt a cow four miles from Castroville he saw some horses coming towards him, and soon discovered that they were being driven by Indians. He hurriedly ran into the brush, left his horse, and came home on foot. The Indians did not see him and failed to find the mare, which he had abandoned so as to be better able to travel through the brush and cactus. A scout returned and found the animal with coat and leggings still on the saddle. The trail of the Indians was taken up, and the party soon came upon two men who had been killed by them. The men killed were old man Grace and his son. Their wagon was standing in the road loaded with pickets. This took place near where Idlewild is now, below La Coste station. Both of the men were shot in the left side with bullets. Between Elm Creek and Medina they killed a Mexican boy. The Indians were overtaken by another party and some of them killed.

CASTRO'S DIARY. PART I.

In getting together material for a history of this famous colony of southwest Texas I have spared no pains in getting the most reliable information, and have been very successful in finding old documents and papers among some of the old settlers, who have carefully preserved them through all these years, and willingly gave me all the information they were possessed of. They are justly proud of their achievement here in the wilderness, and they and their descendants will read with interest their history.

I am under many obligations to the citizens of Medina County for assistance in my work. Among these are Judge Herman E. Haas, of Hondo; Chris Batot, and the Kochs and Neys, of D'Hanis; August Kempf, district clerk of Medina County; Judge M. Charobiny, of New Fountain, and August Rothe, of the large ranch of the Rothe Brothers, on the Seco.

At the time of the incipiency of Henry Castro's immigration scheme in Europe, Texas offered rare inducements to the thousands of sturdy men in the old countries who had to labor for a living to get cheap homes and better their condition in life. Texas was new,—had just emerged from under the misrule of Mexico, and had set up housekeeping for herself as a Republic. She had rich lands by the millions of acres to give away to those who sought homes within her borders. Energetic men went to work to bring in people from some of the old countries to help settle up these vast regions which stretched away towards the setting sun for many hundreds of miles, covered with rich grasses and cut through at almost regular intervals from San Antonio to the Rio Grande by clear, bold streams, as the Leon, Medio, Medina, Quihi, Verde, Hondo, Seco, Ranchero, Sabinal, Frio, Blanco, Leona, Nueces, Turkey, and so on.

Many people from Europe and from the States of the Union who had no part in bringing colonists here wrote to friends and relatives about this grand country and induced many to come. Henry Castro was a man of extraordinary ability and perseverance, or he could never have surmounted the many hindrances and obstacles which were thrown in his way for years before he could begin to see and taste any of the fruits of his labors.

From extracts of memoirs of Henry Castro, which were preserved by his son Lorenzo, we find that when General Henderson was in the city of Paris, France, to procure from Louis Philippe a recognition of the Republic of Texas, he visited the home of Henry Castro.

Castro in his memoirs says: "The Prince of Peace (Godoy), whom I had known after he was exiled from Spain, occasionally visited me. After having risen from a private in the bodyguards of the king to prime minister of Spain, and after having received all favors the king was able to confer upon him, he was reduced to poverty, and was then living in Paris on the income of 5000 francs a month, which he received as the recipient of the Grand Cross of the Legion of Honor, which had been conferred upon him by Napoleon the First. Among the many gifts made to Godoy by the king was the title to the province of Texas, and I then entered into negotiations with him to hunt up the original deed and execute a conveyance to the provisional government of Texas. But all of his property and papers had been declared confiscated by the Spanish government. Although he tried through some friends to procure that document he did not succeed in doing so. It would have been rather strange that Texas should have claimed her recognition through a deed of conveyance of the owner of the soil, the Prince of Peace.

"When I called to see Mr. J. Lafitte (banker) with General Hamilton, of South Carolina, to aid him in negotiating a loan of $7,000,000 for the Republic of Texas, after hearing me with a great deal of attention, he was pleased, and declared that the loan could be affected; but taking me to one side said to me in French, because he did not speak English and the general did not speak French, 'Mr. Castro, please tell me where Texas is situated.'

"On another occasion General Hamilton had an audience with Louis Philippe, who made him sit by his side and conversed with him in the most intimate manner, and having most solemnly promised his support to the projected loan, left the general perfectly delighted. He called upon me and expressed great hopes of success, and we then visited Mr. Lafitte, who, after hearing the general's report of his conversation with the king and his great promises, to our great astonishment he said to us confidentially that without any doubt the king would do exactly contrary to what he had promised the general. Hamilton was almost confounded at hearing Mr. Lafitte, but his prediction proved true, as afterward the king proved false to his word.

"When I first tried to charter a ship to carry immigrants to Texas I found great difficulty, as the coast of that portion of the gulf was hardly known. I could get ten vessels to go to New Orleans, but I could not find one to go to Galveston. I had maps of the coast of Texas, made according to the best data I could procure, which was from Captain Simpson, of Galveston, and circulated it in many parts of Europe. Among the pamphlets published by me, one particularly attracted attention. It was styled 'Coup d'Oeil Sur le Texas,' signed by Hr. Fournel, with a map by A. Bre, geographer to the king, dated 1840.

"For services rendered to the Republic of Texas I was allowed to enter into a contract of colonization to establish two colonies, one situated on the Rio Grande, commencing at a point nearly opposite Camargo and running to Salt Lake (Sol del Rey), thence in a parallel line to a point opposite Dolores, below Laredo. This colony I could not attempt to settle, as Mexican troops occupied in force that portion of the Rio Grande, and claimed all the territory between that river and the Nueces. The other west of San Antonio, including that portion of the country now comprising part of Medina, Uvalde, Frio, Atascosa, Bexar, McMullen, La Salle, and Zavalla counties, is the one I colonized. At the time that my first colonists arrived in San Antonio, in February, 1843, no settlement existed west of the San Pedro Creek to the Rio Grande. I met with great difficulties in procuring immigrants in France, because the government was trying to turn the tide of immigration toward Algiers. After great expense and arduous labor, I succeeded in sending my first ship, Ebro, Captain Perry, from the port of Havre to Galveston, Texas, with a load consisting entirely of French immigrants and a full cargo of merchandise subject to duties."

Henry Castro having landed one shipload of colonists in 1843, the following is his report to the President of the Republic of Texas in regard to his work of colonization:

"Washington, Texas, July 12, 1844.

"General: The period has arrived when I am bound to render you an account of the honorable mission confided to me, namely, the colonization by Europeans of a portion of the county of Bexar.

"At the time your excellency executed a grant in my favor, on the 15th of February, 1842, you were likewise pleased to appoint me consul-general of Texas for the kingdom of France. On that occasion the honorable Secretary of State wrote to me as follows: 'The President of the Republic has been pleased, in consideration of the services you have rendered to the cause of Texas, as well as from your known zeal for her interests and ability to protect and advance them, to appoint you consul-general of the Republic of Texas for the kingdom of France.'

"I lost not a moment's time, and on the 15th of May was in the city of Paris busily engaged in the execution of my contract by every means possible within my reach. My early efforts were in some measure frustrated by rumors of the invasion of the county of Bexar, which were widely and industriously circulated. These rumors were, however, contradicted by a letter addressed to me by your secretary, which read as follows: 'The President desires me to say to you that he hopes that recent occurrences may not incline you to defer the execution of your plan of settling your colony in our western confines. Its position for commanding internal trade and its capacities in points of soil and climate will make it a most desirable part of our country.'

"The encouragement given me by your excellency strengthened my determination to proceed in the work of colonization, and on the 3d of November, 1842, I was able to dispatch from Havre the ship Ebro, with 113 colonists. This first expedition was followed on the 10th of January, 1843, by the departure of the ship Lyons, and on the 27th of the same month the ship Louis Philippe sailed from Dunkirk with a number of colonists, accompanied by my agent, E. Martin, and by the Abbe Menetrier, chaplain to the royal chateau of Versailles. The voyage of Mr. Menetrier was undertaken with a view to examining the country, both on my account and that of his family, which had preceded him.

"These expeditions are authenticated by lists containing the names, ages, and professions of the colonists regularly transmitted by each vessel to the honorable Secretary of State.

"On the 14th of January that gentleman wrote me as follows: 'It affords to the Governor of Texas much satisfaction to be informed that you are carrying out your contract in good faith and with much apparent success, and I have great pleasure in assuring you that every proper facility will be extended to you by this government in the prosecution of an undertaking so manifestly adapted to promote the interest of the country. The President is fully aware of the obstacles of the late predatory incursions in Texas by Mexico and the various unfounded rumors of invasion by that power have thrown in your way, and he directs me to assure you that he will not fail to give to those circumstances a due consideration as connected with the fulfillment on your part of the conditions of the same.'

"This manifestation of kindness remunerated me for the innumerable difficulties by which I was surrounded in France and in Texas,—difficulties to dishearten and deter me from the execution of my arduous enterprise. I am fortunately so constituted that obstacles call forth my firmness and power of resistance, and impelled by these feelings I redoubled my exertions, trying to overcome all opposition and to justify the generous confidence you had reposed in me. I therefore continued boldly on the execution of my contract, and succeeded in forwarding from Antwerp the following vessels: October 25, 1843, the Jeane Key; December 11, 1843, the Henrich; April 12, 1844, the Ocean; May 4th, the Jeanette.

"The names of the persons composing each expedition are invariably entered upon a list regularly transmitted by each vessel to the honorable Secretary of State.

"These four expeditions, added to the three already mentioned, constitute altogether seven vessels transporting over 700 immigrants, of whom the great majority are tillers of the soil. In selecting colonists I have uniformly required certain conditions, such as good character, the necessary clothing and farming instruments, and means of subsistence for one year as near as possible.

"The difficulties inseparable from my first efforts, and erroneous statements of many of the immigrants may have affected to a great extent the rigid execution of this plan. The arduous and at the same time expensive exertions have incontestably laid the foundation in Germany and France of immigration to Texas.

It is beyond all question far more practicable at present to transport to Texas 7000 immigrants than it was to induce one-tenth of that number to engage in the enterprise at the time I commenced the fulfillment of my contract.

"A complete organization having been effected, will now secure a regular succession of expeditions, the first of which will leave the port of Antwerp in August and September next, so that taking it for granted that the last expedition arrived about July 15th, there has not been nor will there be any interruption in the process of settling the country.

"If I have been able to endow the country with vigorous arms for the cultivation of the soil, I have not been less instrumental in contributing to improve the financial condition of the Republic. ' The vessels already sent to this country brought full cargoes of goods subject to tariff duties, and those which may be expected during the winter will be loaded with large amounts of merchandise. The experience which I have acquired during more than two years of practical exertions in the undertaking intrusted to my care has convinced me that Texas can only be promptly settled by immigrants possessing the qualifications mentioned in a preceding paragraph. The poor, to whom money may be advanced on a promise of repayment in labor, are unsuitable persons for colonization, because the laws of this country refuse to recognize contracts by virtue of which the time and services of a party are engaged beforehand. The capitalist will naturally decline advancing funds on the sole guarantee of a promise.

"Farmers in easy circumstances rarely immigrate, and this remark applies to France more than any other country, hence the difficulty of obtaining settlers. By the terms of my contract I was to transport to Texas 200 families by the 15th of July, 1843. I believe that in spite of every obstacle I have.

"With regard to the occupation of the lands, that is a point which has not been under my control, and it has been retarded by various circumstances the existence of which was beyond my power to prevent. If required, I can quote the language of the honorable secretary in his letter of January 4th last, already alluded to: 'The president is fully aware of the obstacles thrown in your way, and he will not fail to give to those circumstances a due consideration as connected with the fulfillment on your part of the conditions of your contract.'

"My report would not be complete without I submit to your excellency a detailed statement of the expenses incurred, amounting already to $40,000, which are increasing the more rapidly because I am personally superintending the operations that could not be accomplished during my absence.

"I have laid before your excellency a statement of facts. I submit them for your consideration and for that of the government. What I have already accomplished under the most serious obstacles which could possibly be encountered will enable you to form an opinion as to my future success. I indulge in no vain boast or promises; they are valueless in an undertaking in which action alone is called for. I shall continue, therefore, my labors, with the courageous perseverance belonging to my character, and with incessant confidence in your justice and in that of the government. In 1841 you were pleased to acknowledge that I had rendered services to the country. I enjoy the conscientious conviction of having since that period pursued absolutely the same course, identifying myself with the cause of Texas and devoting to it my time, my fortune, and the future prospects of my family. I entreat your excellency to assist me in taking possession of the lands granted to me in organizing my colony and securing to every settler the protection he has a right to expect, by designating proper authorities in conformity with the laws of the country for the administration of the judiciary and the maintenance of order. HENRY CASTRO."

When Mr. Castro addressed these letters and statements to the which had been granted to him, and was in eastern Texas at old Washington on the Brazos, and it seems entertained some fears that he would have trouble in getting possession of the lands.

CASTRO'S DIARY. PART II.

Came to Texas in 1843.

After Henry Castro had sent his first colonists on to San Antonio he remained at Washington on the Brazos until he could communicate with some of the government officials in regard to taking possession of his land grant, and when this was all arranged he set out on the 13th of July, 1844, for San Antonio, in company with Mr. Louis Huth, and arrived there on the 18th of the same month. His arrival created quite a sensation when the fact was made known. In his memoirs he says he stopped with a native of Genoa named Antonio Lockmar, and that he kept the best house in the city. He says that in Don Antonio he found one of the best, most courageous and obliging men he had ever met with in his many travels. On the 19th he called his people around him, who had been anxiously awaiting his arrival, and thus addressed them:

"Henry Castro, to the colonists holding grants of land derived under his contract with the government of Texas: I have made you partake, within the limits assigned to me, with all the advantages that the government of Texas has made me by granting to me a large and fertile tract of land in the county of Bexar. Circumstances independent of my will have prevented until now the taking possession of these lands. To comply as much as possible with the terms of my contract with you, I have come among you to aid you in your labors and to constitute the colony where our hopes are to be realized. We live under the patronage of a liberal government, among the most hospitable and intelligent people of the earth, having at our disposal lands situated in a healthy locality and of notorious fertility. What have we to do in order to enjoy these advantages? We have only to labor with courage, unity, and perseverance. Let us then go to work at once without hesitation or loss of time. I have taken care that we should be in sufficient numbers to conquer all obstacles of locality. My incessant labors in Europe for the last three years have secured me numerous and good colonists, who will arrive here next fall. At this time the ship Jennette Marie, which left

Antwerp May 15th, and which has just arrived at Galveston, brings us reinforcements. Among all the concessions made by the government, the one to which you belong is the only one respected, on account of my efforts to fulfill the conditions of my contract. The land that you will acquire will in consequence of this exception be of more value. The Almighty has created us to work; let us fulfill our destiny if we desire to secure the welfare of our families. I will give you the example of courage, patience, and labor. You are associated in my enterprise. I will aid you with all my might and my resources. Actions and not empty words have always been and always shall be my rule of conduct."

The next few days were busy ones with Castro, making preparations to visit his lands and take a look at them for the first time. The famous Texas ranger, Capt. Jack Hays, was there and furnished Castro an escort of his men, which we see from his diary, which we quote now:

"July 20th, 21st, 22d, 23d, and 24th.—I received many visitors, explained my plans to my colonists, and made preparations to visit the colony lands.

"July 25th.—Left San Antonio with five men of Captain Hays' company of rangers. Our party consisted of seven, making in all twelve men, and well armed. Camped first night on Medio Creek, twelve miles west.

"July 26th.—Mr. John James, who accompanied us, killed three bears on the Potranco Creek; saw many wild horses. James Dunn, one of the rangers, ran them and killed a fine stallion Crossed the Medina River and killed two deer and one alligator and caught some trout; camped on the Medina.

"July 27th.—Recrossed the Medina. At 7 o'clock we had an alarm; one of the rangers reported having seen some mounted men, and not being able to make out who they were, six men left our camp to reconnoiter. They returned without any result. My grant begins four miles west of the Medina. The first thing I saw on my grant was a bee tree full of honey. Reached Quihi Lake, ten miles from the Medina. This point has water, timber, hills, and prairie. It is a good location for a settlement. Camped on the Hondo Creek; also another good place for a settlement.

"July 28th.—Reached the Rio Seco, twelve miles west of Hondo Creek, still on my grant; caught some trout and killed two deer.

Ascended the Seco to the foot of the hills and camped at a water hole below the hills.

"July 29th.—Rode across the country and again reached the Hondo, where we gathered some persimmons and wild grenadines. Camped three miles from Quihi Lake.

"July 30th.—Followed the banks of Quihi Lake, which valley possesses all the advantages for a colony; procured honey and fish in abundance. Camped on the Medina.

"July 31st.—Returned to San Antonio. Two of our rangers were taken sick with a fever.

"I have during this excursion of seven days seen 160 miles of country, which can only be compared to an English park, without meeting a single settlement. No dangerous wild animals were found, but herds of deer and wild horses. With coffee, sugar, and flour, we have lived well from the product of our hunting and fishing, and always had plenty of honey. I had left my colonists all quiet and full of hope, and on my return from this little exploration of part of the colony I found Prince Solms and his companions, with ten or twelve followers, had arrived at San Antonio a day or two after my departure, making a great noise and show, producing upon the modest people the same impressions as a circus troupe in their middle-age costumes. They did not have much trouble in gathering my colonists around them, as they spoke German and showed them certain liberality in the way of drink. Every one spoke of going and settling on the prince's land and following him wherever he should lead. Although the prince, acting as a gentleman, did not have anything to do with these maneuvers personally, still he manifestly sustained his agents in their course. He was much seconded by a desperate character by the name of Rump, who belonged to Captain Hays' company of rangers. Prince Solms having been informed that I intended to establish my first settlement on the Quihi Lake, ten miles from the Medina River, which was four miles east from my colony line, listened to certain propositions that were made to him regarding a seventeen-league tract of land belonging to a citizen of San Antonio known as John McMullen. He started with his party to explore said tract of land. I understood that if he negotiated for the occupation of such tract of land my enterprise would be ruined, and taking advantage of his absence, I entered into negotiations with McMullen, and with the assistance of one of our most able and honorable attorneys, Mr. Vanderlip, made a contract with the said John McMullen to colonize on certain conditions his grant. When the prince returned to San Antonio he certainly was disappointed. On the 12th of August I made my colonists the following ad- President of the Republic of Texas he had never seen the land dress:

"First. In order that each colonist remain in the true path that his interest commands him, it has become my duty to let him know what he would lose if he abandons it. You will have through me, first, a concession of 320 acres of land per family, and 160 acres for each of the single men, within thirty-five miles of San Antonio, in the vicinity of Quihi Lake, in a section of country where you will find good water, timber, prairies, and hills, the land being of the first quality.

"Second. A house gratis, for which you will have nothing to do but aid in its construction; during the occupation you will be fed at my expense.

"Third. A sufficient number of cows will be furnished to those who have not the means of purchasing stock; all the milk they may need the first year.

"Fourth. Work oxen, plows, and farming implements will be furnished by me free for the first year.

"Fifth. To those who have not sufficient means of subsistence, rations will be furnished until the first crop is gathered.

"Sixth. Labor will be given you in building up what buildings are necessary for the colony, for which labor salary proportioned to the ability of each will be paid you. I will also arrange the distribution of labor so that it will be equitably divided.

"The above is my profession of faith and my address to you. Should you ignore them, you will act contrary to the interest of your families.

"San Antonio, August 12, 1844.—I will only remark here that I had to contend with powerful enemies who were trying all their might to seduce my colonists, and that it took more than ordinary energy to fight against those enemies in a wild country far away from my associations. On August 20th I informed my colonists that in two former notices I had called their attention to their duties, that certain parties were trying to persuade them to ignore by the meanest kind of proceedings. I defy those who direct these maneuvers to avow them. If they did so they would receive at my hands the chastisement that cowards deserve. To day I make known to you that in order to facilitate your settlement of our first establishment I have bought sixteen leagues of land on the Medina at certain conditions of colonization. We will settle there. I will grant to each colonist that will accompany me forty acres of land and one town lot on the same conditions that I have obtained for myself. The balance of the 320 acres granted to heads of families and of 160 acres granted to single men will be taken up on the lands of the colony grant. This new liberality on my part exceeds the promises of my contract with you. I hope that you will appreciate it to its just value. I gather you around me for a last communication.

"I wish to repeat to you that I have secured for you the following advantages. [The same already above mentioned.] Those advantages exceed the conditions of our contract, and are granted to you to accelerate our settlement and our prosperity.

"Aug. 23d.—Information reached Prince Solms that his confederates in Germany had entered into a contract with Fisher, and instructions received to abandon all projects of settling Bourgeois Dorvane colony. Yellow fever bad at Galveston and New Orleans."

CASTRO'S DIARY. PART III.

In writing the history of Castro's colony, I again quote from his diary:

"August 25th.—Some of my colonists who had left Galveston in the early part of July will not reach this place as soon as it was expected on account of sickness. At Santitas' ranch, forty miles from San Antonio, the Indians attacked a cart which had unfortunately remained behind the convoy. A young colonist aged 19 by the name of Z. Rhin was killed. The driver, who was an American, made his escape. The Indians burned the cart and all its contents. Afterwards in the ashes was found the gold and silver that was in the trunks. The silver had melted and the gold had only been blackened. The driver remained in the woods the following day, and although the Indians numbered twenty he kept them at bay with his long rifle. One of the hands of poor Rhin was found nailed to a tree. He was probably the first martyr of European emigration by Indian brutality in western Texas.

"August 26th.—To-day five or six Comanches came within two hundred yards of the house I occupy on Soledad Street and succeeded in capturing eleven mules that were grazing in the inclosure. Alarm was given in the town and the robbers were pursued, but without any result. The mules were lost. Such acts of audacity on the part of the Indians intimidate my colonists and tend to injure my enterprise.

"Four volunteers who were sent by Captain Hays to reconnoiter on the Nueces River ninety miles from San Antonio were surprised while bathing in the river by a large party of Indians. Two were reported killed. The other two reported that they had undressed themselves and with horses unsaddled they were bathing in the river when they were fired upon from the bank of the river. The attack was so sudden and unexpected that seeing their comrades fall and fearful of being surrounded, they fled, leaving their arms, clothing, saddles, and bridles in possession of the Indians. You Texans who read this may know what our friends suffered riding naked bareback a distance of nearly one hundred miles in the hot month of August, but they however reached this place in safety.

"The conduct of this scout sent as explorers in a portion of the country then full of Indians was certainly very imprudent."

(This surprise of the rangers which Mr. Castro has thus described occurred at the three forks of the Nueces, as the place was then called by the rangers, and was in Nueces Canyon. The men were Kit Ackland, Rufe Perry, James Dunn, and John Carlin. The two last named were in bathing when the attack was made on their camp and they went to San Antonio and reported Ackland and Perry killed, but they, although badly wounded, made their way back to San Antonio on foot.)

I quote again from Mr. Castro. He says:

"In the month of July last Captain Hays with twelve of his company encountered near Corpus Christi seventy-five Comanche warriors. A fight ensued which I am told lasted fifty minutes, nearly hand to hand. Thirty Indians were killed and many others wounded and routed. This victory was greatly due to the use of Colt's revolvers that the Texans used for the first time in this engagement, to the great astonishment of the Indians, who fought bravely."

There is a difference of opinion as to where the revolvers were first used in conflict with the Iidians. Capt. Mayne Reid, in his book, "Hays', Walker's and McCulloch's Rangers," says it was in the Pedernales battle. The writer had an uncle, Andrew Sowell, who was in the battle which Mr. Castro describes, and says they used the revolvers (five-shooters) there, and he thinks for the first time. No doubt it was the first time this band was fought with them. Tom Galbreth, another old Hays ranger, says it was in Nueces Canyon; at least they used them on another bunch there for the first time.

Again Mr. Castro says:

"August 27th.—I hastened as much as possible the preparation necessary to my leaving this city, believing that I had the sympathy of the inhabitants of the place, but here again I met with a bitter deception. I had against me without my knowledge the merchants and large real estate owners. The first, because they feared that a new town started west of theirs would take away most of their trade with Mexico, and the others because they had received the services of many of my colonists at low rates, and because they found in them industrious and intelligent laboring men. As long as it was thought that my proposed settlement was all talk, no opposition was made, but when it was found out that my departure was certain, rumors were circulated by those interested that my people would all become an easy prey to the Indians; that they would not make a crop for a year to come; that the heavy rains that would set in about October would prevent them from constructing their houses. How could they live in that desert? They were going to leave a certainty for an uncertainty; they would certainly return, when they would find the situations they now filled occupied by others, and a most deplorable misery would be the reward of their removal. Those new enemies were not the least dangerous to encounter. However, I was inspired to give them a terrible blow by proclaiming that in my first attempt to settle the colony I would only accept men to accompany me; that the families should remain in the city until otherwise decided. That satisfied everybody.

"August 28th, 29th, 30th, and 31st.—These few days were employed in preparations for our expedition. On the 31st all the colonists who were to form part of the expedition, with their families and many of my American friends, were invited by me to participate in a farewell dinner, which went off exceedingly pleasant, and toward evening, owing to the great number of toasts drunk, became very enthusiastic. September 1, 1844, at 4 o'clock a. m., I had gathered carts numbering twenty-two. The farming utensils, baggage, and provisions being ready to be loaded in the town, some of my employes informed me that rumors had been maliciously circulated that we would not start on that day owing to the small number composing our expedition, and to give it more weight, it was said and reported that I had stated that we would be at least fifty men strong, but that I could not fulfill my promise, etc.

"I immediately sent ten men on horseback in all directions to contradict such rumors, assuring everyone that had enrolled his name to form part of my expedition; that nothing but death would prevent me from starting on the appointed day; that I would fulfill all of my promises at any cost and hazard, and that we would be fifty men anyhow at our departure. Although I made every effort in my power my adherents came in slowly, making many excuses under various pretenses, but always assuring me of their intended fidelity to their engagements.

"My position became critical, for in delaying my departure I encouraged the efforts of my enemies to discredit my promises and take away from me the colonists I had brought to this country at so much trouble and expense. Many unfortunately had allowed themselves to be persuaded. It was 2 o'clock in the afternoon, and rain was falling by torrents, as if to create me more embarrassments. It became necessary to supply the number of colonists missing with Mexicans paid by me. On this occasion my friend Don Antonio, with his numerous friends, secured me the number of men that I wanted, owing to the high pay granted them, and I must say to his credit that all of them were good men and behaved well in all circumstances. Although it was raining by torrents at 4 o'clock, having kept all day an open table well supplied with meat and drink, I managed to retain those who would take the trouble to come and inform themselves of what was going on. It appeared to me a proper time to call the roll of the colonists. Of those to be present only twenty-seven were there, but with my Mexicans we were fifty. The train of carts being then loaded, I ordered it to start. When we mustered I found thirty-five colonists and Mexicans well armed, who followed on foot. I accompanied them with about twenty men, all pretty well armed and mounted. This departure was fortunate, and was really one of the greatest triumphs that I obtained over the overwhelming difficulties I had to overcome in my enterprise of colonization. It entirely restored confidence in myself and my enterprise.

"September 2d.—On the Medina River. Started with a party to reconnoiter the point where we were to form our settlements. We only returned to camp at midnight. I caused my people to create an alarm by firing their guns and pistols, and was afterwards satisfied that the lesson was not entirely lost.

"September 3d.—Crossed the Medina River at about 8 a. m. at the actual crossing (now opposite Castroville), a beautiful location. Our camp was shaded by large pecan trees, at the foot of which ran a beautiful stream having plenty of game and fish. The improvised kitchen of my French colonists was soon filled with dishes which, aided by the drink I contributed, soon brought everybody in good humor, and the evening was spent in a gay manner.

"September 4th.—Built a shed in which to place our commissary. Arrival of Deputy Surveyor John James.

"September 5th.—A dispute arose between the French and German colonists, which I fortunately settled amicably.

"September 6th.—Labor more regularly organized.

"September 7th.—Messrs. Dr. Cupples and Charles de Montel leave for San Antonio to bring Bishop Odin.

"September 8th.—Storm during the night, which surprised us and gave us a good ducking. Drank twice a little brandy during the night and smoked a pipe, contrary to my habit.

"September 9th.—Arrival of three colonists. One of my mounted men reported having seen a trail of fifty Comanches. Information sent to Captain Hays and precautions taken against a surprise from the Indians. Built a guard house.

"September 10th.—Cut timber to construct a large shed to shelter every one temporarily. Discovered the kind of grass proper for roofing. Our camp abounds in game and fish. Arrival of Bishop Odin, Rev. Oge, Captains Hays and Chevalier.

"September 11th.—Departure of Captains Hays and Chevalier. To-day my table was set on the banks of the Medina, under the rich foliage of the pecan and walnut. Besides my customary guests we had the bishop and Rev. Oge, whom I did my best to please. Amongst the novelties we had for our fare we had several bottles of wine made from the mustang grape by one of the colonists from the Rhenish provinces. Without doubt it was the first wine manufactured on the Medina, and it was considered very fair.

"September 12th.—An election was held by the authority of the county judge for two justices of the peace and one constable to constitute the authorities of our new precinct. I acted as president of said election. Messrs. Louis Huth and G. S. Bourgeois were elected justices, and Louis Haas constable.

"On the morning of the same day we proceeded to the ceremony of laying the cornerstone of the church of Saint Louis (king) by the Rev. Bishop Odin, accompanied by his grand vicar and followed by all the little colony. Discharges of musketry, bonfires built, and the usual libations ended this well-occupied day.

"September 13th.—Departure of Bishop Odin, whom I accompanied part of the way. The bishop was pleased to deliver me the following certificate:

"'I, the undersigned, bishop of Claudiopolis, affirm to whom it may concern, that upon the invitation of Mr. H. Castro, who has received from the government of Texas a large grant of land in the county of Bexar, I visited, accompanied by Abbe Oge, of my diocese, his settlement situated on the Medina River, twenty-five miles west of San Antonio de Bexar, to lay the cornerstone of the first Catholic church to be constructed in the first settlement of the said Castro, and that we placed the same under the invocation of Saint Louis. We have seen a good number of colonists at work building their houses with a view of forming a solid and permanent settlement.

"'In faith of which I signed and affixed my seal to these presents.

"'ODIN, Bishop of Claudiopolis.

"'Castroville, Sep. 12, 1844.

"'Seen for legalization of the signature of Odin, bishop of Claudiopolis.

"'F. GUILBEAU,

"'French Consular Agent at San Antonio de Bexar.'"

The document signed by Bishop Odin and dated Castroville, September 12, 1844, is no doubt the first time that the name Castroville was ever signed or printed, as it come into existence at that time.

CASTROVILLE FOUNDED.

1844.

After the colonists had become somewhat settled in their new habitations and their town named after its founder, the following document was drawn up and signed by those who had remained with him:

"Process verbal of the possession taken of the lands situated on the concession made to Mr. H. Castro by the Texan government, on the 15th day of February, 1842, situated in the county of Bexar, and of other lands belonging to him.

"We, the undersigned colonists engaged in France by Mr. H. Castro to participate in the advantages of the grant above mentioned within the limits assigned by the government of Texas, the terms of which are more particularly set forth in a contract passed between us and the said H. Castro, do declare:

"That the said Castro having assembled us at San Antonio de Bexar as our leader, conducted us on that which had been assigned and given us by him, in consequence of which we left San Antonio on the 1st of September to go to the Medina River, twenty-five miles west, which place we reached on the 2d instant. We declare that, independently of our contract and without any obligation on his part, Mr. H. Castro has made us the following advantages hereafter expressed, in order to facilitate to us our speedy settlement."

Here follow the advantages above mentioned:

"First. To each of us forty acres of land of his property on the Medina.

"Second. The necessary transportation and our rations secured until our houses shall be constructed.

"Third. Horses and oxen until next crop.

"Fourth. Bacon and corn to those who may want it until the next crop is gathered.

"Fifth. The use of his milch cows.

"We declare that Mr. John James, deputy surveyor of this district, came and surveyed the lots assigned to us. We declare since twelve days that we have reached our destination our labors, being well conducted, promise to give a comfortable shelter for ourselves and families within seven or eight weeks. We are satisfied, by the experience that we have acquired, that the climate of Bexar County is among the most salubrious, the water exceedingly good, timber sufficient, and the land appears to unite the qualities needed for a great fertility. Such is the protection under which we have established ourselves and which forms the base of our hopes. We have unanimously resolved to name the town of which we are the founders Castroville.

"Done at Castroville, on the Medina, in the county of Bexar, September the 12th, 1844.

"Signed: Jean Batiste Lecomte, Joseph Haguelin, N. Rosec, Theodore Gentil, Auguste Fretelliere, J. S. Bourgeois, Zavier Young, Louis Huth, George Cupples, Charles Gouibund, J. Fairue, N. Forgeaux, P. Boilot, C. Chapois, J. Macles, Leopold Menetrier, Michel Simon, Theophile Mercier, Antony Goly, Louis Grab, G. L. Haas, Joseph Bader, Bertold Bartz, Charles de Montel, Sax Gaspard, J. Ulrich Zurcher, George Spani.

"Certified to at Castroville, September the 12th, in the year 1844.

"G. L. HAAS, Constable.

"Louis Huth and J. S. Bourgeois, Justices of the Peace.

"Republic of Texas, County of Bexar.—I, the undersigned, do hereby certify that Louis Huth and J. Simon Bourgeois are justices of the peace and G. L. Hass constable for Castroville, in this county.

"Given under my hand and official seal at San Antonio de Bexar, this the 5th day of October, A. D. 1844.

"DAVID MORGAN,
"Chief Justice of Bexar County.

"Seen for the legalization of David Morgan's signature, the consular agent for France ad interim.

"FAUTREL AINE.

"Recorded by T. Hos. Addicks on the 7th day of October, A. D. 1844, in the records of Bexar County."

All of Castro's colony did not arrive until some time in 1847, but came as they could get ready and shipping.

The following are the names of the ships and the captains who commanded them, date of sailing, etc.:

CASTROVILLE FOUNDED. 139

1. Ebro, Captain E. Perry, from Havre to Galveston, 1842.
2. Lyons, Captain G. Parker, from Havre to New Orleans, 1843.
3. Louis Philippe, Captain Laborde, from Dunkirk to Galveston, 1843.
4. ———, ——— ———, ——— to Galveston, 1843.
5. John Key, Captain De Paw, from Antwerp to Galveston, 1843.
6. Henrich, Captain Andries, from Antwerp to Galveston, 1844.
7. Ocean, Captain Rochjen, from Antwerp to Galveston, 1844.
8. Jeannette Maria, Captain Perischke, from Antwerp to Galveston, 1844.
9. Probus, Captain Deonis, from Antwerp to Galveston, 1845.
10. Prince Oscar, Captain Azoerken, from Antwerp to Galveston, 1845.
11. Marcia Claves, Captain Caiborn, from Antwerp to Galveston, 1845.
12. Alberdina, Captain Matling, from Antwerp to Galveston, 1846.
13. Euprosina, ——— ———, from Ghent to Galveston, 1846.
14. Talisman, Captain Loomis, ——— to Galveston, 1846.
15. Diamant, Captain Baller, ——— to Galveston, 1846.
16. Cronstadt, Captain Hatch, from Antwerp to Galveston, 1846.
17. Carl Wilhelm, Captain De Schelling, from Bremen to Galveston, 1846.
18. Louise Frederich, Captain Kniggs, from Bremen to Galveston, 1846.
19. Neptune, Captain Starsloppe, from Bremen to Galveston, 1846.
20. Leo, Captain Goerdes, from Bremen to Galveston, 1846.
21. Bangor, Captain Leighton, from Antwerp to Galveston, 1846.
22. Feyen, Captain Kruse, from Bremen to Galveston, ———.
23. Duc de Brabant, ——— ———, from Antwerp to Galveston,

24. Schanungza, Captain Patton, from Antwerp to Galveston, 1847.

25. ——, —— ——, from Bremen to Galveston, 1847.

26. Creole, Captain Wessels, from Bremen to Galveston, 1847.

27. Creole, Captain H. Hall, from Antwerp to Galveston, 1847.

There are but few of the original colonists now alive, but the writer has found and interviewed some of them, and will write biographical sketches of these. They have a very interesting tale to tell of the hardships and dangers they had to undergo, both in coming across the waters and from Indians on the frontier after they arrived at their destination. Some were lost at sea, others died en route after landing, and many were killed by Indians. Mr. Castro lived to enjoy the fruits of his labors. His wife and son Lorenzo died at Castroville, but himself in Mexico, and there is no relative in this country that bears his name.

I am indebted to Mr. Louis Haller, of Castroville, for a list of names of the ships, which he has preserved for many years.

JOSEPH BURRELL.

Came to Texas in 1844.

Mr. Joseph Burrell, who lives on the Medina River above Castroville at this date (1898), is one of the original colonists of Henry Castro. He was born in Aldorf, France, in 1829, and started to Texas in March, 1844.

The start was made from Antwerp to the promised land, and the trip was uneventful. The ship sailed fast, and made a much quicker trip than many others which came about the same time. The first landing was made on Texas soil at Galveston, but like nearly all the immigrants, those who were bound for west Texas re-embarked again for the port of Lavaca. Mr. Burrell says it took them a long time to arrive at the last mentioned port, and that a strange thing happened on the way. One day they landed on an island, and all of the officers on the ship went away and did not return for a week. The passengers could not tell where they went or what the meaning was. They could only wait and watch for their return. When the officers returned they gave no explanation of their conduct, but got under way again and arrived all right at their destination.

From Port Lavaca the Castro colonists went to Victoria, and there saw their first Indians. They were in large force, but seemed to be on good terms with the whites. The balance of the journey from here to San Antonio was made in ox wagons. Many of the immigrants by this time were sick from exposure, and two of them died on the way. Two oxen were lost on the San Antonio River, which caused some delay and extra expense to purchase more. Some friendly Indians had paid them a visit while in camp, and that circumstance likely accounts for the missing oxen. On the way out there was some talk of settling at Goliad. They had a surveyor along to lay off the land, but they abandoned this idea and moved on to their original designated place to settle. While in camp when the oxen were lost, most of the men scattered out to hunt them. The elder Burrell had one yoke of oxen, and with these he carried the women and children and those of the men who were sick to a Mexican ranch two miles away. One man was left in camp with the other wagon, and while here alone was attacked by the Indians and killed. These pretended friendly savages then burned the wagon.

This first victim of the inoffensive German immigrants to savage cruelty was named Rehen. On this same day the subject of this sketch, then a boy 15 years of age, was out hunting the lost oxen on horseback, and coming to the San Antonio River started to ride down to the water's edge for his horse to drink, but suddenly the animal wheeled back and tried to run away. Young Burrell succeeded in checking him and looked back. The cause of the fright of the horse was now apparent. A band of Indians was on the opposite side of the river, and they at once commenced crossing towards him. He now let the pony run and made his escape from them. These same Indians went on to camp and did the mischief before noted. The driver of the wagon came in sight while the wagon was burning, but was afraid to venture near, so ran away and gave the alarm.

The unfortunate colonists finally, by purchasing more oxen, made their way to San Antonio. Henry Castro and quite a lot of his people were at this place, not having as yet commenced his settlement, which was to be on the Medina River, twenty-five miles west from San Antonio, at the present site of Castroville. The Burrell family was among the first to go out and help to erect a shanty out of poles. It was a rude affair, but large and capable of sheltering all the people until they could get their individual houses erected. This primitive shelter was covered with grass, which made a good roof, turning water like shingles. The people all stayed in it at night for fear of the Indians. Castro himself came out with them, but went back to San Antonio and left Louis Huth in his place to see to the interest of the colony. His son now has a store in San Antonio.

Mr. Burrell knew Capt. Jack Hays, and says when he first saw him he thought him quite young to be in command of a company of rangers.

Mr. Burrell describes the country at that time as being very beautiful. No brush, only scattered liveoak and mesquite trees on the high ground, and large timber in the valleys. Many fine pecan trees were on the river, and high grass everywhere. All the streams were running high. The branch he now lives on was fed by a large spring, and emptied into what was called the

Pecan waterhole, which was always full until the Spring branch quit running, a number of years ago. This place was the camping-ground of a large band of Indians when Mr. Burrell first came to the country. There is a well now on the original site of the spring, which affords plenty of water.

In 1846 Mr. Burrell joined a company of rangers commanded by Capt. John Conner. They moved their camp many times on the lookout for Indians, but had no fight with them. When a trail was struck the Indians would burn the grass behind them to cover it.

During this time the war with Mexico broke out, and Captain Conner carried his company to Mexico and joined General Taylor at Monterey. This was in 1847. On the way, and before they reached the city, they came upon the remains of a United States government train which had been captured and destroyed by the Mexicans. There were about 200 wagons, all of which were burned and the drivers all killed except one, who made his escape and carried the news of the disaster to General Taylor. Mr. Burrell knew a great many of the teamsters who lay dead beside the road. The Mexicans carried away the mules.

When the time of their enlistment had expired Captain Conner's men were discharged, and Mr. Burrell joined the company of Captain Veach and remained until the war was over. He was discharged at San Antonio, and now draws a pension for this service of $8 per month.

He next obtained a job as government teamster to assist in opening a road from San Antonio to El Paso. From the latter place he and others were sent seventy-five miles north to cut timber for the purpose of building forts. Beeves and goats were carried along to eat.

After arriving at the scene of their labors a place was selected in a secluded little valley in which to keep the beeves and goats. A heavy snow, however, soon fell, which covered the valley a foot deep, and which lasted several days. During this time the Indians succeeded in getting the beeves and goats out of the valley and carried them off. There were not sufficient horses in camp on which to pursue the marauders. The baggage wagon had been drawn to their present camp by oxen. These resolute fellows, however, determined to follow the Indians, and here commenced one of the most unique pursuits of Indians that has ever been recorded in frontier history. They hitched oxen to the baggage wagon and followed them in that. One reason which induced them to attempt a pursuit by this slow locomotion was the fact that the Indians would have to go slow with the goats and beef cattle. Not knowing the country, however, they soon got into a dry country and could find no water. The supply with which they started was soon exhausted. The oxen also gave out and lay down. They had one wagon, three yoke of oxen, and eight men in this strange expedition. The men now scattered in different directions on foot to hunt for water. In his rounds Mr. Burrell came to a clear lake, and being almost dead with thirst, lay down on his stomach and commenced to drink very fast. He soon sprang up in terror, for it was alkali, and came near killing him. He now found some prickly pears, and cutting out the inside, obtained some moisture by chewing them. On this same evening two of the other men found good water on the Sacramento Mountains, and came back to let the others know where it was. They all got together by firing pistols, and then lost no time in getting back to the water. Here they stayed three days, and were then loath to leave, as it was two days hard walking back to the wagon. The oxen had all been turned loose when the search for water commenced, but on the second day after the men had assembled on the mountain all of the oxen came up straight to the water. One man had started on the expedition on horseback, but had turned back when the water gave out. A man named Cotton, from San Antonio, was in charge of the timber cutting outfit, but had stayed in camp when the pursuit of the Indians was inaugurated, and he was informed of the situation by the man who returned on the horse. Cotton at once came with two men to hunt for them, and found them at the waterhole on the mountain. They now killed one of the oxen to eat and drove the balance back to the wagon, hitched two yoke to it, and drove the odd one along. The country was sandy, and the team could not well pull the wagon through it, so three men would push, one drive, and three rest until it came their time to push. Cotton and the men with him went on back to camp, taking the other wagon and some teams which had been left in camp, and went across to Donna Anna, thirty miles away.

The men came on with their slow and tedious way of moving.

If one ox gave out the odd one was put in until the other could rest, and so on. Finally, however, all of the oxen gave out, and they had to leave the wagon and oxen except one, on which they put their blankets and other things, and traveled that way until the ox gave out, and then the men had to make pack horses of themselves. Having no water was the cause of the oxen giving out. The men were without water on this return trip three days. Burrell had brought a five-gallon keg from the mountain, but it gave out three days before reaching their old camp from which they started in pursuit of the Indians. They stopped one day at the old camp and drank water. Next day one of the oxen which had been left arrived in camp. By this time the men were hungry again, and killed the ox for food. They remained one more day and ate beef.

Cotton went to a new camp where timber was better, and supposed the men would follow him when they returned. Some of them did so, but Mr. Burrell and two others went to El Paso, eighty miles distant. They had to make this journey on foot, and took some of the ox meat along to subsist upon by the way. It was thirty miles to the first water, and there they rested awhile. It was fifty miles to the next, El Paso. They were badly worn out. After resting awhile they built them a house, Mexican fashion, and went to farming by irrigation. Their crop, however, was never finished on account of the Indians stealing their teams. They now quit El Paso and started to California. There were fifteen wagons in the outfit, some of them containing whole families. This was in 1850. On the route the Indians stole part of their teams before they reached the Gila River. The Indians were pursued, and this time with success. The stock was all retaken and brought back. When the party arrived at the Gila a halt was made and Mr. Burrell went on alone. When he arrived at the Colorado River, on the line of New Mexico and California, he fell in with a friendly Indian who told him where to cross the river, as it was very dangerous. A party of white men now came along who seemed to know the fords, and Burrell crossed with them, but in doing so his horse was drowned. There was a train camped on the other side whose captain knew Burrell, and wanted him to remain and go with them. He stayed with them one night, but next day set out again alone. On the way he fell in with another train which was going his way, and journeyed with them.

At Santiago he got on a boat and went to San Francisco, and from there to Sacramento. At the former place he again met Capt. Jack Hays, who had removed to California after the Mexican war and had been elected sheriff of San Francisco County. Burrell bought tools at Sacramento and went out to the mines and got into a job at $6 per day. It snowed here a great deal. There was at this time great excitement on Scott River, and Mr. Burrell went over there. On the way, however, his pack mule was stolen and he had to carry his pack on his own back. The snow was so deep he soon had to stop, and went to mining again at $8 per day. When the snow melted off he went on to the Trinity River and found better diggings there. There were six in his party now, and they soon heard news of a better place further on. Burrell and two others went on, but soon run short of means and had to return to the old camp. The other men by this time had gone and nothing was there. They went on down the country, and soon lost all they had in an Indian raid. Burrell then went back to Sacramento and from there to Oregon. He stayed here nearly a year and tried farming, but made nothing. Salt was $16 per sack, and flour could not be had at any price. He had to eat beef without bread. His partner was sent off on a horse with money to buy provisions, but he went on into California and did not return. He secured another partner and went into the mining business again. One day while at work there was a cave-in and he was partly covered with rocks, and had to remain in that condition until his partner could go half a mile and return with help. He thought Burrell was dead. After the rocks were removed he was not able to stand, nor could he see. He was carried to a shanty, and did not walk for many days. Nine other men were buried in like manner the same day, and most of them died. He quit mining then and went to building rock houses.

He came back to Texas by way of New Orleans, and again arrived at Castroville in 1855. Soon after getting back the Indians made a raid and stole some good horses from him, and also some from the ranch of Ed. Braden. The latter lived in San Antonio, but had a ranch on Calaveras Creek. Burrell and one of his brothers and a man named Huffman were up in the hills and saw the Indians with the horses, and Burrell wanted to make a charge and try to recover them. The others would not agree to this. He then said he would shoot and see if he could hit one at long range. The Indian's horse was hit, and he sprang on another and got away. It was one of Braden's horses that was wounded, and he was captured and brought back. Braden soon came and wanted Burrell to go with him on the trail of the Indians. The trail was taken up, and after circling about some went straight towards Westfall's ranch on the Leona. When they arrived at this place they found a dead man and a dead dog in the yard. They did not know who the man was, but knew it was not Westfall. The same Indians they were trailing had attacked the ranch. They quit the trail here, as the Indians were too far ahead to overtake them. They learned afterwards that the dead man was French Louie, and that Westfall himself was badly wounded, but had made his way to Fort Inge.

After this he joined a minute company commanded by Capt. George Haby. The Indians made one raid and stole horses all over the country. Captain Haby took twenty men and followed them. The trail was struck at a place called "Mescal camp," where some Mexican liquor had once been made. Here the Indians killed and ate a horse. They were overtaken at the head of the Hondo River, with 101 head of horses. Burrell tried to cut them off from the horses, but was prevented by a deep creek. The Indians left the horses they were riding and escaped into the brush. After a great deal of search and trouble the stolen horses were all rounded up and carried back to the owners.

Mr. Burrell used to live near the Medina River, but in 1871 was badly damaged by high water and wanted to move to the hills, but his wife's mother said no, it would never be this high again. Next year came a worse rise and he lost everything. He now lives on a high hill, a mile from the river. The wind took the roof off of his house here. Mrs. Burrell was a Haby, and came from Alsace.

INCIDENT OF RANGER LIFE.

1844.

The facts in the thrilling incident of ranger life now about to be narrated were furnished the writer by the old Texas ranger, Thomas Galbreath. While Mr. Galbreath was not a participant, he was a member of Capt. Jack Hays' company of rangers at the time, and well remembers all of the particulars of this frontier episode.

In August, 1844, about a month after the fight in Nueces Canyon, Captain Hays sent four of his men back to the canyon to see if there was any fresh sign of Indians there. The men sent on this rather hazardous mission so far from the settlements were Kit Ackland, Rufus Perry, James Dunn, and John Carlin. The four rangers went a westerly course until they arrived at a point in the prairie north of where the town of Uvalde now is, and then turned northwest towards the mouth of Nueces Canyon.

For some time no signs of Indians were seen, except the remains of some of those killed in the previous battle, until they came to what the rangers called the three forks of the Nueces. Here about noon, after a hard ride, the men dismounted, unsaddled their horses, put them out to graze, and prepared their noonday meal. After dinner Ackland lay down to rest awhile before continuing the scout, and Perry stood guard. Dunn and Carlin took their horses down to the river to wash them and cool them off, and to take a swim themselves. The rangers had not stopped on the main river, but on a little creek with high banks several hundred yards from the main Nueces. Dunn and Carlin left their saddles in camp, and when they came to the river stripped off their clothing and rode their horses into the stream. Perry was a good and experienced ranger and Indian fighter, but even his exeperienced eye failed to detect a band of Indians who were concealed near by and intently watching every movement of the scouts, and as soon as two of them went off the Indians slipped down the bed of the small creek, keeping hid from view by the banks, until they arrived opposite the camp of the rangers. Their presence was not detected until they suddenly ascended the bank and sent a flight of arrows at Perry, who fell with three wounds, two in the body and one in the face. Ackland at once sprang to his feet with his gun, but was fired on and hit in three places with bullets and arrows, one of which was in the mouth with an arrow, which knocked out some of his teeth and badly lacerated the flesh. He did not fall, however, but quickly aimed his gun at an Indian's face close by, who had his head above the bank of the creek, and fired. The charge hit the Comanche full in the face and he fell backward. The Indians had the advantage of the bank of the creek, which they could dodge back behind when they fired, but seeing the wounded condition of the two rangers, began to come out in large numbers and to charge them. Ackland, without backing, drew his revolver and fired on them with such deadly effect that they again sought cover. During this close combat the wounded Perry drew his pistol, and although unable to rise, turned on his side so that he could see the Indians, and by his shots helped to put them back in the ravine. Ackland now sprang to Perry, lifted him on his shoulder, and started in a run with him to the river, where Dunn and Carlin were. Ackland, although a powerful man physically, was nearly exhausted from loss of blood when he arrived at the place where his other two companions were and laid Perry down. Dunn and Carlin were brave men and had been in many fights with Indians, but failed to come to the assistance of their comrades in their terrible need, but sat on their horses and watched the battle at their noonday camp. Their plea was that it was useless to make an attempt against such a large band of Indians, many of whom they could see in the ravine from their position on the river, and knew they would be cut off before reaching their companions. They had stripped off their clothing and were in the water when they heard the fight commence at camp, and at once came out and mounted their horses without their clothing, ready for flight in case the Indians were too strong for them. By the time Ackland got to the bathers the Indians were yelling loudly and plundering the camp. Although the wounded rangers had pulled the arrows from their bodies they were bleeding profusely, and left a trail of blood from their camp to the river. The two unhurt and mounted rangers, seeing they could do no good, took Perry across the river at the suggestion of Ackland, and then waited until Ackland crossed. A brief consultation was now held, and Perry asked Dunn to load his pistol for him. Dunn took the pistol and ascended a tree to see what the Indians were doing, but failed to load it, as he dropped it on descending, and exclaimed: "The valley is full of Indians, and a large band of them are coming this way." He and Carlin now set out for San Antonio, naked as they were and bareback on their horses. We will not judge the action of these two rangers too harshly. They said it was useless for them all to get killed. They looked upon Ackland and Perry as already dead,—badly wounded and no horses to escape on,—and they would hasten on and inform Captain Hays of the situation. It indeed seemed that there was no chance for the two wounded rangers, left alone on the banks of the clear, beautiful river, with a horde of yelling savages on their trail. Under the circumstances some men would have given up in despair and met their fate without an effort, or, in the position of Ackland, told his disabled friend good-bye and made his own escape if possible. Not so in this case, however, with the lion-hearted ranger. He determined to save his friend or die with him. They had no chance to defend themselves except with knives. The blood had dried and clotted around Perry's eyes so that he could no longer see even his brave friend, who was now bending over him and trying again to lift him on his shoulder. "What are you going to do now, Kit?" asked the wounded Perry. The loud yelling of the Indians denoted their near presence when this question was asked, but they were on the opposite side of the river tracking Ackland by his blood, like a hunter would a wounded deer, and were not yet aware that the rangers had crossed the river, and no doubt expected each moment to come upon them and have an easy time taking their scalps. Ackland was very weak from loss of blood, and his mouth was so badly swollen that he could hardly talk, but managed to tell his friend that he was going to secrete him somewhere and then hide himself, as that was the only chance. He succeeded in getting Perry on his shoulder, but staggered to and fro as he went off with him down the river. Ackland was careful in his flight to leave as little sign as possible. The blood had quit flowing from their wounds, and their saturated garments clung to their bodies. When almost exhausted and ready to sink in his tracks, Ackland came to a large drift that covered an acre or more of ground which had been deposited there during some great rise in the river, and this afforded a good hiding place. Crawling in under the drift he dragged Perry after him as far as he could go, and then explaining to him what kind of a place it was, said he would go and hide somewhere else, so that if one was found likely the other would escape. It was agreed that if either one recovered sufficiently and was not discovered by the Indians, to set out for San Antonio at once and bring help for the other. Ackland said he would not be far from the spot where he left Perry. The Indians could still be heard, and pressing the hand of his friend, the fearless Kit crawled away and was soon lost to hearing. After getting clear of the drift, he covered the trail he made going in and out by throwing leaves and sticks over it, and then stepping on stones, chunks, and logs as he went away from the place.

Ackland now went further down the river and secreted himself. Perry lay under cover where he was left and listened to the Indians. After a short time he could tell that they had crossed the river and were evidently on the trail of the rangers, and would soon be at his hiding place. For some time all was perfectly still, and then he was aware of their presence by low talking near by. The Indians had begun to hunt more cautiously, not knowing but that likely the other two rangers were also in hiding and had their guns and pistols. He could also hear the Indians walking over the brush, and finally they got onto the drift under which he lay and walked directly over him. O how he wished for his eyesight and gun and pistol well loaded; but he was helpless and lay still and listened, thinking that each minute would be his last. The drift covered so much ground and had so many openings in which a man could crawl that they failed to find the right one, and finally went on down the river.

Perry was now uneasy about Ackland, fearing the Indians would discover him. He listened intently, expecting each moment to hear the exultant whoop which they would utter in case they found him. He could tell this from the occasional yell of pursuit. His mind was greatly relieved as the hours passed by and he failed to hear the ominous sound come from the savages, who were anxious to avenge the braves who lay dead up the river, and one at least whose ugly face was badly mutilated by a rifle ball from Ackland's gun.

As the evening wore on Perry suffered much from his wounds and thirst. He could hear the river running near by, and was tempted to risk the Indians seeing him and try to get to it, but yet he waited and listened. He could tell by the birds singing that night was not yet approaching. After what seemed almost an age to him everything became still. He could no longer hear the birds, and all animal life seemed hushed except the hoot of an owl or the scream of a panther or wildcat. He now determined to leave his hiding place and make an attempt to crawl to the river. Slowly and in darkness he came forth, feeling his way and guided in the right direction after he got clear of the drift by the sound of running water. Many obstacles were encountered,—logs, tree tops, and large rocks,—so much so that many detours had to be made to get around them. Finally, however, he arrived at the edge of the water, and no one who has not experienced the same sensation can realize his sufferings or his pleasure while drinking the cold water, after dragging himself over rough stones and logs, guided by the rippling water to its brink. He now bathed his head and washed the clotted blood from his eyes so that he could open them and once more take a survey of the situation. It was indeed night. The dark mountains loomed up on both sides of the canyon, and the stars shone bright overhead and cast their reflection in the clear water at his feet. After his hot, fevered head had been cooled by frequent applications, and his thirst appeased, he felt strong, and for the first time since he felt the shock of the missiles which struck him that day at noon he was able to stand on his feet. One of the arrows had struck the lower part of his body and paralyzed it up to this time, except the use of one leg. He now thought of his wounded companion, whom he knew was not far away, but they dare not signal to each other for fear it might attract the Indians. Perry feared that when the reaction came upon Ackland, after his terrible efforts to save him, and the bad wounds he had received, it would prove fatal to him or render him incapable of making his way back to San Antonio, which was about 120 miles. The brave Perry now determined to make an effort to reach San Antonio himself and send back succor to his wounded friend. He was satisfied that Captain Hays would send men back to search for and bury their bodies, but as they had left the place where Dunn and Carlin had last seen them they would not know where to hunt. That night he set out on his painful, slow, and almost hopeless journey. We can not describe, but can only imagine, what he suffered from wounds, hunger, thirst, and the burning sun of August, impelled on by not only a desire to save his own life but that of his friend, if he yet had a chance for life. Suffice to say that in six days and nights of travel he arrived in San Antonio. Dunn and Carlin had arrived two or three days before in a most deplorable plight, being sunburned and badly worn out by riding so far without saddle or clothing. They reported Ackland and Perry both killed, as they thought it would be impossible for them to escape. Captain Hays at once sent back a scout of trusty men to rescue his two gallant boys if possible, and if not, to find the bodies and give them decent interment. Great excitement prevailed when Perry got in, and another scout was at once detailed to go and hunt for the other wounded ranger, as they had a better idea of where he might be found from a description of the place as given by Perry.

Where now was the gallant Ackland? All felt an interest in him, and men hurriedly made their preparations to start. Before this scout could get off, however, Ackland solved the problem of his fate by walking into town about two hours after Perry. He had left his place of concealment and started to San Antonio that night after he could no longer hear the Indians. They passed close to the place where he lay and went on down the river, but continued to circle and hunt until night. He and Perry started about the same time, and evidently were not far apart during the trip,—Ackland exerting himself the same as his companion to get to San Antonio to send succor back to the other. Both were in a horrible condition with wounds and starvation—three festering wounds apiece, and both their faces lacerated and badly swollen; even their messmates failed to recognize them on first sight. The best medical aid that San Antonio could furnish at that time was secured, and they were slowly nursed back to health and strength. The room in which they lay while under medical treatment was just north of where the large dry goods establishment of L. Wolfson now is, on the north side of Main Plaza.

The men who went back to look for the unfortunate rangers did their duty, but of course did not find them. They went to the battleground and saw plenty of blood on the ground where Perry fell and where Ackland stood over him with the blood streaming from his face, and could trace their flight by the blood where Ackland ran with Perry to the river. They could not track quite as well as the Indians, for it is evident they trailed to the drift where Perry was concealed, but were baffled there by the skill of Ackland. The rangers could not start the trail from where the two wounded men were left, but found Perry's pistol.

James Dunn was censured by Captain Hays and others of the company, but he was a good ranger, and had no chance in this affair. He was looked upon as one of the most daring men Hays had. He was in the fight at Bandera Pass, in which he and Ackland were both wounded, and also in the big fight in Nueces Canyon, and there did well. Kit Ackland and Rufe Perry had more scars on them than any other men who followed Jack Hays in Texas or Mexico. Ackland died in California and Perry in West Texas in 1898. The latter had more than twenty scars on his body made by bullets and arrows.

LOUIS HALLER.

Came to Texas in 1845.

Mr. Louis Haller, one of the pioneers of Castro's colony, and who still lives at Castroville, was born in France, in Upper Alsace, in 1831, and started to Texas in 1845. He came in an English ship called the Queen Victoria, commanded by Captain Randle. His father was a soldier under Napoleon and saw a great deal of hard service, following the fortunes of this famous Corsican over the bloody fields of Europe. The Victoria was three months making the trip from the old country to the shores of the new. Her captain lost his bearings and sailed around the shores of Scotland and Ireland, then to the West Indies, from there to Mexico, and then to New Orleans by way of Key West, Fla. The sailors on board the ship bet young Haller $25 that he could not climb to the top of a mast, but when he had accomplished this feat they would not pay the bet. From New Orleans he went to Port Lavaca. He saw Galveston as he passed, but did not land. One lady died on shipboard while crossing the ocean. She had six children, one of them being born on board the ship.

From Port Lavaca Mr. Haller came to Seguin by way of Victoria and Gonzales, arriving there in 1845. A Swiss by the name of Hipp kept a store in Seguin at that time, and Haller could understand his language, but could not speak or understand English. Mr. Hipp hired young Haller to clerk in the store for him. Of the settlers living at Seguin at that time, Mr. Haller can remember the Johnsons, Calverts, Kings, Sowells, and Nichols. On one occasion he went down on the river fishing near town with the Johnsons, and left them for a short time to look at some hooks which had been put out lower down the river, and was chased by a band of Lipan Indians. He had no gun to shoot with and they gave him a good scare, but he dodged them very adroitly and made his escape. These Indians at that time were at peace with the whites, and did not intend to kill him. Next day they came to Johnson's and told about running the boy, and said he was the smartest young white man they had ever seen; that when he ran away from them he left no trail by which they could find him. Haller had ran upon the rocks, jumping from one to the other, and leaving no trace of his flight. When out of sight he hid, and the Indians came very close to him. They told Johnson that they did not want to kill him, but wanted to make a servant of him for a squaw of their party. These same Indians tried to get guns from the white men to go and fight the Mexicans when the war broke out in 1846. But there were no guns to spare, and General Taylor thereby lost a few volunteers.

In 1846 Mr. Haller left Seguin and went up to New Braunfels, and from there by the way of San Antonio to Castroville. At this time there were a good many people there and not much work to do, so he went back to San Antonio and clerked in a store for Nat Lewis. In 1850 he came back to Castroville and settled. His people had bought stock and he came out to attend to them. He spent many years in the woods and on the prairies and lost much stock by Indian depredations, and altogether had quite a hard time. He says the Indians were very bad around San Antonio while he stayed there, and one morning killed a Mexican boy near the plaza. The Comanches did this, and when they began their retreat back to the mountains they were followed by the friendly Delawares, and a severe battle took place in which the latter were the victors, killing many of the Comanches and taking their horses. The rangers under Hays had gone to Mexico, hence this daring raid. While in San Antonio Mr. Haller wanted to join the rangers who were commanded by Capt. Jack Hays. The captain told him he was brave enough and could ride a horse fairly well, but was afraid that he could not shoot straight. Haller then took the captain's rifle and showed him how he could shoot, and was complimented on his marksmanship by the great ranger captain. Soon after this Hays carried his men to Mexico, and young Haller went scouting on the frontier after Indians. He was on one scout with Big Foot Wallace, but his horse gave out at D'Hanis and he had to come back. Wallace went on and had a fight with the Indians at the head of the Big Seco Creek, in the mountains. This was about the commencement of the civil war. Soon after the war the Indians killed Valentine Guerly on the Francisco Creek. Mr. Haller helped to bring in and bury the dead man. Guerly was armed and fought the Indians. He was shot all over and scalped. They first buried the body at Castroville, but afterwards it was taken up and reinterred on the Francisco. These same Indians ran three men who were in an ambulance. There was also a wagon along, and a fight ensued in which one Indian was killed. The men in the ambulance left it and ran to the brush and made their fight there. The men were Joe Meyer, Jack Bendeler, and Joe Kruest. The latter had a bullet shot through his hat. He had taken the horses out of the vehicle and was trying to make his escape with them, riding one and leading the other, but the led horse pulled back and broke his rope. The Indians tried hard to get the loose one and ran him very close, yelling loudly and shooting at Joe; but the horse was so badly scared at the yelling that he ran close behind the one ridden by Kruest, and the Indians could not cut him off. They all got safely to the brush without losing a horse or man, and there beat the Indians off, killing one of their number.

Mr. Haller's uncle, Valentine Haller, was killed on Lime Creek, or Clay Creek as some call it. This was seven miles south from Castroville. The old man was alone when killed, and the people hunted for him a long time before his remains were found. His bones were brought to Castroville and buried. The grass in those days grew very rank all over the country, and if a man was killed while alone his body was hard to find. The bones of Mr. Haller were not discovered until the grass burned off. His remains were identified by some bits of clothing which had escaped the fire. It was evident that he was lost at the time he was killed. His hearing was also defective.

A boy named Frank Gephart was stolen, or captured rather, on the Francisco by Indians, and was never heard from again by his people. His stepfather, Joe Murry, was with him, but fought the Indians and made his escape.

Mr. Haller was an old friend of Rube Smith, and remembers well when the Indians killed him on the Hondo. He also knew F. G. Tinsley, was an old-time friend of his, and said he was a justice of the peace in the frontier days of Medina County. He remembers the time when the man above Castroville beat the brass kettle all night during an Indian alarm.

In 1867 Joseph Meuret and Frank Gephart, who lived near Castroville, went out to hunt oxen between Black Creek and Francisco, and while on a cattle trail saw four or five men driving horses and coming towards them. These men had on hats, and it was supposed by the two ox-hunters that they were settlers. Their mistake was not discovered until the two parties came near together, and the Indians, for such they were, commenced yelling and shooting and charging upon them. Frank Gephart, who was but a boy 12 years of age, began to cry, but his elder companion told him not to be afraid; that they had good horses and could outrun the Indians. They ran about a mile, and the man told the boy to keep in the trail, and he rode behind and whipped his horse. In this way they got within 300 yards of the Moore ranch, when another trail crossed theirs, which was washed out to a ditch. The boy's horse would not jump this, but turned and ran to one side; while the man was turned and shooting at the Indians, thinking at the time that the people at the ranch would hear his shots and come to their assistance. No one came, and by this time the Indians were among them and seized the boy's horse by the bridle. Others were shooting many arrows at the man, but by dexterous dodging and wheeling his horse was not hit, but many arrows were picked up there afterwards. The hard-pressed man now went to the Moore ranch, but no one was there, and he went back home and raised the alarm. A party followed the Indians but they were not overtaken, and the boy was never seen or heard of again.

JUDGE BERNHARD BRUCKS.

Came to Texas in 1845.

Judge Bernhard Brucks, the subject of this sketch, was born in Westphalia, Prussia, in the town of Cossfield, in 1835 He started to Texas with his father, John Bernhard Brucks, and his mother, in 1845.

They came on the ship Albertina from Antwerp by way of the English coast, and lay up for some time at Brookhaven, which he says was a great place for fish. At Brookhaven they took on more passengers, and had a long trip of sixty-two days to the coast of Texas, landing at Galveston. Here they stayed two weeks, and then took shipping for Port Lavaca. The ship was very old and leaked badly, necessitating a continual working of the pumps. While in this condition a furious Texas norther came from the land and blew them off from their course. It was impossible to cook anything on account of the pitching of the ship, so when they came close to St. Joseph's Island the passengers wanted to land and cook something to eat, but the captain objected to it, and there was a mutiny on board. The commander was taken prisoner and guarded on the ship by part of the men with guns, while others landed in boats and cooked. They stayed here one day and then got under way again, all being satisfied, after their hunger was appeased, to proceed on their journey.

The next landing place was at Corpus Christi, where they stayed two months. The time was in 1846, and their destination was Castro's colony. General Taylor was there with his army, and the war was just commencing with Mexico. Before leaving this place the colonists had to send to San Antonio for Mexicans and carts to transport their effects to their destination. The carts were of the old primitive type, with huge wooden axles that could be heard creaking a mile when moving. They had no oil for the carts, hence the fearful noise they made. While en route they split open prickly pears and greased (?) with that. While at Corpus Christi Mr. Brucks saw his first Indians—300 Comanches whom General Taylor had sent for and wanted to enlist them to fight the Mexicans. This the Indians refused to do, and went back to their hunting grounds. At that time they pretended to be at peace with the whites, but were ever treacherous, as their name implies, which means "Snake-in-the-grass." The immigrants had a hard trip to San Antonio. It rained a great deal, and all the streams were overflowed. One cart was washed away while crossing the Nueces River. It was recovered, but the goods it contained were badly damaged. They had plenty of deer meat and turkey on the trip, but had no bread, using boiled rice instead.

When they arrived in San Antonio the Mexicans would go no further, and ox teams had to be hired to carry themselves and effects on to Castroville. The Brucks family stayed there one month, and then went out with a party to settle Quihi, still further west, but on Castro's grant and under his jurisdiction. This was on March 4, 1846. The town had already been laid off, and ten families were the first installment. While at Castroville Mr. Brucks saw Capt. Jack Hays and his company of rangers. They were stationed for awhile on the Medina River above Castroville.

The people who settled at Quihi, on the creek of the same name, had town lots in addition to their other land, and on these they soon erected temporary shelters. The hostile Indians soon found out this new settlement, and two families were killed by them in one week after the settlement was begun. Mr. Brucks heard the Indians howling in the night, and some heard the guns when they were killing the families a mile away. A man named Koch came to Quihi and told the news. The Indians took two boys captive, and great confusion prevailed among the people during the night. Mr. Brucks was a boy at the time, but can distinctly remember hearing one of the captive boys crying and calling for his father as the Indians passed near the Brucks tent, but all at once he ceased his lamentations and they heard him no more. The Indians had killed him.

The elder Brucks had brought a church bell from Europe, and it was at this time hanging on the limb of a tree near his tent. Here the men rallied to fight the Indians, and one man was appointed to ring the bell all the time. The bellringer became badly frightened, and would ring a few jerks and then run to the tall grass and lie down a few moments, and then run back and ring the bell again, and then back to the grass, and so on.

Next morning the boy whose cries were heard the night before calling for his father, while in the hands of the savages, was found dead one-half mile from the Brucks tent. He had been killed by a lance thrust. The other boy, who did not cry, was carried on and was not killed. He stayed with the Indians six months and was then sold to a trader, who carried him to San Antonio, and he was sent from there home to Quihi. His people were all killed the night he was taken except his old grandfather, and he was badly wounded and died soon after. The boy could not or would not talk much in his own language when he came back, and being very young, could give no detailed account of his captivity. At first he said the Indians tied him behind an Indian on a horse that had long ears (mule), and also stripped and painted him. The boy did not like to have the paint on him, and the first opportunity that offered washed it off. The Indians whipped him for this, and then painted him again. This happened after they arrived at their far away retreat in the mountains. The squaws would take him out of camp, tie a rope loosely around his body, fill it full of wood, and make him carry it to camp. He said the Indians while traveling ate all of their meat raw, but when they stayed in camp they cooked it. They had plenty of deer meat and honey. The boy did not know where the camp was, but said it was a long distance towards the northwest. One morning the Indians tied their captive to a tree, and then all left camp. In the evening they came back and a white man was with them, who bought the boy and untied him from the tree, and then carried him to San Antonio. The name of this boy and the one killed was Brinkhoff.

On one occasion a boy named Henry Snyder, 12 years of age, who was herding cows one mile from his father's tent, was captured by Indians, carried off, and never heard from again. The cows were herded to keep them out of the crops, for as yet no fences had been made.

After the Indian raid in which the Brinkhoff families were killed the people all collected together and built a brush fort on the bank of the big waterhole in Quihi Creek. It was simply a high brush fence in a half circle, the deep, wide pool of water making the other side secure from attack. Inside of this rude fortress the people would sleep at night.

Mr. Brucks was at one time badly scared by friendly Indians when a boy and out after the cows. He was riding a mule, and had all of the cows in the trail ahead of him on the way home. Finally he took a fancy to walk, and let the mule follow the cows in front of him. During this time he heard the sound of an ax in the brush and scrubby timber near by, and at once left the trail to see who it was chopping out there so far from town. What was his surprise and terror, when he arrived at the spot from which the sound of the the ax proceeded, to walk directly into a camp of Indians. He was so close to them he was afraid to run, and stood and looked at them until an Indian came and took him by the arm and began to talk and motion all round in a circle with his other hand. Young Brucks could not understand what he said, and stood there in mortal terror. The Indians had plenty of deer meat, skins, and honey, and gave the boy some meat. Their honey was put up in deer skins. The old Indian chief took a piece of meat himself, and dipping it in the honey would put that end in his mouth and cut the piece off close to his lips. The boy thought he was a prisoner and had to follow suit, so he dipped his meat in the honey and ate like the Indian did. The chief then took Brucks out into the opening and showed him the way home, thinking he was lost. Young Brucks now made lively tracks and caught up with his mule, who seemed to be in no hurry, and was slowly making his way along the trail. Mounting now in hot haste, Brucks made his slow steed wake up, and as he expressed it, "made him git for home." These Indians were Lipans, and had a permit to hunt and carry skins to San Antonio.

The Indians all finally became hostile, and were so bad that the elder Brucks carried his family to San Antonio and boarded with an Italian named Locomer, who had once been a pirate under the famous Jean Lafitte. The Texas rangers were also quartered at this place, and one day in sport brought an Indian chief with them to dinner. They called the chief "Old Santa Anna," and had a good deal of sport with him, as he was very drunk. The landlord, as was his daily custom, was also drunk. The red chief was very awkward at dinner, and the rangers could not make him eat with knife and fork, but persisted in putting the meat and other edibles in his mouth with his fingers. Old Locomer did not like this, and hit the Indian over the head with a pistol, knocking him down. "Old Santa Anna," as the boys called him, was very mad at this treatment and went away, but soon came back with his bow and arrows and a big knife, and said he had come back to kill the white man that hit him. Locomer stood behind a half-open door, and as the Indian came in he grabbed him and held him against the wall, and took his bow and arrows and knife away from him. This Indian was one of the Lipans who came to San Antonio to sell skins under the treaty stipulation.

San Antonio at that time had no houses with a board or shingle roof. One house, called the "Plaza house," was being built by Mrs. Elliott and covered with shingles, but it was not finished. Mr. Brucks knew John Glanton, the famous gambler, and saw him cut a Mexican to pieces one day for spilling water on him. The Mexican, although badly hurt, got well.

After Mr. Brucks moved back to Quihi the Indians were still hostile, and he had many narrow escapes. On one occasion while out hunting on foot, three miles from home, he shot a deer, and when it fell his dog ran up and caught hold of it, but it got up and ran away, followed by the dog. This dog would never bark on a trail or when he caught anything, so Mr. Brucks ran through a thicket to see which way they went, as it was open beyond in the direction they were headed the last he saw of them. Before getting to the opening himself, however, he saw an Indian standing in the bushes watching the dog catch the deer. Brucks now secreted himself without being seen by his dusky foe, and reloaded his gun. Not knowing how many more might be near, he slipped away into a larger thicket and lay down and listened, intending to fight them there if they came upon him. While lying here he happened to think that his dog would trail him, and by following the dog the Indians would come upon his hiding place, so he crawled out and made tracks for home. About a mile from home the dog overtook him and was very bloody. At first Mr. Brucks thought the Indians had wounded him, but it proved to be the blood of the wounded deer which the dog had caught. The alarm of Indians was raised when Mr. Brucks arrived at the settlement, and a crowd of men went back to investigate. Only a portion of the deer could be found. The red hunter had taken the balance, but he could not be found. It was now evident that only one Indian was there, and if Mr. Brucks had known this he could easily have killed him.

In 1849 the elder Brucks died of cholera, during the prevalence of the great epidemic of that year. He had a hay contract with the government, and had established his camp between the Medio and Leon creeks. The contract was finished, and Mr. Brucks went to San Antonio to get his money and buy some goods. All this was accomplished and he started home, but had caught the dread plague and died on the road at Medio Creek. Another man with him, named Leinweber, also died. At this time young Bernard Brucks was county commissioner at Castroville, and had the cholera himself. Many people died.

In 1861 Mr. Brucks joined a company of rangers commanded by Capt. James Paul, and was stationed at Camp Verde. On one scout they got seventy-five head of horses from the Indians which these red thieves had stolen and driven off from the settlers. On another occasion Captain Paul lost his spectacles while on an Indian chase, and when it was over had the whole company looking for the lost glasses. A cedar limb had jerked them off, but a whole company of Texas rangers failed to find them. The famous Indian fighter and slayer of the "Big Foot" Indian, Ed Westfall, was their guide and trailer. Judge Brucks says that Westfall would follow Indians until his horse gave out, and then would abandon him and continue the pursuit on foot. In one camp they found seventy-five head of horses, but no Indians were around. They were off in the D'Hanis settlement stealing more horses. One shield was hanging on a limb in camp. These Indians were pursued from D'Hanis and the horses recovered which were stolen from that place.

In 1880 Mr. Brucks was appointed county judge of Medina County, and was then regularly elected to that office for fourteen years. He now lives at Dunlay, on the Southern Pacific road, and is strong and hearty.

Capt. James Paul was a lawyer and private secretary of Henry Castro. He lived to be quite old, and died at Castroville in 1897.

INCIDENT IN THE LIFE OF COL. J. C. CARR.

Came to Texas in 1845.

Around the old town of D'Hanis, situated two miles east of the Seco Creek, in Medina County, and on the line of the Southern Pacific railroad, cluster many historic incidents of the long ago, when these valleys and prairies were covered with rank grass, and herds of deer and antelope and wild horses called mustangs roamed over them instead of the domestic animals of civilization, as now.

At the time of which we write, a struggling little colony of German immigrants brought here from the old country by Henry Castro were fighting for existence and trying, it seemed almost in vain, to sustain themselves from incursions of hostile Indians and all the ills of an isolated frontier life, cut off as it were from the outside world. By pluck and perseverance, however, they weathered the storm, and now their children,—for there are very few of the old ones left,—enjoy the fruits of their labor and hardships in the possession of nice residences and beautiful and well laid out farms and ranches. Only a few of the low grass-covered huts remain to mark the footsteps of the pioneers.

In 1859, although the country had undergone a change and times were more prosperous, and a good deal of the hardships of frontier life had been overcome in the twelve years' existence of the colony, still it was the frontier, and Indians raided constantly upon them, killing the settlers, carrying some into captivity, and driving off many head of stock, especially mules and horses, to their strongholds in the mountains or on the "Staked Plains."

At the time of which we write (1859), Capt. Joe Ney, Sr., one of the first settlers, was still alive, and kept a hotel, store, and stage stand at old D'Hanis. In the fall of the above year the Indians made a raid on the town at night and succeeded in getting the stage horses and other stock which were in the corral, to the number of nearly thirty head. To illustrate with what sly and stealthy movements an Indian can work and not be detected, we will say that the inclosure from which the stock was taken adjoined the storehouse and hotel, and no one was disturbed or the presence of the Indians detected until the morning came and disclosed the fact that the corral was empty.

On the night of this daring raid there was a lone man camping on the Seco Creek, near D'Hanis, named James C. Carr, now known throughout the State as Colonel Carr, or "Locomotive," the noted depredation claim agent of the Alamo City. Early on the morning after the raid Colonel Carr, or "Buckskin" as he was then called by the settlers, on account of a suit he wore made out of that material, went to D'Hanis and there found Capt. Joe Ney, "Seco" Smith, Riley, and other citizens of D'Hanis preparing to go in pursuit of the red marauders. "Buckskin" was never too busy or in too great a hurry not to waive all other considerations and go in pursuit of Indians when they raided in the vicinity where he was, so he at once joined Captain Ney and set out after the hostiles. The trail led in a northwest direction to a point on the head waters and mountain creeks of the Medina and Guadalupe rivers. Here the trail suddenly turned towards the southeast, going in the direction of the little frontier town of Bandera, situated on the Medina River. These experienced frontiersmen from D'Hanis soon perceived, from the signs and general direction traveled, that the horses were now in the hands of white men, who were evidently making for Bandera. This surmise was correct, for when Ney and his party arrived at Bandera they found all of the horses in possession of a scout who had just arrived in town a little ahead of them. Captain Sauer and other citizens of the town and vicinity had struck a trail of Indians who had been raiding in their settlement, but abandoned it and were returning home when they struck this band of Indians who had raided D'Hanis, and gave them battle. The Indians failed to make much of a fight, and soon abandoned the horses and fled into a cedar brake. While considerable shooting was indulged in by Captain Saner and his men, it was not known if an Indian was killed or wounded, on account of the thick brush and rocks where the skirmish took place. The horses were all collected and driven to Bandera. This fight took place at the point where Ney's men noticed the acute turn the trail assumed, and at once surmised that here the Indians had met with white men and been defeated and the horses recaptured. Captain Saner said his men were tired, thirsty, and hungry when they met the Indians, and after routing them and rounding up

JAMES C. CARR (BUCKSKIN).
One of Capt. Joe Ney's scouts in the early 50's.

the horses, not only those which were taken from Medina County, but as many more which had been stolen elsewhere, came at once back home.

Captain Ney and party having cut out their horses, left Bandera in the evening, coursing their way without a road across the mountains in the direction of D'Hanis.

Late in the evening Colonel Carr, or "Buckskin," sighting a fine herd of deer, stopped behind to get a shot. The game was shy on account of the open country, and he had some trouble to get in good range. Finally, however, between sundown and dark, Carr took a shot at a fine buck. At the crack of the gun the stricken deer, which was standing about 100 yards away, came bounding towards him, and almost fell at his feet. His horse, which was being held by the bridle, took fright, jerked loose, bounded away, and was soon out of sight in the gloaming. The horse went in the direction Ney and party were going. "Buckskin" could have trailed his horse and followed the right course had daylight lasted, but night coming on this was impossible. He stood over the deer a few moments, loath to leave it, but as nothing could be done with it said to himself, "Good meat, adios." It was impossible to follow the trail, and it grew darker and darker. No direct course could be followed, and "Buckskin" soon realized that he was lost, and would have to spend the night alone in the trackless woods.

Captain Ney and his party camped a little after dark, and the horse ridden by Carr, true to the instinct of his animal nature, followed true on their trail and soon arrived in camp with saddle and bridle, but minus his rider. It was at once believed by all that J. C. Carr was killed by Indians, and falling from his horse, the animal had escaped. Thinking that a band of Indians was in their vicinity, like all prudent frontiersmen they built no fires or gave any signal to the missing man. Guided by a few dim stars, "Buckskin" wandered nearly all night in a vain endeavor to get the right course for the settlement at D'Hanis. At last, seeing all his efforts were futile, he lay down to rest but not to sleep. At daylight he ascended a mountain peak and got his course for D'Hanis, which was about ten miles distant. This was on Sunday morning. Captain Ney and his party had also made a daylight move and reached town early in the morning, ate breakfast, and then raised a large crowd for the purpose of hunting for the body of Carr, thinking they would find his mutilated remains and likely have to fight a band of Indians. Before they started, however, they sighted a lone pedestrian in the distance, coming straight to town. By his garb they soon recognized him, and a wild shout went up as many galloped to meet him. They dismounted, took him on their shoulders, and came shooting and yelling back to town. He was carried to the hotel of Captain Ney, where was spent one Sunday never to be forgotten by those who were at that time citizens of the old town of D'Hanis. So much for this raid, fight, and loss of but one (buckskin) man. Col. Locomotive Carr came to Texas in 1845 from his native State, Tennessee, and has resided in the Rio Grande border counties ever since 1857.

JOHN L. MANN.

Came to Texas in 1846.

John L. Mann, the subject of this sketch, and one of Castro's colonists, was born in Upper Alsace. Mr. Mann, in company with the Habys, started to Texas in October, 1846, on the ship Duc de Braband, and made the trip in forty-eight days, which was considered fast time in those days. Other ships which started two weeks before the Duc de Braband were beaten two weeks in making the passage. In December the ship landed at Galveston. The immigrants went from there to Port Lavaca, arriving at the latter place on Christmas day. There were 200 passengers aboard, about one-half from Alsace and the others from Wittenburg. They did not celebrate Christmas, but spent the day unloading the ship. Mr. Mann had no relatives on the vessel, his parents having remained in Europe. Old man Joseph Haby helped to pay his passage from the old country to Texas, and he says was like a father to him. His father was taken sick in Germany the day he landed in Port Lavaca, and died on New Year's day. In 1851 his mother and brothers and sisters came to Texas and lived in the Haby settlement. Mrs. Mann, the aged mother of John L., lived to be 85 years old, dying in 1892. When Mr. Mann and the Habys arrived at Port Lavaca with other immigrants they had no way of coming to Castro's colony, and Nichalus Haby bought a horse and rode all the way to Castro's colony, a distance of nearly 300 miles, to procure wagons and teams, and then went back after his people and some others. The Habys had brought two wagons on the ship from Europe, and Nichalus procured oxen at Castroville to work to these wagons and drove them all the way to Port Lavaca for this purpose, and also carried one more wagon and team, and with these they came on out to the colony, arriving there on the 2d day of February, 1847. Mr. Mann's father told him when he went to sail for America to stay with the Habys, but 1847 was a very dry year, and the Habys not having much work to do, John left and went to San Antonio and there obtained work on the Alamo. After the Mexican war was over the people in San Antonio heard that Col. Jack

Hays was coming with his regiment of Texas rangers, who had so distinguished themselves in various battles in Mexico, and great preparations were made to receive him and his men, who were going to enter San Antonio from the east, coming by way of Seguin. When the news was spread through the town that the rangers were in sight, Mr. Mann and many others ascended to the top of the Alamo to see them pass through the Alamo Plaza. Thousands of people were present, and as the sunburned, warworn veterans entered the town cheer on cheer rent the air. A regular salute of twenty-one guns was to have been fired, but the cannon which they had ready for the occasion got out of order after a few shots, and this part of the program had to stop. Colonel Hays and his men marched on through the Alamo Square, crossed the river at the bridge, and passed up Main Street to the square in the central part of the city, followed by the shouting, cheering multitude all the way.

After night another cannon was procured, and Mr. Mann hitched two horses to it and proceeded to Main Plaza, followed by the men, who were going to try again to fire the salute to Colonel Hays and his men. Arriving in the center of the plaza, Mr. Mann unhitched the team and carried them away so that they would not be frightened when the big gun was fired. This time the salute was a success; boom after boom made the old town echo and re-echo again and again.

In 1849 Mr. Mann was employed by the government and sent to Port Lavaca after wagons. The government already had mules and oxen down there. Before arriving at the port, news was circulated that the cholera was there. Mr. Mann, however, did not believe this report, and proceeded on into town and found out that it was not true. When on the way back to San Antonio a rumor came that cholera was in that place, but this was also looked upon as a fake. While in camp, however, on the Salado Creek, four miles from the city, the report was confirmed. The dread epidemic was indeed there. Mr. Mann had started with a mule team, but had exchanged with another driver on the road for one of oxen, and as grass was good and water plenty, he remained here in camp until the dread disease had run its course. Many people died, and when he entered San Antonio he missed many faces of friends who had succumbed to the epidemic.

The wagons were now loaded with supplies for the post at El

Paso, which was under command of Maj. Martin Van Horn. A guard of soldiers went with the supplies, and also a party of engineers to work on the road, which was almost impassable in places, and which caused delays of many weeks. Two weeks were spent at Devil's River cutting down the bank before the wagons could go down into the channel. The mail at this time from San Antonio to El Paso was carried by Big Foot Wallace. He had guards with him, one of whom was Mr. C. Pingenot, who now lives at Kline, in Uvalde County.

On the way back from El Paso, and when about half way to the Pecos River, they met Howard's private train loaded with goods which were to be transferred to the government train and carried on. Mr. Mann's wagon was loaded with part of these goods and he went back to El Paso. The wagons were then sent up to Santa Fe and the teamsters discharged, but Mr. Mann got employment two months at the post. In May he came down on a pony in company with five teamsters who were driving government wagons to San Antonio. In June he was employed by Dr. Lyons of San Antonio to drive a wagon in his train up to El Paso. Mr. Nat Lewis of San Antonio also went up with a train about the same time, composed of wagons and carts. Mr. Mann knew all points well in regard to water, and was guide or general adviser in regard to travel and camps. The train arrived at El Paso all right, and started back on the return trip, arriving at "Dead Man's Pass" with five wagons and thirteen men. This is believed by a great many people to be an unlucky number. Eight other discharged men on horseback had been with the wagons, but had left them and went on, seven mounted and one on foot. At the pass the teamsters found one horse of this party which had given out, so this left two of them afoot. Three other wagons were behind, but had not arrived in sight yet. There was a long stretch of road ahead in view, and Mr. Mann saw some one on a hill in the road walking, and thought it was some of the party mentioned before. This person, however, was an Indian who had gone on the hill in the road to see how far the party of horsemen were ahead, for here the Indians had laid a trap to capture the train. Part of the Indians at this time were hid from view by the thick, tall bear grass on one side of the road, and the balance were behind a hill out of sight of the road on the opposite side, and mounted on their horses. The men in the party of teamsters who were now about to experience one of those fearful frontier tragedies so often enacted were John L. Mann, Ben Sanford, Emory Givins, John Crowder, ——— McDonald, Charley Hill, Jerry Priest, ——— Brown, Charles Blawinsky (Polander), Nick Andres, and others whose names can not now be recalled, among whom was a blacksmith.

John Mann's wagon was in the lead, and walking ahead of him in the road about thirty steps was Jerry Priest and the blacksmith. The latter had lost his mind while on this trip, and at this time was perfectly crazy, but harmless. The wagons were now inside of the ambuscade, and the Indians began to show themselves on both sides of the road. Priest stopped and began to look to the right and left, and Mann said to him, "What is the matter there?" "Indians," said Priest, and at once ran back to the wagons. The poor demented blacksmith made no attempt to run, and was killed in his tracks by the first fire from the Comanches.

The Indians kept firing, and soon killed the near wheel steer in Mann's team, and also shot many arrows at him in a few moments. Thinking that his gun was in the rear end of the wagon, he jumped out and ran back there and felt where he always kept it, but it was gone, so he and Priest ran back to the next wagon. Some confusion now ensued, but most of the men left their teams and ran together, and the long, desperate battle commenced. The man Brown was an old Indian fighter and took things very coolly, standing near a wagon wheel and putting in his shots as fast as he could load his rifle and take aim. The balance of the men who had guns were doing the best they could against such odds. The Indians would make close, daring runs, yelling loudly, and on one of these occasions Brown killed one, and he fell from his horse and lay on the ground within thirty yards.

The Indians were shooting both bullets and arrows, which were almost continually striking the wagons, especially the one at which the men had concentrated. A ball finally struck Brown, and he fell. Some of the men who were inside of the wagon and shooting from there saw Brown when he was hit, and knew from the way he fell that he was killed. The Polander had stood by Brown on the outside and was still fighting, but at length he was hit and fell mortally wounded.

The situation now looked desperate, indeed; three of the men already killed and the Indians still numerous and exultant. Some of the men now proposed they make a sally from the wagon and bring the bodies of Brown and the Polander in; the latter they knew was not dead. This was at once and quickly done. Brown was dead, and his unfortunate comrade was writhing in agony. Nick Andres, who had been outside fighting near his own wagon, now got in the wagon with his gun and aimed it over the wagon-bed to shoot while the Indians were making a charge and were very close, but a ball struck him in the throat before he could pull his trigger, and he fell back and died in a few moments. It seemed now that there was no chance for the beleaguered men. One of their party lay dead in the road thirty steps away, two lay dead in the wagons, and another dying. An old man whose name is not now remembered, and who was in the wagon with Andres but had no gun, took the dead man's gun, jumped out of the wagon, and came to the other men during a charge by the Indians, and was wounded in the knee by a bullet. Besides him, Crowder and Givins were both wounded in the arm.

There were some squaws in the fight, and they used bows and shot arrows into the wagon time and again, sticking them into the wagon sheet and wagon bed. During the hottest part of the fight, when so many men were being killed and wounded, McDonald said he was wounded, but an examination of his person failed to find a scratch. The Indians captured the wagon in which the dead body of Andres lay, and carried it off and scalped the unfortunate man. Mr. Mann's wagon was also ransacked and a lot of beef taken out; also his gun, which he failed to get in his hurried search when the fight first commenced. It was a fine rifle, and cost $25. Mr. Mann had no gun during all this trying time, except as a comrade was shot and could no longer continue the fight. He made many narrow escapes from the balls which were constantly hitting the wagon. One rifle ball passed through his hair, but did not break the skin on his head. Mr. Mann had shot a beef with his gun the day before and had not loaded it, thinking he would do that when he got to camp, so the Indians had no chance to shoot his gun on account of their powder being too coarse. They loaded, however, and tried time and again that night to shoot it.

The fight commenced as the sun was setting, and the Indians stayed around and shot at the wagons at intervals until 2 o'clock in the morning. The brave Polander lived on through most of the night, but finally succumbed to the terrible wound which he had received. During the night Mr. Mann cut a hole through the wagon sheet, so he could tell something about the Indians and shoot when occasion offered. During these times he could hear the Indians popping caps on his gun, trying to fire it at the wagon, but could not do so on account of the coarse powder, which would not go down into the small tube of the rifle. Late in the night the Indians quit firing, and only occasionally shot arrows. Mr. Mann said to the men, "The Indians are out of ammunition for the guns and will soon quit and go off, and we will be saved."

Soon after this the Indians went into camp about 400 yards off, and building fires proceeded to cook and eat the beef which they had taken from Mann's wagon. It was a long and grewsome night the survivors of this fearful fight spent in the wagons among the dead men and hundreds of savages camped near, whose fires they could plainly see. When daylight came, however, not an Indian was in sight. The dead one who had lain near the wagon at dark was gone. Many other Indians were seen to fall during the fight, but had all been carried away during the night. Not seeing any Indians in sight, Charley Hill got out of the wagon, and taking his gun ascended a small hill near by to take a look. This was the hill behind which most of the Indians were concealed the evening before. As soon as Charley arrived at the crest of the ridge he saw some mounted Indians coming towards him, and at once ran back pursued by them, shouting as he came, "The Indians are coming again, boys!" He was fired at before reaching the wagons, and one ball just barely missed him.

Four of the Indians went up the road in the direction the wagons came from, and the others went back out of gunshot. Mr. Mann now left the wagon and went and turned his ox loose, which had stood there all night yoked to the dead one. The Indians had taken off the balance of the teams from the other wagons, and Mann said they could have this one, too. The ox commenced eating grass, like that was all he was thinking about during the night. As soon as he fed out of gunshot of the wagons the Indians got him. Some of the oxen had been turned loose from the wagons in which the men were fighting to prevent them from moving them, and all were taken by the Indians.

Besides the three wagons that were behind there was also a train of Mexican carts, and about 9 o'clock seven mounted Mexicans made their appearance, riding ahead of the carts. The Americans thought they were another band of Indians and almost gave up hope, but at once made preparations to fight another battle. They were greatly relieved and encouraged when the horsemen came up to them. They now explained the situation to the Mexicans, and they sent a runner back to hurry up the carts. The Indians had seen the Mexican train coming and had left. The Mexicans were not aware of this, and made ready to help the Americans to fight them. The white men during the night had brought two of the wagons up and had stopped them one on each side of the one they were fighting from, which afforded great protection and no doubt saved the lives of some of the men, as many balls and arrows struck these empty wagons. The Indians had got two, and carried them off a distance. The Mexicans moved the wagons around in a triangle and piled up rocks between the spokes, fixing for a regular seige. Jim Fisk was in charge of the Mexican train, and when he came sent a Mexican after the soldiers at Beaver Lake, but he met them coming this way and they got to the scene of the battle a little after dark. Next day the soldiers took the trail of the Indians, but never caught up with them. The teamsters were very much in hope they could get their own oxen back, and blamed the soldiers for not following faster and further.

The dead men were buried on the spot where the battle was fought. Brown and the blacksmith were both shot through the heart, and the Polander was hit lower down. Andres, as before stated, was struck in the throat. Dr. Lyons was behind with some other carts, and when he came up gave Mann a fine red blanket, as he was in his shirt sleeves and had nothing to sleep on. The Indians had pillaged his wagon and taken everything he had. The doctor took this blanket from around his own shoulders and gave it to Mann. When the other three wagons came up one man had a small one, and this was taken to pieces and placed in Mann's wagon and the team hitched to the latter, and his wagon carried along in that way. The balance of the wagons were left until Nat Lewis could send for them. Mr. Mann gave the teamster $25 to bring his wagon in the way described to Fort Inge, on the Leona, just below the present town of Uvalde, in Uvalde County. Mr. Mann tried to get pay from the government for the loss of his team, but failed.

He now went back to Haby's and made a crop, and selling his corn, bought another team and commenced freighting and made plenty of money. In 1853 he married Miss Magdalena Burrell and stayed one more year with the Habys, and then moved to where he lives now, on the Medina, above Castroville, and built a log house. He has a good residence now and a fine farm, and has plenty, although he has lost a great deal of stock from Indian depredations. He was with Mr. Charobiny the day his house was robbed and Mrs. Charobiny carried away captive. He says when they arrived at the house the yard was covered with feathers where the Indians had ripped the bedticks and scattered them and took the cloth along.

The writer received a hearty welcome at the house of Mr. Mann, and was entertained in the old-time frontier hospitality. May he live long to enjoy the fruits of his labors, and rest in peace at last.

ROBERT WATSON.

Came to Texas in 1846.

The subject of this sketch was born in Habersham County, Georgia, on the 23d of January, 1821. When 17 years of age he enlisted in the army under General Jesup to fight the Seminole Indians. They had made a break from the swamps of Florida and ravaged the lower part of Georgia. As soon as an organized force went against them they retreated back into the swamps and everglades of Florida, and thence the army followed them. In the Walklesassy swamp a hard battle was fought and an Indian town burnt. Mr. Watson was wounded in the left shoulder by a ball during the battle, and Sergeant Jennings of his company was killed. The ball struck him in the head, cutting his hat band. A negro man was captured who was with the Indians, and the soldiers sent him to the widow Jennings of Georgia as a gift. Seventy-five Indians were killed and wounded. Mr. Watson was in many skirmishes during the balance of the campaign.

He came to Texas in 1846 and first settled in eastern Texas, but moved from there to Llano County. He soon after joined Capt. John Williams' company of minute men for frontier protection. Dave Cowan was first lieutenant and his brother Gid was second. While this company was in service the Indians made a raid on the San Saba and killed a man named Jackson, his wife, and one daughter, and carried off two of the children—a girl and a boy—captives. The minute men got on the trail and followed it to near the Wichita Mountains, where they met the two little captives coming on the back track. They said the Indians left them in camp and ran off after some game which came near camp, and they left also and were trying to get back home. The party turned back here and carried the children home. They were entirely naked when discovered. Another band of Indians was also followed, supposed to be the same ones, and overtaken at the head of the Llano. In the fight which ensued the chief and his squaw were killed.

On one occasion, while Mr. Watson was in his field at work,

he was cut off from the house by a band of Indians. His only weapon was a sixshooter, but with it he stood them off until his son could come to his assistance with a Henry rifle, and a lively fight then took place. Several neighbors had penned cattle at his home the previous night, and were still there, and some of them came and helped him in the battle. These were Charley Roberts, Bud (his son), and William Higgins. Charley Roberts had his horse killed, and one of the Indians had his killed near the corner of the fence. William Higgins killed one Indian, and several were hit by Mr. Watson.

About the year 1873 a noted Indian fight took place at the Pack Saddle Mountain. Mr. Watson was not in the fight, but was near by and knew the men who participated in it. The Pack Saddle Mountain in Llano County derived its name from the peculiar shape it assumed at a distance, and which resembled a pack saddle. During a raid by Indians eighteen of them camped in the gap of the mountains and remained there to cook some meat of beef cattle they had killed. Five cow-hunters discovered them, and at once set about to give them battle. They were Robert Brown, Stephen Moss, William Moss, Eli Lloyd, and one whose name is not now remembered. The men were fearless, advanced boldly into the gap, and at once charged them. William Moss was in the lead when they ran in among the Indians, and was soon shot through with a bullet and was supposed to be mortally wounded. He moved back and dismounted from his horse, but the other men stayed with him and continued the battle. The Indians would charge them and fire, but always retired from the fire of the white men. This lasted for some time, until Lloyd and the man whose name is not known were both wounded with bullets. Only two men were now unhurt, but they were not dismayed and still held their position, the wounded men who were able assisting by loading guns or pistols. The Indians were badly hurt, too, and several of their braves lay dead on the mountain and others were sorely wounded. They finally gave up the fight and left the mountain, and the settlers made their way back home, carrying Moss, who was badly hurt. The ball had struck him in front and lodged in his back. A doctor named Smith cut it out, and he finally recovered after a close pull, as did also the other two wounded men.

Mr. Watson was in one fight at the head of the Little Llano

in which two Indians were killed. Captain Williams was in command. He was afterwards killed by Indians in Baby Head Gap, between Cherokee Creek and the Llano. He was on his way to Austin with a drove of cattle, and was cut off here and killed. One of his men also suffered the same fate. Before any settlements were made in Kimble County, where Junction City is now, Mr. Watson moved and settled just above the present town at a place called "The Boggs." On one occasion while here he was out bear hunting on the north prong in the rocks and cedar brakes, and suddenly came upon a camp of three Indians. They were camp-keepers for a larger party, and were engaged in making arrows. At the sight of the white man they sprang to their feet and ran before Mr. Watson could bring his rifle down on them. In a few jumps they were out of sight. Watson did not inspect the camp, but at once retraced his steps and soon after, in a few days at least, went to the nearest settlers and returned with reinforcements. The Indians had not returned, and the camp was as he had left it. In the camp were found three shields, three bridles, three lariats, a soldier's saber, cap, and cape, and also his scalp. There was also one woman's scalp. Her hair was long and black, while that of the soldier was short and light. There was the picture of a white boy painted in the center of one of the shields, with red garters on. On the head was fastened a bunch of hair taken from the scalp of the soldier. The writer remembers hearing Coon Taylor tell about finding the remains of a soldier in a cave on the North Llano while out there with a hunting party. This might have been the man. His comrades may have found his remains and placed them in the cave, as many such incidents happened during the frontier days. Not long after this incident Mr. Watson moved back to the settlements on account of the Indians. He now lives at Utopia, Sabinal Canyon, Uvalde County.

HERBERT WEYNAND.

Came to Texas in 1846.

The subject of this sketch was born in Bigenbach, Prussia, sixteen miles from the Belgian line, in 1822. In 1846, and also prior to that time, many immigrants from Alsace and other points near the Belgian frontier were coming to America and settling on the frontier of Texas, being led hither by Henry Castro.

In March, 1846, Mr. Weynand, in company with about 200 other colonists, started for the promised land, where they were told they could build up happy homes and have all the land they wanted. The colonists were delayed six weeks at Antwerp, and then set sail on the American ship Bangor. They were seventy-two days crossing the ocean. A boy was born on board the ship during the time, and was named after the ship. One of the party, Jacob Gold, was taken very sick and was left on the coast of the Belgian channel. A purse was made up for him to pay expenses during his sickness. He recovered and came on to the colony, and lived to be an old man and a veteran of the Mexican war, and died below San Antonio. The ship Bangor landed at Port Lavaca, on the coast of Texas, and the colonists scattered. Some came on west to the colonies, while others obtained work along the coast country. The mosquitoes were very numerous, and the travel-worn people presented a forlorn aspect as they stood grouped around the fires in the smoke, with blankets around them, when they were first put ashore.

Mr. Weynand obtained work from the government at $1 per day. Being a young man and without family, he did very well. On the first morning he presented himself for work after being employed the man in charge asked him if he had eaten breakfast. Not understanding the language well, at a venture he said no. He was then directed to the eating quarters, and was told to tell the cook to give him breakfast. Thinking this was something he had to bring to his employer, he delivered the message in the best English he could command. He was greatly surprised when he was told to sit down and eat. Not wishing to cause any more confusion he did so, although it had not been many minutes since he had eaten a hearty meal.

When his time was out he hired a man to bring his effects to Castroville, then recently settled by colonists, twenty-five miles west from San Antonio. The price charged for his freight by ox team was $3 per hundred pounds. He worked here all winter for a Frenchman, and in the following spring attempted to make a crop, but failed, and was finally taken down sick. The people gave him medicine made from some kind of leaves, and he recovered in fourteen days. Mr. Weynand now went below San Antonio and hired to a man named Thomas to cut hay. This work lasted forty-one days.

On the 3d day of March, 1847, Mr. Weynand and a man named Rutinger arrived at D'Hanis, another colony still west of Castroville, on Seco Creek. They worked one month clearing off town lots, and then entered into a contract with a man to make a crop on shares. They had no plows or team, and had to plant corn with a hoe. The man Rutinger was still living in 1898, and was the oldest man in Medina County, being 92 years of age. On one occasion seventy-three Comanche Indians rode into town. They did not attempt to molest anyone, but took Mr. Rutinger's horse and anything else they took a fancy to. At this time the colonists only had meat and water to subsist upon. One of the Indians came and sat down beside Mr. Weynand, and said he was a Mexican, on account of the big wide hat he wore. The Comanches were then at war with the Mexicans.

Not being successful in making any money farming, these two primitive tillers of the soil went back to Castroville to get work. Rutinger finally went to San Antonio and worked for a man named Reese.

By this time the war was going on between the United States and Mexico, and Mr. Weynand enlisted in the American army at San Antonio. His command was the Twelfth infantry, Company E, Captain Welsh. The lieutenant was named White, and Mr. Weynand says he was a splendid man. The regiment was commanded by Colonel Bonham. The lieutenant-colonel was named Seymore.

On June 2, 1847, the command started to New Orleans, and from that place embarked for Vera Cruz. At the latter place the regiment was kept for quite a while, and the men drilled and practiced firing. Here also many of the men were taken sick, and only forty out of eighty of Welsh's men were fit for duty. General Scott was moving towards the City of Mexico, and 200 of the troops at Vera Cruz were ordered to follow in his rear as a rear guard. Mr. Weynand was with this guard, and says they suffered a great deal on the route. Besides having to fight almost daily with scattered bands of Mexican troops, rations were short, and the men had to subsist on crackers and berries. They finally turned and went back to Vera Cruz. Here they were met by 4000 American troops under General Lane, a very young man, Mr. Weynand said. These troops had 300 wagons and plenty of provisions, and all set out together after General Scott. At Jalapa they met Colonel Lawley and his men. Just before getting to the town, and not far from the national bridge, while in camp one night firing was heard in the direction of the bridge, and next morning when the command moved on a dead cavalryman was found on the bridge. He had been sent back by Colonel Lawley to see what delayed the troops in the rear, and was killed by some Mexicans who were ambushing the bridge to cut off small detachments of American troops. The clothing had been stripped from the body of the dead trooper. The troops moved on and came to the pass of Cerro Gordo, where General Scott had just fought a battle and lost many of his men. Many signs of the desperate struggle were seen. The entire command now went on to Perote, and from there to Puebla. All of the beeves had now been killed and consumed, and short rations prevailed again.

A German who could speak but very little English told General Lane that a Mexican army was close at hand. Firing was soon heard, and General Lane ordered the troops to move round a hill in the direction from whence it came. They did so, and came upon the town of Humantla. The advance guard was fighting, and the balance of the troops joined in and the battle soon became general. The troops went from house to house, breaking them open and routing the Mexicans on all sides, who soon abandoned the town and commenced a retreat. The dragoons pursued them, led by Lieut.-Col. Samuel H. Walker, the famous Texan. In this running fight out of town Colonel Walker was killed, and Mr. Weynand saw his body on a horse as it was being brought back to town by his men.

After the battle many of the soldiers went into the saloons and became so badly intoxicated and scattered about town that some were left when the army moved. The Mexicans captured these and kept them four months. On the march Mr. Weynand was in the rear guard behind the train. One day firing was heard ahead, and they soon came upon the wagon-master and one teamster badly wounded with buckshot, and a doctor attending to them. They were shot from ambush, but both recovered.

At Puebla quite a battle was fought, eighteen men being killed out of one company in a close fight on the plaza. Here part of the troops to which Mr. Weynand belonged stayed nine weeks, and were constantly harassed by the Mexicans. It was necessary to fire upon them every day with cannon to keep them at a distance. The main part of the army had joined General Scott. When the troops left here the man who shot the wagon-master and teamster was caught and swung to a limb. There were 2000 men on this march, and they made thirty miles in one day, which is far above the average for infantry. The roads were very good. One one occasion the Mexicans fired on the troops with cannon from a ridge. The cavalry charged up the ridge, and soon carbine firing was heard. Infantry was ordered to their support, but when they arrived the fight was over and threee dead Mexicans were on the ground. The cavalry went in advance of the train, and one day after a creek was crossed sharp firing was heard, and when the train and rear infantry came upon the scene forty dead Mexicans lay on a very small space of ground, where the cavalry had killed them.

When the command arrived at a small town in a valley at night about 9 o'clock they stopped on a hill and planted cannon, and the infantry lay down. Soon, however, the artillerymen commenced firing on the town, and before daylight an advance was ordered and the place captured. Some of the soldiers at once proceeded to rob it, and one of them went into a church and got a suit of clothing which belonged to the priest. It was very fine, trimmed with gold lace, etc. The captain of the company to which the soldier belonged dispossessed him of the fancy suit, and then placed him in jail.

Before the American army got into the City of Mexico they had to descend a very steep place with lakes on both sides, and the men had to keep the road in single file, which made a very extended line. Here the Mexicans had planted a cross, and said they would fight until all were killed; but they failed to do so on the approach of the United States troops. The city was taken by storm, and the army stayed four months. They were drilled every day on a prairie by General Smith. Mr. Weynand was under his command when the army left Mexico.

The writer will state here that in his interview with Mr. Weynand notes were taken, and the many stirring scenes he passed through during the compaign in Mexico are given as he now, at this late day, remembers them. At that time he could not understand much English, and fails to remember the given names of his officers, and also the names of many towns through which they passed.

When the war was over the troops came back 300 miles, and then broke up into detachments to take shipping for the United States. Mr. Weynand came on with 500 troops to New Orleans. They made the trip from Vera Cruz in nineteen days. Five men died on the way, and some in New Orleans. They were paid off here and discharged. Weynand and eleven other men hired a ship for $100 and came to Galveston. From here he and a companion came up to Houston in a boat, where they bought a wagon and yoke of oxen and set out for New Braunfels, in Comal County. The wagon had no bed on it, but his partner made a rough one that would answer their purpose. They were one month making the trip. They only rested here two days and then came on to San Antonio, arriving there the last day of August, 1848.

Mr. Weynand had a town lot and twenty acres of land at D'Hanis, and now told his companion, whose name was Charles Frederick, that he would go out to his land to make a crop, and for him to stay in San Antonio and work and send supplies out to him. He again failed to make anything farming, and had to go back to San Antonio to get work. His companion obtained a job working on the Alamo, but unfortunately fell from the walls one day and was killed.

Mr. Weynand now got a bounty of $100 in lieu of 160 acres of land which was due him, and with this cash he again tried farming, and again failed. In 1849 he went back to D'Hanis. In 1850 he once more tried his hand as a tiller of the soil, and this time made a good crop and times began to get better. The Indians were not so bad, as the Texas rangers had come, and were stationed near the town on Seco Creek, at a point now the home of Mr. Louis Rothe.

After the rangers left United States troops came and built Fort Lincoln, just below the old camp of the rangers.

Mr. Weynand now bought land and built a house upon it on the east bank of the Seco, just opposite Fort Lincoln. The troops at the fort were under the command of Major Longstreet, afterwards the famous Confederate general. Second in command was Lieutenant Dodge, for whom Dodge City, Kansas, was named. By this time Mr. Weynand had a family. In 1866 his son Herbert, George Miller, and August Rothe went out on a cow hunt and camped in Hondo Canyon, twenty miles from home, and stayed there several days. One morning ten Indians came upon them, killed George Miller, and took young Weynand captive. He was but 12 years of age. Rothe alone made his escape and told the news. Mr. Weynand made many trips in search of his boy, but of no avail; he never saw him again. He heard once there was a captive white boy among some Indians in Mexico at San Fernando, and at once set out for that place, paying large sums of money for guides. His horse became sick in Mexico so that he could not travel, and he had to delay several days, and as soon as the horse recovered a Mexican stole him and he had to buy another. Mr. Weynand could not find his son. The captive boy was not his, and he gave up the search. Before starting back home Mr. Weynand discovered that corn was cheap there, and bought ninety bushels for $33\frac{1}{3}$ cents, and hired some Mexicans who were coming to San Antonio with wagons to transport it for him. For this he paid them $15, and sold the corn at home for $2 per bushel.

Mr. Weynand has been very unfortunate with his children. He had a large family, eleven boys and six girls. One of his boys died, another was stolen by Indians, one was accidentally killed by a friend when he was 19 years old, one of the same age was killed by a horse falling on him, another died a natural death, one had his arm shot off, and a daughter caught fire and burned to death.

Mrs. Weynand, who before marriage was Miss Angelina Ney, is a daughter of John Ney, whose father was a nephew of Napoleon's great field marshal, and fought under him at Waterloo. She was born in Prussia, six miles from the French line, at Dillingen, and came to San Antonio in 1846 as part of Castro's colony. When the remains of Col. Sam Walker were brought from Mexico for burial at San Antonio Miss Angelina was living there with the family of Mr. Geo. Paschal, father of Congressman Thomas Paschal, and helped to make the wreaths that were placed on the coffin of the hero of Humantla. Thomas J. Paschal at that time was two years of age.

JOHN W. PATTERSON.

Born in Texas in 1849,

On the Patterson irrigating ditch, near Rio Frio postoffice, in Frio Canyon, Bandera County, lives Mr. John W. Patterson, one of the early settlers of southwest Texas. He was born in Smith County, Texas, in 1849, and came west with his father, Mr. Newman Patterson, when quite young, and first settled on the Sabinal River, six miles below the present Sabinal station on the Sunset road. While Mr. Patterson has had quite an interesting experience on the frontier, the most important was the part he took in helping to rescue a little white girl who was a captive among the Indians. At the time of this Indian raid in which the little girl was captured Mr. Patterson was living in Frio Canyon, not far from the spot where he now resides. The Indians on this occasion, which was about 1876, had been down the Guadalupe River on a big raid, and when ten miles below Kerrville came upon Mr. W. R. Terry, who with his family had just settled on Verde Creek, not far from its confluence with the Guadalupe. The Indians came upon them suddenly and unexpectedly, and Mr. Terry was killed without any chance to defend himself. He was a short distance from their camp, making shingles to cover his house. Two of the children were also killed, and Mrs. Terry fled from the place and made her escape. She was repeatedly fired at, and both bullets and arrows cut her clothing. She avoided the savages by leaping down a bluff. One little girl 8 years of age was carried off by the savages. The Indians, after scalping and mutilating the body of Mr. Terry, continued their murderous journey and succeeded in capturing a negro boy further down the country, and then turned a southwest course towards the Frio and Sabinal canyons. The next place they were seen was on Little Blanco, between Sabinal and Frio canyons. Here they came upon Mr. Chris Kelley and came near getting him. He succeeded in escaping them by leaving his horse, which they captured. The next place they struck and made themselves known was at the mouth of Cherry Creek, where it empties into the Frio. Here they came upon the cow camp of Ed Meyers,

John Avant, and William Pruitt. The men were away on a cow hunt, and the Indians robbed the camp and took off all the horses that were there. They then turned and traveled northwest, crossing the Frio River about where Mr. Joseph Van Pelt now lives. The cowmen on their return to the pillaged camp took up the trail of the Indians and were joined on the route by other settlers, two of whom were Mr. Joe Van Pelt and a man named Martin. The Upper Frio men who lived on the Patterson ditch did not at this time get the news of the raid, but received it later in the day and began collecting to join in the pursuit. Before they got ready to start, the negro boy, who had made his escape from the Indians, came to where the Frio men were assembling. He said the Indians had traveled up Elm Creek, and then, ascending a high mountain overlooking the Frio valley, saw houses in the distance and stopped to look at them, neglecting to keep an eye on the negro boy, who was riding a pony up the mountain in their rear. Seeing their attention attracted to the white settlement, the sable captive slid off his horse and made his escape through the rocks and thick brush. He then told of the captive white girl, and said she was taken from the Guadalupe valley. He was going to mill, he said, when the Indians came upon him. The negro had many stripes on his person where his inhuman captors had whipped him; he was also nearly starved. This tale of the negro, and the little white girl still being a captive among the Comanches, lent new impetus to the movements of the men, and they mounted their horses with alacrity and set off, determined to rescue her or perish in the attempt. Night set in dark and foggy before the trail was reached, and the settlers had to camp to await the light of day to prosecute the pursuit. Next morning they found the trail on the divide at the head of Buffalo Creek, between Main and Dry Frio. The trail led one mile west and then turned north. The settlers could now see to their left into Dry Frio Canyon, and to their surprise and great joy discovered the Indians over there and traveling from them down Mare Creek towards the river. The men now quit the trail, and going down the mountain as best they could, took it up again where they saw the Indians, who by this time were out of sight again. One reason why they came so soon upon the Indians was the fact that the latter had traveled all night in the fog and had lost their bearings, and went round in a circle, which brought them back by daylight to within a mile of where they had passed out the evening before. This fortunate circumstance saved the settlers a long and tedious route of trailing, following the devious windings of the lost Indians in the fog the previous night. If the Indians could have kept a straight course that night it would have been a long chase, and they might have succeeded in escaping the pursuing party.

Five miles from where the trail was taken up in the valley of the Dry Frio they came upon the stolen horses which the Indians had dropped, seeing now that they had to make up for lost time. Half a mile further they came to a cedar brake, and also upon the Indians, who had stopped in the river and were letting their horses drink. The white men present now were only five in number, to wit: William Pruitt, John Avant, Lysander Avant, Jack Grigsby, and John Patterson. The other settlers from below had not joined this party, and were following the winding trail. At sight of the Indians the men all raised their guns at once and fired hurriedly, without taking a good aim. Not an Indian fell from his horse, but all dashed furiously out of the water to the opposite bank and disappeared amid the rocks and cedar. It was evident from the actions of some that they were badly hit. One reason, no doubt, of this bad firing was the fact that the little white captive was riding behind one of the Indians, and some fired high for fear of hitting her. The men dashed across the shallow mountain river after the Indians, and a wild and desperate chase commenced through the brush and over the rocks. The horse being ridden by the Indian and the little girl showed signs of weakening as the white men came in sight again and crowded close upon them, firing rapidly with their Winchesters. The Indian jumped off and mounted behind a comrade, and the little girl soon fell from her position to the ground. John Patterson was the first man to reach her. She was standing on her feet holding the horse by a rope in one hand, and in the other tightly clasping a small piece of blanket upon which she had been riding. She was badly scared when the men dashed up to her. The yelling, firing, desperate ride through the brakes, and the whistling bullets had completely unnerved her, and she stood shaking like an aspen leaf. The kind words of the men, however, who told her not to be afraid, and to stay where she was until they caught the Indians, had a soothing effect, and she said she would not leave. The Indians were again overtaken as they were ascending a hill and a rapid fire was opened upon them, and the rear one, who was the chief, had his horse killed. The chief himself seemed to bear a charmed life. Ten shots were fired at him as he was making off on foot, but he kept steadily on, carrying a long lance in his hand. He had part of a wagon sheet, which had been taken from the cow camp, wrapped about his body, and this he finally threw off. John Avant, to make sure of close shots, dismounted from his horse, and resting his elbow on his knee, fired twice as the chief arrived at the crest of the ridge; but he kept on and went out of sight. The men now crossed a gorge and went on up the mountain, hoping at least to find the Indian at whom so many shots had been fired. The covering which had been discarded by the Indian, and which the white men picked up, was found to be very bloody and had nine bullet holes in it. The Indians outnumbered the whites about two to one, but made scarcely any resistance, and seemed bent only on flight.

In going up the hill John Patterson's girth broke, but he let the saddle slide off without dismounting and continued the chase bareback. As they could see nothing more of the Indians, after going some distance and having things badly scattered, they took the back track to where the little girl was left. Another party of trailers were met on mules and played-out horses, and one of them had the girl behind him. She was where the first party had left her, and the second party had discovered her by being on the trail of the Indians. Both parties now camped together to rest and eat something. The little girl was nearly starved and ate ravenously, never taking a piece of bread from her mouth after the first bite until it was all gone. The last band of trailers had also brought the horses along which the Indians had abandoned on Mare Creek.

After resting their horses John Patterson and some others went back to see if they could find the wounded chief. Not far from the spot where they last shot him they heard a groan, which was shortly repeated, but the rocks and brush were so thick that it was impossible to find the spot that it emanated from, and they were again compelled to abandon the search, as night was coming on. Next morning Patterson and John Avant went back again and found where the Indian had lain on some cedar limbs which had been broken off and a bed made of them. These limbs were very bloody, but the body could not be found. It is evident the Indian died here and that some of his party had returned and carried him away, and likely made the bed of cedar boughs for him.

During the absence of Avant and Patterson, the man who picked up the little girl wanted to leave the crowd and take her on to the settlement, but was prevented by William Pruitt, who said they would all go back together. The little girl said that during the windings of the Indians in the foggy night the horse of one of them fell off a bluff and broke the Indian's leg. They then divided their force, one party going off with the crippled Indian. The negro boy said there were fifteen of them when all together. The white men afterwards found the place where the accident happened, and said the fall was twenty feet.

After the return to the settlement a messenger was dispatched to the Guadalupe to find out about the little girl, and her mother came after her. The captive girl lived to be nearly grown, and then died. Her mother and Joel Terry, her brother, now live in this country.

After this raid the Indians came again into Frio Canyon and stole two horses belonging to a man named Sawyer, who was afterwards killed in Dry Frio Canyon, some say by the noted Bill Longley.

The Indians then went down on the Sabinal below the mountains and killed a Mexican sheep herder. They then started back towards the mountains and came through Ross Kennedy's pasture and stole a horse from William Adams. Then they came on across to the Dry Frio. John Patterson and several others took the trail of the Indians and followed it over into Nueces Canyon. Here they came upon two men named Goodman and Wells, who had been chased and shot at by the Indians. They now joined the party in pursuit. Wells was a great bear hunter. The trail led up the Nueces and was very rough,—no roads or settlements in those days. Some of the men had to return on account of their horses giving out. Patterson and seven others were loath to give up the pursuit, and went on. Their provisions, however, soon played out, and left them in a bad fix. They were many miles from any settlement, and entirely unacquainted with the country. They knew that by going in a certain direction they would strike the Fort Clark road, and by taking either end get to some place where provisions could be procured. They could kill game and eat it without bread and keep from suffering, so there was no uneasiness on that score, and they continued the Indian hunt. Before coming to the Fort Clark road they came upon an Indian campfire which had been but a short time before abandoned. Five miles further on, in the draws of Devil's River, they came upon the Indians in camp in a large liveoak mott about 500 yards in extent and very brushy. The horses of the Indians were grazing in the edge of the thicket, and John Patterson called the attention of the men to something in a tree and smoke in the thicket. The men now circled around the mott to the left and saw an Indian coming, and Patterson at once shot at him. The Indian returned the fire and then ran into the thicket. The settlers kept on around, and soon saw two more Indians on foot running a horse with a pair of hobbles on his neck, which they were trying to catch hold of to stop him. They could run as fast as the pony, and likely would have caught him, but at this time were fired on and ran back to cover. The Indians, it seemed, wanted to get off as light as possible with the whites, and so after a time drove all the stolen horses out of the thicket and gave them a start towards the white men, as much as to say, "Take your horses, now, and leave."

The pioneers were not satisfied with this, and still guarded the covert by placing men on regular watch. John Avant went round on the south side of the thicket and set fire to the grass, trying to burn them out, but they would not come. One of the white men saw two persons coming up the creek and called Patterson's attention to them, who at once pronounced them Indians, and set about to cut them off from the thicket. They were Indian hunters, and had a pack horse loaded with buffalo meat. Some of the men followed Patterson, but the Indians, discovering them, dropped their pack horse and ran. Patterson pursued and got close enough to shoot, and was reaching to pull his Winchester out of the scabbard, when his horse stepped in a hole and fell. Patterson was thrown violently to the ground and his horse ran off. The Indians escaped, but the whites got the buffalo meat, which came to them very opportunely on account of their want of provisions.

The settlers now held a council to determine what to do. Half of the men wanted to go into the thicket and fight the Indians in there, but the balance objected. It was then agreed that those who did not want to go in were to hold the horses of the others, who would make an advance on the Indian encampment. The men went in shooting and making all the noise they could, and the Indians ran away in great alarm, so when the camp was reached it was deserted. The booty was considerable, and the men had to make several trips to bring it all out. It consisted of eighteen blankets, one buffalo robe, one saddle, four shields, two head-dresses, one microscope, and a pass from the Indian agent at Fort Sill for these Indians to go on a buffalo hunt. The pass was old, and here these fellows were down in South Texas, out of the buffalo range proper, killing people and stealing horses. The things were divided among the men, and the shield, which John Patetrson got, had a woman's scalp attached to it. They also got thirty-five head of horses and two mules.

Some of the stock belonged to the Allen brothers and some to Brown and Sawyer. They also found in the camp 500 smooth sticks for making arrows. These the men broke. There were nine Indians in this party, and the number of white men who routed them was eight. Their names are as follows: John Patterson, John Avant, Dick Humphreys, Lon Sawyer, L. L. Green, Dave Wells, Goodman, and A. Blackburn. The four first named are the ones who went into the thicket and captured the camp. Sawyer and Patterson got the head-dresses. They were gorgeous affairs, having a row of feathers reaching to the ground, somewhat like a Sioux war bonnet.

These men deserve a great deal of credit for this trip, and their perseverance and courage to penetrate a wild country, infested with savages, with so small a number, and then invest and rout the savages from their stronghold in the manner in which they did, and bring off the booty and recaptured stock.

They were gone fifteen days and were nine days without bread—three days on buffalo meat alone. A true frontiersman knows how to take care of himself and not starve when out.

JOHN REINHART.

Came to Texas in 1849.

Mr. John Reinhart, who has a fine ranch on Big Seco, in Medina County, is one of the pioneers of western Texas. He was born in Bavaria, town of Orb, in 1832. Came to New Orleans in 1848, and to New Braunfels, Comal County, Texas, in 1849. Moved from there to Cibolo River, and thence to the Seco Creek, near D'Hanis, in 1854. In those days the young German immigrants who had no families did not remain in the colonies long at a time, but sought work anywhere they could find it. Some worked for the government when Fort Lincoln was established on the Seco, and others drove teams or cattle, and in fact did whatever their hands could find to do.

About the time that Mr. Reinhart came to Seco, Mr. John Dunlap was in the country buying up a drove of cattle under a government contract, to be delivered at Fort Lancaster, which was situated at the mouth of Liveoak Creek, where it empties into the Pecos River. Mr. Dunlap lived at Fort Clark. As soon as the cattle were collected a start was made for the fort. Mr. Reinhart had been employed by Dunlap to help deliver the cattle at their destination. Situated as Fort Lancaster was then, far out on the extreme frontier, with no settlements between, and infested with hostile Indians, such an undertaking was extremely hazardous, but there are always found men who will brave any danger and start anywhere. There were but three men in the party to make this long, dangerous trip—Reinhart, Dunlap, and Capt. Joseph Richarz.

Nothing occurred to make the trip of more than normal interest until they reached Howard's Wells, out on the plains. Here, just before going down into the valley with the cattle, they discovered a man on a mountain, and at once began to proceed with great caution, fearing it was an Indian, and that they would lose the cattle. The man in question, however, was a white man, watching the road back towards the east for help. His party had camped the night before at the wells, and that present morning had been attacked by a large body of Indians, and all of their horses and mules taken off. There were nine white men and five wagons of this party. Their horses were out grazing with one man to watch them, when the Indians made a dash from cover to capture the horses. The Indians played a very smart trick to get the white men also, and came near being successful. Dividing their force, while still concealed from view behind the hills, one party charged upon the lone guard at the horses, and, as was expected by the savages, the men at the wagons seized their guns and rushed out into the prairie to save the horses and succor the guard. The other band of Indians now dashed across the open ground on their ponies to cut them off from the protection of the wagons. The white men saw this in time, however, and retreated back to their position. The guard, who was very well mounted, made a wide circle in the prairie, ran around the Indians, and joined his companions. The Indians secured the stock and drove them off, passing within long rifle range of the chagrined owners, who gave them one volley as a parting salute. One of these shots took effect on a horse ridden by one of the Indians, killing the animal in its tracks and throwing the Apache to the ground. He mounted behind another, however, and they all rode away. As the three cattlemen could do nothing for them, having no extra teams, they went on and reported the matter at Fort Lancaster, and the commander of that post sent out teams belonging to the government and brought the wagons in.

After delivering his cattle, Dunlap and his two men started back together, and when they arrived at the crossing of Devil's River met a drove of 150 head of horses. They thought at the time that only three Indians were with them. It seemed an easy job to rout these, and capture the horses, although they were only armed with pistols. They acted upon this impulse and charged, but what was their surprise when seven more Indians appeared on the other side of the horses. They had been concealed, and now dismounted and remounted on fresh horses to give the trio of white men a battle and chase. The horses ridden by the cattlemen were jaded, and the situation began to look serious. They at once reversed the matter, turning their charge into a retreat. The Indians, however, did not follow them, and the white men soon checked up. Dunlap now said: "Boys, I believe the guns of those Indians were wet (it had been raining), and that was the reason they did not fire or charge us, and we can go back and clean them up yet. That would be a good item for a newspaper, that three men whipped ten Indians and took 150 head of horses away from them." So it was agreed, and they turned back to have a fight. The Indians saw them coming back, and all left the horses and came yelling and charging upon them. Once more they beat a retreat, and continued their flight until they were safely ensconced in a big thicket where they could defend themselves, willing to let the Indians and horses go. The Apaches did not pursue far, but soon went back to their horses, and the white men continued their way home, where they arrived without further adventures.

So that the reader who has no experience in such things can more readily comprehend the dangers, seen and unseen, which beset the path of the pioneer, I will relate two incidents of this character.

In the spring of 1859 Mr. Reinhart went from his home on the Seco to the Comanche waterhole, several miles south from him, to look after stock and to kill a deer if chance offered. On the way he rode by a large thicket, and on looking back at it saw something move that looked like a deer, and at once raised his rifle so as to be ready to shoot if it came into plain view. It was an Indian, however, and thinking from the action of the white man that he was discovered, he dodged back from view. Mr. Reinhart was riding a horse which he did not often mount, and he was very sensitive to the spur. The settler knew that he saw one Indian, and not knowing how many more there were, put spurs to his horse in order to make a quick run to a mott of liveoak trees, where he could dismount and better stand them off. Besides his rifle he had a good revolver. This tender horse he rode now commenced to pitch instead of running when he felt the spur. This would have been the time for the Indians to have made their break for him, for it was all Mr. Reinhart could do to sit his horse, and he could not have used gun or pistol. He finally reached the timber and looked back. Quite a lot of Indians were in view on the edge of the thicket. The reason they did not pursue the settler was that they were all on foot, having just come in on a raid, and had not picked up any horses yet. As they did not follow, Mr. Reinhart rode off slowly from the trees and made a circle back home.

On the way back Reinhart met Jack Wolf, and advised him to

go home with him and spend the night. This Jack agreed to do, and next morning he and Reinhart went up to his brother's, Sebastian Wolf, on Huffman's ranch, which was on the Seco, a short distance above the present ranch of Mr. Reinhart. The three now went back to the thicket where Reinhart saw the Indians to see what discoveries they could make. The signs there showed the Indians to be about ten in number, and that they had been secreted while making arrows, and had killed a turkey, the feathers of which were profusely scattered around. The Indians from this place went down the Seco and stole many horses, among which was a very fine one belonging to Billy Doan. Being well mounted now, the Indians made themselves heard from in various places. The three white men went on down to D'Hanis and told the news of the raid. Huffman and his partner, Sebastian Wolf, went west and crossed the Sabinal River not far from the present station of the same name. They then made a circle west in the prairie. Here this same band of Indians came upon them and a desperate running fight took palce, in which the two ranchmen were killed.

It is supposed that the chief rode Billy Doan's horse and was killed off him in the fight by Wolf, as his throat was cut from ear to ear after he had been killed by arrows. The Indians were followed by citizens and defeated in their camp on Blanco Creek, and all the horses retaken.

When John Bowles killed three Indians on the Sabinal, Mr. Reinhart went over to the Bowles ranch and saw the three Indian scalps hanging on a clothesline in the yard.

On another occasion Mr. Reinhart went deer hunting to a noted place called the "cowlick," and while there saw something move which he thought might be a deer. On riding nearer to investigate, a dove flew up, and thinking this was the object which he had observed, rode on in another direction. At the cowlick, among other cattle he noticed one of his work oxen, called Tom, licking at the bank. It began to rain soon, and Mr. Reinhart went back home by way of the lick, and his steer was still there. When he arrived at home himself and gun were wet, and after putting on dry clothes he fired off the gun in order to dry and cleanse it. A man by the name of Webster was stopping at the Reinhart ranch, and came out to where he was working on his gun and told him the cattle had just run home and old Tom was shot with an arrow, which was still sticking in him. "Impossible!" said Mr. Reinhart; "I left him a few minutes ago at the lick, and nothing was the matter with him then." "Come and see," said Mr. Webster. It was even so; the cattle were at the cow lot badly frightened, and old Tom was running around trying to get rid of the arrow. He had to be driven into the pen and roped and tied before the feathered shaft could be extracted. It had penetrated one foot into the paunch. The question was, why did not the Indian shoot Reinhart? He evidently rode near him several times, and no doubt it was a glimpse of him he saw when he thought he saw a deer and the dove flew up, etc. The only solution that offers is that there was only one Indian, and he was afraid of the white man's gun and pistol in case he should fail to bring him down with his arrow.

Mr. Webster afterwards sold goods in Uvalde and was one night killed and robbed in his store.

In 1861 Mr. Reinhart joined a ranging company commanded by Capt. Chas. de Montel. Their station was at Ranger Springs, twelve miles above the present home of Mr. Reinhart, in the Seco Valley. On one occasion the Indians made a raid below the mountains, and runners were sent to D'Hanis to get men to follow them. Mr. Reinhart was in D'Hanis at the time, having been sent from the ranger camp to bring the mail for the company. However, he joined the expedition that was making up to follow the Indians. The trail led back to the northwest or west, in the direction of Sabinal Canyon. They went to the ranch of Ross Kennedy, and from there into the canyon, and took up the salt marsh. Near the head of this place the settlers camped on the trail about where Mr. Calvin Mitchell's ranch is now. Next morning they ascended to the top of the mountains, over which the trail led, and taking a look back into the valley saw a small squad of the rangers following them. They had been notified of the raid and in which direction the Indians were going out. The settlers waited until the rangers came up, and all went on together. The rangers were under the command of Lieut. Ben Patton, and among his men were Jack Davenport, John Kennedy, Pete Bowles, Lon Moore, and several others. The Indian trail led northwest through a very rough range of mountains. At length the trailers came to a cedar brake on the south side of the mountain, and Pete Bowles, one of the rangers, went slowly ahead until he could see into a valley beyond. He then pulled his horse back quickly and said, "There they are." The Indians had camped in the valley on the high ground, between a small creek with steep banks and a deep hollow. In their rear was a cedar brake. The white men now dismounted, and leaving two men with the horses, went round the mountains concealed from the view of the Indians, and then came up the creek through the brush, still hid from view. The Indians were close to a big spring, and there was about an acre of open ground around their camp. When the rangers and settlers came up under the bluff they were very close to the Indians, but could not see them, but could see their horses. The force was now divided and a party went round each way. Some of the men crept up the bank and peeped over, and could see the blankets of the Indians on the bushes. Another cautious step forward and the Indians themselves could be seen. Reinhart now motioned to the men who had not climbed up, and indicated with his finger the exact location of the Indians, and also signaled a charge. Both parties now leaped up the bank in plain view, and not over fifty yards from the astonished savages, and commenced a terrific fire from rifles, shotguns, and pistols. The Indians made but little attempt to fight, and at once scattered into the cedar brake, followed by a shower of bullets which cut the bushes on all sides. After the fusilade was over three dead Indians were on the ground, and one was trailed some distance by the blood, but could not be found. The reason no more Indians were killed was the fact that they had only a few jumps to make to get to cover. The Indians had cooked a quantity of meat, and were fixing to leave. They had their bows and quivers on their backs, and one of them was shoeing a horse with rawhide. This one looked over the horse's neck when the charge was made, and a ranger fired at his head, but hit too low and killed the horse. One man who did not live in this country, but who joined the scout and was in the fight, cut off the ears of the dead Indians and strung them on a string to carry back east with him.

The rangers and settlers now went back to their horses and took the back track for home and the ranger camp.

On one occasion Mr. Reinhart and others followed a band of Indians who had a lot of horses which they had stolen out of the settlement. After a long and hard chase they succeeded in retaking the horses without a fight, as the Indians left them and ran, and they returned with them to D'Hanis. The men were tired and worn out, and put the stock in the horse lot of John Ney, and proceeded to have a good night's rest. The Indians had followed the white men back, and that night got the horses again and carried them off, to the great surprise of the men when they woke up in the morning and realized the situation. They followed them again, but this time the Bandera men had taken up the trail when it passed through their country, and had overtaken the Indians and recaptured the horses. The D'Hanis men carried the stock back again, but this time kept better watch upon them.

CAPTAIN H. J. RICHARZ.

Came to Texas in 1849.

Among the pioneers of West Texas who deserve a place in Texas history is Capt. H. J. Richarz, one of the gallant men who led the famous Texas rangers against the savages on the frontier, and stood between these painted demons and the hearthstones of the pioneers. Captain Richarz was born in 1822 on his father's estate, near Cologne, on the Rhine, being at this writing (December, 1898) 76 years of age. His father was second burgomaster and head of the municipality of the town of Ella, having now a population of 4000 souls; also for a number of years head administrator of Castle House, Ella, the residence of the late Princess Louise of Prussia; and up to his death in 1886, at the age of 92 years, honorary president of the War Veterans' Volunteer Rifles of 1813 and 1815. He was also knight of the Order of the Crown of Prussia, an order for meritorious service from the king of Prussia and the duke of Saxe-Coburg.

Captain Richarz was the eldest son and received a liberal education, first in the town school, and until the age of 16 years at a private academy in the city of Dusseldorf.

At the age of 16 years Captain Richarz joined the same volunteer rifle legion in which his father served through the wars of the allies against Napoleon, and after serving his time out and being three times promoted, quit and took a confidential position as "commissar" of the chief engineer of the Prince Wilhelm Railroad, in the Prussian district of Berg and Mark.

In 1848 he took an active part in the revolution against the absolution and feudal system, having been elected and commissioned as captain of a camp of militia and twice as elector for the representative of the Frankfurt parliament and house of representants in Berlin. He also took an active part in the bloody struggles that followed, and in the meantime married. The merciless, reactionary monarchical side being victorious, Captain Richarz chose to go into voluntary exile, rather than to be fusiladed or imprisoned for years in a military fortress. He evaded the civil and military officers, had his property sold to a younger brother, and arrived safely in Rotterdam. He embarked at Havre, France, and arrived in New Orleans in the fall of 1849. The voyage across the ocean was disastrous, especially along the coast of Africa, and they were finally shipwrecked near St. Thomas, in the West Indies, and had to say there two months before they could again get shipping. From New Orleans Captain Richarz and his wife and two children went to Indianola, on the coast of Texas, and from there made their way to the San Antonio River and bought 500 acres of land opposite the mission of Espade, nine miles below the city of San Antonio. He brought with him some Saxon merino rams, which he was lucky enough to save, and commenced sheep-raising. He was the first man to import this kind of stock to Texas. In the sheep business he had a partner named John H. Herndon, of Velasco.

In 1853 he moved with sheep and cattle to Fort Lincoln, in Medina County, fifty miles west of San Antonio. The fort was situated on the Seco Creek, about two miles from the old town of D'Hanis. Captain Richarz here occupied for two years the quarters of the last commander of that station, Major Longstreet, afterwards the famous Confederate general. He purchased 500 acres of land near here, and established the first postoffice west of Castroville at the D'Hanis settlement, and acted up to the civil war as postmaster. He served one year as justice of the peace during the war, and after that as chief justice of Medina County. Up to the time of the war, Captain Richarz was the leader of the citizen scouts for protection from the bloody inroads of the savages.

In 1861 the brother-in-law of Captain Richarz was killed and scalped by the Indians.

In 1861 he was commissioned by the Governor as major cammanding the independent battalion of mounted home guards of Medina County. Part of this force was always placed in camp along the extreme frontier line, and kept scouts constantly out trailing and fighting the Indians wherever they could come upon them.

Captain Richarz succeeded in those times in checking to some extent the inroads of the savages and taking a good deal of spoils from them. This state of irregular warfare between the Indians and the volunteer organizations lasted until 1870. The country was really without aid from the government. The sparsely scattered garrisons of regular troops along the Rio Grande, mostly negro cavalry, were not adequate to the occasion. Captain Richarz says the Indians would drive off horses in sight of their camps.

In 1870 the State of Texas, under permit and authority from the Federal government, organized a frontier force of rangers, and Captain Richarz was given a commission as captain of E company, to be stationed at Fort Inge, on the Leona River, four miles below the town of Uvalde, and also an order from General Reynolds, of the United States army, to take the efficient warriors of the Seminole tribe of Indians under his command. The tribe at that time was under the control of United States agents, and encamped on the Rio Grande. The captain protested against this measure, and argued that he was well informed by personal observation of the unreliability of these savages and their moral degradation, and apprehending corrupting influence of his men, this plan was abandoned.

Captain Richarz placed his men, carefully selected, in various camps, and only retained enough at his headquarters to make an efficient scout, and kept scouts going constantly along the Rio Grande and various parts of the imperiled frontier, and had regular communications from Laredo to the Llano River. After having some successful expeditions and fights, one of which was near the Rio Grande, Captain Richarz received command of two more companies of rangers. The last bloody battle which the rangers under Captain Richarz had with the Indians was fought with the Kiowas and Comanches, near Carrizo Springs. The scout was commanded by Sergeant Eckford and Dr. Woodbridge. There were fourteen rangers and three citizens in the fight. The Indians numbered seventy, and fought in two lines. Eight Indians were killed, including their chief, who was fantastically adorned, and had four scalps of white women. The wounded of the Indians could not be ascertained. A ranger named Belleger, from Castroville, was killed, and Dr. Woodbridge was knocked from his horse by an Indian and severely injured. So hot was the fire the rangers ran out of cartridges and could not follow up the Indians, and had to return.

The Indians at this time had invaded the frontier in three strong parties, and Captain Richarz was following another band when this battle was fought. About this time Walter Richarz, son of the captain, and Joe Riff, both rangers, were killed on the Blanco by Indians. When the bodies were found, the signs of battle showed with what desperate valor the young rangers had sold their lives.

This was about the last of Indian raids on this part of the frontier. After Captain Richarz left the frontier service he served as justice and attended to his stock and farm. Served one term as representative of the Fifty-second district in the Legislature. His hearing becoming defective, he was incapacitated from further public service, and he spends a quiet life on the west bank of the Seco, in a romantic spot near the foot of the hills, where he attends to his irrigated garden and orchard. He reads the finest print without glasses, and never misses a rabbit or turkey at the distance of eighty yards with a rifle. He has a kind and friendly disposition, and has many friends. His judgment of men and things is astute, and he has a blunt way of talking and expressing himself, but his judgment is seldom at fault. He is a devoted Texan, and liberal in his views.

GIDEON THOMPSON.

Came to Texas in 1852.

Among the first settlers who came to Sabinal Canyon, but few have had a more varied or interesting experience than Mr. Gideon Thompson, who still survives at this date (1899) to tell the tale of frontier days.

Mr. Thompson was born in Hawkins County, eastern Tennessee, on the 3d day of November, 1822. In 1842 we find him in the State of Arkansas, where the same year he married Miss Margarette O'Bryant. He came to Texas in 1852, and in the fall of the same year wended his way to Sabinal Canyon, the extreme limit at that time of civilization in southwest Texas. Mr. Thompson made a short stop in San Antonio on his way out, and says at that time he could have fired the town with a torch as fast as his horse could run, on account of the houses being low and mostly covered with grass.

Mr. Thompson's family was the first white one that came west of the German settlement of old D'Hanis, in Medina County. Capt. William Ware was the first white man to settle in Sabinal Canyon, but he came without his family, and had to return to East Texas for them, and in the meantime Mr. Thompson and family came. About the same time came John Davenport, Lee Sanders, Henry Robinson, and James Davenport. Mr. Aaron Anglin, a young man, came with Mr. Thompson but soon returned to Arkansas, where he married, and came back in 1853. When Mr. Thompson first came to the canyon he had four children in his family, namely, William, Hiram, Robert, and Mary Ann. These were the first white children to cast their eyes over the lovely valley.

The first winter after arriving the five families all lived together at Capt. William Ware's place. He was an old Indian fighter, and said this would be best until they could find out what the Indians were going to do.

In the summer of 1853, as no hostile Indians had put in an appearance, Mr. Thompson moved to the place where he now resides and built a log cabin on the Anglin prong, as it is now called, of the Sabinal River, six miles above Captain Ware's place and five miles above the present town of Utopia. The first post-office in the canyon was at Captain Ware's, and was called Waresville. Mr. Charles Durbin put up a store and sold goods there until his death, which occurred in the early 80's.

Mr. Thompson built his house close to the creek, and says it does not look now like it did then. It at that time was a clear, bold, running stream, capable of running and operating machinery. The banks were steep and the water deep. There is no water at all there now. He thinks the cause of this is that when cattle were brought into the country they made trails down to the water, and the banks commenced washing and caving in, and filled up the channel gradually with soil and gravel. He says where Mr. Dan Harper's place is now, when he (Mr. Thompson) came here, there lay a large cedar tree top and roots, put there by high water. This place is below Mr. Thompson's, and between the Anglin prong and main river. Also on the George Murchison place, below Utopia, lodged against a noted liveoak tree having large, peculiar knots on it, were three large cypress trees, also put there by high water. If such overflows were to come now, many houses would most likely wash away. In the same year Mr. Thompson moved to his place the Tonkaway Indians came and camped at the mouth of the canyon, under the bluffs at the Blue waterhole. They were a friendly tribe, and assured the whites, when Mr. Thompson and others went to interview them, that they were only there for the purpose of hunting bear. They had also camped before this below the mountains on the river about where Mr. Bascom Lyell's place is now. Here they had planted corn and watermelons.

About the same time the Lipan Indians camped and pitched their tepees on the Frio River, near the "shut-in," where now are the farms of Joe Richards and Ed Meyers. The government moved these tribes the same year (before the watermelons of the Tonkaways got ripe) to the Palo Pinto Creek, seven miles from Fort Clark, and there established a reservation. Some of the Lipans soon after left the reserve, and going into the vicinity of San Antonio, killed some of the Foster family and carried one of the girls into captivity. Mrs. Foster made her escape and carried the news into San Antonio. This was the first Indian raid Mr. Thompson heard of after coming to the country. Maj.

Robert Neighbors, Indian agent at that time, was in San Antonio, and learning of the Lipan raid procured a company of soldiers and went in pursuit of them. He had a German sub-agent named Linsell, who stayed at the Palo Pinto reserve, and who had just arrived in San Antonio, accompanied by four Lipan chiefs. These chiefs were compelled by Neighbors to go with the expedition and help to trail their own countrymen. The hostile trail led to the head of the Guadalupe River, and when it was taken up was followed rapidly by the trailers. After several days' hard ride over a rough country, the command stopped at the head springs of the Guadalupe to rest their horses a short time, and while so doing the Lipans went a short distance from camp to take observations, and were charged and run back by a squad of white men from Sabinal Canyon. Among these men was Mr. Thompson. They were out on a scout and looking at the country. As soon as matters were explained to them by Major Neighbors, they left and went back towards home and the soldiers continued the pursuit. The trail led around the head of the Nueces River. They next made a dry camp, but had water enough next morning to make coffee, and while it was being boiled the agent sent the Lipan chiefs and two soldiers to make note of the general course of the trail, who were soon to return and report. The two soldiers shortly came back and reported that the chiefs had suddenly left them and galloped away rapidly towards the Palo Pinto. The troops followed on, but when the reserve was reached the Lipans, having been warned of the approach of the soldiers by the chiefs, had hastily gathered up their belongings and decamped into Mexico. One of the chiefs carried off a horse belonging to Major Neighbors, and wanted to take the horses and tent of Linsell, but were prevented by the Tonkaways, who were always friends of the white man. Strange to say, the old Lipan chief sent the horse of Maj. Neighbors back, but the tribe always remained hostile to the whites and made many raids from Mexico into Texas.

Mr. Thompson does not know what became of the captured girl.

In 1856 the Indians made their first raid into Sabinal Canyon. They came in from the south, and entered the valley from the lower side. They first came upon the ranch of John Fenley, where W. B. Wright now lives, and stole two head of stock horses, one mare belonging to the old man, or Uncle Johnnie as he was called, and one belonging to his son Demp. Early that morning Mr. Thompson discovered there was something wrong with his cattle by their actions, and on investigating found a trail of Indians not far from his house. This was the same band that had raided Mr. Fenley nine miles below. Mr. Aaron Anglin lived about 400 yards up the creek from Mr. Thompson's, and he was at once notified of the presence of the Indians. John Brown, of Tennessee, an old-time friend, with his family, was living with Mr. Anglin. They had just come to the country a short time before. These three at once set out in pursuit of the Indians, who had crossed the west prong of the Sabinal 250 yards below Mr. Thompson's house and kept around the foot of a mountain northeast of his place until they struck a spur of the mountain which extended west towards the river. On this spur was a thicket of shinoak bushes, about the center of which was a sink hole. Here in this depression they built a fire and spent the balance of the night. This was near the spot where G. P. Wheeler afterwards settled. After daylight the Indians came upon Mr. Thompson's work oxen and shot several arrows into them. Mr. Thompson heard his ox-bell rattling violently that morning soon after daylight, and was suspicious that all was not right. In trailing they came upon the spot where the Indians ran the oxen, which changed their course, and they went in a northeast direction. They ran the oxen around the mountain and left them near where Mr. Henry Taylor now lives. Prior to this raid of the Indians, Leek Kelly, Laban Kelley, and Jasper Wish had settled on the main prong of the river on the west bank, opposite to where Mr. Bob Thompson now lives. This was two or three miles northeast from Mr. Gideon Thompson's. These settlers, however, had moved back to Williamson County, and left no one at their place. Some of their effects had been left in the house, among which were two spinning wheels and one room full of corn in the ear. The trail of the Indians led to these deserted cabins, and here they left plenty of sign of their presence. They had fed their horses and left piles of corn in the yard, and broken the two old-time spinning wheels all to pieces. An old sow that had been left behind was killed, and many things broken to pieces besides the wheels. The three settlers took hasty observations of these things and continued on the trail, and coming to the spot where Mr. Nobe Green now lives, found in a thicket a bunch of cattle which had been chased by the Indians and arrows shot into some of them. A short distance further on Uncle Johnnie Fenley's mare was found badly used up, and had evidently been used in chasing the cattle. At this time the Indians were close by in camp, and would have been surprised but for an unfortunate circumstance. A dog had followed the white men, and at this critical moment jumped a rabbit. His yelps alarmed the Indians, who at once retreated with their horses into the mountains. In the camp was a large pile of cobs where the Indians had been shelling corn to carry along with them. Mr. Anglin now said he thought it of no use to go any further, as they could not catch them. Mr. Thompson said: "You two wait here while I look a little further." After going a short distance he discovered six Indians on foot coming towards him in a trot, on the opposite side of a deep gully, but out of rifle range. The other party was now signaled and told to "Come on; here are the Indians." The white men on getting together rode towards the Indians, who began to dance and to rub paint on their faces. They had their horses hid under a bluff, fifteen head in all, to the right of where they had displayed themselves, and three Indians left with them. This was just above where Mr. John Foster now lives. They had shown themselves on the opposite side of the deep gully to decoy the white men away from the horses. Mr. Brown had a long-range gun which was now handed over to Mr. Thompson, who said he could move them if the gun would hold up; but when he dismounted to make the attempt the Indians ran away up the mountain and hid themselves among the rocks and bushes. The white men now crossed the gully on foot and went to the base of the mountain. The Indians then commenced shooting arrows at them. They would rise up quickly and shoot, and then drop down again before a rifle could be aimed at them. These were the days of muzzle-loaders, and no ammunition was wasted by the pioneers without a chance of hitting something. The Indians discharged at least one hundred arrows, all black, but they had no spikes in them. The white men could easily dodge them at the distance they were shooting, and no one was hit. The arrows were finely made, sharpened to a fine point, and then hardened in the fire. A handful of them was picked up. Mr. Anglin finally got into some bushes where the Indians could not see him when he took aim, and awaited a good chance for a shot. One soon presented itself. First the head and then the shoulders of an Indian came up above the rock. A quick aim, and bang! The head went down instantly. The Indians now went further up the mountain, and were so hidden by rocks that they could not be hit by a rifle. Mr. Anglin could not tell if he hit his or not. Mr. Thompson now left the other two again and went on around the mountain to see what had become of the Indians, and saw them high up, but they soon disappeared from view. He kept on, however, and soon discovered an Indian sitting on a rock 150 yards above him. He took as good aim as he could under the circumstances, having to shoot almost straight up, and fired. The Indian never moved, but yelled and said something which was unintelligible to Mr. Thompson, but Mr. Anglin, who also heard him, said it sounded to him like the Indian said "Try again." The settler reloaded his gun and started up higher to try another shot, but the savage beat a hasty retreat. Three more Indians now came from where the horses had been secreted and joined the others. Mr. Thompson had passed the horses, and these three Indians tried to cut him off from his companions, but they warned him to look out. He had discovered them, however, and soon made his retreat back. He saw one of the Indians leading the roan mare which belonged to Demp Fenley. The white men now left and the Indians came back and got their horses, the former not knowing where they were. On the way back home they came upon the wounded oxen. One of them was shot behind the left shoulder, close to the work of the leg, with a spiked arrow, and was in very deep. The spike had become detached from the arrow and was still in the wound, but so deep it could not be extracted without cutting too much flesh. The spike remained in the ox two years, but the wound would not heal. About the expiration of this time the ox was loaned to Mr. Silas Webster to haul corn, but hurt his foot and became very lame. Mr. Thompson said now was a good time to cut the spike out, and it was accordingly done. It was four inches in length and shaped like a dirk, sharp and of good metal. A schoolteacher named Hutchinson put a handle on it and it made a good knife. The ox soon after died. Mr. Thompson went back to the place where he shot at the Indian on the rock, and saw that he had only struck four inches below him, and found the flattened ball where it fell.

Not long after this raid the Indians paid Sabinal Canyon another visit. This time they killed a big fat cow for Mr. Anglin, and were very bold about it. They slaughtered the animal in the night near the house, and in the cow lot. The meat was cut up, packed on an old gray horse, and carried away. Next morning Mr. Anglin raised the alarm and collected the following named men to pursue them: Gideon Thompson, Sebe Barrymore, William Barrymore, Henry Robinson and his son Frank, Silas Webster, Dud Richardson, and Henry Fuller. The last named was a negro man brought to the canyon by Capt. William Ware.

The trail of the Indians led west towards a range of high mountains two and a half miles distant. At the foot of these mountains the men dismounted, and leaving their horses in charge of William Barrymore and Henry Fuller, took the trail on foot up the mountain. It was a hot day and the mountain rough and steep. The men became greatly exhausted, and the trail was finally lost amid the rocks, tangled vines, and bushes. On arriving at the crest the trail could not be found after the most diligent search, and the hunt was about to be abandoned, when a great number of wild bees were discovered. Henry Robinson now proposed that the others sit down and rest while he descended into a gorge near by to hunt for a bee cave. While he was gone Mr. Thompson observed quite a number of buzzards sailing around over a cedar brake, coming close to the tops of the trees, but not alighting. When Robinson came back he called his attention to the peculiar action of the buzzards, and remarked that they were prevented from lighting by the presence of men or wild animals.

An investigation of the brake was now inaugurated, and a rude and freshly made brush fence discovered. Inside of this inclosure the Indians were encamped, and cooking the flesh of the slain cow of Mr. Anglin. They had built this brush screen on the night before, after they had carried the cow to the top of the mountain, so that the settlers in the valley could not see the fire while they barbecued the meat. Evidently they had packed the meat on the old gray horse, and were about to start when the white men came upon them. They became alarmed at some noise the settlers made as they came to the brush, and ran away. The brake was dense and the Indians could not be seen, although they heard them rattling the rocks as they ran. The trail of the old horse was easy to follow. His heavy tread left a great deal more sign than the light moccasined foot of the Indian. Besides this, he scattered chunks of meat as he went. After following some distance, however, and not being able to catch sight of an Indian or the pack horse, the white men halted and abandoned the pursuit, as they were all nearly exhausted by their exertions. While sitting to rest on a rock where they could see over into a valley, six Indians were discovered coming in a trot towards them, but low down on the mountain side, and out of gunshot. The white men all sprang to their feet and commenced to run down the mountain towards them. On coming near the spot where the Indians had been seen they were not visible anywhere, but signs were near by where they had pushed the old horse off a high bank into a gulley, down which they intended to continue their flight. The trail was taken up and soon three Indians were seen lying down, evidently exhausted by their exertions to get clear of the white men. Before a shot could be fired they sprang to their feet and were out of sight in a few moments in the rocks and bushes. The white men at this time were scattered, and the three Indians soon ran close to Henry Robinson and his son Frank, and stopped without seeing them. Henry Robinson carried a double-barreled gun, one for ball and the other for shot. Both father and son fired at the same Indian, and all three were out of sight again in an instant. On coming to the spot where the Indian who was fired at stood, plenty of blood was found, and also a belt which had been cut from his waist by a bullet. His trail was now taken up. It led down a gulley, and blood was profusely scattered and to be plainly seen on the rocks, and very black, indicating a liver wound. A pair of wet moccasins were found on a rock where the Indian pulled them off and left them after wading a small creek. They were heavy when wet, and retarded his flight. At last the white men were completely tired out, and yet the wounded Indian was not found. Dud Richardson had become very sick from exertion and overheat, and was vomiting. The chase was again abandoned. The old gray horse was finally found, however, lost in the shuffle, and taken in custody by the settlers. He came out of the chase with but very little of Mr. Anglin's big fat cow hanging to him. Besides the horse, there were captured one lance, one shield, two bows, one quiver of arrows, five bridles, and five lariats. Night was now approaching, and it was quite dark before they could descend the rough mountain to where they had left their horses. The animals were all right, tied up where they had left them, but the men left in charge were gone.

About one month after this raid the Indians came again, and no doubt for revenge, for it is almost certain that the Indian wounded by Henry Robinson died. As before, they first let their presence be known at the ranch of Mr. Anglin. They came at night and were discovered by the dogs. Mr. Anglin was gone to the Cibolo at the time to see Mr. Pancost about some horses. He lived at Selma, and afterwards sold goods in San Antonio under the firm name of Pancost & Son. One of Mr. Anglin's dogs was very much afraid of Indians, and as soon as he would get scent of one would rush into the house and go under the bed. On this occasion, when the dogs raised the alarm in the yard, this particularly nervous dog in regard to Indians made a break for the house, but as the door was closed he came near butting his brains out against the shutter. "Indians!" exclaimed Mrs. Anglin as soon as she heard the dog make such a frantic effort to get into the house. On this particular night Mr. John Leakey and wife were stopping with the family of Mr. Anglin, and he at once opened the door, pistol in hand, and went into the yard. The other dogs were still barking, but it was too dark to see anything. While Mr. Leakey was standing with his face in the direction of the Indians as indicated by the dogs, an arrow sped from out the darkness, barely missing Mr. Leakey. He now sent several bullets in the direction the arrow came from, and then went back in the house. Lights had been put out when the first alarm was raised, and Mr. Leakey now sat in darkness and kept watch until daylight. Mr. Leakey's home was below the mountains on the Sabinal, in the Patterson settlement. Next morning after the Indian alarm Mr. Leakey, while looking about for the signs of the Indians, found a cap of foxskin hanging to a blackjack limb about 100 yards from the house. It was evident that this was the cap of the Indian who shot the arrow at Mr. Leakey, and lost it in flight when the settler returned the fire. He might have been wounded. Mr. Leakey notified the nearest settlers of the raid, and five men soon collected at Mr. Anglin's house to go in pursuit of them. They were, besides Leakey, Gideon Thompson,

Henry Robinson, Silas Webster, and Sebe Barrymore. They decided to follow the Indians on foot, as the mountains were steep and rough for horses. The Indians were supposed to be some distance away by this time and the pursuit would last several days, but in the end they hoped to come upon them unawares in camp and get the best of them. Mrs. Anglin filled a pillowslip full of provisions, and Mr. Leakey fastened it across his shoulders back of the neck. The sequel will show that these daring pioneers were never to partake of the food which the good woman was so careful in preparing for them.

The trail led southwest to the mountains, two and one-half miles away, and the trailers soon arrived and commenced their ascent. The Indians were on top of the mountain in an ambuscade and watching all the maneuvers of the whites. They had made their trail plain, even cutting bushes with their tomahawks so that the white men would be certain to come into their trap. It was a hot day in August, and the men went up slowly. While ascending, Mr. Thompson, who was always on the lookout for signs, saw buzzards again, and said he believed the Indians were on the mountain. "Not an Indian in ten miles of here," said Mr. Leakey. When the top of the mountain was reached the men were hot and tired. It was a fine place for an ambush—rocks, low brush, and cedar trees. The lead men had penetrated the ambush, and their order as to position when the battle commenced was as follows: Robinson in front, Leakey next, Webster next, Barrymore next, and Thompson last. Mr. Thompson was incumbered with a large Spanish water gourd full of water which was strapped to his left arm. In addition to this he carried a heavy rifle, was very much fatigued, and had not quite reached the top. He had just called to the men to stop and rest awhile, when two shots were fired in front by the Indians at Robinson and Leakey. At the same time he saw an Indian running along a ledge in plain view waving a red blanket and yelling. He was trying to draw the fire of the men in the rear to him, so that, few and tired as the white men were, they would fall the easier victims. As before stated, the two foremost men had penetrated the ambuscade and had been fired on at close range, but without effect. Mr. Thompson thought at the time that these two first shots had been fired by Robinson and Leakey. The Indians now broke cover in many places, and showed themselves to be quite numerous. As the white men began to return the fire the Indians sprang from tree to tree and from rock to rock, and soon encompassed them on two sides. Mr. Thompson saw Mr. Leakey close among the Indians, and pointing his gun vigorously from one to another but failing to fire. The reason for this was the fact that Leakey had borrowed a rifle with set triggers, and he had been used to a single-triggered gun, so in this trying ordeal he had failed to spring the trigger and the hammer could not be pulled down. At this time Mr. Thompson was making frantic efforts to disengage the water gourd from his arm, but failing, was compelled to fire with this weight dangling at his left elbow. The Indian he aimed at was not more than twenty yards from him, but the smoke from his gun when he fired so obscured his view that he could not see the effects of the shot. He now heard Leakey firing, and looking in his direction saw him half bent, leaning towards the Indians, and shooting rapidly with a revolver. He had thrown his gun down. Robinson fired his gun and then retreated past Leakey, telling him to run—there was too many for them. Mr. Thompson made an attempt to reload his gun, but choked it, and was unable to do so. Calling now to Leakey to run, he started back down the mountain. Webster and Barrymore had passed him going back, after discharging their rifles. Robinson, brave as a lion, but seeing the utter futility of making a fight against twenty-five Indians under the circumstances, continued his retreat, after again calling to Leakey to come. Webster and Barrymore were going back the way they came up, Robinson further to the right, and all soon passed Thompson. In going down a limb caught in the strap of Webster's shotpouch, jerking it from his shoulder, and it was left dangling in the air. The Indians at this time were making the mountain gorges echo again and again with fearful warwhoops, and the shots from Leakey were no longer heard. An Indian now came out on a rock with a rifle in his hand where he could have a plain view of the retreating men, and taking aim fired it at Thompson. The ball passed through his hat brim on the right side, went between his ear and head, and passing on hit Barrymore in the hip, coming out at the thigh. This shot was fired from Leakey's gun. An Indian had picked it up where Leakey had discarded it, and knowing how to operate the set triggers, fired it with the result above narrated. The three men now retreated to an open ledge and halted, as Barrymore was continually falling. There was no doubt in their minds that Robinson and Leakey were both killed. All were silent for a short time, and then Leakey was seen staggering down the mountain towards them, and finally sank down. After emptying his pistol he had turned from the Indians and sprang down a ledge, covered with wounds, and made his way back more dead than alive. Mr. Thompson at once went to him and gave him water out of the gourd which he still carried on his arm. The water soon revived Leakey, and he began to talk. The first words he said were, "Damn the gun! I could not make it shoot. I must have broken it in some way. I pulled and pulled on the trigger." He was hit by arrows in nine places, and Mr. Thompson says he was the bloodiest man he ever saw. One arrow had struck near the wrist as he had his arm extended towards the Indians, firing with a pistol, and it penetrated lengthwise of the arm nearly to the shoulder, and was still transfixed. Other wounds were in the neck, face, head, thigh, and body.

Robinson had also sprang from a ledge and stopped in the brush and reloaded his gun. He then rejoined his companions, who thought him killed. After he came an Indian was discovered on a rock looking for them. Robinson at once prepared to shoot him, but Mr. Thompson said, "No, Henry, don't shoot. It will bring all of them on us again, and no loaded guns. Mine is choked; Leakey's is gone; Barrymore is wounded, and his gun not loaded, and Webster has lost his ammunition and his gun is empty." Robinson then desisted and all went down the mountain, Barrymore having to be supported. Thus they got clear out of this most desperate situation without losing a man. Leakey still had the provisions strapped to his shoulders. They were saturated with blood, and were taken off and thrown away. After arriving at the Anglin ranch again Dud Richardson was sent to the Patterson settlement after men, and an expedition was organized to go in pursuit of the Indians. When the reinforcements arrived they at once repaired to the battleground and took the trail of the Indians. How many were killed in the fight could not be ascertained. There was blood on the ground in places, but no doubt some of this came from Leakey's wounds.

The trail led a southwest course towards the town of Uvalde, about forty miles distant. On Bear Creek some dead grass had been burned off, leaving the ground covered with ashes, and in this twenty-two trails of foot Indians were counted. Mr. Thompson thinks they fought twenty-five on the mountain. Besides the trails of the Indians there were fifteen trails of horses. The Indians made one camp on Bear Creek. Here they took Leakey's gun to pieces and scattered the parts around. All of it was found except those parts which had holes through them for screws, etc. The trail was continued on from here in the general direction until they came to the "yellow banks" on the dry Frio, at the foot of the mountains. Here the Indians separated into two parties, and it was afterwards ascertained that the largest party went down the main Frio. The trail here was hard to keep, and the Indians scattered considerably on purpose to retard the pursuit of the whites, whom no doubt they had seen from some mountain top. The smallest trail was finally located, and it tended in the direction of Pilot Knob, at Fort Inge, four miles below Uvalde, on the Leona River. The soldiers had been removed from the fort, and no one was there at this time except old man Griner and his family. The Indians passed around to the left of the fort and kept south. For two days the men trailed through dense brush and pears, and finally lost the trail. It had been put out by numerous wild cattle that had passed over it. The men were now without food and water, and were compelled to quit searching for the lost trail and go to the Leona for water. Some of the men were in favor of giving up the pursuit and returning, but Mr. Thompson and "Butch" Dilliard persuaded them to try one more day. This was finally agreed to, and the trail was found again. The Indians on their way up to Sabinal Canyon on this raid had traversed this part of the country and had roped and tied up three head of wild cattle, no doubt intending to eat them on their return, but failed to do anything with them, likely passing the spot in the night and not being able to find them. When the white men passed two of the cattle were dead, and the other had got loose and made his escape. The trailers also found where the Indians had killed one old male of the wild cattle and cooked the meat. They took the bones along with them until they came to where there was some rocks, and there cracked them to get the marrow. They passed near Westfall's ranch, and when the settlers came to a point on the river about a mile below they heard the Indians singing and making a noise like a gang of Mexicans. The men all dismounted now, and leaving three of their party with the horses, advanced cautiously toward the banks of the Leona, from whence the sounds emanated, led by Henry Robinson and Newman Patterson. The Indians were all in bathing, except two bucks and one squaw. Some were yelling and some singing and making a great splashing in the water. It seems they were of the opinion that the white men had abandoned the pursuit. The surprise was complete. The first intimation they had of danger was the sight of white men standing on the bank shooting at them. The men in front fired first and killed the squaw and one buck. The balance of the men scattered along the bank and poured a perfect storm of bullets at those in the water. The buck who was on the bank and was not killed at the first fire ran to an elm tree, and was shot by Jesse Lewis, a half Cherokee Indian. The hostile then left the tree and ran a short distance and fell, with his bow in one hand and three arrows in the other. Some of the Indians in the water tried to come out and secure their arms, but the fire from the white men was so severe that only one got out on the bank, and he caught up his quiver by the wrong end and his arrows all dropped out as he attempted to run back in the water with it. Mr. Thompson saw one Indian in the water who had been shot, and with his back half exposed was watching to see who was going to shoot at him again. Mr. Thompson shot him again, and he turned over and over in the water, like a snake with his back broken, until he got to the opposite bank, and then got out and went about 200 yards on the opposite side of the river and lay down. Some of the men stripped off their clothing and followed him and killed him. He had on a big sixshooter, two of the chambers of which were loaded. It is somewhat strange that he had it on in the water. Two guns were picked up and were found to be badly overloaded, the charges measuring four inches. An Indian believes in making all the noise he can when in a fight. One Indian made his escape without being hit. He was afterwards seen on a reservation at Fort Belknap by Mr. Black, who was in the fight. Eight Indians were killed on the spot. Mr. Black was afterwards killed in Uvalde. On one of the shields captured was found the missing parts of Leakey's gun—the pieces that had holes in them. This gun belonged to John Richards, and he had but recently purchased it in San Antonio from Mr. Charles Hummell, who dealt in firearms, and is still in that business under the firm name of Charles Hummell & Son. All parts of the gun were finally collected and sent back to San Antonio, and Mr. Hummell put it together again. Besides Mr. Thompson and the others already mentioned, there were in this Indian killing scrape Judge McCormick, John Ware, John Davenport, John Bowles, Joel Fenley, and others. None of the white men were hurt, and all returned safely home.

In 1861 Big Foot Wallace fought the Indians on the head of the Seco, about twelve miles from Sabinal Canyon, and that night came with his men into the canyon with some wounded men, one of whom was William Davenport. He left the Indians in possession of the battleground and about 200 head of horses. He wanted more men to help to pursue and fight them again, and if possible to retake the horses which were stolen below. This band of Indians had penetrated into the settlements as far as Atascosa County and killed many people. Around the little village of Pleasanton they had killed a man named Herndon, wounded Anderson and O'Bryant, and chased several others. On the way back they were fought by a small party of settlers, in which James Winters was killed and others wounded. Further on they killed "Mustang" Moore, near where Moore's station is, and Peter Ketchum, on the Hondo. They also killed Mr. Murray, tax assessor of Bandera County. Others were also killed and wounded by them, and horses gathered up all over the country. Captain Wallace stayed that night at John C. Ware's place, near where Utopia now is. Jasper Kinchaloe was sent up the canyon to notify the settlers who lived above. Late at night he came to Mr. Thompson's house and told the news of the battle and the need of more men. Jack Kelley lived still above, about where Mr. Sam Harper now lives, and Mr. Thompson went to notify him. His horse was out, but they hunted him up in the dark and came on down to Mr. Anglin's house. Here they tried to shoe their horses in his shop, but the wind blew the light out and they could not do it. Next morning seven of the canyon men went to the Cypress spring, where the Bob Harper place is now, and there intended to wait for Big Foot Wallace and his men from below, and in the meantime shoe their horses, as Mr. Thompson had brought his tools along. By the time the shoeing was over a cold rain had set in, and as Wallace and his party had not as yet put in an appearance, Thompson and his men mounted their horses and started back home. After crossing the river, however, and coming to a point about where Mr. Henry Taylor now resides, they came upon the trail of Wallace and his men, who had crossed below and came up the west bank of the river. The Thompson party at once turned and followed their trail, and came up with them at the old Kelley ranch, which has been previously mentioned as the place where the Indians broke up the spinning wheels. Here the whole party stayed until morning, as by this time the weather had become fearfully cold, the rain turning to sleet. Most of the men were not prepared for such a change, some of the Atascosa County men not even having their coats with them. They did very well, however, at the deserted ranch during the night. The following morning was clear and not so cold, and the Indian hunt was resumed with vigor. The intention of Captain Wallace was to get ahead of the Indians and lay an ambush for them. His party was traveling north and the late battleground was east, but the general course of the Indians was northwest, and would intersect that of the whites. The Indians traveled slowly with so many horses and over a very rough country, and no doubt also laid up for the sleet in some cedar brake. Wallace got ahead of them on the divide and placed his men in ambush for them. The impatience of the men, however, and their want of discipline, caused them to fail in their object. Many of them left their places of concealment to look, and when the Indians did come and before they were in gunshot a man named Hilburn fired his rifle and the Indians ran and scattered. Some of the men had left their horses too far, and could not get them quick enough to do any good in the pursuit. The horses, however, were all captured and carried back to the owners by Wallace and his men.

In 1866 the Indians attacked the ranch of Mr. R. H. Kinchaloe in his absence and killed Mrs. Bowlin, a neighbor lady, who was there at the time. They also wounded Mrs. Kinchaloe in a dozen places, and left her for dead on the floor.

Mr. Thompson took an active part in the pursuit of the Indians, but was unsuccessful in getting them. He had the misfortune to get his leg broken after he got to be an old man, but is hearty and carries his years well. He still lives on the place he first settled over forty years ago, but has made many improvements and is well to do. His wife died a few years ago. Mr. Aaron Anglin died at his home on May 15, 1884. His wife, Mrs. Jennie Anglin, died in November, 1894, on Thanksgiving day.

Mr. Anglin was one of the commissioners who helped to lay off the town of Uvalde. His son, Job Anglin, still lives at the old home on the Anglin prong of the river.

CAPTAIN MALCOLM VAN PELT.

Came to Texas in 1853.

Fifteen miles west of Sabinal Canyon, running nearly south, is Frio Canyon, a long, wide, beautiful valley, with the Frio (pronounced Freo) River running through its center. There are many clear creeks flowing into it on both sides, and each of these streams has small canyons containing many acres of rich land which is now (1897) being rapidly settled and small farms opened.

One of the early settlers here is Capt. T. M. G. Van Pelt, who has a fine ranch and farm fronting the river. Mr. Van Pelt was born in the town of Charlotte, Mecklenburg County, North Carolina, in July, 1831. His great-grandfather was a soldier in the war of the revolution, and was killed by the tories and Indians. He was at home at the time when the Van Pelt house was attacked by the red and white savages. His grandfather first discovered the enemy and ran to the house. As he was getting over the yard fence the tories commenced shooting but missed him, and hit the top rails of the fence. In the fight that ensued at the house the elder Van Pelt (the soldier) was killed, but the son made his escape. In the war of 1812 his grandfather was on his way to join General Jackson's army when the battle of New Orleans was fought.

Mr. Van Pelt came to Texas in 1853 and first settled at Gonzales, but soon moved from there and settled at Prairie Lea, in Caldwell County, in 1854. He bought cattle there and drove them to the Hondo River just below where Hondo City now is, the county seat of Medina County. That was in 1855. In 1860 he moved and settled in Frio Canyon, Uvalde County. Among those who were there at the time was E. V. Dale, Richard Ware, and Capt. Theophilus Watkins. The latter was captain of the frontier guards. Mr. John Leakey was the first settler, but had moved his family and was running some freight wagons below. In 1861 Mr. Van Pelt went back to the Hondo to gather his hogs, and while doing so stayed at the ranch of Widow Dean and her son Joe. During that time the Indians made a raid and killed several settlers, among whom was Mr. Pete Ketchum. Mr. Van Pelt helped to bury Ketchum, and also saw nine head of horses the Indians had killed. The hostiles were in large force, and nearly all of the men in the country rallied under Big Foot Wallace to pursue and fight them. The Indians were overtaken at the head of the Seco (Saco) Creek, where they had selected a strong position and had halted to give the settlers battle. Mr. Van Pelt had joined the expedition. Near their ambush the Indians had tied a horse on the side of the mountain near their trail, and in plain view of anyone approaching from the valley. It seemed to be an abandoned horse. Judge Davenport was the first one to see the animal and exclaimed, "To first sight belongs the property," and started up the mountain, followed by several others. Captain Wallace said, "Look out, boys; that is a trick of the Indians," but they kept on and were soon fired upon by the Indians at close range with shotguns and other arms. Some of the men were hit, among whom was a son of Judge Davenport, William. There was a general stampede back down the mountain, and some confusion prevailed amid the yelling of Indians. Mr. Van Pelt says the first sight he saw of the Indians was one rise up on his knee and fire a shotgun. Captain Wallace ordered all to dismount at the foot of the mountain and tie their horses to the cedar trees which grew thick on the bank of the ravine. He also requested some of them who had long range guns to ascend a hill in the rear and fire from there, as they could better see the Indiians, who had now taken refuge from the rifle shots in the rocks, and could not be seen from below, where most of the men were posted. During one charge Mr. Van Pelt had his gun up to his face and was taking aim at the chief when a man named Hilburn fired first and killed him. The Indian fell forward on his face with an arrow in his hand, which he was about to adjust to the bowstring to shoot. The other Indians carried his body up the mountain. He was very brave, and continually charged the whites until he was killed. One Indian was observed with a shotgun which he laid down after discharging it, and commenced shooting arrows very fast. He had on a hat and shirt which reached down nearly to his knees. George Robins fired at him with a shotgun, but he caught the load on his shield and ran, leaving the shotgun. This gun belonged to "Mustang" Moore, whom the Indians had killed on this raid near the place where

Moore's station now is on the International Railroad, and which was named for him. Moore had camped on a return trip from San Antonio. William Davenport, who was wounded and lying under a cedar tree during the hottest of the firing, wanted to get up and join in, but Judge Davenport stopped him, and said, "Lay still, Bill; there are a thousand of them here yet." When the fight was over and the Indians had all gone back on top of the mountain, Mr. Van Pelt asked if there was any man in the crowd that had on a linen shirt. No one had, but there was one found who had linen wristbands on his shirt sleeves. These were taken off and picked to pieces very fine by Mr. Van Pelt, and twisted into a cord and carefully inserted into the wound of Davenport and drawn through, but left there. The wound was in the leg above the knee, and was made by a large ball that went through. The cord afterward was turned frequently until it began to get well. This was to keep the wound cleansed. Judge Davenport wanted to cut the leg of the pantaloons off, but Mr. Van Pelt objected to that, saying the leg would freeze before they could get to the settlement in Sabinal Canyon. By this time it was nearly night, cold and sleeting. The Indian chief killed in the fight was afterwards found in a cave. He was finely dressed, having many beads on his clothing and a magnificent headdress and shield. These things were sold, and the shield alone brought $30. When coming on the trail of the Indians up Seco valley the settlers crossed the bridle road that led from Bandera over to Sabinal Canyon. Captain Wallace said the Indians had run some one along the trail, as the tracks of running horses indicated. This was correct, and the man pursued was Mr. Murray, the tax assessor of Bandera County, who was coming over to Sabinal Canyon to assess, as part of the valley was in Bandera County. Murray was killed, and his body, at the time Wallace and his men passed, was lying not far away on the side of the mountain. The Indians who killed him got back to their companions in time for the battle, in which they lost Murray's pistol, and it was recovered by the white men.

After the fight Wallace and his men went to Sabinal Canyon and spent the night. Additions were made to his force by canyon men, and the pursuit of the Indians commenced again. Mr. Van Pelt says they ambushed the Indians at Ranger Springs, but, as has already been written, Frank Hilburn fired too soon and spoiled it all. Mr. Van Pelt says that Hilburn badly wounded the Indian at whom he fired, although at long range, and that he died and his body was found afterwards. The Indians had many horses, and when the stampede commenced after Hilburn fired a bell was heard on one of the loose horses rattling loudly. Mr. Van Pelt exclaimed, "My bell!" meaning he would have the horse that wore the bell. An Indian had mounted this belled horse, and Mr. Van Pelt gave him a close chase and was about to fire his rifle at him when the Indian looked back to see if the white man was going to shoot, and a limb knocked him off. He made his escape to the brush, but Mr. Van Pelt got the horse and also one of his own, which the Indians had held for more than a year. Nearly 200 head of horses were taken and carried back to their owners.

While Mr. Van Pelt lived on the Hondo, in 1859, the Indians made a raid, and after killing a Mexican herder, chased and killed two cowboys, one Huffman and Sebastian Wolfe. Van Pelt, Mike Whiff, George Johnson, and Jack Wolfe, brother to the one killed, followed the Indians, but were met by Jack Davenport and others who had followed the Indians and whipped them and taken their horses. They had Huffman's mule, saddle, and pistol. The bodies of the men had not as yet been found, but it was very evident that they had been killed. All now went to look for the missing men, and soon found their dead and mangled bodies and buried them. Wolfe's throat was cut from ear to ear. The dead Indian in the tree was also taken down by them.

In 1862 Malcolm Van Pelt, Frank Hilburn, Jasper Wish, Gid Thompson, Joel Fenley, Chris Kelley, Ezekiel Tucker, and James Davenport followed a band of Indians from the Frio to the head of East Nueces, near the head of Ash Creek. There they found a mare killed, with the back skinned where the Indians had cut out the sinews to make bowstrings. Some said the animal had been killed several days, but Mr. Van Pelt knew the mare and said that she belonged to Joe Harrison, and was at his ranch only a few days before. He was confident the Indians were near who killed her. In scouting around through the hills seventy-five wigwams were discovered, and near them a horse belonging to Mr. Van Pelt. He, however, declined to go to him, and said he did not need that particular horse in his business just at that time. The men now went back and camped, as they could not make a fight if all those wigwams had tenants. Next morning in going back to the spot where the dead mare lay it was discovered that the meat had been taken away, only the skeleton remaining. It was afterwards learned that nearly all of the Indians at this time were below on a raid, and those in camp kept hid from the white men, and when they left followed them and tried to ambush them on Patterson's Creek, but the white men passed the danger spot ahead of them. Another party of white men returned to the wigwams, but they were deserted. The Indians anticipated a return of the whites and left. While the men were looking about the camps a smooth, flat pecan stick was found, and on it was drawn the Frio River, nine white men, and four Indians, the white men going down the river and the Indians to the northwest. This was for the information of the war party when they should return from the raid. The pictures of the Indians were drawn with red paint. They also drew a picture of the moon, showing how old it was when the white men were there.

Mr. E. V. Dale, an old San Jacinto veteran, who lived many years in Guadalupe County and died there, was a neighbor of Mr. Van Pelt. They were good friends but entirely different in their temperaments. Mr. Dale was always in earnest and serious on all subjects, and was never known to get off a joke on anyone. Mr. Van Pelt was exactly the opposite, always running over with fun and practical jokes, and when no one else was around would perpetrate them on his friend Dale. On one occasion Dale was invited by Van to take a hunt with him and another neighbor. He consented, and came at the specified time with gun, blankets, and provisions. Van Pelt was to furnish the wagon and team. The wagon had no bed on it, and the things were strapped to the coupling pole. Mr. Dale did not like these arrangements, and wanted a wagon bed put on so a sheet could be stretched over it at night to sleep under, as he was solicitous about his health. This was overruled, however, and they started, Mr. Dale perched astride of the coupling on the bedding. Mr. Van Pelt was on the rocking bolster, where he could control and guide the oxen. The other man was on a horse carried along to pack game to camp on. Everything went on all right until they went to cross the Frio River. It was shallow at the crossing, but deep above. The spirit of mischief now came upon Mr. Van Pelt, and it was almost irresistible to give Mr. Dale a ducking. He had one ox that, if he jumped out beside him and talked quick and loud to him, would swerve sharply in the opposite direction and was hard to control. Just as they were entering the stream Mr. Van did that trick, and the oxen turned sharply up stream into deep water, submerging Mr. Dale and all the bedding. Van Pelt held on to the rope and yelled "Whoa!" with all his might, and of course was wet himself, to make Dale think it was accidental. When they got out Van told his wet friend how it all happened, and when he got through Dale said, "Yes, and you are an old fool." The balance of the day was spent drying clothing and bedding around large fires. Mr. Dale said it would be the death of him. No bad effects, however, occurred from the wetting, and they killed plenty of game and had a good time.

When Mr. Dale was loaded up and ready to move east he drove by Van Pelt's, and calling him out, extended his hand, saying, "Van, I am going to do something for you now that the devil has never yet done for you,—tell you good-bye." Van laughed heartily at this, shook his hand, and they parted friends.

JACK MILLER.

Came to Texas in 1854.

Among the pioneers of Southwest Texas who has endured the perils and hardships, met the dangers unflinchingly, and suffered loss of loved ones at the hands of the savages, is Mr. J. W. Miller, better known as "Jack" among his friends. Mr. Miller was born in Pulaski County, Missouri, near Waynesville, which was the county seat at that time. His grandfather was a soldier under Washington. Jack Miller came to Texas in 1854 and settled in Sabinal Canyon, near the present village of Utopia. He moved from this place and settled at Fort Lincoln, on the Seco, below the mountains near old D'Hanis. While living at this place, on the 29th of January, 1867, his brother George, in company with August Rothe and Herbert Weynand, went up into Hondo Canyon on a cow hunt and camped out several nights below where the Bandera road now crosses the valley. Early one morning the Indians came upon them and the boys ran from camp on foot, not having time to untie and mount their horses. There were no guns in the crowd and but one pistol, and it only partly loaded, carried by August Rothe. Rothe and Miller were about 17 years of age and Weynand about 13. Miller was killed and Weynand carried off a captive. Rothe made his escape to a mountain, and kept the Indians off by aiming the pistol at them when they ran close to him. Keeping his few loads in reserve was all that saved him, the Indians not knowing how badly loaded his pistol was. Young Rothe came to a settler named McCay and told the news, and a party came and carried away the body of Miller in McCay's wagon. A runner was then sent to notify the Miller and Weynand families at Fort Lincoln. The father of the murdered George came and brought the body of his son home and buried it there. (See a more detailed account of this affair in the sketch of August Rothe.)

On one occasion Jack Miller, Ambrose Crane, "Seco" Smith, George Johnson, Charles Richter, and William Wagener were camped on the Seco cow-hunting below where the railroad now crosses the creek. The elder Miller, father of Jack, came down to see about the cattle, and on his return home was run onto by Indians in Seco bottom, but succeeded in getting away from them and back to the boys, and gave the alarm. The cowboys at once mounted and put out after the Indians and soon came upon them. The Indians had forty head of horses belonging to Judge George Harper, who had a ranch on the Hondo River some miles east of the Seco. The Indians ran when they saw the cowmen and a long chase commenced. In about one and a half miles run one Indian was overhauled with a worn-out horse, which he deserted, took to a thicket, and there prepared to fight the white men. All of the cowboys now stopped, as no more Indians were likely to be caught, and concentrated around the thicket where the lone Comanche had made his stand to fight his pale-faced foes, who greatly outnumbered him. Even with only one Indian to fight the men had to approach him with great caution to keep any of their party from being killed. As soon as the Indian would get a glimpse of a man as they circled around trying to see him an arrow would come in quick flight, and some narrow escapes were made. Ambrose Crane, who was a very tall man and could see over bushes and tall grass, obtained a view of the Indian and shot at him with a pistol. Many shots were now fired, the men charging in and firing with sixshooters, their only weapons. The Comanche was badly wounded, having his elbow shot off so that he could not use his bow, and becoming desperate, left his cover and charged the crowd. The pistol balls met him on every side, and he soon sank down and died, with a butcher-knife clenched in his only hand that he could use. Mr. Rolly Miller, father of Jack, and a very old man, who had followed the boys, scalped the dead brave, and his body was left where it fell. Jack Miller gave the Indian one stab with a knife when he left the thicket, and the white men closed around him. The Millers had in mind the dead and mutilated body of a son and brother. Years after some one found the skull of the Indian and carried it away. Judge Harper got all of his horses back. The Indian had selected a bad one on which to make his escape, and lost his life in consequence. There were many horses in the herd that would have carried him away safely. The Indian looked to be about 30 years of age, and was tall and slim.

Jack Miller is one of the successful stock men of Medina County, and has a fine ranch on the Seco. About 300 yards from his house, and nearly opposite, on the west side of the creek, is the site of the old house built by Mr. Myrick, in which Richard Ware and Charles Durbin made their stand and kept off a large body of Indians in the early settlement of the country.

AUGUST ROTHE.

AUGUST ROTHE.

Came to Texas in 1854.

Among the pioneers of the west who have seen wild Indians, fought them, and been chased by them, is Mr. A. C. Rothe, who now lives on his ranch on the west bank of the Seco, about six miles north from the town of D'Hanis.

Mr. Rothe was born in the northern part of Bavaria in 1847, and came to Castroville, Texas, with his father, Henry Rothe, in 1854. They sailed from the old country in the ship Salucia, and landed at Galveston. From this point they came by ox teams to Castroville. Mrs. Rothe was sick on the way, and died in fourteen days after arriving at their new home in this far away, strange, and frontier country. It is always sad to think of a death under these circumstances. These people, cutting loose from all ties of relationship, friends, home, and country; braving the dangers of the deep in a small vessel; landing on a foreign soil among people whose language they could not speak; the long and tedious trip to the west by slow moving ox wagons, and at last reaching the place of long expectation, and then not live to enjoy the fruits of the sacrifices which they have made in order to reach the place where they expected to rest from their toils and build up pleasant, happy homes in the beautiful new country.

The Rothe family first settled on the Medina River, six miles above Castroville, and then moved up near the Haby settlement, six miles further. The Rothe boys were Fritz, Henry, Louis, and August, and one daughter. The Rothes had a hard time of it at first. The boys had gone to school most of their time while in Europe, and had not as yet learned how to work on a farm or handle cattle, which was all that young men could do at that time in the west, except probably freighting or working for the government on forts, etc. The elder Rothe was also unused to this kind of work, being a man of some means, and an officeholder in the old country. However, they soon learned how to manage and raise stock, and farmed until 1862. They then moved to the Seco, near Fort Lincoln, and took charge of the Riley stock of cattle under contract to keep them three years.

In the meantime the civil war had broken out, and the two oldest boys, Fritz and Henry, joined the company of Captain Kampmann and went to the Confederate army and served the cause of the South until the break-up.

August and Louis had to fill the contract with Riley's cattle, and they had a hard time of it. The Indians constantly depredated upon them and kept stealing their horses, so that they could hardly keep ponies enough to handle the cattle. Horses were high and hard to get. In the three years they were engaged in handling the Riley cattle they lost $3000 worth of horses. After this contract was finished, and the other boys coming back from the war, the Rothes brought their cattle from the Medina and commenced to raise cattle on an extensive scale, and were very successful. August saw his first wild Indian in 1863. In that year he and his brother Louis and Charles Richter, all boys, went on a cow-hunt to the Cedar waterhole, on Seco, some distance above the settlement. On the way they came upon three head of cattle which had been killed by Indians. Two of the stock had arrows in them, and the boys dismounted and pulled these out and carried them along with them.

At this time Jacob Sauter, Tobe Sauter, and Mike Schreiber had gone up to the Cedar waterhole to cut grass. The boys went up there and told them to look out, "the Indians were in." The grass-cutters said they had seen a man running horses, and Tobe Sauter said it was an Indian, but the others thought not; that the Indians would not run horses in daylight that close to camp, and then kept on with their work. It seems that the Indians had not as yet discovered the presence of white men, so that when one of them commenced to whet a scythe blade he looked towards them quickly, and then left the horses and ran across the creek out of sight. The three boys now made a circle in the prairie not far from the present residences of August and Fritz Rothe, and then came back towards the waterhole. When near there they saw four saddled horses in a liveoak grove. Not knowing for certain that it was Indians, they rode on and came near them. An Indian now jumped up from among the horses and gave a keen whistle. He had heard the noise of the horses' feet on the rocks. When he whistled, three other Indians came from cover near the waterhole and advanced rapidly towards their horses. Two of these Indians had guns. One mounted and sat on his horse and the others stood on the ground, the one with his gun ready to shoot, all four intently watching the young cowboys as they slowly rode around them. The boys only had two six-shooters in their party, and some of the loads of these had been fired at a fox before they knew that Indians were around. The Indians all mounted now and rode off across the creek, and the boys went back to the grass-cutters and told them of the Indians. One man was just preparing to start with a keg to the waterhole for water, and would have been killed by the Indians if the boys had not come upon them and caused the Indians to leave their ambush and go away. The hay camp was not at the water, but near enough to get their supply there. The Indians were watching for some one to come after water.

The Indian alarm was raised in the country, and a scout made up which followed the trail into the mountains, but the hostiles made their escape.

In the spring of 1865 August Rothe, George Miller, Herbert Weynand, and Jacob Sauter left the settlement on Seco, near Fort Lincoln, and went to hunt oxen on the Hondo at a place called "sink of the water." These places are at or near the mouth of all the canyons through which these mountain streams flow. The water sinks here in the accumulation of heaps of gravel that for ages has been piling up. Sometimes the water will break out again many miles below.

The boys were all young. Weynand was about 12 years of age, and the youngest. The others were some years older. They made their camp at the sinks, and then commenced to hunt their oxen. Sauter found his oxen the first day, and went home.

The same day, while August Rothe was hunting his oxen in the mountains, about 2 o'clock in the evening, he found old man Ludwig Mummie, who had been lost part of two days and a night. He was very hungry, and almost delirious. He had lost his way trying to come through the mountains from Bandera to D'Hanis. Rothe took him to their camp, and when he had been refreshed with food and coffee he mounted his horse and went on home, although the boys begged him to stay. He had a good gun, pistol, and plenty of cartridges, and had he stayed would no doubt have averted the terrible tragedy which was enacted the next morning at this camp, in which one of the boys lost his life and another was carried off into captivity, never more to return, and which caused two families to mourn the loss of loved ones. After Mummie left, Rothe went to see about the horses, and soon heard firing in camp. He at once hastened back, and found that George Miller had nearly emptied Rothe's pistol at a tree. The pistol was the only weapon in camp. August said, "George, you should not have done that. I have no more loads, and now suppose the Indians should come upon us." Weynand spoke up and said he had a little powder and two buckshot in his pocket. There was one load left in the pistol, and August took the two buckshot, and by patching them like loading a rifle, charged two more chambers of the pistol, making three in all. Next morning after breakfast Rothe and Weynand went to get the horses, which had gotten a mile and a half from camp with hobbles on, which was an unusual thing for them to do. It consumed about two hours to find the horses. Rothe tied his horse and Miller's together and led them back. Weynand had his bridle with him, so he mounted his horse and rode back. The camp was situated on the bluff bank of the Hondo, and in the rear was a small rocky hill. Four hundred yards further was a high, rocky mountain. When Rothe and Weynand got near the small rocky hill in the hear of the camp, and before they could see the latter, they met George Miller coming in a run with a scared look upon his face, who said that a lot of Indians were under the bluff watering their horses. At first Rothe thought that Miller was trying to fool them, and stood a few moments, but soon saw by his pale face that it was no joke. Miller said he was lying down smoking a pipe and heard the rattle of the rocks as the Indians came up the bed of the creek to the water, and not knowing what it was, walked to the bluff and looked over, and was very close to them. Up to this time the Indians had not seen the camp, but saw Miller when he looked over the bluff at them, and then turned to run.

The Indians had to run down the creek bed a short distance before they could find a place where they could ascend the steep bank. While Miller was telling this, they heard the rattling of the rocks as the Indians were coming out of the bed of the creek to chase Miller, not having as yet discovered the other two boys. In a very short time the Indians were close upon them, eight in number and all mounted. Rothe had no time to untie the two horses so that he and Miller could make their escape on them, and said to George, "We must run for the mountain. If we get to it before they kill us we may get away." He then told young Weynand to run up the road as fast as he could to McCay's ranch, several miles distant. The boy did so, and he and Miller set off at full speed to the mountain, pursued by five of the Indians. Three ran after Weynand. The Indians came close, yelling, and Rothe drew his pistol and waved it as he ran. When near the base of the mountain Miller gave out and said he could go no further. "Run! run!" said Rothe, as he pointed his pistol back at the Indians, who were close upon them, and still continued himself to make desperate efforts to reach cover. The Indians were afraid of Rothe's pistol, and would dodge when he aimed at them, and this would give him a chance to make another spurt ahead, and in this way he succeeded in getting a short distance up the mountain. He then stopped, nearly exhausted, and looked back. The Indians saw Miller was not armed, and one of them caught hold of him just as Rothe looked back. The boy jerked loose, and again ran towards the mountain. An Indian then ran up to him and struck him over the head with a lance. George staggered from side to side, but still continued to try to run. An Indian then ran ahead of him and aimed a lance at his breast, and Miller stopped. Rothe thought that Weynand had made his escape, but at this time heard him scream, and looking in that direction saw an Indian have him by the hair and pulling him out of some bushes. Whether the boy fell off the horse or jumped off could not be told. This was the last Rothe ever saw of him, for he himself was compelled again to run. Two of the Indians had carried Miller back to camp, and the other three were coming up the mountain on their horses after him. The Indians were all on sorry horses but one, and he came so close to Rothe that he recognized the horse as belonging to Cosgrove, who had a ranch on Seco where John Reinhart now lives. This fellow, whom Rothe thinks was a Mexican, had on a hickory shirt. His face was brown, nose flat, and he said in fair English that he was going to have the white man's scalp. The others he knew were all Indians; they wore the garb, and had long black hair. The other two flanked the hard-pressed youth and tried hard to get around him, but the way was steep and rough and difficult for horses to ascend. The one on the Cosgrove pony came so close that Rothe concluded to risk one shot at him, and stopped and aimed his pistol. The fellow, however, wheeled his horse quickly behind some liveoak bushes, but at the same time sent an arrow which hit the muzzle of Rothe's pistol, glanced down, and went through his pants leg, just grazing the skin. The other two now commenced shooting, and the arrows came from both ways, but their aim was bad, owing to the strained position they were in on the steep hillside. Rothe could hear the arrows pass him, and once more made an effort to reach the top of the mountain, pointing his pistol as if about to fire when they came close, and thus gaining a little time and pushing on. The Indians seemed to be very much afraid of the pistol, but if they had konwn the true condition it was in would have crowded upon him and no doubt have succeeded in getting his scalp, for on examination afterwards it was discovered that one of the loose-fitting buckshot had dropped out in his flight, and the good load, as he supposed, failed to fire when tried. The only shot he had was the other buckshot that still remained in the chamber. Two Indians now went back down the mountain, and the one on the brown pony tried to pass around Mr. Rothe and turn him back. The hard-pressed man, although nearly exhausted, managed to keep ahead of him. The Indian when he discovered that his two companions had quit the chase and gone back beat a hasty retreat himself. When Mr. Rothe finally succeeded in reaching the top of the mountain, which was quite elevated and steep, he stopped and looked back into the valley below, but could see nothing of the Indians. He now continued his flight and went down the mountain on the other side, and finally laid down in a dense thicket, and there came near dying from over-exertion. When sufficiently recovered to travel he went to McCay's ranch and also to that of Miller, to tell them the news. McCay got four men together, and led by Rothe went back to the camp. The first thing they saw when they arrived there was Miller's shoes, close together, like a man would place them in retiring for the night. A short search, and Miller's dead body was found under the bluff near the water, where the unfortunate young man had first seen the Indians. He was stripped except as to one sock, and his hands were tied behind him with a pair of hobbles so tightly drawn that the flesh was cut to the bone. He was lanced in the left side and the jugular vein in the neck was cut. He was not scalped or in any other way mutilated, except the bruise on the head where he was hit with a lance at the time of the capture. Mr. Rothe said that when he went to tell the Miller family of the death of George, he would rather have faced the Indians again that have done so. Young Miller was well liked by all who knew him. Before they got to the camp McCay said he did not believe the boys were killed, as he thought they could have killed August and George both before they got to the mountain if they had wanted to. They never shot at Rothe until they saw he was about to make his escape. The body of Miller was taken to Fort Lincoln and buried. A scout followed the Indians from D'Hanis under Captain Joe Ney, and they were overtaken, but they scattered into the mountains and nothing could be done with them. Some horses which they had stolen at Quihi were recovered, and also the horse, saddle, and bridle of Herbert Weynand, but the captive boy was never heard of again by anyone in this country.

August Rothe was several days recovering from his over-exertion, and drank water almost constantly for three days. These were the same Indians who killed Buchaloe on the Sabinal, and then came on down and got Cosgrove's horses.

It seems that everything worked against the two unfortunate boys, Miller and Weynand, and that they were doomed. In the first place, had Mummie remained with them, well armed as he was, they might have kept the Indians off. If the horses had not been so far from camp that morning the Indians would only have found a deserted camp, as they intended going home as soon as the horses could be caught up and saddled. There was a place below called the Mustang waterhole, and to this place the Indians went first to water their horses, but it had dried up, and they moved on to the next at the camp. This was ascertained by following their trail. Had not Miller looked over the bluff when he heard the rocks rattle the Indians might not have discovered the camp, etc.

August Rothe saw Dr. Woodbridge three days after the fight at Carrizo, and said the back of his neck was badly swollen and bruised, the effect of the blow from the Indian which knocked the doctor from his horse. Dr. Woodbridge said the Indian hit him with a bow, which came near breaking his neck. In 1872 the father of the Rothe boys died. In this same year August and his brother Fritz started to Bandera, and at Quihi Pass came upon five Indians and a sharp fight ensued, in which fifteen shots were fired. The Rothes were armed with Winchesters, and by some means so were the Indians. Fritz was riding a young horse, and he became so badly frightened at the yelling and firing as to be unmanageable, and his rider was not able to work his gun properly. The Indians had twenty-five head of horses, and were first seen by the white men. Fritz said, "Who are those over yonder?" August said, "Indians!" his brother thought not. About this time the Indians discovered the white men and dropped back behind their horses so as to get together. They now made a charge, and the Rothes ran up a bare hill where there was no protection, but stopped to make a fight. One Indian came very close and August shot at him, but the Indian was keen-sighted, dodged behind his horse, and avoided being hit. Another shot was fired quickly, which struck under the horse and caused the Indian to straighten up very suddenly, as he was hanging low down on the opposite side of his horse. The Indians now divided, and some went around the hill so as to cut them off if they attempted to come down. All of this time the Indians were firing rapidly. August saw one whose body was exposed sitting upright on his horse with his gun in the act of shooting, and both fired at each other about the same time. The ball from the Indian's gun almost grazed Rothe's head, and the Indian fell to the ground, bringing his saddle with him. He succeeded in crawling to a tree, but left his gun where he fell. The other Indians now came back to this one, and the white men left the hill and continued their course to Bandera. They had not gone far before they discovered two Indians in ambush ahead of them. August held up his gun and advanced upon them, and they gave way without a fight.

In 1873 August had one more bout with Indians near the Medina River. They tried hard to ambush him and cut him off into a trap, but he outgeneraled them and got clear. These were the last wild Indians he ever saw.

The Rothe brothers, by strict attention to stock, have been very successful, now having 100,000 acres of land, 85,000 of which is fenced. They have had at times 16,000 head of cattle and many hundred head of horses. While the writer was at the house of Mr. Fritz Rothe he related a circumstance of early times out west, which shows what kind of a country it was at that time as to game and wild animals. Mr. Jack Davenport was out hunting one day, he said, near the Sabinal River, and killed a deer. There was a large mesquite tree near, and to this he dragged the deer and proceeded to skin it. Two more deer now came up and snorted at him. Jack reloaded and fired until he killed both of them, and brought them to the same tree. While stooping over at work he suddenly felt something clutch at his shirt collar behind. Turning quickly, he saw a large panther reared up behind him. His gun was not loaded, and he backed off, loading as he went, the panther following. He killed this one, and happening to glance up the tree saw another, which he also killed. Three deer and two panthers under one tree, you might say, killed in a pile.

J. W. GARDNER.

Came to Texas in 1855.

J. W. Gardner, who lives near Big Foot postoffice, in Frio County, is one of the many Texans who bear scars on their bodies, relics of wounds put there by the heavy hand of the red man as he retreated, delivering his blows against the pale face in a desperate but futile effort to stay the advance of civilization toward the great west.

Joseph G. Gardner, father of the subject of this sketch, was a native of middle Tennessee, but moved from there to Lousiana, where his son J. W. Gardner was born in 1851. The family came to Texas in 1855 and settled in Atascosa County, but again moved in 1861 and settled near "Old Frio Town," in Frio County. They stayed at that place four years and then moved to Guadalupe County, settling fifteen miles south from Seguin, in the Sandies country. Here, in 1869, the elder Gardner died, and was buried at the "Sandies Chapel Church." The widow Gardner with her children now moved back to Frio County and settled where Mr. J. W. Gardner now lives, seven miles south from Devine and three miles from Big Foot postoffice. Here, in 1871, young Gardner hired to Mr. Simpson McCoy to drive cattle out to the Nueces River near where Cotulla now is, or to be more exact, seven miles above, at the Lago Cochina, or Hog Lake. About one week after arriving at this place the Indians made a raid in the vicinity of the ranch. This was about the middle of the summer. The people here were not aware of the presence of Indians in the country, and were not as much on the alert as they would have been otherwise. On the morning that this frontier episode which we are now about to narrate took place, J. W. Gardner went out very early in the morning on foot to hunt some horses which were to be used that day in their business of handling stock. The men at the ranch at this time were Simpson McCoy, A. F. Gardner, J. C. Gardner (brothers of J. W.), W. M. Wilkins, John De Spain, Joe Culp, Howell, and Burk—two last given names not remembered. Besides the men above mentioned, there were the families of McCoy, A. F. Gardner, John

De Spain, and Duncan Lemons, the latter being absent at the time. When young Gardner had left the ranch house about half a mile he discovered a man on horseback ahead of him and coming in his direction. He was a curious looking fellow, and Gardner, thinking it was an Indian, turned to run, but the man said in a loud voice in the Spanish language, "Parity! parity!" (stop! stop!). Thinking now by his language that it was a Mexican, and from having on a hat, Gardner stopped and looked back, but discovered that the supposed greaser was drawing an arrow from the quiver at his back, and had a bow in his other hand. Being now thoroughly frightened, the youth turned and fled, pursued by the Indian, who adjusted an arrow to the string as he ran, and on coming within range let it fly at the boy, who had gotten about seventy-five yards from the starting point. This first arrow wounded him in the left arm, and passing through also inflicted a wound in the side.

By this time twelve more Indians had shown themselves, all on horseback, and commenced closing around Gardner in a circle. Seeing there was no chance to get through them, he ran into a thick clump of persimmon bushes and stopped. One Indian rode up close to him and by signs demanded his hat. This was promptly obeyed, and then signs were made for him to run and the direction to go. Looking that way, the boy saw an Indian sitting on his horse whom he supposed was the chief from his head dress, which was profuse with feathers.

Up to this time the Indians had been very quiet, not wishing to alarm the men at the ranch, for no doubt they had investigated and knew the situation and were looking for the ranch horses, and also expecting to catch some settler alone and kill him, which now seemed to be the fate of Gardner. The young man had called several times for help, but was made to hush by the Indians after he was wounded and they caught up with him. The rest of the Indians stopped a short distance off, some with their horses' heads turned one way and some the other, leaving an open space between them of ten yards or more. Gardner, although badly wounded and bleeding, fully took in the situation at a glance, and made up his mind to make a desperate run through the open space between the Indians and try to gain the ranch.

In an attempt to carry out this plan he darted forth, at the same time calling loudly for help. The Indians followed on horseback and one of them shot him with an arrow, striking the right side under the shoulder blade, and then ran his horse over him, knocking him down. The boy arose and still attempted to flee, calling at the top of his voice for help. The men at the ranch heard the cries and soon McCoy, Culp, Howell, De Spain, and A. F. Gardner came to his assistance. The Indians, seeing the white men coming, no longer tried to conceal their presence, but commenced to yell and fire pistols at Gardner, and the one who ran over him with his horse came close and aiming a pistol at the back of his head at close range fired. The ball struck on the right side of the neck, barely missing the neck bone, and came out under the jaw. Many other shots were fired, but this was the only bullet that hit him. By this time the ranchmen were on the scene, and taking trees on the Indians commenced firing on them. When struck by the pistol ball young Gardner fell to his knees, but regained his feet and ran about thirty yards further, and then commenced staggering—the earth, trees, everything faded from sight, and he felt that he was going down. Deafness to some extent came on. The yelling of the Indians and firing of guns sounded far away, although they were so near. About this time he was jerked clear off the ground and he felt that he was going through space, tightly grasped by a strong arm. His brother, older than himself, had made his way to him in among the Indians, and taking him up under one arm and holding his gun in the other hand, made his way back, amid a shower of bullets and arrows, to the men who were fighting the battle. The nearest Indians to A. F. Gardner when he picked up his brother were within thirty steps, and although fired at repeatedly, he was not touched except in his clothing. He had no time to stop and shoot until he gained the position of McCoy, who was the leader of the frontiersmen.

The Indians soon gave up the fight and left, and the white men went back to the ranch with the wounded boy, who, besides the three wounds on the body, had seventeen holes in his clothing made by bullets and arrows. Seven of the settlers soon obtained horses and went in pursuit of the Indians and overtook them twenty miles from there on the Nueces River, and another fight took place, which wound up in a standoff. The guns and pistols of the white men were in poor condition, and some of them could not be made to shoot at all. During the fight Mr. Burk, before mentioned and given name not known, was hit in the top of the shoulder by a bullet, which penetrated the neck and lodged against the neck bone. The ball was cut out by J. A. Gardner with a pocket knife.

After the Indians left the place where they wounded Gardner they crossed the Nueces River and killed a Mexican who was herding horses for Jesse Laxson. The body was not found for some time after, as the Mexican made a run and was killed in the brush.

It took young Gardner six weeks to recover sufficiently to be carried home. A runner was sent at once to notify his mother when he was first wounded, and she started at once to go to him, but in the meantime there had been a great rain, and when she arrived at the Nueces River it was one and a half miles wide and her son was on the opposite side. Here she stayed several days and nights, but as it continued to rain there was no chance to cross. Men, however, swam back and forth every short while to let her know how her boy was, and when he was on the road to recovery and out of danger she went back home to take care of the smaller children. As this was below the mountains the country was low and flat and the waters ran off very slowly, sometimes remaining overflowed for several weeks at a time.

Mrs. Gardner died in 1882. Mr. Gardner still lives on the old homestead place, and has a good farm. He has been married twice. His first wife was Miss Jennie Holmes, sister to Mr. Sam Holmes, who was killed in his store at Utopia by a burglar several years ago. His second and present wife was a Miss Lucy Wingate.

JESSE LAWHON KILLED BY INDIANS.

1855.

The following detailed account of an Indian raid in Comal County and the killing of Jesse Lawhon I get from an old copy of the Seguin Mercury, published by R. W. Rainey, and bearing date of July 21, 1855. The account is furnished by the Hon. William E. Jones, and is as follows:

"Mr. Editor: It is a painful duty devolving upon me to communicate to you the particulars of an Indian outrage just committed in this neighborhood. On Saturday morning last Mr. Jesse Lawhon, who has been living with me for nearly two years in the capacity of overseer and manager of my farm and stock, went out accompanied by one of my negro men to drive up some oxen. About 11 o'clock the negro boy ran home afoot and barefooted and wet to the hips, and told me he feared that Mr. Lawhon had been killed by the Indians; that Mr. Lawhon and himself were riding together in search of cattle, and when descending a hill into the valley of one of the branches of Curry's Creek, near the foot of the mountains, they were attacked by five Indians who emerged from the bed of the creek and rushed upon them at full speed. They did not discover the Indians until within forty or fifty feet yards of them. Mr. Lawhon wheeled and ran in the opposite direction, while the boy dashed towards home. A large Indian, mounted on an American horse, pursued the boy. On arriving at the creek his horse plunged into it and fell. He jumped off and ran up the bank, when the Indian fired at him, the ball striking the ground beyond him. He then saw the other four pursuing Mr. Lawhon very closely on the hill, and then jumping into the channel of the creek, made his escape, and saw no more.

"He stated from the beginning that one of the party was a white man and the other four Indians, naked and armed with guns. The white man was dressed in dark clothes with a white hat. He saw most distinctly the one that pursued him. After he had shot at him, and being not more than twenty steps from him, he thinks he can not be mistaken in saying that he was an Indian and not a Mexican. The boy has often seen Indians in Texas and has mixed a good deal with Mexicans, and as his statement is thus far the only evidence of the character of the party which we have, I thought it more proper to give them more fully than I should have done under other circumstances.

"In the meantime the alarm had been given in the settlement and a party of men repaired to the scene, taking the boy along with them. On arriving there the Indians had left and Mr. Lawhon could not be seen, but the statements of the boy being all substantially confirmed by the horse tracks and other signs on the ground, they proceeded to search for him. His hat was found near the starting point; his saddle, with the skirts and stirrups cut off, was found on the trail of the retreating savages about one mile off. Then they found the trail of his horse from the place where he was attacked, and followed it until they found the dead body in a thicket. He had been shot through the heart with a large ball, and his body and face otherwise bruised and cut. A blunt arrow was found by his side. He was wholly unarmed and compelled to trust to his horse for safety, and the horse he rode, although large and strong, was not fleet. He had evidently made a desperate struggle to save his life.

"From the point at which he first discovered the Indians, he had turned westward in the direction opposite to that which they came, but soon being overtaken by his pursuers he wheeled by a short circuit, and leaping a large ravine, passed the place from which he had started, crossed the creek at the point from which the Indians had first issued, and ran up the hill on that side in the direction of home. Being overtaken again by his savage pursuers, he dashed back again into the creek valley lower down, and there, among the small thickets and brush, he seemed to have been surrounded and hemmed in in an angle made by the creek impassable here, it being a perpendicular bluff. Wheeling again, he burst through the Indians and regained the elevated ground, followed by the whole pack, and once more faced home. After running 400 or 500 yards across the heads of ravines he appeared to have been again overtaken, when in utter desperation he plunged down a bluff thirty feet high and nearly perpendicular, part of the distance his horse tearing up the rocks and crushing the brushwood in his downward course. At the foot of this bluff he landed in one end of a long thicket, and possibly might have escaped if he had abandoned his horse. None of the Indians followed him down the bluff, but the horse tracks indicated that a portion of them turned the point of the bluff and met him as he emerged from the point of the thicket and shot him.

"Mr. Lawhon was an industrious and most worthy citizen, sober, moral, and of unimpeachable integrity, universally esteemed by all neighbors and acquaintances. He was about 25 years of age, of manly person, and gave the highest promise of usefulness to his country and honor to his family. He left a wife and two small children, who were in his lifetime dependent on him for their maintenance."

The writer will say here that Judge Jones was a prominent man in West Texas in his time, was a good lawyer, and held the position of district judge with dignity and ability. He presided at the first term of district court ever held in Seguin, and the house is still standing where it convened. It is now known as the Rust property. When the grand jury was impaneled on this occasion, there being no jury room, they assembled under a live-oak tree north of where the court was being held, and there proceeded to business. The first bill they found was against one of the petit jurymen. This spot is now the property of G. W. L. Baker.

The Jones family were brave, patriotic people, and did their part when Texas needed brave men on her border, where Mexican and Indian depredations were so frequent.

When Capt. James H. Callahan organized an expedition into Mexico in 1855 to chastise a band of Indians who had taken refuge there after a raid in Texas, one of Judge Jones' sons (Willis) went with Callahan and was killed in the fight with Indians and Mexicans near Piedras Negras.

Capt. Frank Jones, a brave and gallant ranger captain, was also a son of Judge Jones, and was killed a few years ago in a desperate fight with Mexican robbers near the Rio Grande. Capt. Frank Jones was once a citizen of Uvalde.

1. Charles Meadows. 2. James Finch. 3. Walter Franks. 4. Albert Finch.
A GROUP OF TEXAS COWBOYS. ATASCOSA COUNTY.

EARLY SETTLERS OF ATASCOSA COUNTY.

Created in 1856.

During the days of Indian raids in the west and southwest, Atascosa County did not escape, and has her bloody chapter in the frontier history of Texas.

The county was created from Bexar in 1856, and named for the Atascosa Creek. The Navarros, Salinas, and others established stock ranches inside the present limits of the county at an early day, but were broken up during the Texas revolution and the Navarros moved further east and established ranches near the present town of Seguin, in Guadalupe County.

In 1853 permanent settlements began to be made, and by the time the county was organized quite a number of settlers were located, among whom were Justo Rodrigues, Judge J. S. Fern, Calvin Horton, the Askins, Yarbers, Tumlinsons, Brights, Slaughter, "Scotch" Jim Brown, Franks, Spears, James Lowe, Charles Hood, old man Terry, McCoys, and Dan Arnold.

The first county seat was called Navatasco, and located twelve miles above the present one of Pleasanton. The land on which it was built was donated by Col. Antonio Navarro and named by him. The first half, it will be observed, was part of his own name, and the last the middle half of the name of the county of Atascosa. The first court was held here in the spring of 1857. Jose Antonio Navarro was a grand and noble man. He was born in San Antonio in 1795. His father was from Corsica. In 1834-35 Antonio was land commissioner for Bexar district and De Witt's colony, a member of the convention of 1836, and one of the signers of the declaration of Texas independence. He loved Texas and her institutions, and was always ready to take up arms in her defense. He was in the unfortunate Santa Fe expedition as one of the commissioners, and was carried a captive with the balance of the Texans to Mexico, and there confined for years. Santa Anna hated him because he was of Spanish origin and a friend to Texas, and when the Americans of the expedition were released, kept him in chains in the strong castle of San Juan d'Ulloa. While he was chained down to a stone floor in the dark, damp dungeon, Santa Anna offered to release him if he would renounce all allegiance to Texas and become a citizen of Mexico. The grand old man, with his gray locks damp with dungeon mold, scornfully rejected it and taunted Santa Anna with his perfidy, saying: "I am a Navarro. No traitor's blood runs in my veins. You can only do your worst with me. I will die chained on this prison floor before I will for a moment entertain a thought of accepting your insulting proposition." When Herrera became President he released Colonel Navarro and allowed him to return to Texas. He died in San Antonio in 1870, loved and respected by all who knew him.

In 1858 a new county seat was laid off on the west bank of the Atascosa Creek and named Pleasanton, after General Pleasanton. John Bowen donated the land and named it. He was an intimate friend of the general. It is situated thirty-five miles south of San Antonio. Many settlers soon began to come in. The first one to settle and build a house was E. B. Thomas, who also put up the first store in the prospective town.

Soon after the town was laid off came Tobias Kelly, Calvin S. Turner, Judge Ferryman, J. H. Dorsey, Capt. John Tom, Rev. W. W. Whitley (Methodist preacher), John W. Stayton, and V. Weldon. The two last named were brothers-in-law and partners in the blacksmith business, and also young law practitioners. This same V. Weldon came prominently before the people a few years ago in the congressional race against W. H. Crain in the Eleventh District. Dr. Pyrtle came soon after, and also another blacksmith named Garlinghouse and a German named Slickum. The latter put up a saloon and grocery store, backed by his partner, Louis Zork, a capitalist of San Antonio. The first county officers were: County judge, or chief justice, as it was then called, Marcellus French; sheriff, James H. French; county and district clerk, Daniel I. Tobin, brother of Capt. William Tobin, of San Antonio; assessor and collector, Ed Walker. W. H. Long was elected to the last named position, but for some cause did not serve. The first commissioners were Eli J. O'Brien, Levi English, James Lowe, and J. A. Durand. The first district attorney was James Paul, and the first district judge E. F. Buckner. The first grand jury were William N. Gates, James McDonald, Jacob Ryman, Sexto Navarro, Gil Rodrigues, James Brown, Jesus Hernandez, James Feeder, Rich Hilburn, Isaac Cavender, Drake Gillelland, Thomas R. Bright, Tryon Fuller, Cullen Benson, and Calvin Horton. As far as is known, none of this first grand jury are now living. Calvin Horton died in February, 1898, at a very advanced age.

About 1859 the Rev. Uzzel came and settled, and also a mechanic named Carter.

In the Somerset settlement, near the Bexar County line, were the Ducks, Klemkes, Millers, and Louis families. At Gates Valley were the families of Rutledge, Gardner, Gates, and Williams. Of the Spanish families were the Navarros, Flores, and Tiriens. The Musgroves, Barksdales, and O'Briens lived in town. Below town, on Laparita Creek, lived Juan Palacia, Captain Fountain, Jesse Lott, the Cook boys, and Dan Brister. On the Laguilinas were the Marshalls, Odens, Newtons, Lease Harris, and Tom Kerr. On Galvan Creek were R. G. Long and the Cavenders.

Mr. Eli Johnson, one of the early settlers, and who still survives, came from Montgomery County, Alabama, to Texas in 1856, and first stopped in Guadalupe County, near Seguin, with the Sheffields and Olivers, but the same year came on out to Atascosa County with Ed Lyons and Jake Young. They settled on Salt Branch, seven miles from Pleasanton.

In 1860 Mr. Johnson joined a company of rangers commanded by Capt. Peter Tumlinson. They were stationed on the Sabinal River below the mountains. Their camp was attacked one night by Indians, who were beaten off without loss.

On the 22d of May, 1861, he was married to Miss Melissa Tucker. She died on the 16th of March, 1865. In 1869, on the 22d day of February, he married the widow Mary Adams, whose maiden name was Lawhon. She died April 22, 1892. He again married, and his present wife was Miss Mildred E. J. Hurley.

Mr. Johnson passed through all the exciting times when the country was raided by hostile Indians, and now lives on the Atascosa Creek three miles below town, where he is engaged in farming and stock raising. He has 200 acres of land in cultivation, and a fine artesian well near his residence flowing fifty gallons of water per minute; also a fine orchard of ten acres. No man stands higher in the estimation of the people who know him.

Mrs. Amanda Turner, also one of the early settlers, and widow of Calvin S. Turner, still lives in Pleasanton, near where they settled in 1858. She was the daughter of Ezekiel Tucker, and a native Texan. She was also one of the first settlers of Hays County, living there on the Little Blanco when very young. She was married to Calvin S. Turner in 1851, and moved to Guadalupe County, near Seguin. In 1858 she came to Pleasanton. Mrs. Turner had four brothers—Columbus, George, Napoleon, and Marion. The latter went off with the Walker expedition, and never returned. There were three sisters of them: Polly Ann married James C. Carr, now the rustling agent for the San Antonio *Express;* Melissa married Eli M. Johnson, of Pleasanton. Mrs. Turner kept hotel for many years and is known far and near. She has eight living children, four boys (Gilbert, Robert, Thomas, and Albert) and four girls (Sarah, Dallas, Anna, and Dora). Sarah married William Franks, who died at Eagle Pass; Dallas married William A. Purgason, now merchant at Amphion; Anna married Gus Clark, merchant of Pleasanton. Two have remained single—Gilbert and Dora.

Calvin S. Turner was the son of Maj. Wiliam Turner, who came to Texas in the early 40's. He was a soldier under General Jackson, and participated in the battles of Talladega, Tallahassee, Horseshoe Bend, and New Orleans. He was twice severely wounded. Calvin was a ranger under Jack Hays, and took part in the battle of Salado in 1842. In this fight he was wounded in the head by a musket ball. He served through the Mexican war of 1846 in the famous regiment of rangers commanded by Col. Jack Hays, his old captain. He took part in the battles of Monterey and Buena Vista.

After returning from Mexico he received a commission from Gov. P. H. Bell as second lieutenant in the ranger company commanded by Capt. Henry E. McCulloch. He engaged in stockraising after coming to Pleasanton, and also opened up a hotel. He served under Capt. John Tom part of the time as minuteman to repel Indian incursions, and participated in the Indian battle on San Miguel Creek. During one raid near town his Mexican herder was killed by Indians. During the civil war he was a lieutenant in Captain Maverick's company, Wood's regiment. He died in 1872, honored and respected by all who knew him.

In 1861 the Indians made one of the most daring and extensive raids ever known in Atascosa County. They were in large force and scattered all over the country, killed fourteen people, wounded many more, and carried off a large lot of horses. They did not confine this raid to Atascosa alone, but spread death and destruction on their trail as they went back to the mountains. They killed "Mustang" Moore where the station of that name is now, on the International Railroad; James Winters on Black Creek, and Murray the tax assessor of Bandera County. At Pleasanton they killed William Herndon and a negro belonging to Marcellus French, and wounded Alexander Anderson and Eli O'Brien. These last named were all out from one to two miles from town, hunting stock, etc. Napoleon Tucker was with Herndon, and being on a fast horse made his escape, at the earnest solicitation of Herndon, and brought the news of the presence of the Indians to the people in town. They first made their appearance in the settlement above, and Ed Lyons sent Alex Anderson on a fast horse to notify the people at Pleasanton. The Indians came upon him a mile from town and ran him in, shooting an arrow into his back. News now came fast, and there was great excitement. One of French's negroes was killed and another captured. Men continued to run in wounded, or their faces badly torn by limbs in their desperate flight from the Comanches.

One of the most remarkable escapes was that of Eli O'Brien. He had gone out on that morning to hunt stock without gun or pistol, and had been warned by a neighbor, William Dillard, that it was not safe to go unarmed. His reply was, "There are no Indians in the country," and he went on. When about two miles from town he came upon a band of Indians in a blackjack and postoak timbered country. The Indians were sitting on their horses under the trees, and as some of them had on hats which they had procured from men they had killed or chased, O'Brien thought they were cowmen. When they started towards him yelling he cried with a loud voice, "No use, boys; you can't scare me." When they came out from among the trees so that he could see them plainly and began to string their bows, the settler at once realized who they were and the great danger which now confronted him. Wheeling his horse, he started at once towards home with them in pursuit. His horse was a good one and they failed to run on him at once, and so divided their forces, running parallel with and to the right and left of him. He watched both sides closely and saw that he was gaining some on them, but failed to look behind until he felt the wind of an arrow near his head. Turning, he saw an Indian close behind him, and at the same time got an arrow in the back. His only weapon was a butcher knife, which he now drew when he saw that the Indian was going to get up beside him. Two more arrows, however, came in quick succession and fastened in his back. The Comanche now yelled loud, and making a sudden spurt came alongside of him and reached to pull the stricken man from his horse. O'Brien, with the strength of despair, made a stab at the Indian with his knife, who barely interposed his shield in time to catch the blow, and then stopped. The town was near, but the other Indians still tried to ride around the white man and turn him back. A most serious difficulty now came in the way, which caused the white man's heart to sink within him, and the Indians to yell loudly and urge their horses to greater speed. The cause of this was a deep and wide gully directly in front, ten feet across and the same in depth. There was no way to turn to avoid it without being cut off. I will say here that this is the reason that Indians in chasing a man run to the right and left of him, so if any obstruction comes in the way and he is bound to turn, they can get him either way he may turn. One or more on good horses run straight behind so that he can not double on his track and dodge them or gain time. In this case the only chance for O'Brien was for his horse to safely leap the gully. If he fell the man was gone. It will be understood that all of this was done very quickly. There was no intermission in the speed of the horses; all were doing their utmost, and the two miles from the place where the chase commenced had been passed over in a few minutes.

When the Indians perceived that the white man was going to attempt the leap they yelled louder and fiercer, so as to terrify the horse and make him overdo himself or stumble or leap too quick, or anything which would be in their favor. When the brink was reached and the spring had to be made that meant life or death to him, O'Brien held his bridle lightly and let his horse jump naturally making no extra motions with hands or feet, and the gallant animal passed safely over and had several feet to spare. No Indian attempted to follow, and all went back and gave up the chase. O'Brien was hardly able to sit on his horse, and was swaying to and fro in the saddle when his horse dashed into the assembled and excited crowd in town. When he passed William Dillard's house, who had given him the advice that morning, and who knew from his speed that Indians had been after him, he exclaimed, "What's your hurry, O'Brien? There are no Indians in the country." The arrows were removed, the spikes cut out, and the wounded man recovered. The horse was kept in the O'Brien family as long as he lived, and tenderly cared for.

Eli Johnson and others went out and brought in the body of Herndon. The citizens, not thinking they were able to cope with such a body of Indians alone, sent a runner east for help, and 200 men came from Gonzales and Guadalupe counties, under command of Captain Rabb. Eli Johnson with a minute company, aided in scouting, and it was perceived that the Indians had left the country and gone back to the mountains, kiling people and capturing stock as they went. They were not to get back, however, without a battle. Big Foot Wallace, with the Hondo and Sabinal settlers, defeated them in a battle in the mountains and recaptured 200 head of horses from them.

Judge A. G. Martin, who still lives at Pleasanton, was one of the early settlers of Atascosa County. He came to San Antonio in 1849, and was with the first train that ever went through to El Paso. The same year he went to Seguin and located there. When he arrived at Seguin a big Methodist meeting was in progress, and this fact was the real cause of his settling there. He stopped to attend it, and liked the people and country so well he concluded to make his home there. For a while he worked in the county clerk's office under Paris Smith, and in 1854 was elected district clerk over John F. Gordon. He came to Atascosa County in 1856, built a house, and then went back for his family and returned in 1857.

In 1864 he was elected county clerk, but during the days of reconstruction he was removed and another put in his place. He was disfranchised, not allowed a vote, and as the judge expressed it, "Not given a negro's chance." When restored to citizenship, he was elected district and county clerk in 1873. He held this office seventeen years, and was elected county judge and held one term, refusing to be a candidate for office any more. The present county jail was built during his term of county judge and under his supervision. It is one of the best jails in the west. It is built of red sandstone and brick, the stone being on the inside. It is two stories, commodious, and with strong iron cages. The first jail here was a hole in the ground, with some roofing overhead to keep the rain out. It was twelve feet deep, and was covered with a raised trap door and fastened with a padlock. The writer was here in 1872, and saw the sheriff put a man in this hole.

Judge Martin has four sons. The eldest, J. L. Martin, was born at Seguin. By profession he is a lawyer, and at one time was county judge of Kinney County. He served in the Twenty-fourth Legislature, and in 1897 was appointed district judge of the Thirty-eighth Judicial District on the death of Judge Eugene Archer, who held that position at the time of his death. When the next election came off he was elected to that position, and is the present incumbent.

The second son, H. G., was elected district clerk of Atascosa County. The third son, John B., is a printer by trade. The youngest, J. R. G., at this time is in Louisville, Ky., studying medicine.

A. M. Avant, present sheriff of the county, was born and raised in Gonzales County. He came here in 1886, and is now serving his second term as sheriff.

The present county judge, N. R. Wallace, better known to his friends as Jack Wallace, came to Seguin, Guadalupe County, in 1876, and did a banking business there. Here he married Miss John Irvin, niece of the old San Jacinto veteran, Capt. John Tom. She has a sister named Tom, so you see their two names make that of their beloved uncle, John Tom, for whom they were named. They are called Johnnie and Tommy by their intimate friends. Judge Wallace came to Pleasanton in 1880, and was elected sheriff in 1883. He was elected county judge in 1894, and still holds that position.

Judge W. H. Smith came to Pleasanton in 1867, and was elected to the office of presiding justice. He was then elected county judge, and held that position eight years. Was then tax assessor for one term. Held the office then of treasurer. Is now practicing law, and is the oldest male resident of the city.

MRS. R. D. KENNEDY.

Born in 1856.

At this writing (1889), in Sabinal Canyon, Bandera County, there lives the daughter of a famous Texas ranger who followed the fortunes of Jack Hays on the Texas border and stood by his side during many bloody encounters, both with hostile Indians and treacherous Mexicans. This daughter is Mrs. R. D. Kennedy, wife of Mr. Houston J. Kennedy, and daughter of George Jefferson Neill, who died in Travis County a few years back. Her grandfather was the Colonel Neill who commanded the artillery at the storming of San Antonio in 1835. He bombarded the Alamo to draw the attention of the Mexicans from Col. Ben Milam, who was entering the town on the other side with a storming party. Mrs. Kennedy was born in Comal County, Texas, in 1856, on York's Creek, near the Guadalupe and Hays County line. She was married to Mr. Kennedy at Seguin, Guadalupe County, in 1875, Rev. Buck Harris performing the ceremony.

Her father, George Neill, while a member of a ranging company commanded by Jack Hays, participated in the famous Indian fight at Bandera Pass. The rangers on that occasion were ambushed in the pass, and a most desperate fight took place, in which five of the rangers were killed and some wounded. Among the latter was Uncle Ben Highsmith, the old San Jacinto veteran who still survives, and now lives in Blanket Creek Canyon, Bandera County. A more detailed account of this fight is given in the sketch of Mr. Highsmith. Mr. Neill was also in the charge on the battery at the Hondo, when the Mexicans halted to fight the pursuing Texans after their disastrous defeat at Salado. It was Jack Hays and his rangers who made this charge and captured the cannon, shooting the gunners down with their pistols.

Mr. Houston Kennedy, while not being a noted Indian fighter, was a cowboy in his young days, and made four trips with cattle up the Chisholm trail to Kansas, when that route was infested with hostile Indians, and has had many narrow escapes.

While on one of these trips, after they had crossed the Texas line and entered the Indian Territory, ten cattle herds were encamped near each other on Pond Creek. This traveling of the herds close together on the trail was for mutual protection, and accounts for so many herds getting through to Kansas without being captured by the hostiles. This number of herds generally had more than 100 cowboys with them, most all of them being brave and good Indian fighters. The bands of roving Comanches and Kiowas would not dare face a band of Texas cowboys like this, but would wait for an opportunity to catch two or three together on the back track after lost horses, or ahead hunting water, or anything else that would carry them away from the protection of their comrades. In charge of one of these herds at Pond Creek was Mr. Ed Chambers, an old cattle boss. The trail forked here where his herd had stopped, and he in company with two cowboys went a considerable distance ahead to see which trail the majority of the herds were following. The country was mostly prairie, with depressions here and there deep enough for men to conceal themselves on horseback. Suddenly out of one of these draws in front of them rode ten Indians. The two cowboys wheeled their horses and started back rapidly, pulling their sixshooters as they ran. Chambers, thinking they were friendly Creeks or Caddoes on a buffalo hunt, galloped slow, telling the boys to stop, the Indians would not hurt them. In a short time the Comanches, for such they were, came close upon them, yelling and shooting. These Comanches were on a buffalo hunt, and had long-range and large bore guns. Chambers fell from his horse the first fire, shot through the body, and some of the band stopped and soon finished him and scalped him. The other two men, seeing they could not assist their dead companion, put their horses to their utmost speed to make their own escape. One Indian came up with the hindmost of the fleeing men and almost yelled in his face. The cowboy had his pistol ready and promptly shot him from his horse, and the balance turned back. When the two cowboys arrived in camp and told the news a detail of one man from each herd was sent back after the body of the unfortunate boss. From the Perkins herd, the one to which Mr. Kennedy belonged, they sent J. C. Neill, brother-in-law of Mr. Kennedy. When the party arrived at the scene of the chase the Indians were gone, and had carried off the body of the one the cowboy had shot. It seems that the Indian was not quite dead, as a place was found where the others had rolled him around on the ground and had probed his wound with coarse straws of prairie grass, the blood on the straws showing they had probed six inches. On examining the body of Chambers it as found that the Indians had taken neither his watch nor money. The body was taken back and buried on Pond Creek, where the herds were camped. This was about twenty-five miles from Caldwell, on the Kansas line.

Mr. Kennedy also tells of many exciting buffalo chases on these trips.

The writer has had some experience on the frontier as a ranger, and learned that it is best when a few men have to fight a superior force of Indians, unless they can get to a good cover, to make as long a run as possible, in order to scatter the Indians in pursuit and fight them in detail, as they do not all ride horses of the same speed. In this way they only fight the Indians on the fastest horses. If a stand is made without cover, they all get around him.

Mr. Kennedy was born in Jackson Parish, La., in 1847, and came to Texas in 1869. He is on his mother's side, who was a Perkins, related to Gen. Joseph Warren, who was killed at the battle of Bunker Hill at the commencement of the revolutionary war. It may not be generally known to Masons that General Warren was at the time of his death grand master of all Masons in America. In regard to this I quote from "History of Freemasonry in America," by Z. A. Davis, page 284, published in 1846:

"In the year 1773 a commission was received from the right honorable and most worshipful Patrick, earl of Dumfries, grand master of Masons in Scotland, dated March 3, 1772, appointing the right worshipful Joseph Warren, Esq., grand master of Masons for the continent of America.

"In 1775 the meetings of the Grand Lodge were suspended by the town of Boston becoming a garrison.

"At the battle of Bunker Hill, on the 27th of June, this year, Masonry and the Grand Lodge met with a heavy loss in the death of Grand Master Warren, who was slain contending for the liberation of his country.

"Soon after the evacuation of Boston by the British army, and previous to any regular communication, the brethren, influenced by a pious regard to the memory of the late grand master, were induced to search for his body, which had been rudely and indiscriminately buried on the field of slaughter. They accordingly repaired to the place, and by the direction of a person who was on the ground at the time of the burial, a spot was found where the earth had been recently turned up. Upon moving the turf and opening the grave, which was on the brow of a hill and adjacent to a small cluster of sprigs, the remains were discovered in a mangled condition, but were easily ascertained by an artificial tooth, and being decently raised, were conveyed to the State house in Boston, from whence, by a large and respectable number of brethren, with the late grand officers attending in procession, they were carried to the stone chapel, where an animated eulogy was delivered by Brother Perez Morton. The body was then deposited in the silent vault without a sculptured stone to mark the spot, but as the whole earth is the sepulchre of illustrious men, his fame, his glorious actions, are engraven on the tablet of universal remembrance, and will survive marble monuments or local inscriptions.

"In 1777, March 8th, the brethren, who had been dispersed in consequence of the war, being now generally collected, they assembled to take into consideration the state of Masonry. Being deprived of their chief by the melancholy death of their grand master, as before mentioned, after due consideration they proceeded to the formation of a Grand Lodge, and elected and installed the Most Worshipful Joseph Webb their grand master."

JOSEPH M. VAN PELT.

Born in Texas in 1857.

Although not an old man when the writer interviewed Mr. Van Pelt in 1897, still he was one of the early settlers and pioneers of Frio Canyon. He was born at Pririe Lea, Caldwell County, Texas, on the last day of May, 1857. This is a noted year to old Texans, and is still called by some of them the "starving year." This was the year of the great drought, when no crops were made, and many families went without bread for weeks at a time. The writer well remembers that hard year, and what a struggle it was to get bread. To get meal was out of the question after the supply which was on hand at the first part of that year was exhausted. There was no flour or wheat in the country, and there were no railroads in Texas to bring supplies. Ox teams had to be sent to Port Lavaca after flour, and it took a long time to make the round trip of 500 miles or more. The struggle was to keep from starving until the wagons could get back. This has reference to the upper San Marcos and Guadalupe country. People living further east did not have quite as hard a time.

One can imagine what rejoicing there was in the settlement when the flour wagons, as we called them, arrived. The flour came high, $18 per barrel. The neighbors in a settlement would raise money enough to load several wagons with flour at the port, and some of those who had large wagons and five or six yoke of oxen would make the trip, and they were paid so much per barrel for hauling. If my memory is not at fault, it quit raining about the last days of February, and none fell again until the 5th day of August. Creeks dried up, there was no grass, and cattle died by the thousands all over the country. We could not even get beef to eat or milk to drink.

The Van Pelts moved to Frio Canyon in August, 1860, when Joe was about 3 years old. That was at the time of the great flood in the Frio River, and the house in which the Van Pelts spent their first night in the canyon was surrounded by water. When morning came there was no chance to get out to high ground, and they were compelled to remain until the water fell. Fortunately the house was not carried away. One of the first things Joe became familiar with as he grew up was moccasin tracks and the almost constant alarm of Indians in the settlement. He went on many scouts after Indians when quite young, and grazed danger many times. Indian tracks were often seen in the field where they stole potatoes and roasting ears.

In 1878 Joe went to Uvalde with his father, Capt. Malcom Van Pelt, and on their return had quite an exciting time with a band of Indians. They first passed a drove of sheep belonging to W. B. Knox, being controlled by Davy Brown and herded by a Mexican. The Van Pelts stopped and got a drink of water from the herder, who gave it to them out of his canteen. About one mile from where they got the water was a dense thicket with mesquite brush around it. When opposite the thicket, but out of gunshot of it, three Indians showed themselves in the open brush on the opposite side to them and commenced yelling. Now, Joe was young and not much afraid of Indians, as he had said many times, and really wanted to have a fight with them. As soon as he saw the painted and feather-bedecked hostiles he jumped from his horse and pulled his Winchester to make his threat good of being change for any reasonable number of Comanches. The old captain, however, had fought Indians before, so pulling his gun and making ready to shoot, told his son to get back on his horse. One of the Indians, who rode a bald-face horse, was very conspicuous in his endeavors by yelling and other demonstrations to induce the white men to run to the thicket. To run was the very thing the captain intended to do as soon as he got Joe mounted again, but not to the thicket. He feared more Indians were around, and being on good horses, thought best to make a run for it down the road and see what it would develop. When Joe got on his horse he made for the thicket near by, but his father told him not to go in there, but to hit the road and warm up that pony behind with his quirt. The young frontiersman acted on this advice and soon a lively chase commenced, the old man bringing up the rear with his carbine ready to shoot if crowded too close. The captain told his son to dismount in the big thicket about a mile ahead. When Joe arrived at the place designated to make a stand he rushed in, but could not find a place that looked thick enough to stop in. In fact it seemed to him at the time that a jack jabbit could not find cover there. It seemed to Joe that he could hear a score of Indians coming at full speed and yelling at his heels, but in fact the hostiles had turned back, yelling defiance, and no one but the old man was crowding him. Not finding a place suitable in the thicket to dismount, he kept on, and he and the captain arrived at home safely. It was found out afterwards that the Indians were ten in number, and seeing the two white men coming down the road, seven of them went into the thicket first mentioned in ambush, and the three were to give them a scare from the opposite side of the road and run them into the ambuscade. Shortly after the chase the Indians all got together and went to where the Mexican herder was who a few minutes before had given the Van Pelts water, and killed him. They were seen shortly after by another man, and there were ten of them together, and the tracks of the seven were found in the thicket.

This same night Silas Webster, a merchant of Uvalde, was killed in his store for his money, but no clew to the murderers could be found.

Shortly after this incident the Indians crossed Frio Canyon not far from where Joe Van Pelt now lives, and went on towards Dry Frio west, having a negro boy and a little white girl captive. Joe was one of the men who followed these Indians, but his horse gave out and he and several others had to return. The Indians were overtaken by another party and the captives rescued.

About 1880 the Indians made their last raid in the vicinity of the Van Pelt settlement. They were followed by men from Frio and Sabinal under command of Henry Patterson. The Indians made a wide circle back to the Rio Grande and killed sixteen people. They killed a Mexican herder in the employ of Joe Ney shortly after leaving Sabinal Canyon. He made a desperate fight with them, and killed one Indian. They scalped him, pulled off one shoe, left him face downward. The body was warm when Patterson's men arrived on the scene. Both arms of the unfortunate man were also broken.

Two men were killed at Crouch's ranch a short time before the trailers came. One of the slain men had bled a great deal. They had six fine sheep tied in a hack, which the Indians also killed and cut the tongue out of one of them. Another man was killed on the Nueces River near Westfall's ranch. He had made a fight and also killed one Indian, and they did the same to him as they did to Ney's herder,—they pulled off both his boots and one sock, and left him on his face, scalped. The trailers were out of provisions, and coming upon a herd of sheep the captain told Joe Van Pelt to shoot one of them for the men to eat. Here Joe made quite a remarkable shot. His ball hit one sheep behind the ear, and then it went on fifty yards and struck another behind the shoulder, and killed both of them. Most of the people killed on this raid were Mexicans.

The pursuit was kept up to the Rio Grande, the boundary line of Texas and Mexico, and Captain Patterson intended crossing and continuing the pursuit, as he had been joined by some United States soldiers, but there was a heavy rise in the river, and they had to return without sighting the Indians.

Mrs. Melod Van Pelt, wife of Joseph M. Van Pelt, was born in Taylor County, Virginia, and was the daughter of Richard Johnston, who was a cousin to the famous confederate leader, Gen. Joseph E. Johnston. She is also a niece of Dr. Johnston of San Antonio, and by marriage of some of her family connections related to Gen. U. S. Grant. Mrs. Van Pelt has literary talent, and is now completing a book entitled "Truth Stranger and Sadder Than Fiction," which will no doubt be very interesting when completed. Mr. Van Pelt has a beautiful home, situated on the high bluff of the Frio River, whose sparkling and leaping waters are a relief to the eye by day and music to the ear at night. East and west are the mountains clothed in living green by the dense cedar brakes which start from the valley and climb the rugged, rocky heights to the crest of the highest peaks. Here for fifteen years Mrs. Van Pelt has lived and gathered many curiosities from the hills and caves around, and with them beautified and bedecked her home with artistic eye and hand. It was here in this far-away frontier valley, so unlike the old Virginia home, with these strange surroundings that the outlines of her book developed, which under other circumstances might never have been created or written.

INDIAN FIGHT ON DOVE CREEK.

1865.

In the winter of 1864 a large band of Kickapoo Indians left their reservation on the Kaw River in Kansas, and with all of their women, children, and worldly possessions started for Old Mexico. The reason of their exodus from Kansas was the fact that they had been called on to take sides in the great civil war which had been raging for some time between the Northern and Southern States. It seems that some of them had enlisted and done some service for the cause of the Union, for they were well armed and munitioned with government guns and knew how to use them, as the sequel will show, in their desperate battle with the Texans at Dove Creek. They crossed the Indian Territory all right, but when the border of Texas was reached their large force of several hundred warriors, besides their women and children, caused uneasiness among the scattered frontiersmen on the Texas side of Red River. Runners were sent far and near to notify the settlers of their approach, and men were collected to dispute their passage through Texas. The Kickapoos, not wishing a collision with the Texans, kept far out on the border after crossing the line, intending to skirt along the edge of the "Staked Plains," and thus make their way safely into Mexico. They crossed Red River about where Clay County now is, and pushed on through the "Panhandle," crossing the Clear fork and main Brazos above all forts and settlements. Texas scouts, however, followed their trail, while men were collecting further east. The place where the different companies formed a junction was at the head of Yellow Wolf Creek, under the following captains: From Bosque County, Capt. Sam Barnes; Hamilton County, Capt. ————; Comanche County, Capt. James Cunningham; Erath County, Capt. Gullentine; Brown County, Capt. Matron; Palo Pinto County, Capt. Totton. Capt. Henry Fossett also commanded a company, and some say he was in command of the whole force of near 500 men, part of whom were Confederate soldiers. Others say that Totton was in command. James Mulkey and Brooks Lee were the main scouts.

The trail of the Indians was taken up at Yellow Wolf by the main force, and as it was large and plain, was followed rapidly.

The Indians were overtaken at the mouth of Dove Creek, near its confluence with the Concho River, in the present limits of Tom Green County, Fort Concho at that time being not located or an abandoned post, on account of the civil war. The Texans halted about three miles from the Indian encampment and sent scouts to find out the situation. The scouts returned and reported the Indians well posted in the timber and thickets bordering Dove Creek and just above its mouth. They also said it would cost the lives of many men to rout them, and they believed also that they were friendly Indians. The officers in command, however, seemed determined to hazard a battle, come what might. The looked upon the Kickapoos as armed invaders and enemies, even if they were from a Kansas reservation, but they likely did not know of this fact at the time, for some thought they were Sioux under old Red Cloud. Be that as it may, on the 8th of January, 1865, the whites moved forward to the attack, some no doubt thinking the day was a good omen, as it was the anniversary of General Jackson's great victory at New Orleans. The Indians were watching all the movements, and remained perfectly quiet until the Texans began to enter their position, when the warwhoop was raised and a deadly fire opened upon them. A fierce charge was now made on the part of the whites, many of whom dismounted and tied their horses so as to better get at the Indians through the brush. After a short and sharp struggle the Indians gave way and retreated with great loss. The camp and all loose horses were captured. But at this moment the Texans made a sad and fatal mistake, the same that Captain Bryant made many years before, and which has gone down in history as "Bryant's defeat." Those that were still mounted left their horses and all commenced to pillage the camp, thinking the Indians were utterly routed and scattered. The Kickapoos rallied, however, and seeing the unorganized condition of their enemies, turned back and fiercely charged them, aiming their rifles with fatal precision. The white men were now at great disadvantage,—dismounted, badly scattered, and many with empty guns. The Indians came among them in great numbers and a panic ensued. Frightened and wounded horses were running in every direction, and many of the men were unable to mount. Ropes and bridle reins snapped on all sides, and the liberated horses galloped over friend and foe. In vain brave men tried to stay the tide and bring order out of chaos and confusion, but in vain; all were carried along by the impact of the general stampede. Those who could mount their horses as a general thing put spurs to them and left the field. But many brave and heroic deeds were performed—friends stayed with wounded friends and helped them to mount horses, or died with them in the bloody fight. The Kickapoos mounted all the horses they could lay hands upon and pursued the white men for some distance, and many were killed and wounded. The loss of the white men can not be accurately ascertained. The following names of some of the slain have been obtained: Don Cox and Tom Parker of Comanche County; Capt. Sam Barnes of Brown County; and from other counties, Albert Everett, Noah Gibbs, John Stein, James Mabry, Joseph Byars, William Epps, Capt. Gullentine and his son. Among the wounded were, W. W. Pierce, Captain Maton, John Brown, and Emms Adams. After the pursuit was over the white men scattered back to their various homes and the Indians went on to Mexico. It is a pity that all the long-haired, painted scoundrels could not have been killed before they crossed the Rio Grande, for the writer knows that these same Kickapoos raided Texas from their secure retreat in the Santa Rosa mountains in Mexico, and caused untold suffering along our border for many years.

A FRONTIER TRAGEDY.

1865.

In 1865 occurred one of those sad frontier tragedies, where the settlers were unable to sustain themselves in an Indian battle, and wives and mothers were made to mourn for loved ones who never returned except as mangled or inanimate bodies. This noted fight occurred on the 4th day of July in the above named year, near the mouth of the Leona River, in Frio County. The settlers in the vicinity at that time were the Martins, Odens, Franks, Bennetts, Hays, Parks, Levi English, and Ed Burleson. These were all in what was known as the Martin settlement.

On the morning in question Ed. Burleson went out a short distance from his ranch to drive up some horses. He was unarmed and riding a slow horse. Suddenly and very unexpectedly to him he was attacked by two Indians who ran him very close, one on foot and the other mounted. The one on foot outran the horseman and came near catching Burleson, but he ran through a thicket, and coming out on the side next his ranch arrived there safely. Quite a lot of people had collected at his house—men, women and children—to celebrate the Fourth and wind up with a dance at night. Ere the sun went down on that day, however, the festivities were changed to mourning. Instead of the gay tramp and joyous laughter of the dancers, wailing and the slow tread of a funeral procession were heard. Excitement ran high when Burleson dashed in and gave the alarm. Most of the men present mounted in hot haste to go in pursuit, and others were notified.

When all the men had congregated who could be gotten together on short notice they numbered eleven, and were as follows: Levi English, L. A. Franks, G. W. Daugherty, Ed. Burleson, W. C. Bell, Frank Williams, Dean Oden, Bud English, Dan Williams, John Berry, and — Aikens. Levi English being the oldest man in the party, and experienced to some extent in fighting Indians, was chosen captain.

When the main trail was struck the Indians were found to be

in large force and going down the Leona River. They crossed this stream near Bennett's ranch, four miles from Burleson's. They then went out into the open prairie in front of Martin's ranch, ten miles further on. The settlers first came in sight of them two miles off, but they went down into a valley and were lost to sight for some time. Suddenly, however, they came in view again, not more than 200 yards away. They were thirty-six in number and mounted two and two on a horse. The Indians now discovered the white men for the first time, and at once commenced a retreat. The white men were all brave frontiersmen, and made a reckless and impetuous charge and commenced firing too soon. The Indians ran nearly a mile, and thinking likely they had well nigh drawn the fire of the settlers, checked their flight at a lone tree at a signal from their chief, and each Indian who was mounted behind another jumped to the ground and came back at a charge, and for the first time commenced shooting. The mounted ones circled to right and left and sent a shower of arrows and bullets. Some of the Indians went entirely around the white men, and a desperate battle at close quarters ensued. The red men had the advantage of the whites in point of numbers and shots. The latter having nearly exhausted their shots at long range, had no time to reload a cap and ball pistol or gun in such a fight as was now being inaugurated. Captain English in vain gave orders during the mad charge, trying to hold the boys back and keep them out of the deadly circle in which they finally went. Dan Williams was the first man killed, and when he fell from his horse was at once surrounded by the Indians. English now rallied the men together and charged to the body of Williams, and after a hot fight drove them back, but in so doing fired their last loads. The Indians were quick to see this, and came back at them again, and a retreat was ordered. Frank Williams, brother to Dan, now dismounted by the side of his dying brother and asked if there was anything he could do for him, and expressed a willingness to stay with him. "No," said the stricken man, handing Frank his pistol; "take this and do the best you can. I am killed—can not live ten minutes. Save yourself." The men were even now wheeling their horses and leaving the ground, and Frank only mounted and left when the Indians were close upon him. The Comanches came after them, yelling furiously, and a panic ensued. Dean Oden was the next one to fall a victim. His horse was wounded and began to pitch, and the Indians were soon upon him. He dismounted and was wounded in the leg, and attempted to remount again, but was wounded six times more in the breast and back, as the Indians were on all sides of him. Aus. Franks was near him trying to force his way out, and the last he saw of Oden he was down to his knees and his horse gone. The next and last man killed was Bud English, son of the captain. His father stayed by his body until all hope was gone and all the men scattering away. The Indians pursued with a fierce vengeance, mixing in with the whites, and many personal combats took place, the settlers striking at the Indians with their unloaded guns and pistols. In this wild flight all the balance of the men were wounded except Franks, Berry, and Frank Williams. Captain English was badly wounded in the side with an arrow; G. W. Daugherty was hit in the leg with an arrow; Ed. Burleson in the leg with an arrow; Aikens in the breast with an arrow, and W. C. Bell in the side with an arrow.

In this wounded and scattered condition the men went back to the ranch and told the news of their sad defeat, and the long, piercing wail of women was again heard on this far-away frontier. Other men were collected and returned to the battleground to bring away the dead, led by those who participated but escaped unhurt. The three bodies lay within 100 yards of each other and were badly mutilated. The Indians carried away their dead, how many was not known, but supposed to be but few, on account of the reckless firing of the men at the commencement of the fight. Bud English was killed by a bullet in the breast, and there was also one arrow or lance wound in the breast. The head of Dan Williams was nearly severed from the body, necessitating a close wrapping in a blanket to keep the members together while being carried back. Oden and Williams were brothers-in-law, and were both buried in the same box. Eight out of the eleven men were either killed or wounded.

Aus. Franks, who gave the writer the particulars of this fight, now lives in Atascosa County.

Dean Oden was born on Mill Creek, in Guadalupe County, and was known to the writer years ago, but he never knew what became of him until getting the particulars of this Indian battle.

FIGHT WITH INDIANS AND RANGERS.

1870.

In 1897, in Frio Canyon the writer interviewed Mr. B. F. Payne, an ex-ranger, who had some interesting experience while serving on the frontier. Mr. Payne is a native Texas boy, and was raised near Austin, Travis County, being born there in the early 50's.

In 1866 he, in company with his father and several others, among whom was William Rutledge, went out on a cow hunt. At this time the Indians still raided the western portion of the counties bordering Travis on the west and northwest, and cowhunters going in that direction generally went armed, especially with revolvers. One day about noon, before the cow-hunt terminated, the party came upon a band of Indians who had stopped in the bed of a dry ravine and were eating dinner. The white men, who were on the high ground above the Indians, were not discovered by them, and they kept on with their repast, which consisted of meat of some animal, wild or domestic, slaughtered by them. The white men at once made preparations to attack them, and drew back under cover and held a council. They did not wish to let the Indians escape without a fight, but Mr. Payne was concerned about his young son Frank, for fear that he would get hurt. The boy was about 12 years of age, and was not carrying any arms. The elder Payne finally told his son to remain where he was and not to leave the spot until the fight was over and some of them came back to him.

These arrangements being now agreed upon, the white men advanced and charged upon the Indians, who at once mounted their horses and fled. The whole party of whites and Indians were soon lost to sight of Frank across a low range of hills. The cowmen, being on good horses, soon came within pistol range and the fight commenced, the Indians giving shot for shot and warwhooping as they went. Young Payne, from his position in the rear, heard all this commotion and became very anxious to witness the combat. Accordingly he put spurs to his pony and galloped to the top of the ridge where he could have a plain view, not intending to go any further. When he arrived at the crest of the elevation, however, he met a loose and terror-stricken horse coming out of the fight, and the boy's horse took fright at him and ran away, and instead of going back the way he came, ran straight ahead and followed in the wake of the Indians. The white men were scattered and one of them unhorsed, and the boy soon passed all of them and ran into the Indians. Mr. Payne saw the peril his son was in, and when he passed called out, "Hold up, Frank; hold up!" That was what the boy was trying to do with all of his strength, but the pony had the bit in his mouth and was beyond control. The Indians evidently thought this a daring and intentional charge on the part of the young white brave, and, yelling loudly, prepared to fight him. The boy passed some of the Indians, who shot at him and threw lances from all sides. Finally a bullet, arrow or lance cut his bridle rein in two. His horse then increased his speed and soon got clear of all the Indians. Frank now took the rope from the horn of his saddle, and making a loop leaned forward and secured it over the nose of his horse, finally stopping him.

In the meantime the elder Payne had followed his son as fast as he could in order to try and save him, and fought his way through the Indians, assisted by some of his companions. He succeeded in killing some of the Indians and scattering the balance. Young Frank made a circle and came back. Besides having his bridle reins severed, two arrows were sticking in his saddle. Only one of the cow-hunters was wounded. He was able to ride, and when his horse was brought back he mounted, and the party arrived at home without further incident.

In 1870 Frank Payne, although still young, joined a company of rangers commanded by Capt. Rufus Perry. The captain was an old Jack Hays ranger, and was the same who had such a fearful experience in Nueces Canyon when he and Kit Ackland were so severely wounded. Captain Perry's company was stationed at a place called Little Red River, near Camp San Saba Springs. While there the rangers received information that a large body of Indians were raiding below and had carried off a drove of horses near Dripping Springs, in Hays County. The rangers lost no time, and were soon at the scene of the raid and on the trail of the redskins. The trail was discovered near Shovel Mountain, and was so plain and fresh the rangers knew the Indians could not be far ahead, and dashed on as rapidly as the nature of the ground would admit, all eager for the battle. When nearing the base of the mountain a white man was discovered running at full speed and being pursued by Indians. The latter stopped on seeing the rangers and turned back, and the hard pressed settler made his escape to the ranger boys. The Indians had 100 head of horses, and were going slow on account of the rough country. The rangers now made a flank movement to the right, kept under cover of the brush until near the horses, and then making a sudden dash cut them off from the Indians in a narrow place. They ran them back south against the foot of Shovel Mountain, and left three men to hold them there until the battle was over. The rangers knew they would have to fight the Indians, as they were in large force and yelling loudly. It seems that during the excitement of running the settler the Indians and horses had become scattered, and the rangers, taking cover and coming out in an unexpected place, by a bold, quick dash had secured the horses. The Indians collected in plain view of the rangers and began to divest themselves of blankets and outrigging, and to pile them up on the ground. The rangers now advanced and dismounted in a post oak ravine, tied their horses, and filled the magazines of their Winchesters full of cartridges, and awaited the charge which they saw the Comanches were about to make. The Indians numbered 125, as near as could be ascertained, and the rangers 28, besides the three who were holding the herd of horses against the mountain. The Indians when they did charge made a turn and tried to recapture the horses, but the rangers charged in turn and opened such a rapid fire that the savage warriors retreated back to their position. The three plucky fellows who were with the horses remained at their post and also opended fire. The Indians could not get to the horses without passing within gunshot of the position occupied by the main body of the rangers. The next charge of the Indians came close to the rangers, and a short but desperate fight took place. The Comanches, however, soon gave back before the galling fire of the Winchesters. They fought with muzzle-loading guns, bows and lances. Captain Perry was a good Indian fighter and handled his men well. The Indians killed in this charge were carried off by daring fellows on horseback, who would lean from the saddle, and taking them by their long hair drag them back to cover. In the third charge the Indian chief was killed and his horse ran in among the rangers with the dead body, which was held to the saddle by a strong strap of leather. If the horse had gone back the other way the body of the chief would not have been captured. The Indians evidently overrated the force of rangers on account of the number of shots fired. The Comanches finally left after suffering heavy loss. The dress and rigging of the dead chief were taken to Austin and placed in the capitol building. Of the men in the fight the writer can only get the names of Captain Perry, B. F. Payne, Frank Enoch, the three Bird brothers, Griffin from Austin, Page from Blanco, and a man named Cox.

The three Bird brothers displayed great bravery and exposed themselves in every charge to the enemy's fire. One of them was killed and the other two wounded, one in the nose and the other in the ear, with arrows. Other rangers and horses were wounded. The dead ranger was carried to Birdtown and buried. The stolen horses numbered 100 head, and were carried back and turned over to the owners. The rangers in this fight were all young men, none being over 25 years of age.

INCIDENTS OF FRONTIER LIFE.

Desperate Indian Battle, 1870.

Among the many interesting incidents connected with the early settlement of Old D'Hanis, the following facts were collected from Mr. Chris Batot, one of the original first settlers:

In 1861 a band of Indians came in near D'Hanis and stole a lot of horses. Before the people knew they were in the country an old man named John Schreiber went out one morning on a mule to hunt a yoke of oxen. Some time in the day the mule came back without his rider and an arrow sticking in him. Great excitement prevailed in the settlement, as all were satisfied that the old man was killed. A large crowd assembled at D'Hanis to organize a search for the body and to fight the Indians if they should come in contact with them. These people were very particular to comply with and adhere strictly to the formalities of the law, and therefore made arrangements to hold an inquest over the body when found. They had no justice of the peace to act in the capacity of coroner, but Mr. Schalkhausen, their school teacher, was an educated man, and they supposed he could hold an inquest as good as anyone. He agreed to go with them, and soon all things were ready. A wagon and team had been procured, and in this the teacher rode with the driver. The balance of the party went ahead on horseback to search for the body. When they arrived about the place where they supposed the old man had been killed the mounted men separated to hunt, and it was understood that the one who should first find the body of the unfortunate settler would make it known by a loud call to the others. A man named Deckard first came upon the body, and gave the signal. The searchers soon collected together on the spot, and Mr. Chris. Batot was sent to inform Mr. Sauter, son-in-law of the man killed, who was in company with the teacher coming with the wagon. When Mr. Batot met the wagon and told the news of the finding of the body to Mr. Sauter, and how he should drive to reach the spot, he rode back to the assembled crowd. The wagon had passed the spot where the body lay, and had to turn back and go up a ravine to get there. This was back towards D'Hanis, and Mr. Batot said as he rode off, "You can see us when you get up the ravine opposite the body." Mr. Batot says the driver had only to put on the bridles of the horses, as they had not been unhitched while Mr. Sauter was waiting for the dead man to be found and informed where to drive to. Now a strange and most unaccountable thing occurred. While Mr. Sauter was adjusting the bridles to the horses the teacher got out of the wagon and followed Mr. Batot on foot, while the driver carried the wagon up the ravine as instructed. When the wagon arrived the men were around the body ready to hold the inquest, but the teacher had not as yet arrived. After a short time waiting, two men went to see what was delaying the professor. They were gone about twenty minutes, and then came back and reported that they could not find him. Fifteen men now set out on horseback and scattered in various directions to search for the man of letters, shouting and shooting for six hours, but no response came from the missing man. He had disappeared as completely as if the earth had opened and swallowed him up. By this time a cold norther had come upon them, and as the men were without coats the search had to be abandoned. The dead man was placed in the wagon and carried back to D'Hanis and buried without the inquest being held. The body was lanced and scalped, but had not been shot with either bullet or arrow. The wounded mule must have dodged into a thicket and eluded the Indians. The old man evidently fell from him or was dragged off by a limb. The mule came in with saddle and bridle on.

After returning home the men got their coats and some provisions and returned to the scene of the killing, and there searched in wide circles for three days without success. The missing man was never seen or heard of again by them. It was surmised that the Indians who killed Mr. Schreiber were concealed near by watching the searching party, whom they were afraid to fight, and seeing this man alone and on foot and not armed, he was captured and carried off. It is all shrouded in mystery, however, as it does seem that so many men scattering in various directions would some of them have come upon the Indians, even in their ambush. The teacher was a man of 60 years of age, well educated, had a good school, and would have had no occasion to voluntarily absent himself without letting some one know it.

Six months after this startling frontier episode, Mr. Deckard, the man who found the body of Mr. Schreiber, was himself killed by Indians under like circumstances. He was not found until the body was reduced to a skeleton by wolves and vultures, and the bones were put in a sack and carried to D'Hanis and buried. The remains could only be identified by the shoes and some camp outfit.

Mr. Batot says that in the year 1870 the Indians invaded the west as if they were going to take the whole country. There were Indians everywhere. At this time Mr. Batot belonged to the ranging company commanded by Capt. Joseph Richarz, and they were stationed at Fort Inge, four miles below Uvalde, on the Leona River. At this time news came to the rangers that a large body of Indians were stealing horses on Turkey Creek, twenty miles west of Uvalde, beyond the Nueces River. There were but sixteen men in camp, two scouts already being gone, one under Captain Richarz and the other under his lieutenant, Sevier Vance. The only officers in camp were Dr. Woodbridge, company physician and surgeon, and Sergeant Eckford. The doctor took command and at once set out to hunt for the Indians, leaving only one man in camp. Court was going on in Uvalde at the time, and Mr. Batot, being a witness in a case there pending, and could not go with the scout, and therefore missed being in the desperate battle near Carrizo Springs which followed. The rangers took up the trail of the Indians on Turkey Creek and followed its tortuous and scattered windings through the chaparral and thorny catclaw brush for two days, and then made the discovery that they had lost a man. It was useless to hunt for him in this brushy and uninhabited country, so the scout pushed on to Carrizo Springs. There was one lone ranchman near this place named English, and he said the scout was a long ways behind the Indians, as they had passed there two days before. This man said that if the doctor and rangers would take his advice he might tell them of a plan by which they could get a chance to fight them. This was agreed to, and English took the men eight miles west, entirely leaving the Indian trail, which was going south. Here about dark English told the men to stop and camp. The idea of English was that the Indians would again turn north when their raid was over and pass near this place.

Next morning English took two of the rangers and went out to see if there was any sign of the Indians having passed in the night. This left Dr. Woodbridge with twelve men. One hour later he sent two men out on a hill as spies, and in a valley to the south they discovered a large band of Indians coming towards them and driving a herd of horses which they had stolen. The two spies at once put back to camp and informed the doctor of the situation, and he gave orders to saddle and mount. The rangers soon came in sight of the Indians going over a ridge, and a charge was ordered. The rangers at this time were armed with Winchesters, and thinking they could sustain themselves, boldly advanced with twelve men against the Indians' sixty. The Comanches had discovered the approach of the rangers, and as soon as they got over the ridge they turned and formed for a fight in two lines and came back at a charge and met the white men on the crest of the ridge. The looks of the Indians and their fearful warwhoops were appalling, and two of the rangers ran. Ten stood their ground, however, and met the onset. The fight was fierce and at close quarters. A gallant ranger named Bedinger, who was in the thickest of the fight, was seen to reel and fall from his horse, and Dr. Woodbridge was struck and knocked from his horse by the Indian chief. The fight seemed hopeless against such odds and the rangers retreated, firing as they went. Dr. Woodbridge at this juncture was seen standing behind a prickly pear shooting at the chief, who was securing the doctor's horse. Two of the rangers, Blakeny and Whitney, went back to the assistance of the doctor and charged the Indians. The other rangers also made a stand and continued to fire. The two rangers above mentioned were in a perfect Vesuvius of fire. No two men, it is thought, ever fired so many shots in so short a space of time. Blakeny's gun became so hot that he could not touch the barrel without getting burned, and all the time during this conflict he and Whitney returned yell for yell with the Indians.

The Comanches had never met such a fire before, and did some most dexterous riding and dodging, but nine were seen to fall from their horses to the ground. Whitney's horse was wounded, but still he advanced to the side of the doctor, who was dazed from the blow he had received, and was slowly retreating and firing. He succeeded in mounting behind the ranger, who bore him safely back to the other men, the retreat being covered by Blakeny, who still continued to yell and fire. The other rangers had formed near and still continued a brisk fire, and the Indians went back, not daring to risk another charge in the face of such a fire. The Winchesters were all that saved the rangers; they would have been crushed if muzzle-loaders had been their arms. The Indians scalped the dead ranger while the fight was going on, as he fell in the hand-to-hand fight, and his body remained in their possession when the rangers fell back. The men had nearly exhausted their supply of cartridges, especially Whitney and Blakeney. The former was short eighty after the fight. The rangers went back to their camp, and next morning a party went back to the scene of the battle and buried the dead ranger. He was hit three times in the breast by bullets. The Indians got his horse and saddle, Winchester, pistol, and belt of cartridges. They also got the doctor's horse, saddle, and bridle, but the chief's horse was found dead on the ground. The Indians had carried off their dead, but the bloody ground where they fought told the tale of what they suffered.

These same Indians after the fight continued their course, and came upon English and the two men who went to look for the trail, and a long running fight took place with them, but the rangers, being on good horses, made their escape to camp. Joe Brierly was behind in the chase and fired repeatedly at the Indians, who also fired many times at him, but appeared afraid to come closer.

The chief's horse which was killed in the fight was a gray, and well known to the rangers as belonging to a ranchman below. One shield was picked up on the ground with a bullet mark on it and a woman's scalp attached. The shield and scalp were sent to Austin. The ranger who got lost while trailing found his way back safely to the camp below Uvalde.

The ranchman English, who was with the rangers on this occasion, afterwards commanded the settlers in a disastrous battle with Indians near old Frio town, in which his son and two other men, Oden and Williams, were killed, besides a number wounded.

FIFTIETH ANNIVERSARY OF THE SETTLEMENT OF D'HANIS.

1897.

The morning of May 1, 1897, was a grand day for the people of D'Hanis and surrounding country. The sun rose clear, ushering in the fiftieth anniversary of the settling of Old D'Hanis, one mile east of the new town of the same name on the Sunset Railroad. Here at the former place the pioneers of fifty years ago unloaded their wagons on the prairie by the side of a clear-running little creek. In the early morning of this present occasion of the celebration a cool wind blew from the north, and everything was propitious for a nice day. At an early hour busy preparations were being made for the day's festivities.

In company with John Gersdorff of San Antonio the writer at an early hour repaired to the barbecue grounds, which were in the rear of the two-story rock store house of Mr. John Fohn. The entrance was through a wide gate which fronted on the main road to Hondo City. Already many people had arrived, but still the horsemen, footmen, and vehicles continued to pass through the entrance from the country, Hondo City, and other points until a vast multitude had assembled within the grounds. During the gathering of the people, Dr. Bradley of Hondo City brought the news of the death of Dr. Cummings of Uvalde, who was well known here, and many regrets and much sorrow was expressed at his sudden demise. Last year he was elected county judge of Uvalde County, and was very popular among the people.

The barbecue grounds was about 300 yards from the spot where fifty years ago the travel-worn pioneers unloaded their wagons and said, "Here we rest." The country was more pleasant to look upon then, as far as scenery is concerned, on account of the thick undergrowth which has since sprung up all over the country. Then towards the west were no settlers. The country was rolling prairie, covered with grass. Along the Seco Creek were small hills and some timber. Towards the north, ten miles of open country and the blue mountain ranges of Seco, Sabinal, and Hondo could be seen. In other things, however, the contrast is just as great. The settlers then had poor teams and clumsy wagons, with no houses and no material at hand to build with, except short pickets and prairie grass for roof. Now we see fine teams and costly carriages, nice houses, and good farms.

On this day the old settlers group together and talk over old times, while the young ladies and gentlemen are in high glee over the anticipated pleasures of the day. There was nothing stronger than beer to drink, and that popular beverage was partaken of freely but not to excess by anyone. Lighter drinks, such as lemonade and soda water, were on hand to be dispensed to those who preferred that kind of refreshment.

When the hour for the parade arrived, the marshals formed the people in line and the start was made from the gate in front of the Fohn building. The line of march was south. First came Mr. Chris. Batot, one of the first settlers, bearing a Texas flag of the days of the Republic, with the legend inscribed on the blue ground: "D'Hanis' Fiftieth Anniversary." Next came a wagon containing a string band, which discoursed sweet music as they went marching along. Next in order were forty little girls bearing flags; then old setttlers, citizens, and visitors of all ages and sizes. In the procession also was an old settler named John Rudinger, bearing a United States flag. The procession was quite extended, the objective point being the old town, where the grass-covered shanties were first erected, some of which were still to be seen. Along the route they passed the residence of Mrs. Fohn, one of the first settlers, who at this time was dangerously ill in San Antonio. The procession returned by a circuitous route, and again entered the grounds. The Texas flag was furled and laid away, and the stars and stripes planted at the gate, where it flapped in the breeze the balance of the day. Trains coming from both ways continued to bring visitors from points along the railroad. Among the people present on the ground was a son of Capt. Charles de Montel, who commanded a company of Texas rangers in the early days and did good service with his men along the border. The younger Montel is a lawyer by profession, and resides at Hondo City, county seat of Medina County.

Dinner was announced at noon, and all repaired to the long tables near the meat pits, and ample justice was done to the fat beef, bread, coffee, and pickles. This feast was quite in contrast with fifty years ago. The old settlers were not possessed of guns sufficient to kill large game, and often suffered with hunger, subsisting many days at times on meal and water made into mush. It will be remembered that these early settlers came direct from Europe, and had never lived in a new country. Their firearms mostly were small bird guns, and not all had them. Sometimes the Indians, who at this time professed to be friends, would come and take what meal they had.

The number of people present today was estimated to be between 1200 and 1500, and 200 vehicles. At 3 o'clock speaking commenced, Judge S. B. Easly first occupying the stand, which was on the balcony at the head of the stairs on the outside of the Fohn building. Judge Easly, in his remarks, paid a glowing tribute to the people of D'Hanis as brave pioneers, honest, law-abiding citizens, and said that no D'Hanis boy had ever been sent to the penitentiary. Mr. Easly was loudly cheered on leaving the stand.

Mr. Chris. Batot, one of the first settlers, now came before the people and rehearsed the history of the colony from the start in Europe up to the time when the country had passed out of the wilderness state into an epoch of more prosperous times. The people listened with great interest and with many cheers, interspersed with peals of laughter at some of his humorous sallies. It seemed almost to make the contrast more perfect, while Mr. Batot was telling of the slow, toilsome march with weary teams across the prairie following the trail of the surveyor's wagon through the high grass, that a fast train dashed by not more than 300 yards from where the speaker stood, and the scream of the locomotive would have drowned the yell of the Comanche of whom he had just been telling. This closed the speaking, and was followed by music from the string band, baseball in the evening, supper at sundown, and dancing in Fohn's hall at night. During the dance Miss Ida Durban of Utopia met with a painful accident by a splinter penetrating her shoe and going deeply into her foot. The young lady was at once conveyed to the depot, where the services of Dr. Patterson, also of Utopia, were secured and attempt made to remove the splinter, but without success, as the doctor was in attendance at the celebration and had no instruments with him. Dr. Bradley of Hondo was now sent for and the splinter removed. It was large, being two inches in length. Miss Durban suffered great agony for more than two hours.

Below are the names of the first settlers who are still alive, and who were of all ages at the time the colony came here. Some were very young: Joseph Finger, Joseph Wipf, Chris Batot, John Reiderman, John Deckert, L. Essen (92 years old), John Batot, John Rudinger, Mrs. F. A. Lutz, Mrs. L. Zurcher, Mrs. Jos. Wolf, Mrs. H. Weynand, and H. Weynand. There were twenty-nine families originally, and numbered about 100 persons. But few of those who were grown at the time of arrival are now alive.

D'Hanis is in the western part of Medina County, on the east bank of Seco Creek.

RICHARD M. WARE.

Came to Texas in 1829.

Mr. Richard Ware was born in Arkansas on the 20th of October, 1828, while the family were en route to Texas. His father, Capt. William Ware, settled in Montgomery County, Texas, in 1829. In 1835, when the war between Texas and Mexico broke out, his father raised a company and went to San Antonio with Gen. Ed. Burleson. When Col. Ben Milam called for volunteers to storm the city, Captain Ware and his men went in and materially aided in capturing General Cos and his army. During the fighting around the Veramendi house, on Soledad Street, Captain Ware was severely wounded in the hand. After the fall of the Alamo and the setttlers commenced their retreat from the Mexicans the Ware family went to Natchitoches, on Red River, ready to cross if the Mexicans were successful. Captain Ware and his company was with Houston's army and fought at the battle of San Jacinto, which gave peace for a time to Texas, which was now organized into an independent Republic.

In 1842, after San Antonio was captured by General Wall, Captain Ware joined the Somervell expedition for the invasion of Mexico, but turned back on the Rio Grande with a great many others.

In 1851 the Wares started west with a drove of cattle. Winter came on when they were in the vicinity of San Marcos, Hays County, and they concluded to stop and hold their stock until spring opened. Some one informed them that if they would go south to the Yorks Creek country, in the Sowell and Turner settlement, they would find some vacant houses which they could occupy and it would be a fine place to spend the winter. This they did. Grass was fine and the stock did well, but many of them were lost on account of their mixing with wild cattle in the big thickets. These wild cattle were not domestic gone astray, but original wild cattle, smaller than the common breeds or home cattle, and all one color—brown. The writer remembers when a boy and living in Hays County, on the Blanco, of seeing a great many of them. They were wilder than the deer.

In the spring of 1852 Captain Ware moved his cattle on west and settled in Sabinal Canyon. The old cabin is still standing, built by himself and his boys, and should be preserved. The elder Ware did not long enjoy the new home, dying the following year.

In 1856 Richard Ware had his first experience with Indians. On that occasion the Indians made a raid into Sabinal Canyon and were fought by John Leaky, Gid Thompson, and others, the particulars of which have been described elsewhere. Mr. Ware joined the force that pursued these same Indians, who were overtaken on the Leona River while in bathing and all killed but one. They had no chance to make a fight, as the settlers were on the bank right over them before they knew it, and they had to dive in trying to avoid the shots. Mr. Ware says when it was over the water was very bloody. This affair has also been described more fully in another article.

In 1859 Mr. Ware was living in Frio Canyon when a raiding band of Comanches came through, having a lot of stolen horses which they had taken in the Guadalupe valley. A party of twelve was made up and pursued them. Of this number were John Daugherty, captain; Wm. Russell, Geo. Patterson, John Williams, Dan Turner, Henry Courtney, Richard Ware, and — Lambert. The trail of the Indians led west to the Nueces Canyon, and the first night the settlers camped without water. They were on the trail again early next morning, and when they came to the Nueces found themselves on a high bluff. It was level on the opposite side of the river and open country for some distance, and the Indians were discovered going across the valley towards the foot of the mountains. The only chance to continue the pursuit was to go on foot. It was decided to do this, and Lambert and Courtney were left with the horses. The other men had some difficulty in getting down the bluff themselves, but finally succeeded and crossed the river without being discovered by the Indians. They went on about two miles and discovered a smoke coming out of a cedar brake, and knew the Indians had camped. Their plan now was to creep upon them and make an attack. They advanced to a water hole not far from the Indians and discovered some one coming towards them.

after water. All lay close in the brush, and as the Indian, as they supposed, came in range two rifles cracked and he fell in his tracks. A rush was now made for the camp, but the alarm had been given and the Indians were scattering through the brake without attempting to make any fight, and none of them were killed. Eight head of horses were taken, and the men went back to the waterhole and examined the dead body there. They now discovered what a sad mistake had been made. It was a captive white boy they had slain. Who he was or where he was captured they could not tell. Evidently he had been with the Indians some time. He was badly sunburned and his hair very long. Around his waist was a belt and knife, and he had two bullet wounds in the breast. By his side lay a water vessel made from the paunch of a cow or horse, and the Indians had sent him to the pool for water. Even if he had been an Indian the settlers made a mistake in killing him at this time, as the fire of the rifles alarmed those in camp and spoiled their plans. Being nearly night and some distance from their horses, and nothing to dig a grave with, the poor unfortunate, whoever he was, had no burial, and was left where he fell by the white men, food for vultures and coyotes. He seemed to be about 14 years of age. With some difficulty a place was found by going below and the recaptured stock brought out of the valley to where the two men and horses were. The return back was made without incident, and the stolen horses returned to their owners on the Guadalupe.

In 1858 a stockman named I. C. Isbel, who lived on the Frio at the foot of the mountains, had eighty head of horses stolen by a band of Indians. The alarm was given and twenty-one men assembled at the Isbel ranch to go in pusuit of them. In the party were six United States soldiers from Fort Inge, under the command of a sergeant. The settlers were commanded by Capt. Henry Robinson. The trail of the Indians led in a northerly direction toward the divide at the head of the Sabinal and Frio rivers. The country there was open postoak and blackjack. The Indians ket a spy back to watch for pursuers, and Captain Robinson, knowing they were in the habit of doing this, made a wide circle to the left so as not to be seen, and came upon the Indians between two noted watering places called the Postoak and Frio waterholes. The white men outnumbered the Indians, but in their first onset made a mistake by all firing their guns at once. The Indians took notice of this, and turning, boldly charged the settlers. The writer has heard men say that Indians in the early days had a poor chance in fighting men who were armed with rifles and they only using bows. This is a mistake, and until repeating arms were invented the Indian had the advantage. A brave when on the warpath carried from forty to sixty arrows in his quiver, and if he could by dodging and the use of his shield avoid the shot which the white man fired at him from a muzzle-loading gun, would then boldly charge him. If the settler did not happen to have a brace of pistols, he was bound to run or be stuck full of arrows unless he could take shelter somewhere until he could reload. This was the situation in this case. The settlers ran and took shelter among the trees until they could reload their rifles. A crisis was avoided by John Leaky and some others who had revolvers and met the charge with a rapid fire. Two Indians were killed on the spot at this place, and John Cook was wounded with an arrow. He was on horseback when hit, and the arrow went through his thigh and pinned him to the saddle. Two of the Indians' horses were also killed. One Indian was shot through both hips and fell in a sitting position on the ground, but pulled an arrow and was about to shoot when a soldier fired at him with an army gun carrying a buck-and-ball paper cartridge. The shot struck the Indian high up on the forehead, tearing off the top of his skull and exposing the entire brain. During the battle the loose horses were badly scattered, and some of the men who dismounted to fight let their horses get away from them. One Indian displayed great bravery and a tenacity of life that was remarkable. He came close to the white men and was twice shot down, but regained his feet each time and continued to battle until the other Indians ran off and left him. He was shot six times by John Leakey with a revolver, and as he went off on foot to follow his comrades was fired at by every man who had a loaded gun. He was very active, and could dodge many shots aimed at him. Henry Courtney followed him on horseback and fired a load of buckshot at him from a shotgun, but the Indian kept on. John Daugherty now mounted a horse, and with a loaded revolver in his hand once more caught up with the brave to give him battle. The badly wounded Indian was still game, and turned back on Daugherty, uttering a warwhoop and sending his arrows with such precision that the settler dismounted behind his horse to avoid them. An exciting and strange battle now took place. The Indian advanced until nothing but the horse separated him from his foe, and both used the animal for a breastwork. Daugherty tried in vain to bring the Comanche down with repeated shots from the pistol until the chambers were empty. He had thus far avoided being hit himself, but was now at such a disadvantage without a load left, and the Indian with arrows yet in his quiver, that he turned and ran to some trees for better shelter, and the redskin mounted the horse and rode off. This Indian had on during the most part of the fight a large piece of cloth, like sail duck, closely wrapped around his body, which he now threw off, and it was picked up by the white men. It was covered with blood and had many bullet holes through it. He also lost his shield, which was spattered with blood.

Richard Ware was in this fight, and came near killing one of his comrades while they were at close quarters and men hurrying here and there and passing in front of one another. He aimed at an Indian, and when about to pull the trigger saw a white man's head through the sights of his gun, but lowered it in time to save him. The man had stepped directly in front of him. The Indian who got off with the horse and saddle also got a good overcoat and a canteen full of water. Several Indians were killed on the ground and most of the balance went off wounded. The horses stampeded badly during the fight, but were collected and driven back to the settlement.

In 1866 Mr. Ware was again living in Sabinal Canyon, but in the meantime had married Miss Slaver, stepdaughter of Mr. Gideon Thompson. Mrs. Thompson and she were the first white women that saw Sabinal Canyon. Captain Ware's family were the first here, but his girls were small, and Mrs. Ware died in eastern Texas. Mrs. Richard Ware saw Mrs. Bowlin after she was killed by the Indians, and helped to wait upon Mrs. Kinchaloe, who was wounded at the time.

In the above named year Mr. Ware was living on Onion Creek, in the canyon, and was engaged in opening a ditch to irrigate a small piece of land situated some distance below the house. While here alone he was attacked by six Indians. He heard the Indians coming through the brush, but thought it was cattle, as they watered near here. When he looked around the Indians were in ten feet of him, and one was aiming his gun to shoot. Mr. Ware had no gun with him, but had his pistol, and being quick to draw and fire, got in his shot with the Indian, who missed Ware, but was himself badly wounded. He then started for the house, shooting as he went, followed by the Indians, who yelled a good deal but did not crowd him close. There were several men living near Mr. Ware, and some at his house at the time, and all heard the yelling and shooting, but no one got to him except his brave wife and John Ware. The wife met him with his gun, knowing he had only a pistol. The Indians got five head of horses and took their departure. At this time there was a boy named Buckaloo captive among the Indians, who was taken from this country, and knew the horses when they were brought in. They said they lost one man in the fight when they got the horses. This was the first one Ware shot. Mrs. Ware saw the Indians when she came to her husband with the gun, and said the hair on their heads, which was very long, "flopped up and down when they galloped their horses."

In this same year Mr. Ware and Charles Durbin went to Bandera after meal. The distance was forty miles, and it was the nearest mill from this canyon. On the way back, and when nearly home, in the lower part of Seco Canyon they saw a drove of horses coming up the valley towards them, driven by a band of Indians. Just ahead of them, about where the old Bandera road crosses Seco, a man named Myrick had built a house, but it was now vacant. To get to this house for shelter was the best thing to do, and the horses were whipped into a run to reach it. The Indians saw them and came yelling to cut them off. The white men beat the race and got inside. Mr. Ware could not find a crack inside the house that he could see through, and after waiting awhile ventured outside to take a view of the situation. Now the Indians were sharp and thought that one of the white men would do this very thing, so posted one of their men behind a tree near by with a gun to shoot anyone that ventured out, while the others drew back and kept silent. After Ware got outside he looked cautiously around the corner of the house trying to see what had become of the Indians, and was startled by the loud report of a gun very near and a ball passed just over his head. Smoke from a liveoak told where the shot came from. The Indian was lying behind it waiting for this opportunity. Ware came to the corner of the house handling his gun as if about to shoot, and the Indian shot too quick, thinking likely he was discovered. The tree stood on the brink of a ravine, and just the glimpse of the Indian's black head was seen as he went over into it after shooting. Mr. Durban, who could not see very well and remained in the house, was under the impression when he heard the loud report of the gun that it was Ware who shot at an Indian, and exclaimed, "Did you hit him, Richard?"

The Indians kept them here all night but did not venture near enough to get the horses, which were tied near the door; but they got the sheet from the wagon, which was left further away. The besieged men left next day, without seeing any more of the Indians.

On one occasion Mr. Ware and some others were in Nueces Canyon looking for some white men who had killed another and were hiding out. At this time there were scarcely any settlers in this far western valley. A few daring men had brought their families there and were living in camps preparatory to forming a settlement. Among these were the Cox family, on Westprong. Ware and his party went to the Cox camp, and found everything torn up and the people gone. To the practiced eye of these frontiersmen it was soon apparent there had been a battle here. Among other things they found a newly made grave, and digging into it with their knives found the body of a little girl, one of the Cox children, who had been killed in the fight. In a waterhole near by they found the dead body of an Indian. Blood and many other signs of the fight were there.

Mr. Ware has had many reverses in life, but he and his wife at this writing (January, 1900) still live in Sabinal Canyon.

Mrs. Ware was born in Shawneetown, Ill., in 1839. Her father's name was David Slaver, and he died when she was quite young. Her mother then married Mr. Gideon Thompson, with whom she came to Sabinal Canyon in 1852.

AUNT MARY DAVENPORT.

Came to Texas in 1830.

Among the many pioneer women of Texas but few have passed through a more varied experience than "Aunt Mary" Davenport, as she is generally called by all that know her. The writer found the good lady at the house of Mr. Monroe Fenley, her son-in-law, who lives two miles east of Sabinal Station. Mrs. Mary J. Davenport was the daughter of Capt. John Crane, and was born in Hardeman County, Mo., in 1823. Her father was a companion and playmate of Sam Houston, and both enlisted in General Jackson's army in Tennessee when the war broke out with the Creek Indians. The two took part in the famous Indian battle of the Horshoe Bend. Houston was a lieutenant, and was severely wounded. After the battle was over Mr. Crane and another young man came upon the body of a dead squaw with a live babe beside her, and they were at a loss to know what to do with it. At this time another soldier came up, named Nick Baker, and they asked him what would be best to do with the Indian baby. "Kill it," said he. This they declared they would not do. "I will, then," said Baker, and thereupon he snatched up the swarthy infant and dashed its brains out against a tree. This man had suffered many things at the hands of the Indians. He had seen them do his little brothers and sisters the same way, and also kill his mother and father. He alone made his escape during the terrible slaughter, and had declared war against all Indians, regardless of age or sex.

John Crane came to Texas with his family in 1830 and settled in Nacogdoches. From there he moved in 1834 and settled about where Huntsville is now. A friend came with him, named Pleasant Grey, and they agreed to lay off their land adjoining and build close together, so they could be near neighbors.

In 1835, when the Texas revolution broke out in a war with Mexico, Mr. Crane raised a company and went to San Antonio, and was one of the captains with his men who entered the town under Ben Milam and helped to capture General Cos and his army. Captain Crane was a relative of Capt. William Ware, who also commanded a company. After the fall of the Alamo and General Houston was retreating before the exultant Mexicans and settlers were fleeing, Captain Crane stayed with his and Captain Ware's families, and the latter went on to San Jacinto and led a company in the battle.

Captain Crane carried the families from near Montgomery and crossed over the Sabine at Natchitoches, La., and remained there until the battle was fought, and then came back with the families to Montgomery, where Captain Ware joined them. Captain Crane then stayed three months in the service, until times were settled and all the troops discharged. He then moved to Walker County and settled about ten miles from Huntsville. While living here a war broke out with the Cherokee Indians, and Captain Crane went out under General Rusk against them. In the battle which ensued he was killed—shot just under the heart by rifle ball. His body and that of a neighbor who was killed at the same time and fell with him were buried on the field by John Robbins and Ben Highsmith. The Indian chiefs who led the Cherokees were Bowles and Big Mush, both of whom were killed.

In 1839 Miss Mary J. Crane married James Elkins, of Walker County. He died in 1844, and in 1848 she married John M. Davenport, in Kaufman County. They moved from there to Sabinal Canyon in 1852 with Capt. William Ware. In 1854 they moved below the mountains and settled at the German settlement of D'Hanis, and from there to Ranchero Creek and engaged in stock raising. In 1858 Mr. Davenport was captain of a minute company and had a fight with the Indians on the Leona River, below the town of Uvalde. The Indians were surprised in camp and all killed but one.

Shortly after this Captain Davenport started early one morning to make a trip of several miles west to Blanco Creek to see some parties about cutting hay for him. When he started Mrs. Davenport cautioned him to keep a sharp lookout and to not let anyone get near him before he found out who it was. "All right," he said. "You take care of yourself and the children, and watch good when you go to the creek after water." This was the last time "Aunt Mary" saw her husband alive. He was killed that evening by Indians near where Sabinal Station is now. Mrs. Davenport pointed out the spot to the writer as

THIS ROCK MARKS THE PLACE WHERE JOHN DAVENPORT WAS KILLED BY INDIANS.

we sat on Mr. Fenley's gallery. The country then was mostly open prairie, with here and there motts of timber and thickets. Now it is covered with mesquite. Mr. Davenport was in three miles of home when the Indians came upon him, and the desperate fight he had with them was witnessed by some Mexicans, but they were afraid to venture to his assistance. When the Indians left they went to the spot and found Mr. Davenport just dying, and not able to speak. They pulled some arrows out of him, and one of them carried an arrow to Mrs. Davenport and told her the sad and startling news. Another Mexican carried an arrow to Mr. John Kennedy, and told him the news. Runners were now sent to alarm the scattered settlers, and Mr. Kennedy came to the Davenport ranch. Mrs. Davenport wanted to go at once to where the dead body of her husband lay, and was about to start in company with Mr. John Kennedy, when Ross, his brother, came up and prevailed upon the bereaved wife to desist, as she might also be killed by the Indians, who in this short time could not be far away. The two Kennedy brothers now rode off together, and John assured Mrs. Davenport that he would go and stay with the body of her slain husband until the settlers who lived below could get together. He took a lantern with him, and when night came lighted it and sat by the body with gun and pistol. When enough came an inquest was held by the dim lantern light, and before day the body was moved home. This was the first inquest held over a person killed by Indians.

As soon as daylight came John Kennedy took some of the assembled men, and going back to the scene of the killing took the trail of the Indians. The others dug a grave and buried the dead man. The trailing party was joined by citizens of Uvalde and soldiers from Fort Inge. They overtook the Indians and had a fight with them, and obtained the pistol of Mr. Davenport. It was learned afterwards from a boy who was a captive at that time in Mexico that Davenport shot one Indian in the arm, one in the body, one in the hip and shoulder, and that one of them died of his wounds on their retreat. This was told by an Indian to the boy. This Indian also said that they killed one white man in the morning that had no gun or pistol, but the one they killed in the evening fought like the devil. The man they killed in the morning was John Bowles. He was a brave man, but not being armed had no chance to fight.

Davenport was killed about 4 o'clock in the evening of the same day. He was riding a mule that day, something he seldom did. He wanted to trade the mule; that was why he was riding him. The Mexicans who witnessed the fight said the Indians rode furiously around Davenport in a circle, yelling, lying low on their horses and shooting arrows. It was with difficulty he could hit them with his pistol, but fought them until he sank down full of arrows.

Mrs. Davenport has spent many sleepless nights on account of Indians. She saw a band near the house once running horses. She remembers well how General Houston looked, and at one time made coffee for him.

J. A. BOALES.

Came to Texas in 1834.

Mr. James A. Boales, one of the early settlers of Texas, was born in Christian County, Ky., August 17, 1829, and came to Texas with his father, Capt. Calvin Boales, in 1834, and settled on the Brazos River at a place afterwards known as Old Nashville. This place was named by the immigrants from Tennessee who settled there. The Boales family started to Texas from Lawrence County, Mississippi, in company with the Tandy family, their relatives. There was also of this party Billy Smith and Billy Moore. On the way they fell in with Jerry and John Bailey, and they all came on together. There also came about this time the Powers and McCanlis families. When the party arrived at their destination only two settlers had preceded them, and they were living in a camp. One of these was James McLaughlin. When the Boales party arrived at the Brazos, opposite the place where they wished to settle, they had to stop and build a boat before they could cross their effects to the prairie and bluff on the other side. Like all Texas at that time, it looked wild and romantic. High grass covered the country in all directions, game was gentle and plentiful, and there was no lack of fresh meat at all times. Bread to these daring settlers was the greatest object in regard to food supply, and they soon learned to do without that without any great inconvenience when they could not obtain it. The soil was very rich, and small patches of corn were planted at the proper season. Before they could get plows and other farm utensils, these primitive Brazos farmers cleared off the high weeds and cane in the bottoms and planted their corn with handspikes, and then without much cultivation fair crops were made. When the corn was matured and well dried they made mortars to pound it in. Although the meal thus made was coarse and rough these people were happy and contented, and really saw more pleasure and enjoyed life better than most people do at this day and time. One great trouble they had to contend with while their crops were growing was the game. They had to guard against bear, deer ,and turkeys to keep them from destroying the growing products before time to harvest.

Among others with whom Mr. Boales came to Texas was Rev. Mr. Smith, a man who became noted in religious and educational work in Texas, and who died mourned by all with whom he came in contact during his long and active life upon the wild frontiers of Texas. At the time of his appearance in Texas he was young, irreligious, and had no education, and for some time worked as a striker in a blacksmith shop at Old Nashville. During a revival meeting he was converted, and showed so much zeal for the cause of Christ that he was taken in charge by two Baptist preachers, Garrett and Fisher, and educated. He it was who founded the famous college at Independence, which was afterwards moved to Belton. He was also a relative of the Boales family.

When these first settlers pitched their camps and built their cabins along the banks of the Brazos they had no trouble with the Indians, who were quite numerous and often visited and traded with the whites. Peace and quiet, however, did not long remain. Mexico had trouble with her American colonies, which soon burst forth into open hostilities. After the fall of the Alamo the settlers all had to retreat before Santa Anna's army until the famous battle of San Jacinto was fought and won. The old settlers called this flight the "Runaway scrape." The party with whom Mr. Boales, then a boy, made his escape was composed of about seventy-five persons. They went into camp on the west side of the Trinity River at Clapp's ferry. There had been a great deal of rain during the flight, and the river was very high. Here, in anxious expectation, the settlers who had stayed with the women and children for their protection awaited news of the battle which they knew General Houston and the brave men with him would fight before they turned their backs on the soil of Texas. While in this condition of anxious solicitude a man named Love came in hot haste with the astounding news that Houston's army had been cut to pieces and almost totally annihilated, and that they had better cross the Trinity at once and continue their flight. What could the wretched people do under such circumstances? The impassable river was in front and the fierce Mexican army in the rear. After some consultation the few men of the party concluded to fight, and commenced the erection of breastworks. On the heels of this messenger, however, came an express from Houston telling the people he had Santa Anna a prisoner and had killed and captured most of his army, and for them to return to their homes. Despair was now changed to joy, and shout after shout went up from the camp. Some say that the man Love was only in sight of the battle, and saw Houston's men prostrate themselves to avoid a discharge from cannon in the charge and thought they were all killed, and reported accordingly as he made his way east. The people at once commenced their westward march, and those that lived at Old Nashville arrived in due time.

Shortly after these events Indian troubles commenced. A man and his brother named Riley moved further up the country with his family, intending to settle on the Gabriel, but were attacked by the Indians. In the fight that ensued one of the Rileys was killed, but his brother bravely continued the fight and succeeded in keeping off the savages and bringing away the body of his brother. While the fight was in progress the family made their escape into the brush and succeeded in getting back to Nashville on foot. There was also one man in the party who ran off when the fight commenced and made his escape. He reported that all of the party were killed.

In 1837 Captain Erath with a small company of men had a desperate fight with the Indians on Elm Creek. Among others of the settlers who were killed in this fight was Frank Childress, with whom Mr. Boales was well acquainted. Erath County was named after this famous Capt. George B. Erath. He often stopped with the Boales family when down in that country.

In 1838 a family named McLelland lived in a camp on Little River and were attacked by Indians. McLelland was gone, and the Indians took possession of the place, killed an infant child by dashing its brains out, and treated Mrs. McLellan with the most monstrous indignities. During the plundering of the camp the Indians found a quantity of whisky and all got drunk. When the effects of the liquor died out they all went to sleep and the woman made her escape in the night with three remaining children of the Folk family, whom she had taken to raise. Their names were John, Charley, and Elizabeth. Mrs. McLelland hid herself and these three children in a drift near the bank of the river. When the father came home he found the dead infant, his only child, and feathers were scattered where the Indians had ripped the beds and poured them out. They were gone, however, and McLelland, not knowing where his wife and the other children were, went down to the settlement and gave the alarm. A party came back with him, and his wife and the children were found nearly dead with hunger and exposure through several nights in the drift, fearing to come out.

In this same year an election of some kind was to be held at Old Nashville, and McLelland and his neighbors who had moved up around him concluded to go down and vote. The men with him were Sam Jones and his two sons, Eli and Wiley, Isaac Standifer, and Solomon Long. McLelland went ahead of the others, against their advice, for they cautioned him to stay back with them, as the Indians might attack him if alone. He said: "No; I will go on; the Indians will not kill a Scotchman." (It seems he had a faster horse than the others.) About ten miles on the road above Old Nashville there are some peculiar shaped mounds called "sugar-loaf hills." Here the Indians attacked McLelland and killed him, and his body was found by the other men when they came along, who took it on to town and buried it.

Mr. Boales was acquainted with most of the men who took part in the famous Indian fight called "Bird's Victory." This was fought on Little River, about three miles from the present town of Belton, county seat of Bell County. The settlers far and near would occasionally get together and fort up at Old Nashville during some extensive Indian raid or series of raids. The ladies of Nashville, Tenn., had taken up a subscription and bought a small cannon and sent it to the settlers at this place to help defend themselves. It is thought that the presence of this little cannon saved the town from being attacked. The settlers would fire it occasionally at sunset or on holidays, and no doubt the Indians were near enough at times to hear it, and knew it was there.

In 1838 or 1839 five of Captain Erath's rangers were killed at a place called Postoak Island, or grove. This was a dense mott of postoak timber surrounded by open prairie, not far from the road which led from the upper settlement to the town. The Indians had been making raids incessantly for some time, and Captain Erath thought it was best for the people to move down to town until something could be done to check the Indians. Some of them were not prepared with teams and wagons to go, and the captain sent five of his men to Nashville to procure wagons and teams for these people. After having accomplished what they went for, the rangers started back up the country, and were attacked by a large force of Indians in the open prairie near this grove. The particulars of this struggle can not be given, as none were left of the white men to tell the tale, but from the signs of the fight it must have been desperate. The names of the rangers were Dave Farmer, Clabe Neill, Jesse Bailey, Aaron Cullins, and Sterett Smith. The delay of these men in returning caused Captain Erath to send more men to see what the cause was. This scout came upon the scene of the battle and found the bodies. The bodies of Cullins and Smith were found in one of the wagons, and the other three were scattered on the prairie between the wagons and mott of timber. It is likely the Indians discovered them some distance off and hid their force in or behind the mott, and when they charged out and cut the rangers off from this protection, they had made a desperate effort to fight their way through the Indians to it. It is likely also that some confusion reigned and there was no concert of action, as the scattered position of the bodies would show. The rangers either went down in one wagon and then each drove one back, or else they rode their horses down and worked them back thus far in the wagons, or some of them. The Indians got all the teams, guns, pistols, etc.

About this time old "Grandpa" Neill was killed by the Indians within 300 yards of the house of Mr. Boales. The morning was foggy, but when the report of the gun was heard that killed him, the neighbors seized their weapons and went to his aid. They found his dead body, but his slayers were gone in the fog and could not be found. One of the sons of the old man named William was killed by Indians on Battle Creek while out with surveyors. Dr. Hill was also in this fight, but made his escape. James Shaw, a representative man of the people, was wounded, and a negro man belonging to Holtsclaugh was killed while out on another surveying expedition. This negro's master and others made their escape.

About 1840 a mail route was started between Old Nashville and Washington and Independence. A man named Joe Taylor carried the mail, and often had narrow escapes from the Indians. On one occasion they pursued him so close to town that the citizens heard his calls for help and came to his aid in time to save him. His old flint-lock gun had failed to fire, and the Indians ran on both sides of him and tried to catch his horse by the bridle. They also shot him in the shoulder with an escopet, and he shot one of the Indians with a large holster pistol he carried. They were not likely aware he had this pistol, and ran close upon him when his gun failed to fire. In the chase the mail bag was lost.

In 1841 three families lived on Walker Creek, where Cameron is now. They were Capt. Dan Walker, Billy Smith, and a man named Monroe. The Indians being very bad, they concluded to move down to the big settlement on the Brazos, and were all fixing to start from the same house when they were attacked by the Indians. The men had just commenced to lift a big box into a wagon when the savages made their appearance, and dropping it ran into the house and a battle commenced. Now, it seems that all the money wealth of the Smiths was in the box, and when the Indians advanced toward the wagons to take shelter behind them Grandma Smith ran out under fire and lifting the lid off the box secured the money and ran back without getting hurt, leaving the box lid standing up. An Indian had a curiosity to know what was in the box and crawled up behind the standing lid and reached his hand around to feel in the box, but at this moment a ball from the rifle of Uncle Billy Smith put an end to his existence. He made the calculation as to the position of his body, and shot him through the box lid. The Indians had enough of the battle now, and left, dragging their dead companion away, and the settlers finished loading and came on down to town. The Smiths were related to the Boales family.

Mr. Boales knew the old pioneer Baptist preacher, Z. N. Morrell, and attended a camp meeting held by him once, and during a service, while the people were thick under the arbor, a band of mounted Indians dashed by and fired into the crowd, killing two men. Some of the white men had guns and returned the fire, but no Indian was killed. Mr. Boales' father, Calvin Boales, was captain of a company of rangers and did good service on the frontier. Mr. Boales says he used to camp with his wagon where Hearne is now, and no one lived there except Billy McGrew. He knew Fort Sulivan when there was no one there except Sulivan, his negro man Dennis, and a man named Poole. He voted in Bee County the first election held there, and after moving further west voted in Edwards County at the first election held there. He was in Milam County when Burleson was cut off.

When the Civil War broke out Mr. Boales joined the Confederate army and served on the Texas coast in Hobby's regiment. P. H. Breeden was his captain, commanding company C. He was in the fight at Corpus Christi and Fort Esperanza. After this the regiment went to Galveston, and was quartered at Bolivar Point until ordered from there to Virginia Point to guard the bridge to keep deserters from crossing. This was about the wind-up of the war, and soon after the regiment was disbanded.

He was made a Mason in 1864, while stationed at Bolivar Point. The lodge was called Hobby Lodge.

In 1881 he moved westward and settled in Frio Canyon, Edwards County, 120 miles west of San Antonio. He arrived in August, a few months after Mrs. McLauren and Allen Lease were killed by the Indians. He has made several short moves around, once to Uvalde and then to Dry Frio, and is now back in Main Frio Canyon.

The writer has spent several nights with "Uncle Jimmy" and his good lady. They are old-time Texans, and one can sit and listen for hours to "Uncle Jimmy" without tiring of his truthful statements of the pioneer days.

F. G. TINSLEY.

F. G. TINSLEY.

Came to Texas in 1834.

Fountain Gillespie Tinsley was born in Barren County, Kentucky, November 23, 1832, and came to Texas with his parents in 1834. His father, Dr. John Turner Tinsley, was in the battle at Gonzales in 1835, when the Mexicans came there to take the cannon, an account of which is elsewhere mentioned.

In 1836, after the Mexicans had stormed the Alamo and Gen. Sam Houston was at Gonzales with his army, he made the Tinsley house his headquarters. Mr. F. G. Tinsley could remember seeing General Houston and sitting in his lap. When the army left Gonzales on the approach of the Mexican army under Santa Anna, Dr. Tinsley materially aided the cause of independence by making a trip to the coast after ammunition and intercepting the army of Houston on their line of march with the powder and lead in time to be used in the famous battle of San Jacinto, which was fought soon after. Dr. Tinsley and his wife Nancy both died at Gonzales at a very advanced age.

The subject of our sketch was in the famous flight before the victorious Mexicans after the massacre of the heroes of the Alamo, and rather indistinctly remembers the terrible hardships endured by the fleeing families from Gonzales towards the Sabine, in the rain, mud, and water of that wet month of April.

After the victory at San Jacinto the Tinsley family, among many others, came back to Gonzales and erected new homes over the ashes of their former ones, which had been burned. When General Houston left Gonzales with his men, and all the families were gone, he left two men with instructions to burn the town on the approach of the Mexicans, which they did.

Mr. Tinsley grew up to manhood at Gonzales. He was of a lively disposition, fond of music and dancing, and was a fine performer on the violin. He was much liked and a general favorite among all the young people. He had three sisters — Mary, Amanda, and Virginia—and one brother, John. The eldest sister, Mary, married a Mr. Sweeny; Amanda married Crockett Jones, and Virginia married Andrew Moore. John married

Miss Dora Houston of Gonzales, and still lives there, as does also Amanda. The others are dead. F. G. Tinsley married Miss Sarah Almedia Davis, at Gonzales, on the 29th of June, 1854. The ceremony was performed by Justice of the Peace John Goss. Just prior to the Civil War Mr. Tinsley moved westward and settled on the Hondo River, in Medina County. Here he raised stock, taught school, and for some time served Medina County in the capacity of justice of the peace.

This was a frontier country, and Mr. Tinsley with his young family passed through all of the exciting times of Indian raids, murders, and alarms, and forting-up of the scattered settlers for protection. In one Indian battle his brother-in-law, Nathan Davis, was severely wounded with an arrow. Wild animals were numerous, and their roars and screams could be heard at night as they came out of the jungles of chaparral and prickly pear down to the Hondo River on the opposite side from the house to quench their thirst. There were wildcats, panthers, tigers, and Mexican lions. These larger ones were shy in daylight and could seldom be seen. They depredated constantly on young stock and were very annoying to the stockmen. One of these, Gip Tilley, conceived the idea of having a large steel trap made, with which to catch a lion or any other of the larger animals. With this purpose in view he went to San Antonio and succeeded in getting one which weighed about seventy-five pounds. The animals had a regular beaten trail from the thickets to the water, and in this trail Mr. Tilley set his trap, but failed to drive a stout stake near to fasten the chain to. A Mexican lion got caught, but ran away with the trap on his foot. Next morning Mr. Tinsley and Mr. Tilley trailed him for several miles where he ran, and in places where the ground was soft holes were made several inches deep where he shoved the trap into it. He ran over prickly pears and tore them down as if a cart had passed over them. The trail was finally abandoned at a place where the pears and brush were so dense that a person could not advance any further without crawling. The time will come, perhaps, when these thickets will be cleared up, and some farmer will plow up a steel trap with the skeleton of a foot in it.

On one occasion Mr. Tinsley and others were out on a cow-hunt and camped in a draw with low brushy hills around and hobbled out their horses. One of the men killed a deer near by, and the hams were cut off for use and the balance left. Next morning Mr. Tinsley went to get his horse, and passing by the spot where the remains of the deer were left discovered that they were gone. Not seeing his horse in the draw, he started through the brush and Spanish daggers which covered a small hill to look in a little valley on the other side. He had proceeded but a few yards, pressing through the undergrowth, when a fierce growl, deep and guttural, came from about the densest portion of the jungle in front of him. He had on a revolver, but backed out the way he came and went on around and got his horse. This was no doubt a lion, and it had the remains of the deer in there. When the other men were informed of the fact it was at first decided to make an assault on the thicket and route the animal, but some of the older men said it was best to leave him alone, not that they had any fear of the beast, but in those days only cap and ball arms were used, and the men only had their sixshooters along, and ammunition was scarce, and a battle with a lion with navies would exhaust all of their shots, and afterwards the party might be attacked by a band of Indians. So the monarch of the jungle was left alone with his prey.

On another occasion Mr. Tinsley was out alone hunting stock, and as frontiersmen sometimes will do, left his firearms at home. He saw no Indians, but found a big black bear up a low tree, and conceived the idea of roping him and pulling him out and then trying to kill him with a pocket knife. The bear was fat and lazy and made no attempt to get down and try to escape, and the noose was thrown nicely over his head and he was pulled out. Mr. Tinsley was riding a trained cow pony, and now circled rapidly around the struggling bear and soon so entangled him in the coils of the rope that he was helpless, and lay panting and growling on the ground. Mr. Tinsley now dismounted and opened his knife, and while his cow pony held the rope taut, cut bruin's throat. The animal would weigh several hundred pounds, and a pack horse had to be brought to carry it all away. In the meantime, however, a great alarm had been raised in the country. A man on his horse on the top of a hill a long distance off had witnessed the roping and killing of the bear by Mr. Tinsley, and reported Indians in the country, and that he had seen them kill one man in the valley of Black Creek. Runners were sent all over the country, and men gathered at different ranches to organize a scout. A messenger came to Mr. Tinsley and informed him of the raid, and when he learned about the man seen killed at a certain place on Black Creek, told his informer to go back and counteract the alarm, as it was himself killing a bear, and he had just brought it in.

In 1861, when the Indians made the big raid, penetrating the settlements as far as Pleasanton, in Atascosa County, men gathered from all over the country to fight them, and Mr. Tinsley and his brother-in-law, Nathan Davis, and other Hondo settlers rallied to the call and joined the men from Sabinal and Seco, and all to the number of thirty or more went under command of Big Foot Wallace in pursuit of them. The account of the trailing and battle at the head of Seco has been fully described elsewhere. Mr. Tinsley was with the main body when the fight commenced in front on the side of the mountain, and when the boys were hurled back on the second squad, went back in the retreat and dismounted and tied his horse with others at the foot of the mountain on the bank of a cedar-timbered ravine. Captain Wallace and others took shelter under cedar trees and a rock ledge to the left, but a more advanced position. The Indians were firing continually at them both with firearms and bows. Mr. Tinsley took shelter behind a cedar tree, but soon perceived that some one had picked him out and was firing at him especially. He soon located his man, who was about 200 yards away, half up the mountain, and firing with a rifle. He would conceal himself to load and then step between the rocks to shoot. He had on a hat and a white shirt. They had killed many people on this trip and had stripped them of their arms and clothing, and were using the weapons now in this battle, and some had invested themselves in the shirts and hats of the slain settlers. Mr. Tinsley had a short, heavy rifle, and fired two shots at the fellow, but perceived that his bullets were falling short. The Indian cut off one limb an inch thick with one of his shots, within a foot of Mr. Tinsley's head. He now poured two full charges of powder in his gun, and when loaded and capped laid the rifle in a fork of the tree and awaited for another opportunity to shoot at his man. When the Indian again appeared to fire, the white man fired first, aiming high at the white shirt front. The double-charged rifle made a loud report, and kicked back under the arm of Mr. Tinsley, and the breech struck the ground a yard in his rear, making the small gravel fly in various directions, and the hammer going back at a full cock. The white-shirted man was seen no more. A few days after the fight a party of Sabinal men went over the battleground, and among other things picked up a hat near the spot where he stood to shoot.

When the fight was over Wallace and his men went to Sabinal Canyon. It was cold and sleeting, and before morning Mr. Tinsley had a very sore throat, and did not go on the trip to cut the Indians off at the head of the Sabinal, but loaned his pistol to Mr. Bob Kinchaloe, who went.

Soon after this Mr. Tinsley enlisted in the Confederate army and served in the regiment of Colonel Woods and in the company of Capt. Josiah Taylor. He removed his family to Gonzales, and they remained there until the close of the war. Mr. Tinsley was in most of the fighting in Louisiana, including the big battle of Mansfield. Before this engagement closed quite a number of Federals were captured and sent into the city of Mansfield near by, with a strong guard to hold them until the battle was over. Among this detail of guards was Mr. Tinsley. The prisoners were held in the courtyard, and during the time a citizen of Mansfield came riding up on a fine horse to look at them. He was very fleshy, and sat back in his saddle with a very important and pompous look on his face, for he was very wealthy, and commenced cursing and abusing the captured soldiers. He shook his fist at them, and said he had a good mind to get down there and cut every one of their throats. Mr. Tinsley walked up close to his horse and said: "Look here, my friend; these are prisoners. Do you hear those cannons down there? Go down there and you can get accommodated. Where those guns are firing men are in that business—cutting throats. Go down there and take a hand, or truck back the way you came." The fellow looked for a moment at the little black-eyed man who thus addressed him, and then, wheeling his horse, went back up the street in the opposite direction to the sound of rifles and cannon. After he was gone one of the prisoners who was standing near, and who wore the shoulder-straps of a colonel in the Union army, asked Mr. Tinsley his name and what State he was from, and on being given the information took out a notebook and pencil and made an entry of it.

When the war was over Mr. Tinsley came back to Gonzales and moved to his old home on the Hondo, but did not remain long. His stock were mostly gone or badly scattered and wild, and he again returned to Gonzales County. From here he removed to Guadalupe County and remained several years, and again moved west, settling near Benton City, in Atascosa County. During the last eight or ten years of his life he preached the gospel of Christ under the auspices of the Methodist church. He died at his home, twenty miles south of San Antonio, on the 13th of February, 1896. He was long afflicted and confined to his bed the last six months of his life, but accepted the chastening hand of God as a child of God, thanking his Creator for the many manifestations of his mercy and love.

Mr. Tinsley was the father of nine children, all girls. Their names were as follows, according to age: Mary, Almedia, Nannie, Emma, Betty, Cordelia, Sopha, Mattie, Eddie. Mrs. Tinsley still survives and lives with a married daughter, Cordelia, near the old home. Those that survive of the children are all married. The eldest, Mary Lillian, married the writer; Almedia married a brother, Leroy P. Sowell, who lives in San Antonio; Nannie married Andrew Wildman, son of a Baptist preacher who lives near Devine, Medina County; Emma married David Calk, and they live in San Antonio. Betty died when she was about eighteen years of age, unmarried; Cordelia married Pearl Briggs, son of a Baptist preacher; he kept the store and postoffice at Segler, and died there in 1898; Sopha married William Pue, son of a Baptist preacher, and they live in San Antonio; Mattie married Emmett Huett, and they live in San Antonio; Eddie died when she was two years of age.

Mary Lillian Sowell, wife of the author, was small when her parents lived on the Hondo, but can remember when one of their neighbors, Rube Smith, was killed by Indians, and the settlers forted-up at his house, while part of the men followed the Indians and fought a battle with them. One of her uncles, Nathan Davis, was badly wounded in the fight. She can remember how the dead man looked. She and some other little girls were afraid to go close to him. He was scapled and very bloody.

THOMAS GALBREATH.

Came to Texas in 1837.

In Medina County, three miles north of Devine, lives one of Jack Hays' old rangers, Thomas Galbreath. When we find one of the old-time rangers who followed Ed Burleson, Jack Hays, and other border leaders in the 30's, 40's, and 50's, we get information that is of more than passing interest. They tell of the time when they used flintlock rifles and heavy single-shot pistols. During some of these years percussion locks had come in use, but still many used the old-time flint which their fathers carried in the last British war.

Mr. Galbreath was born in Macon County, North Carolina, on the 22d day of March, 1823, and came to Texas in March, 1837. In the fall of the same year the Galbreath family settled at Bastrop, on the Colorado River, which was then the outside settlement. The Indians were so hostile and made such frequent raids that these isolated settlers at times almost despaired of sustaining themselves. Gen. Edward Burleson, who had already distinguished himself in the Texas revolution, lived seven miles below Bastrop, and to him the people looked for protection and advice in these perilous times. Burleson said, "We must defeat the Indians in a general engagement, or else leave the country." It was decided by the settlers to endeavor to give the Indians a battle, and to do this they must invade their stronghold, which was in the mountains far up the Colorado. General Burleson was asked to lead the force, which was soon raised, of men and boys who could load and shoot a gun and had a horse.

About one hundred settlers assembled at Bastrop for the expedition. Among this number was Thomas Galbreath, then a boy of 15 years of age, and carrying his father's old flintlock rifle. He had only that year come to Texas, and had never seen a wild Indian.

General Burleson led his men up the Colorado to the mouth of the Llano, and there came upon the Indians in their village in large force. Besides the warriors there were many squaws and children. The Comanches were aware of the approach of the white men, and met them half a mile from their village to give them battle. Burleson formed his men in one line, and the Indians came at a full running charge and yelling loudly. They presented a formidable appearance, riding good horses, their shields on their left arms, and a quiver full of arrows protruding above the left shoulder. All had on the fierce-looking war paint, and many of them had buffalo horns on their head. Their long black hair waved in the breeze like streamers behind them. Their looks, loud yells, and impetuous charge was enough to strike terror to the hearts of men who had never met them before. Young Galbreath felt uneasy, and said if he had seen anyone else run he would have followed suit. He looked at the men around him. Some had fought Indians before, and seemed in nowise put out by this demonstration on the part of the Comanches. General Burleson passed close to Galbreath with fire in his eye and giving his commands short and quick, in about these words: "Dismount now, men, and stand to them. They are not going to run over us. Hold your rifles ready and don't shoot too quick. Take good aim. We will scatter them the first fire." Many of the Indians were nearly naked. They came as if they were going to run over the settlers without making any halt. The loud, clear voice of Burleson was heard, "Fire, boys, fire!" There was a rattling, cracking volley all along the line, and the Indians divided, circling right and left all around the white men. They lay low on the opposite side of their horses and shot arrows as they went. The effect of the fire from Burleson's men could be seen in front. Horses were down and struggling amidst dead and crippled Indians, while others were running riderless with the charge. Others turned back, bullet stricken, and galloped in terror from the field. Some of the Indians who had been fatally hit were falling from their horses as they passed around the settlers. "Load quick, men; they will come again," said the commander. The fight lasted some time, the Comanches making four charges in all. When the quick eye of Burleson perceived that they had begun to weaken, he ordered his men to mount with loaded guns and charge them. The Indians gave way and began their retreat across the open prairie towards the mountains, not even stopping at their village. The running fight lasted two miles, and then the pursuit was called off. The settlers came back by way of the village and took possession of a number of horses, eighty head in all. The squaws looked sullen and would not talk. They were mad because the warriors had been whipped and had run away. The horses which were taken belonged to the settlers around Bastrop. None of Burleson's men were killed on the ground, but many were hit with arrows and some died afterwards. The Indians had no firearms. Many of the settlers' horses were wounded. Mr. Galbreath says this battle caused the settlement to start where Austin is now, but it was then called Waterloo. During the fight he fired his rifle four times. The Indians moved further west.

Living near Bastrop was a man named Manlove, who was the owner of a fine pair of gray horses which were stolen by the Indians. He was greatly distressed about his buggy team, and called on his neighbors to help recover them. Mr. Galbreath and several others responded and at once set out on the trail. They had Tonkaway John with them, who was a good trailer and also fighter. He was a Tonkaway Indian, and lived with General Burleson. The trail of the Comanches was followed rapidly by John, and on the evening of the same day the party started the hostiles were discovered. They were camped in a ravine cooking meat, and the smoke from their fire betrayed them. The white men charged into the ravine, but the Indians discovered them in time to make their escape and carry one of Manlove's horses with them, but leaving the other. The men had ridden all day without anything to eat, and at once proceeded to appease their hunger upon the roasted meat left by the Indians. While engaged in this they heard an Indian yell, and soon discovered him on a hill mounted on Manlove's horse. When he perceived that the white men were looking at him he yelled again and began to wheel the horse in a circle. There was a man of the party named Hutch Reed, who was riding a very fast horse, and Tonkaway John said if Reed would let him have this horse he would catch the Comanche and bring his scalp and Manlove's horse back. Reed said, "All right; but don't you loose my horse." The Tonkaway mounted the fast horse with a sardonic grin on his face and set out, only carrying in the way of arms his bow and arrows. When the Comanche saw John coming to chase him he left the hill and galloped off across the valley, yelling defiance, thinking he could easily get away. When John got clear of some ravines and rocky places and turned his horse loose the

Comanche began to get uneasy and kicked and whipped very energetically. It was no use, however; the gray was no match for Reed's horse. The hostile Indian, seeing that he could not save himself by flight, strung his bow, and a battle with arrows commenced between the two red men. It was evident the Comanche was rattled and shot wild, while John soon filled him full of arrows in spite of his artful dodging and dextrous use of shield. When the Tonkaway finally came up alongside of him the Comanche threw away his bow and begged for life. John paid no attention to this, but taking him by the hair pulled him from his horse, and dismounting, repeatedly stabbed him with a long knife and then scalped him. Remounting now and catching the gray, he came galloping and yelling back to his white companions, leading Manlove's horse with one hand and waving the bloody scalp with the other. Manlove was profuse in his thanks, and dilated on the bravery and prowess of John.

From Bastrop Mr. Galbreath moved to Cedar Creek, ten miles from town, and there hunted and farmed until the

BATTLE OF PLUM CREEK.

This was in 1840. In this year the Comanches, smarting under the defeats inflicted on them by General Burleson and by Col. John H. Moore, made a raid on a large scale through Texas. They penetrated to the coast, sacked and burned the town of Linnville, partly destroyed Victoria, killed and captured some of the settlers, and then commenced their retreat back to the mountains with a great deal of plunder. There were about 600 warriors, besides squaws, and as the settlements were scattering in those days and chiefly confined to the watercourses, it was some time before men enough could assemble at any given point to successfully fight them. In going down from the mountains the Indians had kept between the rivers, where there were no settlements, and consequently were not discovered until a short time before their attack upon Linnville. Runners were sent to the various settlements, and men began to cut across the country in small squads from the valleys of the Colorado, Guadalupe, and San Marcos. Mr. Galbreath heard the news at his home on Cedar Creek, and mounting his horse dashed away to the Colorado, where he found General Burleson at the head of a large company and just starting for the scene of action. Joining him, the command started across the country towards the San Marcos and Guadalupe country, hoping to intercept or cross the trail of the Comanches, who were said to be traveling between the San Marcos and Colorado, going west. On this route they intercepted Guadalupe and San Marcos men, who were already on the trail of the Indians. Among these men were Matthew Caldwell, Jack Hays, Ben McCulloch, Henry McCulloch, Dr. Switzer, Aulcy Miller, French Smith, Ezekiel Smith, Andrew Sowell, John Sowell, James Nichols, Wilson Randle, Barney Randle, and others.

Among the Colorado men were Z. N. Morrell, the Baptist preacher, and Ben Highsmith, the San Jacinto veteran.

The combined forces now numbered more than one hundred men. Nine miles from where the Colorado and Guadalupe men consolidated they caught up with the Indians. This place was at Plum Creek, within the present limits of Caldwell County, and about three miles from Lockhart, the present county seat. Two Indians had been left on a ridge as spies, and sat on their horses and watched the approach of the white men until they were almost within gunshot of them. Both of these fellows had on plug hats which they had obtained at the looting of Linnville, and presented a most comical appearance. A hat never becomes a wild Indian. With his thick, long hair it never fits, and he looks as if he was masquerading with one on. Among the front men of the whites was George Neill, who had a long-range gun. Dismounting, he said he would move them, and aiming high, fired. At the crack of the gun the Indians wheeled their horses quick to run, and both lost their plug hats. An Indian's head is not shaped right to wear a hat, and it is hard for him to keep it in place. The writer, while a ranger in 1870, remembers seeing the friendly Indians who were in the government service as scouts at Fort Griffin wearing hats, but they had to tie them on, otherwise every time their horses jumped or a puff of wind came off they would go. Before the battle came off many more men came, until about two hundred were following the Indians. A large company came from down towards the coast, under the command of Gen. Felix Huston. The Indians made one general stand, but soon broke before the terrible fire of the rifles, and the balance of the battle and pursuit was quite extended, covering several miles of country. Many of the Indians had on fine coats and boots, and some of them carried umbrellas over them. They had many horses and mules packed with goods, and these were rushed on ahead by the squaws, while the warriors fought the battle. At a mott of timber the Comanches rallied in large force and a sharp fight ensued, but they again fled and scattered. Mr. Galbreath says that here he saw a white woman and a negro girl who had been killed by the Indians when they began to retreat from the place. He says another woman was shot with an arrow, but was not killed. He does not remember their names. (These were Mrs. Watt, Mrs. Crosby, and a servant girl captured at Linnville.) It was Mrs. Watt that was killed. Many of the pack animals gave out in the long run and were abandoned and fell into the hands of the Texans. After the Indians left this place they came to a boggy branch, and many of the horses of the Indians stuck fast, and here they left all of the pack animals, with probably a few exceptions, and most of the saddle horses. Some of the hindmost Indians used some of the poor bogged animals as pontoons, and passed over the place on their bodies. The white men ran around the head of the boggy branch and cut off some of the Indians who were on foot and killed them.

The pursuit lasted to the foot of the mountains, between where the towns of San Marcos and Kyle are now, and was there abandoned, as all of the horses were run down, having passed over fifteen miles of country in the chase. The men collected where the fight was severest and most Indians killed, and there camped for the night. Some of the white men were wounded, but none killed. James Nichols, one of the Guadalupe men, received a peculiar wound. He was in the act of firing, when a bullet from the Indians struck him between the middle and forefinger of the right hand and lodged in the wrist. His gun fell without being discharged.

There were ten Tonkaway Indians with Burleson's men, and that night after camp was made they cut off the hands and feet of the dead Comanches who lay near, and roasted and ate them. They also cut one big fat fellow into strips and hung the pieces on a rope.

Many narrow escapes were made by men crowding the Indians too closely when the main body of whites was too far behind and the Comanches turning back on them. Ben McCulloch had an experience of this character. Some were hurt by their horses falling with them.

Soon after the battle of Plum Creek the Galbreaths moved and settled near where the first fight commenced, a few miles from the present town of Lockhart.

In 1842, when San Antonio was captured by the Mexicans, Mr. Galbreath went with other citizens to fight them. Among those he went in company with were the Buntons and Capt. Jesse Billingsly. This party joined the other Texans on the Salado, seven miles northeast of San Antonio. All were under the command of Gen. Matthew Caldwell of Gonzales. Capt. Jack Hays was also there with a company of rangers, having been commissioned by General Houston to raise a force for frontier protection soon after the battle of Plum Creek. General Wall had possession of San Antonio with about 1500 men. Captain Hays with his mounted rangers drew him out to Caldwell's position. Wall crossed his army to the east side of the creek facing the Texans, planted cannon, and the battle commenced. The Texans, 200 in number, acted on the defensive, dodging the pecan limbs which were cut off by the cannon balls and were falling among them. The Mexican commander thought to rout the Texans with this artillery fire, but failing, made preparations to charge them. Cavalry was sent across the creek to cut off their escape on that side, and Cherokee Indians posted on the creek below, and both infantry and cavalry sent above to head off any fugitives in that direction. The Mexicans little knew what kind of men they had to deal with. All were good shots and frontier men, with such Indian fighters as Hays, McCulloch, Walker, Gillespie, Lucky, Dunn, Ackland, Chevalier, Neill, Wallace, Galbreath, Highsmith, and many others equally as good. When the bugles sounded the charge the Mexicans came in fine style and in such dense masses that for a while the situation looked critical. They came almost in among the Texans and fired their escopets. The latter, protected by the creek bank and pecan trees, poured such a volley of death and destruction into their ranks that their formation was broken up and they went back in confusion and disorder to the battery on the elevated ground. A company of cavalry also charged close, but the horses recoiled at the fire, and those who lost their riders went back in confusion, knocking down some of the infantry as they did so. Loud and continuous cheering went up from the Texans. The cannons now opened again, but Caldwell's men only yelled the louder. Several more charges were made, but without success, on the part of the Mexicans, and many were killed and wounded.

Mr. Galbreath said the Mexican cavalrymen had on the largest spurs he ever saw, and when any of their horses were shot down the troopers could not run with their spurs on, and were invariably killed if they happened to be near the riflemen. The rowels were several inches in diameter and dragged on the ground. They would try to run on their toes so as to lift the rowels from the ground. The ground there after the battle looked as if a garden rake had been used over the ground. The Mexicans were badly defeated by Caldwell, but they cut off the force under Capt. Nicholas Dawson of fifty men from Fayette County and almost annihilated them. They were coming to the sound of the firing, thinking the Mexicans were on the west side of the creek, but discovered their mistake when too late. They fought Wall's whole army until nearly all were killed. Two made their escape—Aulsy Miller and Gonzalvo Woods. About twelve were captured. One of these was the young son of Rev. Z. N. Morrell, who was with Caldwell, not knowing at the time that his boy was with Dawson. The following are some of the men who were killed: Captain Dawson, First Lieutenant Dickerson, Zodack Woods, David Berry, John Slack, John Cummins, — Church, Harvey Hall, Robert Barclay, Wesley Scallorn, Eliam Scallorn, Asa Jones, Robert Eastland, Frank Brookfield, George Hill, John W. Pendleton, J. B. Alexander, Edmond Timble, Charles Field, Thomas Simms, — Butler, John Dancer, and a negro belonging to the Mavericks. He had been sent out by Mrs. Maverick to try and communicate with his master, who had been captured while attending court in San Antonio when the place was taken by the Mexicans. The Mavericks were then living on the Colorado, near Ed Manton's. They had sent this trusty slave with Dawson, hoping he might be able to learn something of Mr. Maverick. Poor fellow! Faithful to his trust, he died by the side of Dawson, fighting to the last.

Mr. Galbreath says these were not all the men who were killed that day trying to get to the position of Dawson. They were found killed all over the prairie on both sides of the creek.

He says a man named Butler with eight men heard the firing of the rangers and Mexicans on the west side of the creek during the running fight from town, and thinking it was the main body of Texans, and that they were engaged, crossed over there and were cut off by the cavalry and killed.

The loss of the Texans during the various engagements of the day was less than one hundred killed and wounded, the heaviest being that of Dawson. The Mexicans went back to San Antonio, and becoming alarmed at the result of the battle, hastily decamped for Mexico. They were followed by the Texans, and the rangers under Hays fought the rear guard at the Hondo, but there the pursuit was abandoned and the men returned to their homes.

After the return of Captain Hays from the Somervell expedition in 1843, Mr. Galbreath joined his company of rangers, which was stationed on the Leon Creek west of San Antonio. Not long after joining the company he went on a scout and participated in the famous

BATTLE OF BANDERA PASS.

When Captain Hays went on this scout, his intention was to go out to the head of the Guadalupe River, and then down some of the canyons below the mountains and then back to camp. The scout numbered between thirty and forty men, among whom were Ben McCulloch, Sam Walker, Kit Ackland, Ad Gillespie, George Neill, Sam Lucky, James Dunn, P. H. Bell, Mike Chevalier, Ben Highsmith, Lee Jackson, and Tom Galbreath. The others can not now be remembered. Sam Walker had just returned from Mexico, having made his escape from the Mexicans after the capture at the ill-fated battle of Mier. Some of the old Hays rangers who were also captured at Mier were still in prison, among whom was Big Foot Wallace.

The course of the rangers after leaving camp was northwest. They struck the Medina River above where Castroville is now, and kept up that stream to where the town of Bandera is now. The last camp of the rangers before the fight was made here. Next morning they turned north towards the Bandera Pass, which they entered about 10 o'clock in the morning.

The Comanches had discovered the approach of the rangers

as they came through the open country south towards the Medina, and laid an ambush for them in the pass. They had all of the advantage for the first onset, being concealed among the rocks and short gullies on both sides of the pass, which is about 500 yards in length by 125 in width. This pass runs through a range of mountains which divides the Verde Creek valley from the Medina. The Indians let the rangers get about one-third of the way through, and then commenced firing from both sides at once. The rangers were coming two and three together, and the sudden and unexpected fire threw the front men into a momentary confusion, mostly, however, on account of frightened and wounded horses, which tried to wheel and run back. The Comanches greatly outnumbered the rangers, and for some time the battle was hotly contested. The Indians had guns among them, besides bows and arrows, and men were killed and wounded on every side. Captain Hays was cool and collected, and gave orders as if everything was all right. "Steady there, boys," he exclaimed. "Get down and tie those horses. We can whip them." Many of the Indians came down the pass and engaged the rangers at close quarters. Pistols were freely used, and some hand to hand conflicts took place, in one of which the Comanche chief was killed by Kit Ackland, who was himself wounded by the daring chief. Before the fight was over nearly one-third of the rangers were killed and wounded. The Indians had many killed, and some were carrying them back towards the north end of the pass during the fight. Mr. Galbreath was wounded with an arrow during the severest part of the conflict. He was on the ground facing towards the north, and the arrow came from the right and struck him just above the pistol belt on the left side. The arrow came quartering and went shallow until near the hip bone, when the penetration was deeper, striking the bone and making a severe wound. The hardy ranger made no complaint, but at once drew the arrow and finished loading his gun, which he was engaged in when hit. No one knew he was wounded until the worst part of the fight was over. Lee Jackson was killed at the first fire. Sam Lucky was shot through the body with a ball and was assisted from his horse by Ben Highsmith, who was himself soon after wounded with an arrow.

The Indians, finally seeing they could not drive the rangers

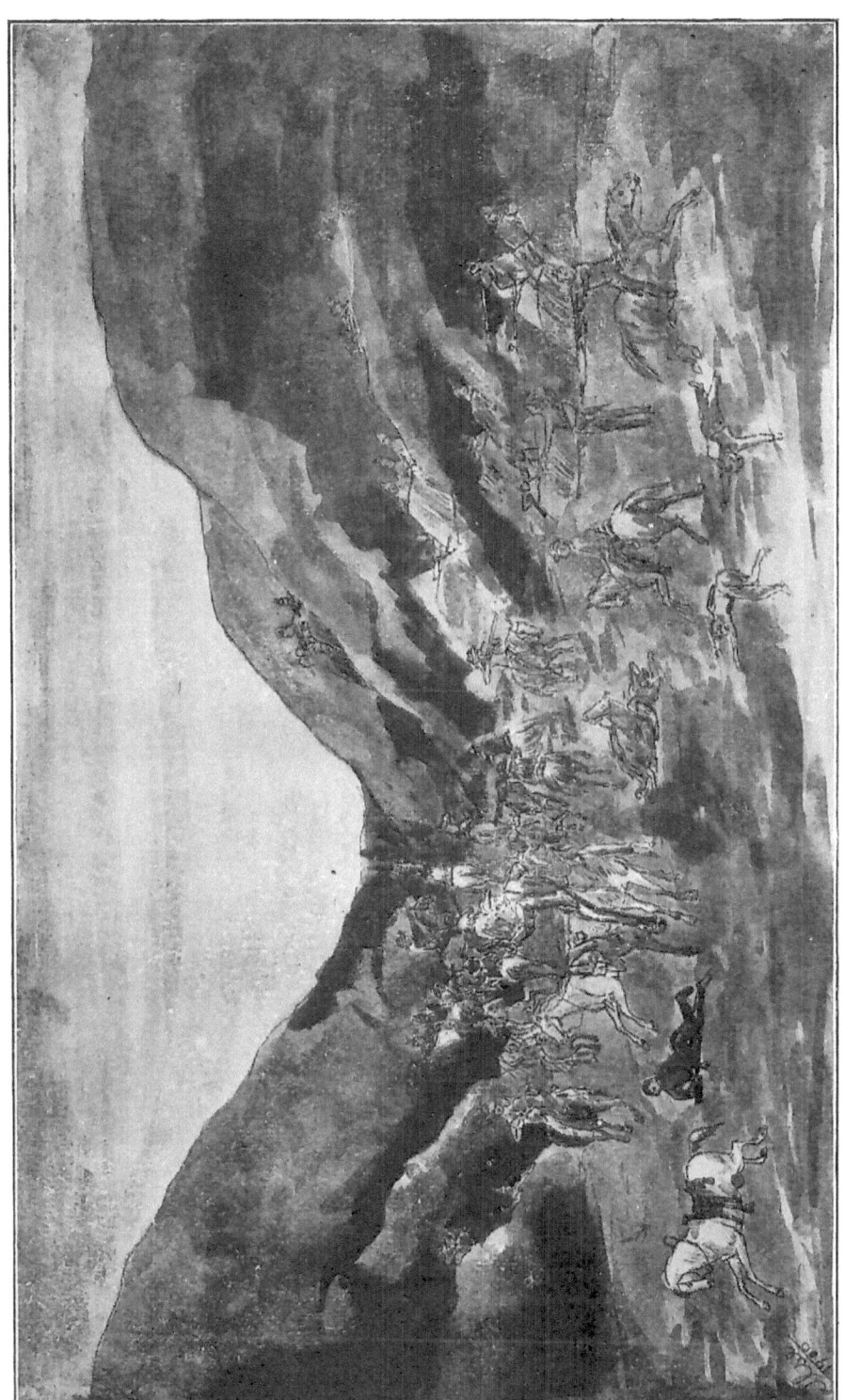

THE BANDERA PASS FIGHT.
From Photo by Steve Surber, Center Point, Texas.

back, withdrew to the north end of the pass, and the rangers went back the other way, carrying their dead and wounded, and encamped at a waterhole near the south end of the pass. Here they buried the dead rangers and attended to those who were wounded until morning. The Indians remained at the north end of the pass and there buried their chief and killed all of their crippled horses and those that belonged to the chief, whether hurt or not. The first settlers in this part of the country will remember seeing these bones. The badly wounded and dead horses of the rangers were left near the south end. There were five rangers killed and six wounded. Mr. Galbreath does not remember their names, as he had not been in the company long enough to become as familiar with them as he did others later. Mr. Highsmith says Jackson was killed there. The wounded were Sam Lucky, Kit Ackland, James Dunn, Ben Highsmith, Tom Galbreath, and some others whose names can not now be recalled. Galbreath and Lucky were carried to San Antonio to have their wounds attended to.

In the following year Captain Hays took fourteen men and went on a scout to the Nueces Canyon. Of these were Sergeant Kit Ackland, Mike Chevalier, Creed Taylor, Sam Cherry, Noah Cherry, Tom Galbreath, and an Irishman called Paddy. The others can not now be remembered. After a long trip out to the head of the river without seeing any fresh signs of Indians, Hays turned back down the canyon and camped one night, and next day traveled until about noon, when some one discovered a bee-tree; and the captain told the men to pull the bridles off, take their ropes down, and let their horses graze, and they would rest awhile there and get the honey. Noah Cherry secured a small ax that was in the luggage on a pack mule, and ascended the tree for the purpose of chopping into the honey without cutting the tree down.

Now it happened that about this time a large band of Comanches were coming down the canyon on a raid, and seeing the trail of the rangers they followed it, and were at this time close upon Hays and his men. The man in the tree, having a good view of the valley, saw the Indians coming and sang out, "Jerusalem, captain, yonder comes a thousand Indians!" They were approaching rapidly on the trail and made a good deal of dust, hence the rather exaggerated statement of the ranger as to their number. Hays had sat down and was watching Cherry chop. He had a listless, tired look on his face, but at the name of Indians he sprang to his feet as quick as a cat and the whole expression of his countenance changed, his eyes flashed, and he gave his orders quick and to the point; first to the man up the tree: "Come down from there, then, quick! Men, put on your bridles! Take up your ropes! Be ready for them! Be ready for them!"

The rangers on this occasion were armed with Colt's five-shooters, besides rifles and a brace of holster single-shot pistols. This made nine shots to the man. When the Comanches came in full view it seemed that the rangers could not sustain themselves against such odds. Mr. Galbreath says that they seemed to be 200 or more. It was characteristic of Jack Hays that he never ran from Indians and was never defeated by them. The Indians came at a full charge, yelling loudly, and thinking no doubt that it would be an easy matter to run over and rout the small squad of white men who were drawn up around the tree and facing them. Some of the men began to raise their guns, and Hays said, "Now, boys, don't shoot too quick. Let them come closer. Hit something when you shoot and stand your ground. We can whip them; there is no doubt about that." When the rangers fired the Indians were close and many fell from their horses, and several horses fell, so much so that quite a gap was made in their front, and the balance divided and ran to the right and left of the rangers, discharging arrows as they went. Captain Hays now sprang into his saddle and shouted, "After them, men! Give them no chance to turn on us! Crowd them! Powder-burn them!" Never was a band of Indians more surprised than at this charge. They expected the rangers to remain on the defensive, and to finally wear them out and exhaust their ammunition. The rangers ran close beside them and kept up a perfect fusilade with pistols. In vain the Comanches tried to turn their horses and make a stand, but such was the wild confusion of running horses, popping pistols, and yelling rangers, that they abandoned the idea of a rally and sought safety in flight. Some dropped their bows and shields in trying to dodge the flashing pistols. The pursuit lasted three miles, and many Indians were killed and wounded. Some of them kept the rangers from powder-burning them by the dangerous thrusts of their long lances. Conspicuous in the chase was Kit Ackland, who ran so close among the Indians trying to carry out the captain's orders that he was lanced three times. He chased one Indian on a blue mule, but it outran his horse. When the fight was over the rangers rode back, and Mr. Galbreath says he never saw as many dead Indians before or since. The Irishman, Paddy, said he saw a wounded Indian go in a certain thicket, and he was going in there after him. Captain Hays said: "If there is a wounded Indian in there you had better let him alone. If you go in where he is, he will kill you before you see him." Paddy hesitated, but concluded to give the Indian a trial anyway. He said the Indian had his leg broken and was not able to do much, and he was not afraid of a crippled Indian, no way. Soon after disappearing from sight he was heard to make a noise or cry out as if in pain, and then all was still. Three or four rangers now dismounted and advanced cautiously in single file and soon perceived a slight rustling in the underbrush, and all fired towards the spot. A squall like a wildcat from the Indian told the tale that he was badly hit, and the four rangers went to the spot with pistols presented. The Indian was dying, having been hit by all four rifle balls. Sixteen feet from the Indian lay the dead body of the ranger with an arrow through his heart and body, the point coming through the skin on the opposite side. The Indian was a large fellow, and had strong arms. He was lying flat on the ground, almost covered up with leaves, and had all the advantage of the unfortunate ranger, who no doubt received the fatal arrow without seeing the Indian. Paddy was taken out of the thicket and buried, and Captain Hays returned to his camp on the Leona.

Many years after this a friendly Delaware Indian named Bob saw the Comanche chief who led his warriors in this fight, and asked the Delaware who it was he fought on that occasion. Bob told him Jack Hays and his rangers. The chief shook his head and said he never wanted to fight him again; that his men had a shot for every finger on the hand, and that he lost half of his warriors. They died, he said, for a hundred miles back towards Devil's River.

Mr. Galbreath can not locate this battleground, but says it was before they got out of the mountains. Mr. Galbreath also says that this was the first time the rangers used the five-shooters in an Indian fight, but some say the Pedernales battle was the place. It was, however, the first time this band of Indians ever had five-shooters used on them.

When the time of enlistment of this company commanded by Hays expired, Mr. Galbreath enlisted in Gillette's company.

During his service with Hays and other captains he remembers the following names of men who from time to time served in the same company with him: Kit Ackland, Shapley Woolfork, Joe Tivey, Mark Rapier, James Galbreath, Big Foot Wallace, Tom Buchanan, Coho Jones, Peter Poe, Mike Chevalier, James Dunn, Ad Gillespie, P. H. Bell, Jeff Bond, James Gocher, William Powell, Leander Herrill, Ed Lofton, Bill Chism, Calvin Turner, James Roberts, Jack Johnson, Sam Holland, Dick Hilburn, William Jett, — Spain, Charles Donoho, Tom McCannon, Ben McCulloch, Henry McCulloch, Sam Walker, Sam Lucky, George Neill, Ben Highsmith, Creed Taylor, Pipkin Taylor, Josiah Taylor, James Taylor, Rufus Taylor, Andrew Sowell, John Sowell, Asa Sowell, Sam Cherry, Noah Cherry, John Carlin, Rufus Perry, John Williams, Joe Davis, Lee Jackson, Leo Huffman, John Saddler, Wesley Deer, Nat Mangum, Stoke Holmes, Heck, Knox, Kaisey, and many others not now remembered.

Gillette's company was stationed in this year, 1845, on the Seco, near D'Hanis, to defend the German settlement there. The first captain being promoted, Captain Warfield was put in command, with William Knox as first lieutenant, Kaisey second, and Lee third. While the company was stationed here Lieutenant Knox went on a scout into Sabinal Canyon and had a fight with the Indians, in which Wesley Deer was killed and John Saddler was wounded. Eight Indians were killed. Mr. Galbreath was not on this scout, but told Wesley Deer in a joking way that the Indians would kill him this trip. Deer was very young, and this was one reason the old ranger spoke to him in this way.

From Seco the camp was moved to the Leona River, about thirty miles further west. The location was three miles below the present town of Uvalde, seven years before it was laid off. Soon after arriving here the captain sent five men to San Antonio after supplies. Of these were Lee, Golsten, Heck, and Huffman. The other one can not be remembered. While in San Antonio a man named Ben Pettit and a negro man were there with corn from Peach Creek, which they sold to the government. The corn was sent out to the rangers' camp, and Pettit and his negro were employed to bring it out in their wagons. The rangers had three wagons containing other supplies. When the five wagons arrived at the crossing of the Sabinal River, where the Sunset Railroad now crosses it, Heck and Huffman went on ahead for the purpose of killing a deer. One mile west of the river they were ambushed by the Lipan Indians and Heck was killed. Huffman, not being hit by the volley that killed his companion, wheeled his horse and ran back toward the wagons. Fifty mounted Indians followed him, and spreading out tried to cut him off from the river. A desperate hard race now commenced. The loose horse of the dead ranger followed close in the rear of Huffman. The Indians shot many arrows at long range, and finally stuck one in the ranger's thigh. He pulled it out and used it for a switch on his horse, wearing it out to the feather. The wagons were at the river, and the men with them seeing the Indians running Huffman, made ready to fight them. The Lipans turned back when they saw the wagons, and the hard-pressed ranger arrived safely. All night the men stood guard. When the Indians went back they picked up Huffman's hat and mutilated the body of Heck. After night came on one of the rangers named Lee volunteered to take chances and go to the ranger camp after help. He made it all right, and Captain Warfield sent thirteen men to their assistance. Of this number was Tom Galbreath. When the rangers got into the prairie between the Blanco and Sabinal the grass was burning for many miles around. The Indians had fired it to cover their trail. It had burned over the body of the dead ranger, badly disfiguring it. The smoke was so dense it was some time before the rangers could find the body, but it was finally recovered and carried to the wagons at the river. It was near day, and the men had spent an anxious night. One of their comrades lay dead on the prairie, another one wounded, and a third in great danger trying to bring succor to them. Besides this, the grass was burning in every direction, and the whole country was lit up. When morning came the body of Heck was buried, and here is a strange story. His grave was already dug and had been for six months. This is the history of the grave: Six months previous to this time a party of surveyors had camped there and one of their number, becoming very sick, apparently died. He was laid out and his grave dug in a small hackberry grove near by. The tent where the body lay was closed up for the night, and the interment of the dead man was to take place next morning. No one stayed inside the tent, but remained until morning just on the outside. When daylight came one of the men looked into the tent, and was almost scared out of his senses by seeing the supposed dead man standing on his feet and gazing about him like a man who had just waked up out of a sound sleep and did not know exactly where he was. The man who made the discovery turned and ran away, but a bolder fellow went in and asked him how he felt. "Very well," he said, "but very weak." He was then taken to San Antonio, and recovered. The grave had remained there open ever since, and in it Heck was buried. No doubt but he had ridden up and looked into this grave while on scouts.

After the last sad rites to their comrade was performed the rangers guarded the wagons past what they thought was the danger line, and then went to hunt the trail of the Indians. They had tried to baffle pursuit by starting north, but had turned back to within half a mile of where they had killed Heck and then went south, burning the grass behind them. The rangers got on their trail all the same and came upon them that evening in the edge of the Leona bottom, on the east side of the river, ten miles below the present town of Uvalde. The rangers at once charged and the Indians ran, but stopped in the bottom and fired on them with guns. The Lipans numbered about forty and the white men thirteen. The latter fired when they charged, and were very close when the Indians fired on them. The rangers being scattered in the charge, the bullets aimed at them did not find many victims, but hit the trees quite lively. One gallant ranger, however, named Nat. Mangum, received a mortal wound from a large bullet. The rangers went back from the charge away from the bottom, dismounted, and tied their horses. Mangum rode his horse back, and was then helped off and laid on a blanket under a tree. It was a drawn battle now. The Indians would not risk the fire of the rangers in the open ground, and the latter could not afford to charge their position with the force they had. Each fired as opportunity offered. The chief had buffalo horns on his head, and could occasionally be seen in the edge of the thicket with a gun in his hand, which he would fire quickly and then disappear again. The sergeant in command of the rangers finally told his men to reserve some loaded guns especially for that chief, and kill him if possible. The next time he appeared nearly all of the rangers fired at him, and he fell.

The wounded Mangum suffered a great deal, being shot through the bowels, and begged the boys to shoot him out of his misery. As he lay under the tree during the fight he called one of his particular friends to sit down by him and asked if he would do him a favor. Thinking he wanted to send some message home to loved ones, he promised. But no; that was not it. He wanted his best friend to shoot him. The other ranger began to cry, and said, "O no; O no. I can not; I can not." Mangum looked straight at him, and said, "Remember, now, you promised to grant any favor I asked you. I can not get over this shot, and I am suffering death over and over again." His friend continued to weep and say, "I can not." "I'll give you my horse and saddle and pistol, and all the wages due me," continued the wounded ranger. "Take your pistol now, my friend, and do what I tell you, or give me mine." Mangum's belt and pistol had been taken off and laid aside. Of course no persuasion could induce the friend to comply. He leaned over him and almost bathed his face and forehead in tears.

About this time another brave ranger named William Lowe came to them badly wounded with a bullet, but laughed and said, "I'll get over this shot all right." It was at this time that some one said, "Look, boys, there he is!" as the chief with the buffalo horns again came into view. A dozen rifles cracked at once and he was seen to fall. Not long after this the Indians were heard crossing the Leona River, and the battle was over. The rangers now entered the bottom lately occupied by the Indians and found plenty of blood, but the dead had been moved. Near where the chief was seen to fall was a pool of blood and a loaded gun, cocked. Heck's gun and hat were also found, and Huffmann's hat. Some one making a close search along the bank of the river discovered the body of the chief in the water wrapped up in blankets, they being lashed close to his body with ropes. When it was taken out and unwrapped the horns were still on his head, and there were seven bullet holes in his breast. The wounded rangers were tenderly conveyed to camp that night, and Mangum died next day and was buried on the banks of the Leona, near Uvalde, and rocks piled over the grave. Lowe got well.

The next fight the rangers had was with the Comanches. The trail of this band was discovered at the foot of the mountains on the Frio River. There were fifteen of the rangers together at the time, and the Indians numbered sixteen. The trail led south across an open country for some distance and the rangers gained rapidly on the Comanches, as they were riding very tired horses. They kept under cover as much as possible, riding in ravines which had bushes and prickly pears around them, whenever they could do so. When the rangers arrived at a dry little creek called Cibolo (buffalo), just above the Laredo road, they came upon the Indians, who were traveling in a ravine but hid from view. The rangers could hear their leggings scraping against the brush. For some distance they rode parallel with them, waiting for a good place to charge. The Indians could also be heard talking. Suddenly they left the ravine and rode out in open view, not more than thirty yards away, and were not aware of the presence of their white foes until fired on. A man named John Saddler fired the first shot, and an Indian fell from his horse. The others attempted to run back to cover, yelling and shooting at the rangers, who charged and cut them off from the ravine. One, however, seemed determined to go back into the ravine at all hazards. Tom Galbreath dismounted, and running to the edge of the thicket and gulley after the Indian had got into it, and getting a view of him, fired and killed him from his horse.

After the Indians had been cut off from the brush they tried to make their escape across the open country—open except scattered bunches of prickly pear (cactus) and catclaw bushes. Some of them were on mules and others on jaded horses, and all were killed, one here and one there as they were overtaken. None of them got more than half a mile from where the fight commenced. One was riding a paint horse, and to him Mr. Galbreath gave chase. The Indian galloped slow, and the ranger soon came alongside of him, but kept about forty steps to one side until he could take aim and fire. One shot was sufficient, and the Comanche fell heavily to the ground. The Indians only shot with arrows, and did but little damage. They were more on the run than fight. One young ranger named Stoke Holmes, who rode a fast little pony, singled out an Indian and said he was going to rope him. While he was running and swinging his rope the pony attempted to jump a large bunch of prickly pears, but reared so high his rider lost his seat in the saddle and fell backwards into the terrible cactus. Some of his comrades, seeing the mishap, killed the Indian and then came to his rescue, as he was unable to extricate himself. His horse had galloped off, but was caught and brought back. The ranger was in a sad plight. His body had thousands of pear thorns in it, and his clothing was pinned to him on all sides. He was almost in agonies with pain. The rangers stripped off all his clothing and extracted all the large thorns, but it was impossible to get out the thousands of needle-like small ones, but with a sharp knife they shaved them close to the skin, so the clothing would not irritate by rubbing against them. He was hardly able to ride for several days.

When the time of enlistment had expired the rangers were ordered back to their old camp on the Seco, and were there mustered out of the service.

Early in 1846 Capt. Henry E. McCulloch raised a company of rangers and Mr. Galbreath joined them. Their station was at the head of the San Marcos River. The officers, besides the captain, were First Lieutenant Story, his son Fred, second, and Asa J. L. Sowell orderly sergeant. The latter was father of the writer.

During this enlistment no important Indian battles were fought, and when the time was out Mr. Galbreath joined Capt. Sam Highsmith's company, which was stationed at Fredericksburg, in Gillespie County. Kijah Highsmith, son of the captain, was first lieutenant and George Gamble second. In three months this company was disbanded.

About this time the war with Mexico had broken out, and Capt. Jack Hays was raising a regiment of rangers for service in Mexico. Many of the old rangers raised companies for the regiment. Among these were Ben McCulloch, Sam Walker, Ad. Gillespie, Kit Ackland, and Mike Chevalier. Mr. Galbreath joined the spy company of Ben McCulloch, and went through many stirring scenes during the war. Being always in advance of the main army, a spy company is exposed all the time to ambuscades, and fight many small battles, besides being in the general engagements. Mr. Galbreath was at the storming of Monterey and the battle of Buena Vista.

After the war he served again as a ranger, and was stationed at San Lucas Springs, between Castroville and San Antonio. Soon after this all of the rangers were mustered out, seven companies being disbanded at San Antonio in one day.

In 1848 Mr. Galbreath married Miss Nancy Jane Wining, and in 1852 settled on Chicon Creek. The next move was where he lives now, near Devine, in Medina County. He was still on the frontier, and had many more scraps with the Indians until they left, never more to return.

In 1875, while living at this place, his son Isaac, a youth of 17 years, was killed by Indians. He went out one morning to drive up the horses, and Mr. Galbreath heard the shots that killed him. He was not sure it was Indians until the horse his son rode came running back to the house. He at once armed and repaired to the spot, but too late to do any good except to bring the dead body of Isaac in. He was shot with firearms and one arrow. There were about fifteen of the Indians. They committed other depredations as they went on, but were not overtaken. Young Galbreath was buried in the Devine graveyard, one mile from town, and was the second person put there. Three others are also buried there who were killed by Indians. George Wheat, brother-in-law to Mr. Galbreath, was killed by Indians. His son Ira was for a long time sheriff of Edwards County.

Mrs. Galbreath died in 1879, and in 1890 he married Miss Mary Shores, his present wife.

Mr. Galbreath relates this rather humorous episode which occurred during the perilous frontier times. On one occasion when several men were out together, among whom was a Mr. Avant, a tolerably old man, and another named Woodward, they came upon a party of Indians, who sprang up out of the grass and commenced shooting at them. Mr. Avant's horse threw him, and he made an attempt to save himself on foot, not being able to get hold of his horse again. All the men ran away except Mr. Woodward, and he stayed with Mr. Avant and pointed his gun at the Indians when they came near, and they would stop and dodge, thereby giving the footman a chance to sprint ahead. This was done several times, and again the Indians came close, and Mr. Avant, who was nearly out of breath, said,

"Aim your gun at them, Mr. Woodward; aim your gun at them. I see it has a good effect." Both made their escape.

Mr. Galbreath was in the ranging service with Big Foot Wallace, and said he could stand more cold than any man he ever saw. He would scout all day in a cold norther without a coat, and then lie down at night on his saddle blanket without cover and sleep soundly all night if not disturbed.

Mr. Galbreath has a good ranch and 300-acre farm.

JACK HAYS.

JACK HAYS.

Came to Texas in 1837.

John Coffee Hays, better known in Texas as Jack Hays, the famous ranger captain, was born in Wilson County, Tennessee, in 1818. He was named for General Coffee, who commanded a brigade in the army of General Jackson at the battle of New Orleans. He came to Texas in 1837, when but 19 years of age, and located at San Antonio. He was a surveyor by profession, and was employed to survey lands on the frontier. His long life on the frontier gave him a hardy constitution, and none were able to stand more hardships and endure more privations than he. His talent as a commander and leader of border men early developed, and he was soon among the chosen leaders of the pioneers in southwest Texas. His reputation as a fighter arose so rapidly he was given the command of the frontier with the rank of major in 1840. This was in part owing to his gallantry at the great Indian battle of Plum Creek, fought the same year, and which has been described elsewhere. If an account was given in detail of all his exploits and battles on the frontier it would make a book within itself.

His two famous battles of Bandera Pass and in the Nueces Canyon have already been given, as also the part he took in the battle of Salado when San Antonio was captured by Wall. He fought one battle west of the Nueces with the Comanches and badly defeated them, and also one near the head of Seco and Sabinal. He was surrounded here for some time, and finally sent one of his men, who slipped out in the night and went to Seguin to notify Captain James H. Calahan, who commanded another company of rangers, to come to his assistance. The messenger rode day and night, as did also the rangers who came back, and the reinforcement soon arrived on the scene, but Hays and his men were gone. Signs of a fierce fight were there, and the dead bodies of sixteen Indians were found. Calahan took the trail and soon discovered that the Indians were in retreat, and that Hays and his men were following them. At the head waters of Sabinal River rangers and Indians were overtaken. The

Comanches were on a mountain and Hays and his men were in the valley, watching them. When Calahan and his men arrived an assault was made on the position of the Indians, and after some firing, in which one of Calahan's men was wounded, the Indians left the mountain and scattered in the roughs and the rangers returned, Hays to San Antonio and Calahan to Seguin.

On another occasion Hays was close upon a band of Indians and located them by his scouts in a cedar brake. The rangers had eaten nothing all day, so hot was the pursuit, and the captain now told them to dismount for a few minutes and partake of some cold bread and beef they had in their wallets, but by no means to raise a smoke. Hays always had a few Mexicans with him, as they were good guides and trailers, but on this occasion, in lighting their cigarettes after eating, they let a pile of leaves get afire, and soon smoke was curling above the tree tops. Hays was furious, and the Mexicans were badly scared and made frantic endeavors to stamp out the fire, he striking some of them with his quirt during the time. An order to mount was now given and a furious run made towards the Indian camp, which was a mile away. It was as Hays had anticipated. The Indians saw the smoke and knew the rangers were on their trail, and had fled, leaving many things in camp, which were taken.

One of the hardest fights Captain Hays had was on the Pedernales in 1844. On this occasion he had gone out with fourteen men about eighty miles from San Antonio northwest in the Pedernales country, now within the limits of Gillespie County, for the purpose of ascertaining the position of the Indians and their probable location.

On arriving near the river about fifteen Indians were discovered well mounted, and they seemed to want a fight. When the rangers advanced upon them, however, they retreated and endeavored to lead them towards a ridge of thick underbrush. Captain Hays was too well acquainted with the Indian character to be caught by their snares, for he suspected an ambush. It was hard to keep his boys from advancing to the attack, among whom was Ad. Gillespie, Sam Walker, and Mike Chevalier. Hays went around the thicket and posted his men on another ridge separated from their position by a deep ravine. This position was occupied but a short time when the Indians discovered who he was, and knowing their man, gave up trying to catch him by stratagem and showed themselves to the number of seventy-five and challenged him to the combat. Hays accepted the challenge and signified to them that he would meet them, and immediately started down the hill with his men toward the Indians, moving, however, very slowly, until reaching the bottom of the ravine, where he was hid from the view of the Comanches by the brow of the hill upon which they had formed. Then turning at full speed down the ravine he turned the point of the ridge and came up in the rear of the Indians and charged them while they were watching for him to come up in front of their position. The first fire of the rangers with rifles threw them into confusion.

The yells, warwhoops, and imprecations that filled the air were enough to blanch the cheeks of the bravest, but Hays and his men had heard such sounds before, and stood their ground unmoved. The Indians, seeing their superior force, soon rallied. Hays now told his men to draw their five-shooters to meet the charge that he saw was coming. In order to resist attack on all sides, as the Comanches were surrounding them, Hays formed his men in a circle fronting outwards, being still mounted on their horses, and for several minutes maintained that position without firing a shot, until the Indians almost came within throwing distance of their lances of them. Their aim was now sure when they fired, and nearly every shot took effect. Twenty-one Indians were killed here before they desisted from hurling themselves on the muzzles of the revolvers. When the Comanches fell back the rangers changed their ground and charged in turn. The fight lasted nearly an hour, each party charging and recharging in turn. By this time the rangers had exhausted the loads in their revolvers, and the chief was again rallying his warriors for one more desperate struggle.

The number of the rangers was by this time reduced, some killed and others badly wounded, and the situation was critical. Captain Hays saw that their only chance was to kill the Indian chief, and asked of his men if any of them had a loaded rifle. Gillespie replied that he had. "Dismount, then," said the captain, "and make sure work of that chief."

The ranger addressed had been badly wounded — speared through the body—and was hardly able to sit his horse, but slipping to the ground took careful aim and fired, and the chief fell

ENCHANTED ROCK.

headlong from his horse. The Comanches now left the field, pursued by a portion of the men, and a complete victory was gained. When all was over on this battleground lay thirty dead Indians, and of the rangers two were killed and five wounded. Sam Walker was one of the wounded, and was also speared through the body.

On another occasion Hays was on a scout with about twenty of his men near the head of the Pedernales at a place called then the "Enchanted Rock." It was of large, conical shape, with a depression at the apex something like the crater of an extinct volcano. A dozen or more men can lie in this place and make a strong defense against largely superior numbers, as the ascent is steep and rugged.

Not far from the base of this hill, at the time of which we write, the rangers were attacked by a large force of Indians. When the fight commenced Captain Hays was some distance from his men, looking about, and attempted to return and was cut off and closely pursued by quite a number of warriors, and made his retreat to the top of the "Enchanted Rock." Here he entrenched himself, determined to make the best fight he could and, as the border men say, "sell out" as dearly as possible. The Indians who were in pursuit upon arriving near the summit set up a most hideous howl, and after surrounding the spot prepared for a charge on the position of the ranger captain. They were determined to get him at all hazards, for no doubt there were warriors along who knew him. For some time as they would see the muzzle of the rifle come over the rim of the crater they would dodge back, knowing it was death to one to face it, and each thought that one might be him. Becoming bolder, however, it was necessary for Hays to fire, and one fell at the rifle shot, and then the revolver went to work, and as they were close, each discharge from the five-shooter found a victim. In those days there were no six-shooters, but these were made soon after. The Indians fell back before this fire, which gave Hays a chance to reload. This was kept up for some time. The rangers heard the battle on the hill and knew it was their captain, and gradually fought their way to him. The Indians below were defeated, and those after Hays fled down on the opposite side when they saw the battle had gone against them in the valley and that the rangers had commenced the ascent of the hill of the "Enchanted Rock."

Captain Hays was glad to see his boys, as the case had become desperate with him. The Indians, maddened at their loss, were drawing closer around him, becoming reckless of life, and would in the end have overpowered him. Five or six dead lay around the spot where Hays fought, and twice as many below. Three or four rangers were wounded but none killed.

When the war of 1846 broke out with Mexico Captain Hays raised a regiment of Texas rangers and fought in nearly all of the desperate battles in Mexico, in which many of the regiment were killed, including Ad. Gillespie, who was captain of a company, and Sam Walker, who was lieutenant-colonel of the regiment. After the war was over Colonel Hays went to California, and was elected sheriff of San Francisco County, and as a matter of course made a brave and efficient officer. He married a daughter of Major Calvert of Seguin, and was brother-in-law to John Twohig of San Antonio, and Colonel Thos. D. Johnson and Alfred Shelby of Seguin, these having married his wife's sisters.

Colonel Hays had his last Indian fight in Nevada in 1860. At that time Virginia City was a mining town, and many Texans, Californians, and others had gathered there. The Piute Indians declared war against the whites and committed many depredations, among others massacred Major Ormsby and his men. There was at this time at the mines an old Texas ranger, Capt. Edward Storey, a man of great courage and very popular among the people. He had fought Indians in Texas under Colonel Hays and Gen. Henry E. McCulloch. Captain Storey at once raised a company, called the Virginia City Rifles, and proceeded against the Indians. Col. Jack Hays heard of the war which his old comrade Captain Storey was engaged in, and came over from California with several companies to help him, and together they attacked the Indians at Pyramid Lake, about twenty-five miles from Virginia City. The Indians were about 1000 strong and well armed, and flushed with their victory over Major Ormsby and his men. They had the advantage of position in the mountains and more than doubled the number of the whites. A complete victory was won by Hays and Storey, but at fearful loss, and among the slain was the brave Captain Storey. This was on the 2d of June, 1860. The dead captain was rolled up in a blanket and conveyed to Virginia City on a pack horse.

Colonel Hays became very wealthy. He never made Texas his home again, but occasionally came on visits to see old friends and relatives. He died at his home near Piedmont, Cal., in 1883.

MRS. M. A. BINNION.

Came to Texas in 1838.

Among the many interesting characters of Southwest Texas was Mrs. M. A. Binnion. While the writer was traveling, hunting up the old settlers, and gathering information from them, he found Mrs. Binnion at the ranch of her son-in-law, Mr. A. J. Davenport, in Little Blanco Canyon. She was then very old and feeble, and on account of failing memory was not able to tell much of the many stirring events through which she has passed —of Indian alarms, massacres, and sleepless nights on the border long before the prairies were dotted with ranches, and when the beautiful canyons were only inhabited by bears, panthers, Mexican lions, and other vicious animals.

Mrs. Binnion was born in Alabama, near Tuscaloosa, in 1818. She was the daughter of Benjamin Phillips, and came to Texas with her husband in 1838, first settling in Titus County. She lived in Burnet County quite a number of years when that was a frontier, and Mr. Binnion was engaged in stock raising. He and the family came to Uvalde County in 1865. Their son Samuel was sent back to the old home in Burnet County to gather and bring the cattle to Uvalde County. That was the last the mother and father saw of the son. He was killed by the Indians while engaged in gathering the cattle. The unfortunate young man was riding a mule at the time, and had no chance to make his escape. The Indians ran all around him and threw their ropes over his head and pulled him from his saddle to the ground, and then ran and dragged him across the prairie. While some were engaged in this others were following and throwing lances into his body. When life was extinct and they were satiated with their savage pastime, the ropes were taken off and the mangled body left.

In 1866, when the Indians made a raid in Sabinal Canyon and killed Mrs. Bowlin and badly wounded Mrs. Kinchaloe in many places, Mrs. Binnion, who was a good doctor and really the only one in the settlement, was sent for. She at once mounted a horse and made a most remarkably quick ride to the scene, and remained fifteen days by the bedside of the wounded woman, attending on her, and she recovered.

In 1870 the Indians made a raid on the settlements and appeared at the Binnion ranch. Mr. Binnion was in bed sick, and could scarcely walk when up. The Indians remained off a distance and watched the house a while, and then one of their number came towards it. Mrs. Binnion now dressed herself in male attire, and getting a rifle sallied from the house to fight the Indian who was approaching. The Comanche acted cowardly and retreated back to his companions. The Indians then rode off down the river toward the other settlement. Mrs. Binnion and her husband now became uneasy about their children, who had gone down to a neighbor's below, and taking their guns followed after on foot. Mr. Binnion being very weak, his wife carried both guns, and still having on a man's clothing. They soon discovered three Mexicans coming around a thicket, and at first glance supposing them to be Indians, sprang to one side and leveled their guns at them. Mrs. Binnion in the excitement of the moment failed to cock her gun, which likely saved the life of a Mexican, for she aimed at one and pulled the trigger trying to shoot. The Mexicans knew Mr. Binnion and called loudly to him not to shoot. They had not seen the Indians, but stayed with Mr. Binnion and his wife to help them fight. One of their sons made a narrow escape. He met the Indians, who chased him, but being on a good horse made his escape. They also ran a Mexican into the thicket, but failed to get him. At another time Mrs. Binnion and another lady kept off a band of Indians by arming themselves with long stalks of the soto plant and aiming them as if about to shoot when the Indians advanced. They dreaded the long rifles of the Texas pioneers and would retreat, not being near enough to detect the deception. In this way the two women who were alone and away from the ranch made their way safely back to it. This sketch is only a faint outline of what this brave heroine of the West passed through, but alas never to be told by her.

CAPTURE OF MATILDA LOCKHART AND THE PUTNAM CHILDREN BY INDIANS.

1838.

In the early pioneer days of southwest Texas Mitchell Putnam and another settler named Lockhart lived on the Guadalupe River below the town of Gonzales. They were industrious, thrifty men, and soon had good homes, and were also blessed with a family of nice, healthy boys and girls. Life ahead of them looked bright and cheerful, but, alas for human hopes and aspirations, how soon was their cup of sorrow to be filled to overflowing and they compelled to drink to the bitter dregs.

One bright day in the fall of 1838 Matilda Lockhart, James Putnam, and his two sisters, one older than he, went to the river bottom to gather pecans. For some time they picked up the nuts, which were in abundance, and their merry laugh continually rang out through the forest. At last it was time to go home; their vessels were full of the rich pecan nuts, and their exertions had given them a keen appetite for their dinner, the time for which had now long passed. The baskets, bonnets, and buckets were gathered up, and the merry group emerged from the bottom to the edge of the prairie. But what a sight now met the eyes of those merry ones! The laughing voices were hushed, and the cheeks which but a moment before had glowed with health and gay spirits, now blanched and paled with terror. There, in a few rods of them, rode a band of wild, painted Comanche Indians, the scourge of the Texas frontier. Escape was impossible. With a wild shout the Indians circled around them, and without dismounting reached from the saddle and secured the screaming victims, and holding them in front dashed away up the valley towards the wilds of the great West.

When the children failed to come home at the proper time the parents became uneasy and a search was instituted in the pecan bottom, whither they knew the children had gone. Their ages ranged from six to thirteen years. Matilda Lockhart was the eldest and one of the Putnam girls was the youngest. Can pen describe the agony of those parents when they come to the spot where the children were captured? It can not. A bonnet here; a bonnet there; an overturned bucket or basket and pecans scattered promiscuously about. A short distance out in the open ground lay little Jimmy's hat. The ground was torn up by horse tracks, and too well these pioneers knew what had become of their loved ones. No time was to be lost. They rushed back and alarmed a few neighbors, who were soon on the trail of the daring red men. Lockhart was furious, vowed vengeance of the most direful nature, and galloped madly on the trail. Putnam was more composed and wanted to be cautious, but he was not lacking in courage, for he fought at San Jacinto in Captain Heard's company, and was one among the foremost in that terrible charge. Among the few men who followed Putnam and Lockhart on the trail of the Indians was Andrew J. Sowell, Sr., uncle of the writer.

The trail led up the Guadalupe River and was hard to keep, as the country became rougher towards the foot of the mountains. The last place that any signs of the Indians could be seen was at the mouth of the Comal River on a sandbar. Here the Indians had halted, and the tracks of the children could be seen in the loose soil. This place is where the German city of New Braunfels now is. Here the Indians entered the mountains and the pursuit had to be abandoned, as the force of the settlers did not justify further advance into the stronghold of the savages. They returned, but only to get a larger force, and this time penetrated the mountains far west of the Comal into the head waters of the Guadalupe, now covered by Kerr County. Here, in a secluded valley, the scouts discovered a large Indian encampment, and that night a daring settler penetrated the Indian village and found out the captive children were there. When the faithful spy came back and reported, Lockhart was for an immediate advance, and it was difficult for his friends and neighbors to restrain him until some plan of action could be agred upon. After some deliberations the plan was to assault the Indian camp at daybreak, as soon as it was light enough for the men to see how to shoot. Lockhart knew no fear, and when the time came led the advance. The loud yell of an Indian announced the fact that the white men were discovered. The time for battle had come, and the settlers made a rush, intending to fight their way to the center of the camp where the children were. The white men were greatly outnumbered, but fought with desperation almost amounting to madness or frenzy. Lockhart led with clubbed rifle trying to fight his way with physical force to his children. Putnam was beside him. The settlers soon saw that the conflict was going against them. Lockhart was wounded in several places, covered with blood, and getting weak. There seemed to be no end to the forces of the Indians, fresh swarms of them continually coming into the battle from the village, only the outskirts of which the white men had reached. Never had such a noise been heard in that valley before. Loud yells rent the air, tomahawks glanced against rifle barrels, and whizzing missiles flew on every side. The settlers could not sustain themselves; the contest was too unequal; valor must to numbers yield. They slowly retreated, fighting as they went, and carrying their dead and wounded comrades with them. Lockhart was loth to give up the fight, but weak, wounded, and bleeding, he allowed his friends to carry him away, seeing all of his hopes of recovering his daughter and the children of his neighbor fade away. After getting clear of the Indians the dead, five or six in number, were buried and the wounded carried back down the valley of the Guadalupe.

In 1840 a treaty was held with the Comanches in San Antonio, in which Matilda Lockhart was recovered, but the Indians failed to bring in other prisoners as they had promised, and the council wound up in a fight in which many of the Indians were killed.

James Putnam after several years' captivity was finally through treaties recovered, but his eldest sister by this time had become the wife of a chief and would not leave, saying that society would not receive her among white people and she would have to spend the balance of her life as an Indian. The other sister had been carried away among a different band of the tribe.

About thirty years after the capture of the children a gentleman named Chenault, who had been an Indian agent, bought a middle-aged white woman during that time and carried her to his home in Missouri. Afterwards he moved to Gonzales, Texas, and brought her along as a member of his family. She was so young when captured by the Indians that she could not remember her name or where she was taken from by them. When, however, she saw the Guadalupe valley in the region of Gonzales she had a dim recollection of seeing the country before, and thus expressed herself. It was now believed that it was the youngest girl of the Putnam children. James Putnam, who lived up the river fifteen miles above the town of Gonzales, was sent for to see if he could by any means ascertain if this was his sister. When he came the fact was established beyond a doubt that it was his sister, by a scar caused by a burn on one of her arms.

How strange that she should be brought back almost to the very spot where she was captured thirty years before, and there spend the balance of her days. The writer was well acquainted with James Putnam, and was at his house many times. He married the widow Nash, and lived on Nash's Creek near the confluence with the Guadalupe. He said the Indians carried him all over Texas, Arizona, New Mexico, and California. Often when he had been left with the squaws and children on some high mountain he could see the warriors fighting with immigrants or Santa Fe traders in the valley below. If they were successful in the fight they came back gleeful and had scalp dances; but if they were defeated, especially with much loss, they beat the prisoners and otherwise maltreated them. He saw many bloody reeking scalps brought in by them of men, women, and children.

Mr. Putnam died near the line of Hays and Travis counties several years after the civil war. His stepdaughter, Louise Nash, married Granville Nicholson, but she died soon after. Mr. Nicholson now lives on the Verde Creek, in Kerr County.

REV. E. A. BRIGGS.

Came to Texas in 1841.

One of the old-time frontiersmen, rangers, and preachers is Rev. E. A. Briggs, who at this writing lives near Seglar postoffice, near the line of Bexar and Atascosa counties. He was born in Amherst, Mass., in 1819, and came to Texas in 1841. His ancestors were in the war of the revolution, and among them were some noted divines and scholars. Mr. Briggs upon first arriving in Texas went to Houston, where he had an uncle, T. P. Andrews, minister to Europe from the Republic of Texas. In 1842 Mr. Briggs was teaching school at Richmond, Fort Bend County, when the news come of the Vasquez raid. There was a good deal of excitement in the country in regard to this invasion of the Mexicans, and a company was at once raised in and around Richmond to go and fight the Mexicans who had captured San Antonio. The school of Mr. Briggs was composed chiefly of young men, and the majority of them joined the company. Their teacher said, "Well, boys, if you are all going to the war I had as well go, too," and he also joined the volunteer company.

These men lived so far from the scene of hostilities that when they arrived at San Antonio the war scare was over. General Vasquez and his men had gone back to Mexico after holding the city only a few days. This raid was nothing more than a plundering expedition, the Mexicans only holding the town long enough to rob it. Here Mr. Briggs first saw Capt. Jack Hays, the famous Texas ranger, and talked with him.

While the settlers were moving west of San Antonio Mr. Briggs was commissioned to raise men for the protection of a German colony which was settling at Quihi in 1846. The war with Mexico, however, broke out at this time, and the rangers were sent to Mexico to assist General Taylor. Mr. Briggs went out under Maj. Sam Highsmith. Out near the Rio Grande, on this side of the river, the rangers come upon a lot of Mexicans who had been attacked and whipped out by the Indians and some of them killed. They had been in camp catching mustangs, and when they were driven out came to the rangers for protection, who at this time were passing near on their way to Mexico. They had lost all of their provisions and the rangers were also out, but all went on together. When the party went into camp some of the rangers were complaining of being hungry, whereupon one of the Mexican women who was with the party of mustang catchers went to the chaparral and soon returned with her apron full of mesquite beans and prickly pear apples, and said, "No starve; plenty to eat." Mr. Briggs said, "How long can a man live on such grub as that?" One of the Mexican men said, "Live on pear all right alone; mix pear and beans, get fat;" and continuing, said, "A man should not want anything better to eat than that."

The Mexicans were protected across the river and the rangers went on to Taylor's army, but arrived too late for the battle of Buena Vista, which had been fought and won. Some of the rangers were sent back to protect the Texas frontier, and Mr. Briggs came with them. There were a great many rangers in Mexico under Hays and Walker. They remained and participated in many battles. Colonel Walker was killed, as was one of Hays' captains, Ad Gillespie. Big Foot Wallace was in this expedition. But a few years before he had been one of the prisoners after the disastrous battle of Mier (Meer), when they had to draw beans for their lives.

Mr. Briggs was altogether three years in the Texas service, part of the time in Captain Cady's company, stationed at Austin to keep the Indians and buffalo out of town.

On one scout the rangers, only a few in number, were sent out to take some observations in regard to a body of Indians that was over on Little River. These Indians were supposed to be friendly at the time, but the people were suspicious of them and wished to keep a watch on their movements. The rangers camped on the same river near the Indians fifty miles from Austin, but did not know of their presence until attracted by the smoke of their camp fires, and even then supposed it was grass burning. Next morning the Indians also discovered the rangers, and two young fellows come out of the timber across the prairie towards them. They made many circles around the rangers lying low on their horses to see if they were going to shoot. They finally straightened up and came to them when they saw no demonstrations were made towards them. They were fierce, devilish-looking rascals, and demanded of the rangers what they were doing there. They thought discretion the better part of valor on this occasion, and replied, "Buffalo hunting." One who could speak a little English said, "Maby so you lie." John Herral, who was in command, said, "Boys, that's hard to take, but we will have to stand it. If we kill these we will never get away from the balance in camp." The whole band numbered about 500. The two young bucks galloped back to their camp and the rangers saddled up and went back to Austin. Of this party, besides Mr. Briggs, was William Winin, who has a brother Edward who lives near the Bexar postoffice, in Atascosa County.

During the civil war Mr. Briggs sold goods in San Antonio with Pancost. The firm name was Ward, Pancost & Co. Mr. Briggs was a member of the firm, the largest at that time in San Antonio. The goods were sold in the Jones building, southeast corner of the plaza. They had extensive stables where the new courthouse now stands. When the business broke up considerable loss was experienced, and Mr. Briggs moved out of town and settled where he now resides, twenty-two miles south of San Antonio, near a noted place called Black Hill. Two young Germans were killed near there after he settled, but he does not remember their names. (See account of this elsewhere.)

He has been in the Baptist ministry now more than twenty years. It was almost a necessity, he said, that he became a preacher out in this frontier country. A frontier preacher named L. S. Cox came and organized a little Baptist church and Mr. Briggs helped him to conduct the services, and finally the people prevailed on him to preach for them. He was ordained, and has been doing the best he could ever since. He has been a member of the Baptist church since he was 16 years of age, and has spent all of his life in a new country in the woods and along the border. He has eight grown sons, four married, one of whom has since died—Pearl, who married Miss Cordelia Tinsley. He kept the Segler store and postoffice near the residence of the Rev. Briggs until a short time before his death. This postoffice was named after James Segler, an old Texas ranger who lives near, and with whom the writer served in the Wichita campaign in 1870-71. Rev. Briggs has one son, Bevy, who is also in the Baptist ministry.

RUDOLPH CHAROBINY.

RUDOLPH CHAROBINY.

MEXICAN WAR VETERAN.

Came to Texas in 1845.

Among the first settlers of Quihi, in Castro's colony, and who still survives, is Mr. Rudolph Charobiny, now living about two miles from the Quihi store south on Quihi Creek.

Mr. Charobiny was born in Zips Comitat, Hungary, in January, 1817, and set sail from Havre, France, in September, 1845, for Texas, as part of Castro's colony. He came over in the ship Deaucalion, which was an American vessel and commanded by an American captain. They were eight weeks on the ocean and had a very good trip, without incident except one fire on shipboard, which originated in the kitchen, but was soon extinguished without much damage being done. The Deaucalion landed at New Orleans and the passengers got aboard the ship Galveston, bound for the city of Galveston, Texas, at which place they landed in November. From Galveston Mr. Charobiny and another young man went on board a steamboat and came up Buffalo Bayou to Houston. It was very cold and the two young immigrants got near the boiler to warm themselves. Now at this time Gen. Sam Houston was on board, and noticing the two young fellows warming themselves at the boiler, took one by each arm and said, "Come, I will warm you up," and leading them into the saloon treated them to a drink of whisky. The general had some fine horses on the boat which he was carrying up the country.

The boys stayed in Houston fourteen days, and in the meantime became acquainted with Dr. Acke, who purchased some drugs with the intention of coming west to practice medicine. Mr. Charobiny and two other young men named Korn hired a man named Alexander to bring them to San Antonio, and they and Dr. Acke journeyed together. The young immigrants intended to join Castro's colony and go to farming. One of the young men, Louis Korn, lives at Kline in Uvalde County at this time, at a very advanced age. The trip from Houston to San

Antonio was with ox teams and very slow and tedious. It rained a great deal; creeks were up and they had to watch constantly for Indians. One of the colonists had already been killed by them while en route from Port Lavaca to San Antonio. The young men had to unload the wagon many times so that the team could pull out of bogholes. They arrived in San Antonio in April, 1846, and at Castroville in May of that year. Mr. Charobiny lived six months in the Republic of Texas before annexation. Henry Castro was planting colonies still further west on his grant of land, and Mr. Charobiny concluded to settle at Quihi, ten miles west of Castroville. The town of Quihi (pronounced Qeehe) being laid off, one lot and twenty acres of land was donated by James Brown, Castro's agent, to the settlers. This was within the town limits. Single men received 320 acres and married men 640 outside of the town. Mr. Charobiny received his 320 acres but did not at once settle, from the fact that about this time he joined a company of Texas rangers, commanded by Capt. John Conner. Dr. Acke, who came up with them from Houston, was also a member of the company as surgeon and physician. He did not, however, serve long in this capacity, from the fact that he was killed in a difficulty at Castroville by a ranger. The company scouted for Indians about two months, and then, the war breaking out between the United States and Mexico, Mr. Charobiny and other rangers enlisted in Bell's regiment of mounted riflemen to aid General Taylor, who had crossed the Rio Grande with an invading army. Texas at this time had been annexed to the United States, and a dispute over her boundary brought on the war.

Captain Conner commanded a company in Bell's regiment, and it was with him as captain that Mr. Charobiny served in the Mexican war. The regiment joined General Taylor at Buena Vista, but too late for the battle there, which had been fought and won. The enlistment was for twelve months, and the time was served out in Mexico. They then returned to Texas and were disbanded at San Antonio. Mr. Charobiny did a great deal of scouting around Monterey while in service in Mexico to keep the Mexicans back from General Taylor's headquarters. The riflemen under Jeff Davis aided in this scouting.

After being disbanded Mr. Charobiny came back to Quihi and

settled on his headright on Quihi Creek, and commenced farming and stock raising. Grass and water were plentiful, with no brush then, but open, lovely valleys. Game and wild honey were in abundance and living cheap. The seasons were good and splendid crops made, and the hardy pioneers began to enjoy the fruits of their labor and sacrifices.

In November, 1847, Mr. Charobiny married Miss Francisco Meyer, and in three months after a band of Kickapoo and Lipan Indians came through on a raid and robbed the house in Mr. Charobiny's absence, who was out on a cow-hunt, and carried off his wife a captive. The same band killed her brother, Mr. Blas Meyer, at his house before they came to the Charobiny ranch. After taking and destroying everything they could, the Indians placed Mrs. Charobiny on a horse and started up towards the Quihi settlement north, about two miles distant. After keeping this course a short while the Indians bore to the left, going a northwest course, and left the settlement to the right. The captive woman had it in her mind to escape if possible, and thought she would try even if killed by them for so doing, dreading captivity among these savages more than death. So when the party arrived at a pecan grove Mrs. Charobiny sprang from the pony and fled, followed by several Indians, who shot arrows at her and succeeded in wounding her badly in two places, so much so that she fell and was unable to rise. The Indians, thinking she was dead and fearing pursuit, rode back and continued their course, without getting off their horses to scalp her or see if she was dead. When Mr. Charobiny came home and found his place torn up and his wife gone he knew it was Indians, and at once ran his horse to the settlement, gave the alarm, and raised men to follow them, and also sent a runner to the ranger camp on the Seco to notify them of the raid. In the meantime Mrs. Charobiny recovered sufficiently to drag herself to the settlement and have the arrows extracted, and by careful nursing finally recovered. The Indians were not overtaken. Major Neighbors, Indian agent, who was then in San Antonio, was also notified of the raid. When Henry Castro heard of this misfortune of the Charobiny family he donated a house and lot in town for them to live in. Castro did all he could to aid his colonists while they were contending with the savages and subduing the wilderness.

The following is a list of the first settlers at Quihi, as given to the writer by Mr. Charobiny: Baptiste Schmidt, John Rieden, Amb. Reitzer, Jac. Ribf, Blas Meyer, K. Bonekamp, H. Gersting, H. Wilpert, H. Gerdes, Jans Sievers, B. Brucks, — Bickmann, F. Bauer, — Boinkhoff, — Opus, — Deuters, John Toucher, H. Schneider, — Rensing, — Gasper, — Eisenhauer, Louis Korn, and Dr. Acke.

Mr. Charobiny draws a pension as a Mexican war veteran, and has lived under five flags. Born under the Hungarian, then under the Republic of Texas, then under the Lone Star, then the Confederate, and also the United States stars and stripes.

He holds commissions as justice of the peace of precinct No. 2, Medina County, signed by three governors of Texas.

The first was by P. H. Bell (his old colonel in the Mexican war), dated on the 6th day of September, 1851. This document winds up thus: "In testimony whereof, I have hereunto set my hand and caused the great seal of the State to be affixed, at the city of Austin, in the year of our Lord one thousand eight hundred and fifty-one, and in the year of the independence of the United States of America the seventy-sixth, and of Texas the sixteenth."

The second commission was signed by Gov. H. R. Runnels, 9th day of July, 1859, and twenty-fourth year of Texas independence.

The third was signed by Gov. Sam Houston, 12th day of November, 1860, and twenty-fourth year of Texas independence.

Mr. Charobiny's pension certificate is No. 14,600, and was issued on the 6th of November, 1894. It states that Rudolph Charobiny was a private in Bell's regiment of volunteer mounted riflemen.

Mr. Charobiny still resides on his headright grant of land donated to him over fifty years ago. His house is on a high elevation on the east bank of Quihi Creek, and commands a fine view of the surrounding country and the range of mountains to the north. He selected this place so that he could have a view of the mountains, which reminded him of his native land. When the writer visited him in 1897 he was then 80 years of age, and was living quietly and pleasantly with his wife and unmarried son, Judge M. Charobiny. The good lady was afflicted with rheumatism which almost bent her body double, and it was with great difficulty that she could get about. A great change has come over her since that trying day when, in the hands of painted savages, she bounded from her horse and ran almost with the fleetness of a deer to make her escape from them. May these good people live long yet to enjoy the evening of life and rest from their labors.

www.ingramcontent.com/pod-product-compliance
Lightning Source LLC
Chambersburg PA
CBHW030225100526
44585CB00012BA/228